# Kabuki Costume

1. *(Frontispiece) Aragoto* costume: Soga no Gorō in *Yanone*. The outer robe is an *atsuwata*. The armor, the *kumadori* make-up, and the elaborate wig are accouterments of the bombastic role.

RUTH M. SHAVER

# Kabuki Costume

Illustrations by Sōma Akira and Ōta Gakō

**CHARLES E. TUTTLE COMPANY**
Rutland, Vermont & Tokyo, Japan

Published by the Charles E. Tuttle Company, Inc.
of Rutland, Vermont & Tokyo, Japan
with editorial offices at
2-6 Suido 1-chome, Bunkyo-ku, Tokyo 112

LCC Card No. 66-15266
ISBN 0-8048-1650-6

First edition, 1966
Second printing, 1990


Printed in Japan

*To*

JACK BRYANT SHAVER

ICHIKAWA DANJŪRŌ XI

*and the*

KIKUGORŌ GEKIDAN

*As this book was going to press, the Kabuki world and its many friends were stunned by the tragic, irreparable loss of Ichikawa Danjūrō XI who died Tuesday, November 10, 1965 at the age of fifty-six.*

# Table of Contents

9

# List of Illustrations

# Acknowledgments

I owe much to the many invaluable friends I have made in the Kabuki theater over a span of some thirteen years. During this time I attended Kabuki performances on an average of six times a month, or a total close to one thousand performances. Among my Kabuki friends, I owe special thanks to Onoe Baikō VII, Onoe Kikuzō VI, Onoe Taganojō III, Ichimura Uzaemon XVII, and Sawamura Tanosuke VI, not only for their special friendship, but for their patient and thoughtful instructions regarding the intricate history and background of their special roles and the costumes that have been worn by them and their predecessors.

I also owe a special debt of gratitude to my teachers, whom I commissioned during a number of years to give me a series of personal lectures from Japanese documentary and other sources to supplement my academic knowledge of Kabuki.

Mr. Akira Sōma, painter, scholar, authority on Kabuki costumes, and son of the noted poet Gyofū Sōma, was an inspiring teacher and a perceptive artist who sketched and painted the majority of the detailed illustrations in this book.

Mr. Gakō Ōta, artist and adviser to the Meiji-za (theater) in Tokyo, instructed me on all forms of Japanese theater arts covering the past thirteen hundred years or more. He was the source of the information given in the chapter on *kumadori*, a subject to which he has devoted more than thirty years of study. The illustrations for *kumadori* are his, as well as some of those for costumes.

Mr. Yasuji Toita, a leading Kabuki critic and author, fascinatingly filled in the missing links in my Kabuki education. I have great admiration for this gentleman, who was very hesitant about taking a foreign woman for a pupil, who was uneasy at the first lectures, but who finally accepted me as a friend and an enthusiast of the theater he knows so well.

To other close and dear friends I owe much for their interest, help, and suggestions. It is a matter of deep regret that one of them will never read this acknowledgment of indebtedness. I owe much to Mrs. K. (Mitsuko) Tamura, who passed away in January 1963, for introducing me to the backstage of the Kabuki. She was my frequent companion at the theater, and it was she who translated into English many of the titles of Japanese plays mentioned in this book.

My utmost gratitude goes to Mrs. Tadayoshi (Takako) Yamada for her intelligent help during the compilation of the information on Kabuki costumes and for her assistance with many matters which only a true friend could give.

To Mr. Jinkichi Narumo, a fine young dancer in the Fujima school of Onoe Shōroku II (Fujima Kanemon), must go my thanks for opening up the delights of the Japanese dance, for acting as interpreter at Mr. Toita's lectures, and for offering suggestions during the writing of the manuscript which helped to clarify the meaning of certain Kabuki details.

I cannot say enough about the family of the late Mr. Yohei Fujinami III—Mrs. Nobuko Fujinami, her two sons, and daughter-in-law—for their kindness in receiving me on several occasions in their fascinating home, where they patiently explained the finer points of fans and swords.

Especial appreciation goes to Mrs. George (Gladys) Savage of the University of California, Los Angeles, who edited the manuscript for clarity, and to Dr. George Savage of the Theater Arts Department of the university for suggestions in editing. The encouragement and help extended by Mrs. Savage has been invaluable.

There is always one person for whom words are inadequate, and such a person is Mr. Tomoyuki Yamanobe, textile and dyeing authority of the National Museum, Tokyo, and member of the Ministry of Education's Commission for the Protection of Cultural Properties. Mr. Yamanobe attended Mr. Sōma's weekly lectures, eventually translated and interpreted them in a most knowledgeable manner, and finally proofread the finished manuscript of this book. For his assistance in many matters, his continuing enthusiasm, his genuine interest, and his sharing of his seemingly inexhaustible knowledge, I am tremendously indebted.

RUTH M. SHAVER

*"Art is a sensitive barometer to measure the buoyancy of spirit."*

—ERNEST F. FENOLLOSA

## NOTE

In speaking Japanese, the five vowels and double consonants are pronounced as they are in Italian, single consonants approximately as they are in English, except that *g* is always hard. Japanese words are pronounced with an almost equal stress on each syllable, except where there is a long vowel sound which is mainly a pitch accent and not a stress accent as in English. Unvoiced consonants sometimes become voiced—for example the change from *s* to *z* in *sakura* (cherry tree, cherry blossom) in the play title *Yoshitsune Sembon-Zakura.*

A noun does not denote gender or plurality except by context of the sentence. The same spelling is standard for singular or plural verbs. The custom of Japanese surnames preceding given names is followed throughout the book except in the Acknowledgments, where all names except those of actors are given in Western style. *Kenkyusha's New Japanese-English Dictionary* and the author's instructors were the authoritative sources for the spelling of Japanese words. All Japanese words other than proper names and those which are widely familiar in the West are italicized. Except in well-known place names, macrons to indicate long vowel sounds have been retained since they are essential to correct pronunciation.

# Introduction

*Kabuki Costume* is designed to acquaint the reader with a little known segment of a great theater: theater costume. The presentation of all phases of Kabuki, or any one aspect completely, within the confines of a single book is an impossibility. It is, however, necessary to give some account of what Kabuki is and how it has developed in order to understand the place and importance of the costumes.

A brief orientation to Kabuki through a discussion of it historically and as an art form will precede chapters on various aspects of Kabuki costume, such as male and female costumes, make-up, wigs, and accessories.

Kabuki is one of the most captivating and fantastic legitimate theatrical forms in the world, though most enthusiasts, both Japanese and foreign, admit it to be a diversion not for the intellect but for the senses. The nobility and warrior classes for centuries rejected this unpredictable, plebeian theater, holding their favorite Nō drama to be the epitome of elegance and good taste. Yet by its own artistic energy, Kabuki long ago raised itself to an admissibly fine classical dramatic expression and today far surpasses Nō in general appeal.

This truly native theater of Japan has been compared to the ancient Greek, to the Elizabethan, and to the Chinese theaters, as well as to the Western opera. Few admit that anything ever originated in Japan. The Japanese are looked upon as the world's most facile borrowers, even in the arts. But Kabuki, composed of dance, song, and histrionics, does not admit to being an offshoot or a development of any other entertainment, other than possibly folk dances of strictly Japanese origin; nor has any serious study of Kabuki proved it to be modeled after a foreign theater. A study of the historical background of Japan at the time of the beginning of Kabuki supports the belief that the art is indigenous.

In Kabuki, the actor is the pivotal force. This is not so apparent to the playgoer upon his first attendance, but the majority of a Japanese audience arrives in a spirit of great anticipation to see how well each role will be reproduced, for invariably comparisons are made of the acting stylizations of the current stars and their forebears. Reputation and popularity are founded on the preservation of a tradition. Only the young ever admit that present-day actors excel the illustrious greats of the past, and the young-in-heart in their dotage undoubtedly will revert to the narrower view of comparisons.

Second in importance to the actor is the over-all pictorial beauty which pervades the stage, and of course the actor's costume is a primary element in composing that beauty. The costume need not necessarily be realistic or logical. Reasonableness is for Western or modern Japanese plays. Until recent times, research was never done to make costumes authentic as to period. The public had little or no knowledge of historical customs and dress. As a consequence, the actors chose to use costumes in current use with which the audience was familiar, because the performers felt that the play would then have a more pertinent meaning.

Psychiatrists say that we see ourselves in characters in dramatic production; we cry and we laugh, usually because of our identification with them. People feel more comfortable if they see traits which they believe to be their own or if they fancy themselves in a similar light. Whether experience, instinct, or the astute Japanese psychology brought Kabuki actors to the realization of what was effective is impossible to say, but when actors used costumes familiar to the people, the audience felt a greater personal concern in the drama, for the playgoers had little vision beyond their own environment. Kabuki therefore developed an imaginative atmosphere of the immediate present which has always endured.

Since Kabuki reached its peak of perfection during the Edo, or Tokugawa, period (1603–1868), practically all the characters, regardless of the age of the play, appear on the stage in costumes of that period. The court beauties of the ninth century, as well as wives of samurai of the eleventh century, are dressed like women in Edo times, and their coiffures also reflect the Edo fashion.

Changes of costumes, materials, and patterns are made for various roles, and costumes are designated in accordance with individual roles. Not only the dress—for garments alone do not make the characterization—but also wigs and make-up fulfill extremely important functions in Kabuki. Patterns are not inflexible. Leading actors do make changes on occasion, but in general most present-day costumes remain identified with those originated by the past masters who popularized the roles. An actor must be a great idol indeed to be able to effect a change or to develop a part in a way that does not conform to the classical tradition.

One of the distinguishing traits of Kabuki, then, is the ease with which habitual playgoers recognize the type of play and the roles by the actors' costumes. The audience depends upon the array of splendid costumes to give vivid impressions of certain characters and to emphasize stage effects.

Some costumes in their original form followed the social trends of the day; others were figments of the imagination, beautified and highly exaggerated. Imitations of costumes worn in the Nō dramas and in the *ningyō-jōruri-shibai* (puppet theater) were used in plays adapted to Kabuki from these media. Even though a plot depends upon a specific period or impersonation of an actual individual, costumes which are not historically correct are used unhesitatingly even today.

It is not unusual to have queer costumes, the like of which never existed anywhere at any time. For instance, the costume called *yoten*—worn in historical plays by brave men, valorous brigand chiefs, and notorious thieves, as well as lowly policemen—exists only on the Kabuki stage. It was never a garb worn in real life. Most costumes worn in the *jidai-mono* (plays based loosely on historical or semihistorical events) and *aragoto* (drama designed for a highly stylized, vigorous form of acting) are not realistic. In many instances they are merely symbolic and grotesque.

In the same scene, some actors may be somewhat conventionally attired, while others may wear unbelievably fantastic costumes—a peculiarity which is accepted as quite natural in Kabuki.

What is the cause of these oddities? One of the principal reasons for the fantastic and imaginative costumes—especially those of samurai and noble classes, since imitation of their dress on the stage was proscribed by law—was that luxurious display of rich materials in Kabuki was strictly banned by the feudal government, so that ingenious methods had to be found to make the costumes theatrical and representative of important personages through color, pattern, and design.

Second, the costumes fulfilled the public's love of glamor, for Kabuki originated among and for the unaffected townsmen and the *nouveau-riche* merchants. Consequently, not only the simple, emotional stories of the plays but also the extravagant costumes satisfied the public's sense of beauty.

Actors made special effort to enrapture their audiences by impassioned acting. In consequence, the costumes, as well as the acting for each role evolved into accepted styles or forms which were completely removed from reality. Thus the weird make-up of *kumadori*: nonrealistic, stylized make-up used for *aragoto* (vigorous, swashbuckling) roles, the costumes exaggerated to a maximum degree for the heroic *aragoto* plays, the supremely colorful richness of kimono for female roles, the costumes of samurai and nobles are all products of the Edo period, resulting from the demands of the nonaristocratic audiences and the sensitive, artistic creativeness of the actors.

Unlike the *jidai-mono* based on ancient events among samurai or court nobles, there is a general type of play, the *sewa-mono,* which has a lowbred offspring, the *kizewa-mono,* which narrates many facets of the daily lives of the lowest commoners, including bad women, thieves, gamblers, prostitutes, vagabonds, beggars, and the like. The actors' dress worn in *kizewa-*

*mono* reflects quite accurately that of the commoners of the lowest strata.

New fashions worn by the townspeople, especially the *kabuki-mono* (outlaws or "free-life" people), were readily adapted to the stage, although usually dramatized for more striking effects. *Kabuki-mono* received their name from one early-seventeenth-century meaning of *kabuki* signifying free life—that is, life without respect for law. *Kabuki-mono* were considered outlaws, and commoners were afraid of these wayward individuals. Yet when such characters were impersonated on the stage, the people adored them—much as today's movie gangsters are esteemed.

Actors often created patterns or selected special colors for their effectiveness on the stage. These subsequently reached the height of fashion for the public at large. Not only the actors' modish kimono but also the intricate tying of the obi, the choice of accessories, and even the way of wearing the costumes were appropriated by men and women alike. For example, the use of *mon* or individual family crests on clothing became widespread during the eighteenth century after the actors had made such devices familiar.

In classic, or pure, Kabuki plays there are no careful recreations of Heian-period (794–1185) dress. The majority of the known Heian styles were those worn by royalty. Therefore, according to law, they could not be reproduced for stage use. Prior to the end of World War II, Bandō Mitsugorō VIII (then Bandō Minosuke VI) wished to appear in a Genji play (that is, a play based on the life and loves of the fictional Heian Prince Genji) for which he had as true reproductions as possible made of Heian clothing, but he was not allowed to appear in the costumes, since doing so was proscribed by law as an act of *lèse-majesté*. He eventually did wear the costumes during the dance recitals of *Nenchū Gyōji Emaki* (*nenchū*, during the year; *gyōji*, festival customs; *emaki*, picture scroll), whose choreography was based on the year's seasonal festivities, but Kabuki itself was no richer in its variety of costumes.

True Heian styles were not introduced to the Kabuki stage until 1951, when two plays in the modern Japanese vernacular were produced: *Nayotake* (Glowing Princess of the Supple Bamboo), dramatized from the story *Taketori Monogatari* (Tale of the Bamboo Cutter) by Katō Michio in 1943, and *Genji Monogatari* (The Tale of Genji), dramatized from Murasaki Shikibu's famous novel of the same name by Funabashi Seiichi, one of Japan's prolific contemporary novelists.

Even though the costumes for these plays have the correct flowing, widely opened sleeve lines of Heian dress, they necessarily are modified for the electrically lighted outsized stage of modern times. Although these costumes give us a visual perception into the past, when overrefinement in wearing apparel was one of the ardent passions of the nobility, they are admittedly of much bolder theatrical design and of brighter-colored cloth than ever was seen in the ancient days, when colors were fixed according to rank.

Heian literature, including the *Eiga Monogatari* (Tales of Prosperity and Luxury of the Fujiwara Family), regales us with stories of noble-women who wore more than twenty layers of garments with *hi-no-hakama* (scarlet culottes) for formal occasions both in summer and in winter, the textiles differing only according to season. This *jūni-hitoe* (literally "twelve-fold costume," although the number of layers was not fixed) was the correct formal feminine attire, but it is not used identically on the Kabuki stage for obvious reasons. Although the sumptuary laws of Edo times had permitted the wearing of such a costume, the actor, swathed in layer after layer of even the most diaphanous of materials, would have been hindered in his movements, and costuming would have been far too costly. In order not to discard the semblance of this lovely old-fashioned ensemble, the ingenious costumers sew layers of edges along the underneath border of the top garments, thereby creating the effect of many robes worn one over another.

The many-layered effect is also used in a most fanciful voluminous costume for the *onnagata*—the female impersonator also known as *oyama* (a less polite term which in the past had some implication of prostitution)— in the role of an *oiran,* the renowned courtesan of Edo days. In appearing as an *oiran,* the *onnagata* never wears more than two *uchikake,* the elaborate outer robe originally worn for formal occasions by well-born women, yet it appears that he could peel off several of these ornately brocaded robes with large rolled and wadded hems and long, trailing sleeves. Again the costumers have deceived the playgoers by their ingenuity.

With relation to sleeves, it should be noted here that "long" or "short," "wide" or "narrow" refers not to the length of the sleeve as measured against the outstretched arm's length but to the length as it falls along the sideseam of the kimono (from shoulder to hem). The conventional kimono sleeve is terminated at the wristbone, which it should normally touch. Certain theatrical roles call for outsized sleeves—sometimes double the width of the material—so that the hands are completely lost in their volume. These garments and their accompanying pieces usually go to extremes. By trailing along the floor, they give the wearer the comic (or terrifying) appearance of an awkward giant.

Unlike Kabuki, the Nō employs certain types of costumes which possibly may have been based on the classic dress of the Heian and Kamakura periods (794–1392). These generally are called *hirosode-mono* or *ō-sode-mono,* the extra wide-open or big-sleeve apparel. Belonging in this class are the *kariginu,* the *nōshi,* and the *chōken.* The *kariginu* (*kari,* hunting; *kinu* —*ginu* in compounds—clothes), a brilliant brocaded outer robe worn in male roles, was used by court nobles in real life as a sporty outdoor dress in the Heian age. After the Kamakura period it became a ceremonial costume among the warrior classes. The *nōshi* was the court gentleman's long silk coat. The *chōken,* an outer robe made of woven silk gauze, is used in both male and female roles that call for a somewhat long and important dance part in the drama, since the large and light long sleeves work effectively for dancing.

Among male costumes of the Nō, the foremost in elegance is exemplified by the *nōshi* and, next to it, the *kariginu*. There is another costume in this category: the *maiginu,* a robe which is a substitute for the *chōken,* made of the same material but somewhat shorter and used in *mai* (dance numbers) by actors portraying women, but never for men's roles.

The *happi* (short coat), worn for men's roles only, comes to just above knee length and has tucked-up sleeves. It represents or symbolizes armor. The character Tomomori wears such a coat in *Funa Benkei* (Benkei in the Boat). The *mizugoromo,* an unlined topcoat, not necessarily elegant, was used by priests, *yūrei* (ghosts), and sometimes by common people as a simple outer garment. In reality, since the *happi* did not exist during the Heian period, it was in all probability devised by the costumers as apparel for the Nō stage.

There are two kinds of *happi* and *kariginu* used in the Nō: for robust characters the costumes are made of elegant gold brocade with lining, and those for refined characters are sewn with exquisite patterns brocaded on gauze without lining, representing the ultimate in splendor, next only to the *nōshi.* The unlined *kariginu* is known as *hitoe-kariginu,* the lined as *awase-kariginu.*

The *kosode-mono,* or *tsume-sode-mono,* are little-sleeve or narrowly-opened-sleeve garments, including the following: the *karaori,* the sumptuous brocaded outer robe worn mostly by upper-class women, sometimes by their attendants, and rarely by aristocratic young boys; the *atsuita,* a kind of *kitsuke* (kimono; see below) for men's roles only, resembling the *karaori* but having a more masculine or a checkered pattern; the *nuihaku,* a kimono imprinted with gold or silver leaf and patterned with embroidery, worn only for women's roles; and the *surihaku,* a kind of *kitsuke* (kimono) of satin, *seigo,* or other silk with imprint patterns of gold or silver leaf and no other embellishment. (*Seigo* is a warp-rib-weave taffeta, the weft threads being thicker than the raw-silk threads of the warp.) These costumes are based on the dress of Muromachi times (1392–1573), when the Nō first appeared on the boards.

The above-mentioned *kitsuke* is a difficult word to explain. It derives from the verbs *kiru* (to wear) and *tsukeru* (to attach), and the meaning is "to attach to the body with an obi." The difference between the regular kimono and the *kitsuke* lies in the manner of wearing the garment. The *kitsuke* is the top kimono, over which the obi is tied, but it is called *kitsuke* usually when a coat or an outer robe is worn over it, sometimes almost concealing it. The term is used in connection with both women's and men's apparel.

The *karaori,* listed first in the above categories of small-sleeved garments, deserves somewhat more detailed attention. It is of two types. The first, for young women, is called *iro-iri* (*iro,* color; *iri,* containing or put in), meaning that the colors include red. The second, for older persons, is called *iro-nashi* (*iro,* color; *nashi,* without), meaning that red is not among its colors. *Karaori* is a word employed originally, and still used, for a particular kind of material imported from China—as Alan Priest describes it in *Japanese Costume,* a "silk (usually twill) brocaded with colored silk floss in large 'float' patterns resembling embroidery, and usually with a separate pattern brocaded in gilt-paper strips." Because elegant robes were made from this material, the robes were also called *karaori.*

The original outline of the kimono was taken from the *kosode,* a short-sleeve undergarment worn next to the skin by people of the middle and higher classes before the Kamakura period (1185–1333). *Kosode* originally meant a short-sleeved or narrowly-opened-sleeved kimono contrasting with the *hirosode,* the kimono with large and widely opened sleeves. In the Edo period (1603–1868), *kosode* referred to the lined and wadded silk kimono with short sleeves worn during three seasons, excluding summer. The same type of kimono without lining was called a *hitoe* or plain kimono, and the *hitoe,* when made of hemp or ramie cloth, was called a *katabira.* These were summer garments. The kimono as we know it today became widely used as an outer garment for men and women from late Muro-machi (1392–1573) or early Azuchi-Momoyama (1573–1603).

It is regrettable that Edo Kabuki costumes have not survived the years. Many exquisite Nō costumes of the Momoyama and Edo periods exist in private or public collections, since the Nō, as the formal theater of the noble and military classes, was well protected by the shōgun (military ruler) and the daimyō (feudal lords), and its refined hand-woven costumes were preserved by aristocratic collectors or by Nō masters. Kabuki costumes, made for the moment, were kept in the theater warehouses or by the actors themselves, eventually to be worn out by repeated use. We cannot, therefore, rely on any actual costumes for the study of the old Kabuki costumes. All of our information comes secondhand and somewhat sketchily from old books, from ukiyo-e or woodblock prints (in which we must allow for some poetic license as to color and design), from costumes made after the Meiji Restoration of 1868, and from word-of-mouth reports handed down from generation to generation within the Kabuki world.

The Theater Museum of Waseda University in Tokyo has the largest Kabuki library in existence, but none of its collection embraces antique Kabuki costumes. Its oldest authoritative information covers costumes worn by Ichikawa Danjūrō IX during the latter part of Meiji (1868–1912). Interestingly enough, what are probably the oldest known remaining costumes—all in excellent condition—are those used by a Kabuki actress, Bandō Mitsue, who died in early Meiji, and are the property of the Tokyo National Museum. It should be explained here that in past generations only the *okyōgen-shi* or women's Kabuki troupe was permitted to perform Kabuki in the *oku-goten,* the innermost palace of a feudal lord's establishment and the precinct in which the wives and daughters of daimyō lived. Although Kabuki actresses were the only ones to perform in the *oku-goten,* they were never permitted to appear in their dramatic roles on the traditional Kabuki stage.

PART
1

# Historical Background

CHAPTER 1

# Early Kabuki

No clearly defined documentation of the actual birth of Kabuki has been found. Some recognized scholars in this field believe Kabuki had its initial performance in Kyoto around the 5th year of Keichō (1600). It was about the same time, 1600 to be exact, when Tokugawa Ieyasu, the founder of the longest reigning dynasty of shōgun (military dictators) in Japan, won the battle of Sekigahara, defeating the generals who had given their allegiance to Hideyori, son of Toyotomi Hideyoshi, considered by some historians to be Japan's greatest military strategist. Hideyoshi, born of humble parentage, rose to become the military ruler prior to Ieyasu's ascendancy but never attained the rank of shōgun because of his plebeian birth. The government instituted by Ieyasu after his victory over the Toyotomi forces is known in Japanese history as the Tokugawa *bakufu* or Tokugawa shogunate. It was destined to continue for more than two and a half centuries.

Other Kabuki scholars believe that Kabuki was not founded until the 8th year of Keichō (1603), which would coincide with the year that Ieyasu assumed the title of shōgun. From that time until the fall of the shogunate in 1868, the age was called the Edo or Tokugawa period, the name Edo signifying that the Tokugawa had established their capital in Edo, the city which became Tokyo in 1869.

The Edo period, like preceding periods, was divided into a number of eras during which Kabuki blossomed from a coarse, erotic form of entertainment into that of classical theater as it is known today. Names of eras were often changed after some disastrous occurrence, such as war or loss of crops. It was a common belief that the adoption of a new era name would usher in a happy, prosperous interval. The over-all era names were not changed except by permission of the emperor. Today there are no such changes, each new era deriving its name from the succession of an emperor.

## OKUNI KABUKI

Caprice has credited a woman with the origin of Kabuki, Japan's time-honored, traditionally male theater. It easily could have been otherwise, for various forms of entertainment which might have caught the fancy of the townsmen prevailed. Yet it was a woman who offered the spark that fired the success of one special form beyond all the others existing at that time.

After a turbulent age of successive wars, there was a relatively peaceful period. The populace gave vent to its long-suppressed desire for pleasure in an era of unrestrained joy. New customs and trends spontaneously erupted. These were commonly called *kabuki,* an abstract noun taken from the verb *kabuku,* which at that time literally meant a "thing leaning"—in other words, an "extraordinary thing" signifying something abnormal, queer, or not common. A person who attracted undue attention by conspicuous traits of behavior, wore gaudy, exaggerated clothing, or swaggered with great bravado was referred to as *kabuki* or *kabuki-mono,* with its nuances of emancipation, pleasure, sensuality, and perhaps lawlessness, since the Japanese are peculiarly bound to the laws of tradition and strict rules of behavior.

In the wake of this new era in public tastes, legend has it that Okuni, a priestess of the great Izumo no Ōyashiro Shrine in central Izumo Province (now Shimane Prefecture), journeyed across the mountains to not-so-distant Kyoto, ostensibly to obtain contributions for the maintenance of the shrine through performances of a prayer-dance. This dance, the *nembutsu-odori* (literally "dance of prayer to Buddha") was an outgrowth of five centuries of teaching prior to Okuni by such priests as Kūya, Ippen, and during Okuni's time by the priest Hōsai, who believed that the principles of Buddha could be most easily understood not by difficult or tedious preaching but by plunging into ecstasy through song and dance. Later the *nembutsu-odori* became familiar as a folk dance.

Okuni's arrival in Kyoto about 1600 is considered a historical event in the annals of popular theater in Japan, for it presaged the beginning of various theatrical forms which gradually evolved into the present-day Kabuki.

Okuni belonged to a class of young maidens known as *miko* or shrine virgins, albeit of questionable virginity, who served the gods of the Shintō shrines, danced before them, and made themselves generally available for any menial task. Since people from all walks of life visited the shrines, inevitably bawdyhouses abounded in their vicinity. The *miko* often performed in these houses after dancing for the gods.

The *miko* did not usually come from aristocratic families, but quite often from the *shake* (the hereditary families of Shintoist priests), a wealthy class who helped support the shrines by donations. However, *miko* could come from any class. These girls did not necessarily enter a permanent religious life. Most of them married young, but a few remained unmarried in the shrines.

Such was the life to which Okuni was inured at the time she gave the first public performance of her dance in Kyoto, captivating the citizenry with her original embellishment of the *nembutsu-odori*. It is believed that she gave performances en route to Kyoto, though no written record exists.

Upon reaching Kyoto, Okuni proceeded to a dry place in the bed of the Kamo River, since it was there that low-class entertainers could perform without being taxed, and the space was free for the asking. At the foot of Gojō Bridge she made use of a *koyagake butai* (outdoor stage) for her performances. This type of temporarily built open stage—made of logs, bunting, and matting—can be seen today at circuses and shrine festivals. The word *koyagake* itself is a very old and popular expression meaning "hut-styled" or "temporarily built."

The townspeople regularly frequented the Kamogawara—that is, the *kawara* or riverbed of the Kamo—to be regaled by debased performances of Dengaku, Sarugaku, and other promiscuous entertainments, and for several centuries after Okuni's appearance there Kabuki actors were weighed down with the ignominious names of *kawara-mono* (riverbed fellow) or *kawara-kojiki* (riverbed beggar).

Only by examining old paintings can we envisage the costumes worn by Okuni. When presenting her first dance in Kyoto, she is thought to have appeared in a priest's black silk robe over an ordinary kimono, both ankle-length. A *nurigasa* (*nuri,* painted; *kasa,* hat; that is, a lacquer-coated, umbrella-shaped hat) covered her head, while around her neck was hung a scarlet breast-length strap of *karaori* (brocaded silk) on which was fastened a *kane* (small metal gong). Okuni struck the *kane* with a wooden hammer called a *shumoku* as she sang the well-known tunes of the day and danced in a most enticing manner.

Many, if not all, of the events surrounding the story of Okuni's life are based on legend. Documentation fails to record accurately where fiction ends and truth begins. So be it what it may, fate stepped into Okuni's life in the form of a handsome man-about-town, Nagoya Sanzaburō, who undoubtedly had been drawn to Okuni by her physical charms and daring exhibitionism. Born in 1576, the seventh child of a samurai, young Sanzaburō, or Sanza as he is popularly known, studied for the priesthood at a Kyoto temple until 1590. Then, at the age of fourteen, already bored with the austerities of priesthood, he gladly became a page to Gamō Ujisato of Aizu, a Christian daimyō. The death of Ujisato in 1595 brought Sanza back to Kyoto with a fortune bequeathed to him by his late master.

Lombard states in *The Japanese Drama* that Sanza "led a life of social freedom, and was popularly known for excellence in social arts, including the Kyōgen" (comic interludes of the Nō). This was the background of the man who it is said became Okuni's mentor as well as lover for a few years.

Sanza, a musician proficient with the *fue* (flute) and *tsuzumi* (hand-drum), taught Okuni popular songs to which he wrote ribald lyrics. Together, they borrowed freely from the Nō and Kyōgen. These performances put Okuni on the highest rung of the ladder of popularity. In these, Okuni donned a man's costume and Sanzaburō a woman's, a reversal of their apparel which made them look ungainly for those times, but which the public nevertheless found exceedingly refreshing and humorous. The male members of the audience in particular found the spectacle of a young woman dancing in masculine attire to be highly beguiling and erotic.

To her Japanese audience with its jaded appetite, Okuni's entertainment was welcome and stimulating. Okuni hastened to capitalize on her popularity by collecting the entrance fees for the dance performances and fees from the eager patrons for her troupe's after-hours profession, prostitution. The shrine's needs were forgotten.

Okuni was the only woman of her troupe privileged to wear male costume. Her costume, after she joined with Sanza, was a wide departure from her original priestlike garb. It was an ankle-length figured kimono, probably made of silk with tie-and-dye and embroidery, without the customary pleated skirtlike *hakama* (culottes), but with full sleeves extending to just below the elbow. The kimono was worn with a simple, narrow, stiff obi tied in *karuta-musubi* style: a flat, oblong bow, the squared loops and knot of which are all exactly the same size.

The tailoring of the kimono was unique. The width of each *mihaba,* one of the four identical sections of the kimono body, was almost double the width of the *sode-haba* (width of sleeves) used today; consequently, the kimono was extremely wide, and when closed in front, overlapped somewhat in the manner of Nō costumes. Okuni's hair was styled in the young man's, or *wakashu,* mode, with a white *hachimaki* (headband) tied around the head. Her accessories included an *ōgi* (folding fan) probably an all-white *haku-sen,* and a leather bag. A small *hyōtan* (the gourd many men carried for holding *sake* or water) hung from the right side of her obi, and a *juzu* (a Buddhist rosary) adorned her neck. To emulate the samurai, Okuni tucked a set of *katana,* the long and short swords, through the left side of her obi. The sheaths and hilts of the swords were gaudy with gilded metal mountings.

It is curious to note that some paintings show actresses of Onna Kabuki, which followed Okuni Kabuki, impersonating Sanza wearing a Roman Catholic rosary with a cross. Though the cross had no definitive meaning to the people in general, and certainly not to the actresses, it was thought to be an exotic accessory. Since the spread of Catholicism in Japan was approaching its zenith, the wearing of a rosary with a cross was not an unusual sight. Whenever a daimyō became a Christian, all of his retainers likewise had to become Christians, and each undoubtedly took to wearing the emblem of Christianity.

When Okuni's form of entertainment reached its peak of popularity, presumably in 1603, it was called Kabuki, with its inference of something degenerate or unorthodox. This appellation was Kabuki written in *kana,* the Japanese syllabary script. Okuni is well delineated by the word *kabuki* or *kabuki-mono,* so that the application of this contemptuous term to the entertainment she popularized seems plausible.

Okuni was the creator of the *Natsu Kagura no Mai* (Dance of the Summer Kagura). The choreography for the dance was based on the Kagura, an ancient religious pantomimic dance form brought down through the centuries in ceremonies performed at Shintō shrine festivals. The costume for the dance was an elegant white silk *suikan,* similar to robes worn by court nobles in ancient days, and red *naga-bakama,* long pleated trousers which trailed for two feet or more, giving the wearer the appearance of crawling on his knees. Her hair was plainly dressed. It was tied chastely just below the nape of the neck and hung free down the back. The simple beauty of this costume was accentuated by a branch of the sacred *sakaki,* the camellia-like shrub used in Shintō ceremonies, carried in the hand. It is probable that Okuni patterned this costume after the masculine white robe and red *naga-bakama* (long trousers) worn by the *shirabyōshi,* the gay professional dancers who flourished during the Heian and Kamakura periods, and who sometimes are said to have been predecessors of the geisha. The *shirabyōshi* wore this costume in imitation of men's wardrobe.

The fact that Okuni and her troupe were occasionally invited to perform before samurai is an indication of the rapidly expanding popularity of Okuni Kabuki. It remained, however, essentially, an expression belonging to the world of the commoner, who had only enough artistic sensibility to enjoy its suggestions of obscenity. He remained complacently unaware of its lack of inspiration or imagination. Denied any stimulus to advance, Okuni Kabuki found it difficult to break through an accepted level of mediocrity. However, Okuni Kabuki with its element of novelty was sufficiently appealing as a performing art to continue as popular theater.

Okuni continued her chosen profession long after her short-lived liaison with Sanzaburō ended. Possibly tired of the gay life, Sanzaburō changed his given name to Kyūemon and became a samurai attached to the feudal lord Mōri Tadamasa at Tsuyama in Mimasaka Province. One of the few instances where fully documented evidence about Sanzaburō is obtainable records the fact that Sanzaburō died in 1604 in a quarrel with a fellow retainer. As for Okuni, historical records mentioning her last years are so confusing that it is useless to speculate when and where she died.

## ONNA KABUKI

During Okuni's ascendancy, troupes of actresses were rapidly formed to capitalize on the popularity of her art. These female imitators achieved such acclaim that their presentations became widely known as Onna Kabuki—that is, women's Kabuki. Improvements in repertoire made by

Onna Kabuki enlarged its audience to include members of many classes of society. Its influence spread rapidly into the realm of the courtesans, who adopted it as another means by which they could charm and attract customers. Courtesan troupes were referred to significantly as Yūjo Kabuki, meaning prostitutes' or pleasure-women's Kabuki. The background connection of prostitution with Okuni Kabuki, Onna Kabuki, and Yūjo Kabuki (the latter two judged to be the same by some authorities) was identical. The link was accepted and ignored until the prostitute-actress became so notorious that, in 1629, all women in any capacity were banished from the stage by the shōgun's order, on the grounds that their appearance there corrupted the public morals.

The real reason behind the banishment of actresses was a little more involved. During the Tokugawa shogunate social grades were kept separated, since the shogunate frowned upon samurai and high officials mixing with people at the lower levels because it often brought about the drawing of swords. Also many samurai lost their full substance when attending the Kabuki, since it cost an enormous amount of money to associate with a courtesan. Therefore the banishment of women from the stage not only stemmed from public-order reasons but social and political reasons as well.

## WAKASHU KABUKI

Wakashu Kabuki, or Kabuki in which *wakashu* (youths of thirteen and fourteen) took leading roles, developed gradually but did not attain prominence until after the ban on actresses (Fig. 2). The term *wakashu* derives from olden times when a youth of *kuge* (nobility) or samurai family, upon becoming an adult, went through a ritual known as *gempuku:* the ceremonial cutting off of the *maegami* or forelock. Youths who still wore the *maegami* were called *wakashu*.

Except for the fact that the actors were young men instead of young girls, Wakashu Kabuki offered little or no change in audience appeal. The sensual dance, executed by the star actor in a provocative and suggestive manner, remained the foremost attraction. Supporting actors merely lined up on the stage to display their handsome faces and figures or danced as a group.

Undoubtedly to offset the inevitable boredom of all-male casts, the role of the *onnagata*—the female impersonator—the ultimate in Kabuki allurement, was born. Murayama Sakon is credited with being the original *onnagata* of an all-male troupe, though Nagoya Sanza previously had appeared in female dress. Sakon first appeared as a woman in Kyoto in 1649. Later he brought his act to Edo, where he danced at the Murayama-za, a theater owned by his elder brother, Murayama Matasaburō. Sakon's innovation was enthusiastically accepted and became so popular that he soon had *onnagata* rivals, among whom the most highly acclaimed during

2. Wakashu Kabuki. Kabuki in which boys in their teens took leading roles attained prominence following the ban on actresses in 1629.

the next form of Kabuki, known as Yarō Kabuki, were Ukon Genzaemon, Nakamura Kazuma, and Kokan Tarōji.

Although the *Kokon Yakusha Taizen* (All about Actors Old and New) furnishes some facts about Sakon, it has little to say about his costumes. It is known only that he wore a silk kimono and a beautifully colored oblong silk cloth over his partially shaven head and that he used cloths of different colors for various roles. It can be assumed that he used female make-up.

Wakashu Kabuki was short-lived. Only twenty-odd years after Onna Kabuki vanished from the scene, Wakashu Kabuki disappeared in the same way. In 1652, *wakashu* actors were abruptly banished from the stages of Edo, Osaka, and Kyoto by the shogunate for the same reasons that actresses had been banned from the theater. During the civil wars *wakashu* had been allowed to accompany warriors to the battle front, where no women were permitted. They were invited for the express purpose of homosexual prostitution, although their agreeable talents as entertainers were not overlooked. The passing of civil strife by no means ended the intimate association between samurai and *wakashu*. Open indulgence in homosexual affairs became common, and the excesses committed ranged from the lurid to the absurd. Finally a public brawl between two samurai over the favors of a young actor evoked the shogunate ban.

To carry out the order of the shogunate, Ishigaya Shōgen, the famous Edo marshal, issued an edict requiring all *wakashu* in the area of his jurisdiction to shave their forelocks in conformity with the adult male fashion. His rigorous order was copied in Osaka and Kyoto.

## YARŌ KABUKI

In 1653, the year after the disappearance of Wakashu Kabuki, the shogunate unexpectedly gave permission, subject to three specific restrictions (to be noted presently), for the reopening of the theaters. This came about, quite probably, in response to earnest appeals made by the theater managers. When the government reinstated Kabuki, however, permits to open were issued to only four of the fifteen existent Kabuki theaters in the city of Edo: the Ichimura-za, Morita-za, Nakamura-za, and Murayama-za. The Nakamura-za was the oldest theater in Edo and bore the name of its actor-owner Nakamura Kanzaburō, also formerly known as Saruwaka Kanzaburō.

Upon the reopening of these four theaters, managers and actors agreed to abide by the following three restraining conditions: that only those whose hair was shaved in front and dressed in adult *yarō-atama* style could appear on the stage; that their performances should not degenerate into a state of immorality; and that *wakashu* should not perform Kabuki, which meant they were not permitted to dance, but could appear in *monomane-kyōgen-zukushi* (realistic drama).

Presumably the government officials concerned with the banning of Wakashu Kabuki understood *monomane* as being a sober, decent, and realistic stage art. They were correct, for *monomane* is the basic art of every dramatic diversion—the art of imitation. *Monomane* was the closest form to a drama, featuring both dialogue and pantomime. Thereafter, Kabuki was referred to by its fourth name, Yarō Kabuki, and so continued to be burdened with the stigma of its name—this time *yarō,* a not too respectable term used colloquially in referring to men of low class.

At the outset the main elements of Yarō Kabuki still were song and dance, but the actors realized that they projected little theatrical magnetism. With forelocks shaven, they felt denuded of much of their physical beauty. The theatergoer might as well stand on the street and watch the passing scene. They recognized also that the public was ready for something more substantial and interesting in theatrical effort.

Through necessity, Yarō Kabuki began to produce plays with simple plots. This was a progressive movement in the history of Kabuki, for the new drama demanded sincere, realistic acting. The study of histrionics and stage techniques was taken up and rose quickly to unprecedented heights. Furthermore, with the development of plots that introduced an array of new roles, actors and others attached to the theaters were afforded unlimited opportunity to display their creative abilities in many ways.

3. Yarō Kabuki. As the successor to Wakashu Kabuki, Yarō Kabuki began to produce plays with simple plots, thus making the first progressive movement in Kabuki's history.

Inherent genius for color and design brought forth a variety of costumes (Fig. 3). These were enhanced by the invention of *katsura* (wigs), which for some inexplicable reason had not been thought of previously. All of these innovations gave new life to the performances of these stage productions.

No one attached to the theater at this time could be called a playwright. The one-act plays, known as *hanare-kyōgen,* were produced from mere outlined suggestions for plots, to which dialogue was added as freely conceived by theater managers and leading actors, and performed ad libitum. Audiences never expected to hear a definite or established dialogue. In successive performances, actors would experiment and improvise according to their diverse whims and temperaments, and such lines or actions as appeared to be well received were retained, until, through repeated use, they became standard parts of a play. One new play followed another.

Eventually a play was so enthusiastically received that the manager had it recorded for repeat performances. The emergence of this script or *daihon (dai,* subject; *hon,* book) was the origin of Kabuki playwriting in

Japan. No scripts of this age are in existence, but fortunately there are records mentioning them. According to these records, a play was never withdrawn from the theater as long as it drew an audience.

There were two distinct types of plays in the first half of the Yarō Kabuki period, the *keisei-kai* (*keisei*, courtesan; *kai*, buying, purchase) and the *tanzen-roppō*. Plays of the first type, the *keisei-kai*, were concerned with the affairs of courtesans and were usually set in the *irozato*, as the licensed quarters of Edo, Kyoto, and Osaka were called. The Yoshiwara district in Edo, the Shimabara in Kyoto, and the Shimanouchi and Minami in Osaka were the *irozato*.

The costumes for the *keisei-kai* plays were most lavish and glamorous, and much of the traditional stage business, settings, and costumes seen in Kabuki plays depicting licensed quarters were founded in this type of Yarō Kabuki.

The second type, the *tanzen-roppō,* delineated a rather bawdy side of life, not for the sake of bawdiness as such but for the excitement in the characterization of people associated with it. The word *tanzen* propounds two entirely different meanings: one is related to theatrical arts or *geigoto* (*gei,* theatrical arts, dance, music; *koto,* matters), with which, peculiarly enough, we are not immediately concerned; the other, which is relevant, refers to a distinctive type of Japanese apparel that became popular in the seventeenth century: the dress worn by the dandies, who habitually lingered in bathhouses.

During the Shōō era (1652–54), in the Kanda district of Edo, in front of the mansion of the lord Hori Tango-no-Kami, there was a public bathhouse frequented by samurai, *rōnin* (masterless samurai), and *otoko-date* (chivalrous cavaliers, swashbuckling street knights) of the city (Fig. 4). This bathhouse became known as a center of relaxation and revelry. Here *yuna* (female bathhouse attendants) not only washed the backs of the bathers but also engaged in less homely tasks. In rooms prepared for such purposes, they played the *samisen* (a three-stringed instrument similar to a balalaika), danced, and were congenial drinking companions as well as amiable bedfellows.

The apparel of the bathhouse addict was singularly fanciful and attracted much attention not only to the wearer but also to his destination—specifically, the bathhouse in Kanda in front of Hori Tango-no-Kami's mansion. The destination, shortened to *tanzen* (literally, in front of Tan's) became the popular designation of the dress. Later *tanzen* was applied to the attire worn by the habitués of any bathhouse (Fig. 5).

The conspicuous figure of the bathhouse dandy came to be known as *tanzen-sugata* (*tanzen,* bold-designed kimono; *sugata,* style, figure; literally, *tanzen*-clad figure). His hair was dressed in the *tanzen-tate-gami* style, a mode born at this time, when samurai who hoped to cover up their identities while they lingered in the plebeian bagnio cunningly tried to pass as patients taking a cure. By deliberately not shaving the forepart of

4. *Otokodate*. The swashbuckling street knight known as *otokodate* (shown here as he appears in *Otokodate Gosho no Gorōzō*) is among the most colorful of the Edo-period types portrayed in Kabuki.

43

5. *Tanzen-sugata*. The apparel of the early-Edo bath-house dandy was singularly fanciful, and his conspicuous style was known as *tanzen-sugata*—that is, bold-designed-kimono style.

6. *Tanzen-roppō*. Taking their name from the *tanzen* attire of the bathhouse dandies of Edo, *tanzen-roppō* (bawdy plays) became a feature of Yarō Kabuki.

the head and allowing the hair to grow stiffly upward about an inch, the *tanzen-sugata* indicated they had been too ill to shave the head properly.

The dandy wore two quite distinctive decorative swords known as *musori-kakutsuba katana* (*musori*, uncurved; *kaku*, square; *tsuba*, sword guard; *katana*, sword)—that is, swords with square guards and uncurved blades—thrust through the obi in *kannuki* fashion: like gate bolts. These swords easily identified the dandy if his elegant manner of walking failed to do so, because they differed markedly from the samurai weapons.

*Tanzen-roppō*—that is, bawdy plays—were first produced in Edo but also became popular in western Japan in the district then known as Kamigata.

It is pertinent to the history of Kabuki to digress here for a brief explanation of the name of this district. Kamigata was the colloquial word for the present-day area of Kansai (*kan*, barrier; *sai*, west), which refers to the provinces west of the old Hakone barrier. This encompasses the large cities of Kyoto, Osaka, and Kobe. Kamigata (*kami*, upper or higher; *kata*, direction) meant the "higher place," or the direction of the emperor, who remained in his capital, Kyoto, in counterposition to the shogunate in Edo (present-day Tokyo). Kamigata ceased to be used as the name of the western provinces when Emperor Meiji moved to Edo in 1868. The eastern provinces were collectively known as Kantō (*kan*, barrier; *tō*, east). Since Edo was the only influential city in the eastern provinces during the Edo (Tokugawa) period, Kantō is not used in the history of Kabuki as is Kamigata, which covers the three important western cities.

Tamon Shōzaemon, an actor, is credited with the introduction of the distinctive style of walking and acting, as well as the costuming and manner of wearing the swords, in *tanzen-roppō* (Fig. 6). *Tanzen* has been transmitted to us today in the *furi*, or choreography, of such plays as *Sukeroku*, *Saya-ate*, and *Modori Kago* and in the dramatic role of Fuwa Banzaemon in *Ukiyozuka Hiyoku no Inazuma*, more commonly called *Nagoya Sanza*.

In 1664, twelve years after Yarō Kabuki emerged, rapid and epoch-making progress was made with the presentation of *tsuzuki-kyōgen:* dramas of two acts. In Osaka, *Hinin no Adauchi* (Revenge of a Villain), written by Fukuoka Yagoshirō, was staged at the theater known as the Araki Yojibeiza. Also during this period, *Imagawa Shinobi-guruma* (the meaning of the title is no longer clear), by Miyako Dennai, was presented at the Ichimuraza in Edo.

As the composition of the drama became somewhat more complex, the staging also changed. For the first time in Kabuki, draw curtains were introduced to mark the change of scenes. With these developments, Kabuki emerged from its formative years to take its place in a new era of cultural enlightenment in which the common man, for the first time in Japanese history, was the focal point. The Kabuki at last had reached maturity in form and could be proud of its name. It was, however, over two centuries before Kabuki was admitted to the realm of classical theater.

CHAPTER *2*

# Genroku Kabuki

Japanese culture attained the peak of bourgeois fulfillment in the fifteen years of the Genroku era (1688–1703), which falls in the middle of the Edo period. This era, though brief, is frequently referred to as the Japanese Renaissance. Its influence was pronounced through the succeeding Hōei (1704–10), Shōtoku (1711–15), and Kyōho (1716–35) eras, covering some thirty-two years of unparalleled maturity in the arts. Even today, aspects of the Genroku era remain.

It has been said that at about this time the writing of the word Kabuki changed from *kana,* the Japanese syllabary script, to *kanji,* Chinese ideographs, though this is not accepted as true by some authorities. The three ideographs *ka* 歌 meaning song, *bu* 舞 dance, and *ki* 妓 woman were used. In this combination, the third character *ki* indicated prostitute, singing girl, dancing girl, or courtesan. During the latter part of the Edo period, the radical indicating woman in the character *ki* was cleverly replaced by the radical for man or person (伎). This changed the meaning of *ki,* in combination with *ka* and *bu* to "skilled person." It did not, however, change the pronunciation of the character or the word Kabuki as a whole. By the time the new meaning was established, Kabuki was composed solely of men.

Sparked by the rapidly expanding influence of the merchant class, plebeian arts reached the zenith of their expression in the Genroku era. The growing self-consciousness of the citizenry demanded beauty and entertainment peculiarly their own. In this milieu, Kabuki found the freedom it needed for creative growth. The imagination, foresight, and great talent for mimicry of the Genroku actors brought forth the basic *kata,* the peculiar stylized Kabuki forms of acting which encompass direction, make-up, costuming, dancing, hair-styling, hand- and stage-properties, musical accompaniment, elocution, and stage settings. During the early years of Genroku, the dramatists wrote plays in several acts and scenes with plots of increasing intricacy. For the first time Kabuki plays were produced in an indoor theater. The roofless theater ceased to exist for Kabuki.

Among playwrights who rose on the crest of the cultural tide was Japan's foremost dramatic poet and first professional dramatist, Sugimori Nobumori, better known by his pen name Chikamatsu Monzaemon. The novelist Ihara Saikaku, the *haikai* (seventeen-syllabled verse) poet Matsuo Bashō, and Chikamatsu formed a trio of the most illustrious writers of the Japanese Renaissance.

Chikamatsu wrote for both contemporary popular theaters: first for the Kabuki; then for the *ningyō-jōruri-shibai,* today generally referred to as Bunraku (the puppet theater). Chikamatsu's great and popularly acclaimed masterpieces were *jōruri* dramas (dramas in which the puppet action is accompanied by a musical narrative) written expressly for the puppet theater. *Jōruri* dramas were readily adapted to the Kabuki stage. Chikamatsu's plays continue to be presented with persuasive appeal to modern-day audiences, much as Shakespeare's plays are performed in the West.

## DANJŪRŌ I AND ARAGOTO

The founder of the ranking dynasty of Kabuki actors in Edo, Ichikawa Danjūrō I, was also the guiding spirit of the stage during the Genroku era. Danjūrō, writing under the pseudonym of Mimasu Hyōgo, was an amazingly versatile playwright as well as an inventive actor. He created the vigorous masculine style of acting called *aragoto,* which was to continue as the *gei* (special art) of the Ichikawa family.

The *aragoto* drama, written to be performed in a grandiose and exaggerated form of acting, is a type of play or sequence of acts in which the central character displays superhuman qualities or spiritual strength and even occasionally represents a divine or an evil spirit. It readily appealed to the masses, who found in the *aragoto* actors substitute heroes for the valiant warriors of the glorious past. This romantic appeal reflected the temper of the Edo populace, which had always shown great enthusiasm for the legendary events in its history. While the theatergoers of Edo accepted without question the highly stylized characterizations of the *aragoto* plays, they rejected the soft feminine love stories of the *wagoto* plays of Kamigata. In *wagoto* plays, acting is noticeably predominant, whereas there is a preponderance of dancing or rhythmic movements throughout an *aragoto* drama. Musical accompaniment with a distinct personal style is therefore essential to *aragoto* drama.

*Kimpira jōruri* (puppet plays about a supernaturally strong man) were the favored dramatic fare preceding *aragoto*. The puppets used in this medium do not exist today; only pictures of them remain. The hero of *Kimpira jōruri* was Sakata Kimpira, a picturesque character who symbolized matchless strength and who destroyed evil characters. Sometimes Kimpira would demolish an entire army single-handedly. When he annihilated demons, he displayed such great power and roughness that the head and limbs of many of the puppets were hurled off into space. It was largely from this vigorous theater that Danjūrō I is said to have taken his *aragoto*, its costumes, and possibly its make-up. Responsibility for the eventual unpopularity of this type of *jōruri* was attributed to the performance of a play entitled *Kimpira Saigo* (The End of Kimpira), in which the sustaining character dies. Without the hero, fans lost interest and deserted the puppet theater for the live theater of Kabuki.

Danjūrō I is credited with originating *kumadori*, the art of special and unusual make-up. *Kumadori* refers not only to make-up of the face but also to make-up of the arms and legs. In 1673, when Danjūrō was fourteen, he made his initial appearance in the role of Sakata no Kintoki in *Shitennō Osanadachi* (The Childhood of Four Strong Warriors or Four Faithful Bodyguards) wearing the first recorded *kumadori,* a weird make-up produced by the use of bold colored lines (see Chapter 23). Danjūrō had his face painted entirely red, and black lines were drawn over this to delineate and emphasize his features. The most prominent features of the make-up were large, fierce, upward-curved eyebrows exemplifying vitality. This style of *kumadori* later became known erroneously as *Genroku-guma. Kumadori* continued to develop during the Genroku era, and Danjūrō was its most versatile exponent.

Danjūrō's costume for the role of the hero Kintoki was patterned with alternating purple and white squares called *dōji-gōshi* (Fig. 71), and to accentuate Kintoki's virility he wore a dark blue obi—an immense, round, wadded obi tied in a *tombo-musubi* (dragonfly knot). *Kumadori* extended to the arms and legs in those early times. Today, flesh-colored tights, or *niku-juban (niku,* flesh; *juban,* underneath garment), on which the *kumadori* pattern is painted, are worn instead of make-up, thus allowing actors to change costumes rapidly without danger of soiling their garments.

*Niku-juban* were devised in 1904 by Kawachi Hanshichi, a maker of *tabi* (bifurcated socks). He offered the *niku-juban* to Onoe Kikugorō VI, who at first was hesitant to use them, feeling that it would be difficult to move his arms with his accustomed grace, but on the advice of Bandō Mitsugorō VII, a great Kabuki dance star, Kikugorō yielded, and *niku-juban* (flesh-colored tights) are now in general use.

The original *niku-juban* covered the body to the elbow. Ichikawa Shin-jūrō, student of Danjūrō IX, is thought to have been the first actor to order *niku-juban* which extended below the elbow to the wrist. Eventually, it was designed to cover the hands. It should be noted here that costumers still persist in making the *niku-juban* with such outmoded knitted material that even on the first day's performance it looks as long underwear does after it has been worn for a number of days. Topped off with a brocaded costume, nothing could be more incongruous or ghastly in appearance.

Although Danjūrō I revolutionized Kabuki with his introduction of *aragoto* plays, he did not confine his playwriting exclusively to this medium.

Three of his dramas still survive: *Narukami* (Thunder God or The Fall of the Recluse Saint Narukami), *Shibaraku* (Wait a Moment), and *Fuwa*, the original drama of *saya-ate*, the "rude challenge." *Saya-ate* (*saya*, sheath of a sword; *ate*, to hit) was the extremely rude and offensive act of a samurai's deliberately bumping into another's sword. If no apology was forthcoming, a fight ensued, for the sword was the embodiment of the spirit of the samurai. For the overly aggressive warrior, *saya-ate* was a perfect means of promoting a fight, and instances of it abound in the drama.

## ACTORS AND ROLES

Kabuki made steady progress under the effective guidance of Danjūrō I and other celebrated actors. Among the most outstanding of these were two Kamigata actors: Sakata Tōjūrō I (1647–1709), a great *tachi-yaku* (actor of leading male roles) whose *kata* (stylized format) was copied by the puppet theater, and Yoshizawa Ayame I (1673–1729), probably the foremost *onnagata* of all time, whose training and style of acting had the greatest influence in molding later *onnagata*. Yoshizawa Ayame I wrote the *Ayame-gusa*, the standard textbook for the female impersonator.

Another famous actor, Nakamura Denkurō I (?–1714), created *saruguma*, the "monkey-type" make-up, in the third year of Genroku (1690), as well as the acting style for the role of Asahina as it is seen today in *Yakko Asahina Ōiso Gayoi* (The Dandy Asahina Haunting the Famed Pleasure Quarter in Ōiso).

The actor Yamanaka Heikurō (1632–1724) was known for his *kataki-yaku* (villain roles), especially those of the *kuge-aku* (wicked noblemen). He also invented a favorite and devilishly effective make-up, variously called *Heikurō-guma*, *hannya-guma*, or *kijo-guma*, for the demoness who appears in the last scene of the dance-drama *Kyō-Ganoko Musume Dōjōji* (The Gay Scene of the Maiden in Kanoko Kimono at Dōjō Temple). Heikurō first presented his demoness make-up in 1705 at the Ichimura-za during his seventy-third year, a ripe age at which to be creative. The costume and make-up for the *kuge-aku* (wicked noblemen) roles of today are taken from those originated by Heikurō and another famous actor, Nakajima Mihoemon (1699–1762), who followed Heikurō.

Ogino Sawanojō I (1656–1704), who later became a *tachi-yaku*, was an *onnagata* and for many years was Danjūrō I's acting partner. He displayed especial brilliance in *waka-oyama* (young woman) characterizations. At the Nakamura-za in 1698, during his second performance of *Onna Narukami* (Priestess Narukami), Sawanojō set a precedent-breaking style by wearing a wide obi for the first time on the stage. Thereafter, the wide obi became fashionable, not only on the stage but also off, and its use has persisted to the present. Prior to this performance, it was the accepted fashion to wear a narrow obi only four or five inches wide and approximately six feet long.

As wigs and make-up developed, the drama became more complex. The full-length *tsuzuki-kyōgen,* plays of several acts, appeared and roles became more diversified. These roles usually fell into one of the following eight important categories, the male roles being generally known as *otoko-gata,* the female as *onnagata.*

*tachi-yaku:* (*yaku,* role) leading male character or man of eminence

*wakashu-gata:* (*kata,* role) young man or boy

*oyaji-yaku:* (*oyaji,* old father) old man

*kataki-yaku:* (*kataki,* enemy) villain

*nyōbō-gata:* (*nyōbō,* wife, although not limited to wife's roles) leading female character, around thirty years of age; later known as *tachi-oyama* (*tachi,* matured)

*kasha-gata* or *fuke-oyama:* (*kasha,* originally a woman servant in a pleasure-house, teahouse, etc.; *fuke,* old) old woman

*waka-oyama:* (*waka,* young) unmarried girl, fourteen to eighteen years old

*ko-yaku:* child's role

Actors were type-cast and rarely ventured from their designated roles. On occasion, however, they would change their roles. An *onnagata* might change from women's roles to become a *tachi-yaku.* The child actors of Genroku were trained to become either *onnagata* or *tachi-yaku.* A *wakashu* or young man's part was not left in the hands of an old man, as neither acting nor make-up had been perfected to the level where an actor could, regardless of his own age, present himself as a character of greatly different age. Many actors bowed from the stage in their prime to enter other fields of endeavor, usually becoming merchants. During Genroku, it was inconceivable for an actor to remain in the theater until feeble in the knees, as did the beloved Nakamura Kichiemon I, who performed until his death in 1954.

Under the aegis of Danjūrō I and his son Danjūrō II, the *kata* took form for two of the most highly esteemed and spectacular plays in the Kabuki repertoire, *Shibaraku* (Wait a Moment) and *Sukeroku Yukari no Edo-Zakura* (Sukeroku's Affinity for Edo Cherry Blossoms, or The Love Story of Sukeroku and Agemaki). The latter play, incidentally, is generally performed in the springtime. The present-day costumes for both of these plays remain almost identical with those of Genroku times.

## SHIBARAKU AND ITS COSTUMES

The flamboyant *aragoto* dramas of Danjūrō I have left an eloquent imprint on the Kabuki world, but none has attained the prominence of *Shibaraku.* The hero of the play, Kamakura no Gongorō Kagemasa, appears in the most enormous and fantastically styled costume and wig, which makes him anything but alluring to Western eyes insofar as color and beauty are concerned. The play, moreover, has practically no plot to impress the beholder, yet it is a tour de force, for it is difficult to discard the remembrance of a mounting so overwhelming in feeling of greatness and power.

Present-day performances of *Shibaraku* are brought vibrantly alive by such actors as Ichimura Uzaemon XVII, Matsumoto Kōshirō VIII, and Kōshirō's younger brother, Onoe Shōroku II. Shōroku is perhaps the most excitingly skillful *aragoto* actor of all by reason of his winning personality, stalwart physique, and full-throated diction, in addition to his superb *kata* (acting format). Some Japanese critics, however, considered the *aragoto* of the late Bandō Mitsugorō VII the most perfected *kata* among contemporary artists. (Mitsugorō died in 1961 at the age of seventy-nine, after seventy-two years of stage life. His real name was Morita Jūsaku.) It is difficult to agree with this opinion, because Mitsugorō was small of stature and had a small, almost childish voice, both of which detracted from the bombastic character of the *aragoto* role in which he played. Perhaps the point in question is one in which the Westerner fails in his concept of Kabuki. He is still looking for some type of reality, be it imaginative or realistic. The Japanese sees the force within the less noisy spectacle.

*Shibaraku's* costuming and make-up were set in the tenth year of Genroku (1697), which saw the initial performance of the play under the title *Sankai Nagoya*. The *Kabuki Nendai-ki* (Chronological History of Kabuki Drama) gives us our only hint of the costume worn by the energetic Danjūrō I in this first performance. The third and final revision, the fantasy we know today, was the creation of Danjūrō II, who wore it on his first appearance in *Shibaraku*, then known as *Jumpū Taihei-ki* (The Story of Peaceful Days like Good Wind on the Sea), at the Edo Kawarasaki-za in 1736.

The first costume in which Danjūrō I appeared was an *atsuwata-no-hirosode* (*atsu,* thick; *wata,* padded; *hiro,* wide opening; *sode,* sleeve): a thickly padded wide-sleeve garment, commonly called *atsuwata,* worn over *yoroi* (armor) under which was a *juban* (undergarment), probably of white silk, and one other garment (Fig. 7). *Kote* (arm protectors) covered the lower half of the arms, and *sune-ate* (leg guards) encased the legs to the ankles. The *atsuwata* was belted with a *nawa* (rope) obi made of oversized wadded cloth rope through which was thrust a single long sword that extended high above the opposite shoulder in the back. The feet were bare. The *katsura* (wig) was dressed in *furiwake-no-sumi-maegami* (*furiwake,* center-parted; *sumi,* corner; *maegami,* forelock) style—that is, with the hair parted in the middle and shaved at the corners of the forehead where the forelock had already been cut in the *gempuku* or *gembuku* (coming-of-age) ceremony. A *chikara-gami* (*chikara,* strength; *kami,* paper), a hair decoration made of fine-quality *hōsho* paper, was tied around the *mage,* the ponytail. Originally it was inconspicuous, but it gradually took on the shape of a pair of bat wings to denote power.

The pattern of the first costume for *Shibaraku* was one of the most novel of Kabuki origin. The reddish-brown *atsuwata* was designed with three distinctive motifs, including a demon's red arm, taken from the story of Watanabe no Tsuna and the demon who lived in the famed Rashōmon gate in Kyoto; a *kinsatsu* or prohibitory sign (from the same story); and the back view of a *kabuto* (helmet) with its laminar folds. The *kabuto* was ornamented in front with the golden "helmet horns" called *kuwagata* (*kuwa,* hoe; *gata,* shape or type) because its shape was taken from that of the lowly hand hoe. The blade end and sides form an outline similar to that of horns.

The second costume of Danjūrō I in *Shibaraku* (Fig. 8) was a blue *suō,* a set of clothing consisting of an *uwagi* (outer garment) with wide-open sleeves and *naga-bakama* (long trailing trousers). The right arm was removed from the sleeve, revealing the bare upper right portion of the torso and arm. Through the left side of the obi was thrust an unusually long sword that curved upward past the shoulder. A huge *kamahige,* a sickle-shaped mustache, rose to meet the *yarō-atama* (adult male hair styling) wig, and a samurai *eboshi* (hat) was firmly fixed to the head. Relieving the severity of the monochrome costume, a *daimon* (large crest) was worked into the center of each sleeve. In this instance, Danjūrō's crest, the *mimasu mon* (*mi,* three; *masu,* dry-measure box; *mon,* crest) was used. The crest is called the *mimasu mon* because the three concentric squares are said to be patterned after three rice-measuring boxes.

The third costume, the final refinement of the *aragoto* costume for *Shibaraku,* was evolved by Danjūrō II and is essentially the costume used even today (Fig. 9). The *suō,* now of enormously exaggerated proportions, is *kaki* or *kakishibu,* a reddish-brown color taken from the color of the astringent juice pressed from the skin of the Japanese persimmon. It is a color that gives an impression of colossal strength, and its sturdiness is sharply enhanced by the use of rough cotton cloth. Probably the most distinguishing characteristic of this *Shibaraku suō* is the out-sized sleeves with the *mimasu* crest set in their centers. Each sleeve stretched out makes a large square by the insertion of cloth-covered bamboo splints. Only a great actor could survive this monstrous costume, which not only completely envelops the man but also extends far beyond his arms and trails behind his covered feet.

The existing *ishō-no-tsukechō* (costumers' notebooks) clearly show that little change has been made throughout the years in the *Shibaraku* costume. In comparison, a costume worn by Ichikawa Danjūrō IX during the November 1895 performance at the Tokyo Kabuki-za and that worn forty-one years later by Matsumoto Kōshirō VII for the January 1936 Kabuki-za performance are found to be almost identical.

The form of the costume was identical, but Danjūrō wore a plain

7. First *Shibaraku* costume: *atsuwata-no-hirosode*. This thickly padded wide-sleeve garment, worn over armor, was devised by Danjūrō I.

8. Second *Shibaraku* costume: *suō*. The second costume chosen by Danjūrō I for his role in *Shibaraku* was a blue *suō*, a set of clothing consisting of an *uwagi* with wide open sleeves and the long trailing trousers known as *naga-bakama* (here drawn up for combat).

9. Third *Shibaraku* costume: *suō*. The third costume for *Shibaraku* was evolved by Danjūrō II and is essentially the costume still used today for the role of Kamakura Gongorō Kagemasa.

10. *Sukeroku* costume. The costume evolved by Danjūrō II for the role of Sukeroku was almost identical with that seen today on the Kabuki stage. The chief difference is that the earlier costume employed the stylized peony crest called *gyōyō-botan mon,* as shown here.

*kaki* (reddish brown) *suō* with immensely long, trailing trousers, whereas Kōshirō's *suō* was designed with lateral stripes of persimmon brown. Both costumes had large *mimasu* crests in white. As usual, the sleeves were made to look like large square shields by the insertion of cloth-covered bamboo splints.

The *kitsuke* (kimono) which Danjūrō wore was fashioned with green cranes in lozenge shape, dyed on white ground and outlined with black-thread embroidery. Black silk banded the wrist hems. Although Kōshirō's *kitsuke* was the same, the dressmaker's book mentions that it was made of white Mōka cotton, a fine cloth made in the Mōka district.

Danjūrō's *juban* had a white *eri* (collar) of cotton with a checkerboard pattern known as *ichimatsu* made with the *mimasu* crest. Kōshirō's juban was made of *rinzu* (figured silk in satin weave) with a *saya-gata* (stylized cross) pattern over which the *mimasu* crest was rendered in appliqué outlined with embroidery.

Danjūrō wore two garments of red silk under the *juban:* the *maru-shitagi* (*maru*, full length; *shitagi*, undergarment) and the *maru-juban*. In this instance, Kōshirō favored two half-length undergarments: the *dōgi* (*dō,* trunk; *ki,* garment), a sleeveless garment of scarlet silk crepe, and the *dō-juban,* also without sleeves but having a white collar.

All the remaining accessories for both actors were reasonably the same. The obi was a black *maru-guke* or rope-style (not flat) obi. The *sekitai* obi with the *suō* had a flat section at each end decorated with white *mimasu* crests. The *chikara* or *niō-dasuki* (*niō*, two Deva kings; *tasuki*, band to hold up sleeves) was made of green and purple bands twisted together. Both actors wore *suji-guma kumadori* (blatant line make-up) with red lines on a white painted ground.

The wig in each case was the *maegami-tsuki-abura-gome-no-gohon-kuruma-bin* (*maegami*, forelock; *tsuki*, with; *abura-gome*, coated and hardened with pomade; *gohon*, five; *kuruma*, wheel; *bin*, sides, sidelocks) decorated with *hōsho-no-chikara-gami* (*hōsho*, thick Japanese paper; *no*, of; *chikara*, strength; *kami*, paper). The *hōsho-no-chikara-gami,* as noted earlier, is a large paper decoration made to look like a bat's wings to denote strength.

Danjūrō and Kōshirō wore the samurai hat called *eboshi*. Danjūrō's was styled with fancy strings braided with red, white, and green skeins of thread and with *himo* (ties) of white silk attached. Kōshirō's *eboshi* strings were colored red, white, green, and purple, and the ties were of twisted green threads.

Today the leading character of *Shibaraku* appears in the Danjūrō version with a plain persimmon-brown *suō*.

•

## SUKEROKU AND ITS COSTUMES

Ichikawa Danjūrō II, like his illustrious father, contributed to the development of Kabuki, especially in the arts of make-up and costuming.

His fresh ideas led to improvements and changes in the *kata* for a number of the Jūhachiban, the eighteen favorite plays of the Ichikawa family. One of these is *Sukeroku Yukari no Edo-Zakura,* first produced in 1713 with Danjūrō II in the leading role of Sukeroku.

The costume for the role of Sukeroku passed through two formative stages before reaching the style accepted as standard. The first costume was a kimono of black pongee on which large bush-peonies were appliquéd from the hem almost to the shoulder. The kimono was topped off with the *mimasu mon,* Danjūrō's family crest. The pattern and color of the obi are unknown, but probably the obi was of the *karuta-musubi* type, broader than a man's yet not so wide as a woman's. Accessories were an orange cotton *hachimaki* (headband) bound around the head, dark-blue *tabi* socks, and one sword, the longer of the usual pair worn by samurai.

The famous *karakasa* (*kara,* China; *kasa,* umbrella; actually a lacquered umbrella), which so unmistakably identifies Sukeroku today, was not used at that time. Instead, Sukeroku, pursuing an enemy, rushed onto the *hanamichi* (runway through audience) brandishing a *shakuhachi* (a five-hole bamboo flute). The *shakuhachi* is still retained, but it is shoved into the obi at the back. Sukeroku wore his kimono in *hadanugi* fashion: the upper part of the outer garment slipped off the shoulders and tucked into the obi. His feet were bare, a Kabuki convention thought to give additional beauty to the *mise en scène*.

A second performance of *Sukeroku* was not to reach the boards until three years later. In 1716, Danjūrō II again appeared in a black kimono, retaining the *mimasu mon,* but with a purple *hachimaki,* as used today. He wore *taka-geta* (high-stilted wooden clogs), and held in one hand a *shakuhachi* (bamboo flute) and in the other a *karakasa,* undoubtedly of the same style as the *ja-no-me,* an umbrella with a double ring or bull's-eye design.

It is hard to understand why *Sukeroku* went begging for thirty-three years before its third performance in 1749, when again Danjūrō II mounted this favorite play. Danjūrō's costume was almost identical with that seen currently except that he used the *gyōyō-botan mon,* a crest containing a stylized peony flower with leaves dyed in many colors (Fig. 10). His garment was not made of pongee but of red-lined black *habutae* (plain silk) without pattern, decorated only with five crests: on the sleeves, at each breast, and at center back.

There is a story, fact or fiction, concerning Danjūrō's use of the *gyōyō-botan mon*. It relates that Misaka, a ranking lady-in-waiting and an enthusiastic admirer of Danjūrō II, presented him with a valuable kimono crested with the *gyōyō-botan* of the celebrated Konoe family of Kyoto. This garment had been a gift to Misaka from her mistress, the daughter of Konoe Iehiro and wife of the Shōgun Ienobu. Konoe Iehiro was considered a fount of knowledge on all matters relating to imperial ceremony and etiquette and therefore had been invited to the Edo court to instruct officials in protocol. The legend may well have authenticity. Danjūrō's wearing of the kimono would have been a subtle compliment to a distinguished lady.

The *shitagi* (undergarment) was put on as one with the *uwagi* (outer garment), the two overlapping and held trimly to the body by a blue obi made of a twill-weave fabric with an over-all woven pattern of *mimasu,* the three nested concentric squares, peony blossoms, and the congratulatory Chinese character *kotobuki.* An *inrō* (medicine box) hung at the right hip. A single sword, the sheath decorated with the tubercled skin of a shark, was thrust into the left side of the obi. The flute protruded from the center back of the obi. *Geta* (wooden clogs for outdoor wear) of Paulownia wood with black *hanao* (thongs), were worn with bright yellow *tabi* socks to form an excellent contrast. Thus garbed, Danjūrō II's Sukeroku was, all in all, an extremely gorgeous fellow—so gorgeous, in fact, that the costume was referred to as *kuramae* (*kura,* storehouse, granary; *mae,* before, in front of) because of its aura of great affluence.

There was in this capsule description of the costume more than a little of the aptness that often characterizes such tags. Kuramae was the name of a street in the Asakusa district of Edo. Facing this street were the government warehouses in which the rice exacted as land tax was stored. The *fudasashi,* or licensed merchants, received the rice from the government, sold it to the ordinary rice dealers, and exchanged it for money for the samurai class. Accordingly, the *fudasashi* were very wealthy and lived in a very extravagant style, and this style, in turn, received the name of *kuramae-fū:* in-front-of-the-storehouse style.

## DANJŪRŌ'S PRECEPTS FOR ACTORS

Danjūrō II kept notes of his so-called secrets concerning his *kata,* but unfortunately his writings were never published. His ideas, however, were handed down by word of mouth or jotted down by other actors and were thus preserved for posterity. Twelve of his precepts are listed here.

1. For *aragoto* roles, the best *tasuki* (cloth band used to hold back kimono sleeves) is braided blue and purple, and the *shigoki* (soft sash) should be purple, as the combination of these colors lends additional feeling of strength to the roles in *Shibaraku* and *Yanone* (Arrowhead).

2. When a short person wears the great pleated *hangire* (wide trousers with stiffened back, copied from the Nō), in order to appear stronger and taller, he should have them styled longer than normal and should wear them high above the waistline. This will give a short actor dignity and authority.

3. In order to appear taller in *aragoto* plays, one should wear high *geta* under the *suō.* (Prior to Danjūrō's time, only short *hakama* were worn with the *suō.*) To avoid clacking the *geta,* pad the teeth (upright supports) with wadded cotton. (Wadded footgear is worn today by the characters Wata-

nabe no Tsuna in *Ibaraki* [Demon Ibaraki] and Gongorō in *Shibaraku*.)

4. Unlined garments should never be worn in *aragoto* plays. To give them body, they should be lined with wadded cotton—never with silk, since silk, being soft, would not give the necessary fullness. The *juban* should always be red, for red is the color most successful in portraying a robust character.

5. One must not wear *tabi* with the *kamishimo*—that is, the combination of *hakama* and a jumper with winglike shoulders worn over the kimono. To be shod with *tabi* when wearing this costume makes a person appear weak. (Danjūrō learned this from his own experience in later years.)

6. White *tabi* make one appear frail.

7. The white base of *kumadori* make-up should be applied unevenly in order to make the *kumadori* appear less flat.

8. Before striking a *mie* (stylized cross-eyed pose), it is best to close the eyes, for when they are opened again they will appear larger. (At first the *mie* appears extremely ridiculous to the Western observer, but it is very much admired and appreciated by the true Kabuki fan.)

9. Portray the feelings and bravado of a child of seven when performing *aragoto*. Do not act in the manner of a good-for-nothing or a gambler, for this leaves only the impression of vulgarity.

10. Use *beni* (red coloring), not rouge or lipstick, on the face and around the eyes, but it must not be too bright. If it is too dark, however, it will look black from a distance. (Lighting for performances was provided by natural light during the day and by candlelight in the evening.)

11. For roles calling for *seppuku* (suicide by disembowelment) or the portrayal of illness, paint the lips white rather than blue, since white lips give a bluish tinge to the face. Also, purse or tighten the lips to make them look narrow, since this gives a person the appearance of suffering or the approach of death. (*Seppuku* is the formal word for hara-kiri: ritual suicide performed in order to die with honor. The samurai performed it by thrusting a short sword into the left side of his abdomen, pulling it across and then up; others by simply cutting from left to right across the abdomen. Danjūrō's advice regarding the portrayal of *seppuku* and illness is still followed today.)

12. For a role that calls for a lost or wounded eye, to keep the eye closed constantly would be difficult and would distort the muscles of the face; so the eye should be painted black, which makes it appear to be blind or wounded.

## GENROKU THEATERS OF EDO

At the beginning of the Genroku era (1688–1703) there were seven theaters in the city of Edo. Only four of these—the Morita-za, the Murayama-za, the Yamamura-za, and the Nakamura-za—were *yagura:* theaters licensed by the government. The remaining three—the Miyako-za, the

Tamagawa-za, and the Kawarasaki-za, which were unlicensed—served alternately as *hikae yagura* (reserve or unlicensed managements) for the Nakamura-za which was in financial straits and could not afford a run. The *hikae yagura* had authority to sponsor stage performances for the *yagura* when they were financially unable to give a scheduled program.

In 1652, the Murayama-za sold its *yagura* rights to Ichimura Uzaemon, who changed the name of the theater to the Ichimura-za. The Murayama-za thereby forfeited its right to resume business under its original name, but subsequently it became a potential unlicensed or reserve management under the name of Kiri-za.

A scandalous love affair between Ikushima, an actor attached to the Yamamura-za, and a ranking lady-in-waiting by the name of Ejima resulted not only in their exile but also in the closing of all theaters in Edo on February 6, 1712. Later three of the previously licensed theaters were allowed to reopen, but the Yamamura-za was excluded. Two of the three *hikae yagura* were re-established, and the third, the Miyako-za, was replaced by the Kiri-za.

The three licensed theaters of Edo, known collectively as Edo San-za (the Three Theaters of Edo) were called *hon* (main) *yagura*. The word *yagura* was used interchangeably to refer to the management and, in its literal sense, to the drum tower which was built on the roof over the main entrance of the theater and from which floated bunting emblazoned with the theater owner's crest. The right to fly his flag actually certified that the theater owner had official permission to give performances.

Friction was inevitable between the *hon yagura* (licensed theaters) and the *hikae yagura* (unlicensed managements), for the *hikae yagura* would refuse to close their theatrical performances when the *hon yagura* reached financial independence. Even though the managements of the theaters changed, actors usually remained with their respective theaters.

Generally performances were given during six alternate months each year: November, January, March, May, July, and September. The acting year began in November with the *kaomise,* the face-showing or formal introduction of a theatrical season, at which the actors were presented. The roles in which they would appear during the season were announced.

The intervening months were equally busy for the actors, who spent this time in intensive rehearsal. They took dancing, singing, and samisen lessons. The theater managers used these intervals to raise the money for the following month's performance. Since banks and moneylending establishments did not exist, management had to turn to prosperous *chōnin* to finance each season's runs. If a production proved popular, the *chōnin* received a percentage of the profits, plus interest on the original loan. For lack of attendance, plays would sometimes close after a week's run. On the other hand, programs that appealed to the public would run until the "beginning of the next season"—that is, a program begun in January might run until March, perhaps for sixty days.

## THE JŌSHIKI MAKU, KABUKI'S STANDARD CURTAIN

Activities of the Edo San-za (the three licensed theaters of Edo) are only memories, but contemporary audiences have a constant reminder of these illustrious theaters in the three colors of the *jōshiki maku,* Kabuki's standard striped draw curtain, which represents these three never-to-be-forgotten playhouses that did so much to further the prestige of the Kabuki. The Ichimura-za, in 1664, was the first to use the three-colored striped cotton curtain of black, *kaki* (reddish brown), and moss green. These same colors are used today in all traditional Kabuki theaters. The Nakamura-za varied the colors, using stripes of black, *kaki* (reddish brown), and white. The Morita-za also used the classic striping but changed the order, using green, *kaki* (reddish brown), and black. It can be assumed that the inspiration for the three-colored curtain came from the five-colored *agemaku,* the entrance curtain of the Nō stage.

An exact replica of the Nō curtain could not be used: the aristocratic Nō actors would have felt it a reprehensible breach of ethics if the "river-bed beggars" had encroached upon their domain. The *jōshiki maku* is an unvarying feature of all pure Kabuki. The curtain is pulled by hand from one side of the stage to the other, from stage left to stage right at the beginning of the play, of an act, or of a scene, from stage right to stage left at the end—or vice versa. The types of plays are not identified by the direction in which the *jōshiki maku* is drawn, but the use of a drop curtain or *donchō,* which was introduced into Japan after 1868, signifies that the drama is not of classic Kabuki origin.

## REGULATIONS GOVERNING COSTUMES BEFORE AND DURING GENROKU

The government kept a wary eye on both costumes and properties of Kabuki from the days of the early Wakashu Kabuki throughout Genroku. This was not unnatural, for the government often issued restrictive bans not only upon actors but also on all other classes of people, including the nobles. To stem the spread of excessive luxury in the spirited Genroku era, the Tokugawa shogunate repeatedly imposed limitations on the wearing of extravagant clothing, on the display of wealth, and on free indulgence in luxury. Such injunctions were often ignored, and this led to additional, more repressive bans.

In January 1662, one such follow-up order was posted to the effect that actors and dancers must refrain from extravagant living on and off the stage; stage properties could not be covered with gold or silver plating; and costumes could not be fashioned from Chinese *karaori* (brocade). Similar regulations were again imposed in March 1668, limiting Kabuki actors' off-stage dress to plain-woven, patternless silk, cotton, or pongee. On the stage, in the same year the casts were permitted to wear costumes of striped silk in plain weaves, *habutae* (the most popular Japanese plain-woven silk), and *tsumugi* (rough-textured pongee). Embroidered cloth and dyed materials, including the customary red linings and purple *zukin* (hoods), were forbidden, since the dyes were very expensive.

Even today, it should be noted, eight pounds of red dye will cost about ¥15,000 or approximately $42.00, a substantial sum by Japanese standards. Red dye or *beni-mochi* is made by crushing buds of the *beni* (a flower similar to a small chrysanthemum) into a paste which in turn is made into small, flat, circular pellets. *Beni-mochi* pellets are now made only in Yamagata Prefecture in the northern part of Japan. It can thus be understood why the Tokugawa shogunate considered red-dyed materials a luxury.

There were two pertinent reasons for proscribing the use of purple. Purple dye was made from the roots of a rare weed and was the most expensive of dyes; and the color was reserved exclusively for the upper classes, such as the various ranks of the daimyō and their overlord the shōgun. Contrary to the belief of some, *murasaki* (purple) never was and is not the color of the emperor. There are two emperor's colors or *kinjiki* (prohibited colors): *kōrozen*, a yellowish brown, and *kikujin*—popularly called *ao-iro*—a yellowish green, said to be the color of mildew on malted rice. In the emperor's ceremonial costume, the *sokutai*, the *hō* (outer robe) dyed in *kōrozen* is the most formal; that dyed in *ao-iro*, the semiformal. These are respectively known as the *kōrozen-no-hō* and the *ao-iro-no-hō*.

As early as 1635, Satsuma Jōun, owner of the puppet theater called the Satsuma-za and initiator of the *jōruri* ballad-dramas in Edo, was sent to prison for using a purple silk-crepe curtain imprinted with the Shimazu crest (a cross in a circle), although the curtain was a personal gift from the Lord of Shimazu, an influential daimyō, to the *ningyō-jōruri-shibai*—that is, the puppet theater—in appreciation of Jōun's artistry. For the *hikimaku* (draw curtain) of the smaller-sized stage of Genroku, the authorities permitted the use of silk crepe or cotton cloth, but the color purple was taboo.

With monotonous regularity, restrictive laws continued to be imposed or reimposed, only to be ignored by those at whom they were directed. Two of these edicts, however, left a decided imprint on classical Kabuki and its *kata* (format).

One order, enacted in 1703, directed that henceforth plays were not to depict current events, especially any activity of the daimyō or the shōgun. Playwrights found the events of the day too fruitful to avoid, and plots based on current events were merely placed in other periods, and fictitious names were used for the characters. Moreover, as most actors and many in the audience had never seen the actual apparel of a daimyō or a shōgun, the costumes for these plays were the creations of fertile imaginations.

By the other order the use of real swords on the stage was prohibited in February 1704, just one month too late to prevent a tragic disaster. Suginami Toranosuke, a talented *wakashu*, became a *tachi-yaku* taking the name of Ikushima Zenjirō. He then became a pupil of Ichikawa Danjūrō I, taking the name of Ichikawa Zenjirō. It is presumed that ill feeling developed between the two, for Danjūrō noticeably neglected his pupil. Danjūrō's actions very much upset Zenjirō's father, Ikushima Hanroku (not to be confused with the Ikushima of the earlier-mentioned Ejima-Ikushima affair). In great anger, Ikushima thrust a sword through Danjūrō. Thus ended the life of one of the most illustrious actors ever to appear on any stage.

## COSTUMES AND MAKE-UP

All actors of the time put on make-up in their own dressing rooms, just as they do today. Dressing was a different matter. With the exceptions of the *zagashira* (head of the troupe), the star *tachi-yaku,* and the *onnagata,* —who used private dressing rooms—actors were dressed in the *ishō-gura,* the costume room located, during this period, next to the *tōdori-beya,* the backstage management office.

It was the accepted practice to behave toward the *onnagata* as if they were women, a courtesy befitting the feminine gentility for which the *onnagata* strove both on and off stage. The Genroku *onnagata* were careful not to expose their bodies. They had separate baths and usually dressed themselves, even tying their own long obi—a time-consuming practice, since short cuts were then unknown. The *onnagata* had separate *toko-yama* or wig dressers, and it was the *toko-yama* who gave them assistance in dressing if it was needed, particularly when they performed a *kayaku* role: one not characteristic of the *onnagata,* such as a male role. At this time, the *katsura-shi* (today called *katsura-ya*), the artisan who made the copper bases for the *katsura,* and the *toko-yama,* the man responsible for dressing and maintaining the wigs during a run, were one and the same.

Actors generally paid for their own costumes, but minor performers were provided for from the *kura-ishō* (*kura,* warehouse; *ishō,* costumes) by the theater management. However, the *kura-ishō*—that is, costumes kept in the theater warehouse—also included full complements of costumes for roles that were often repeated, such as the following:

*asa-gamishimo: kamishimo* (formal samurai costume consisting of jumper with winglike shoulders and short pleated culottes) made of *asa* (ramie) cloth, without lining
*bōzu ishō:* priests' robes
*hitatare:* wide-sleeved costume, based on Nō costume patterned after the real-life formal dress of high-ranking daimyō and the shōgun
*juban:* undergarments, usually red, although not necessarily so
*jūni-hitoe:* many-layered formal dress worn by ladies of the imperial court in Heian times

*kamishimo:* formal samurai costume consisting of jumper with winglike shoulders and short pleated culottes (*hakama*)

*kappa:* raincoat

*kariginu:* set of clothing consisting of a wide-open-sleeve *uwagi*—that is, a coat with an *ate-obi* (*ate,* from *ateru,* to apply or touch; *obi,* sash or belt)—and *hakama,* used only for stage nobleman's costume

*kesa:* surplice worn over outer robe as an official symbol of priesthood

*keshin-mono:* (*ke,* disguise; *shin,* body) animal costumes including those for toads, horses, monkeys, boars, and badgers, which are the property of the *kodōgu* (hand properties) department

*kyahan:* leggings or gaiters

*momohiki:* very tight, long, thick navy-blue cotton trousers, opened at the back, with a lapover so as not to expose the body as the wearer moves

*shikake-mono:* trick costume for bit players (It does not include *hikinuki* costumes—that is, those used for quick changes of costume in view of the audience.)

*suō:* set of male clothing consisting of *uwagi* (coat) with wide-open sleeves and *naga-bakama* (long trailing trousers) or *hakama* (short pleated trousers or culottes)

*tenugui:* hand towel, usually cotton

*tekkō:* long cloth mittens covering lower arms and backs of hands

*yoten:* wide-open-sleeved garments with hems split at sides

*zukin:* ready-made hood (If any other article of clothing is used as a hood, it is not called a *zukin.*)

CHAPTER *3*

# Hōreki Kabuki

The period of Hōreki Kabuki begins with the first year of the Gembun era, 1736, and continues to the end of the Hōreki era in 1764.

Hōreki audiences saw the golden age of the *ningyō-jōruri-shibai*—the puppet theater. Though completely overshadowed by this flourishing theater, Kabuki did not let puppet domination destroy the strong spirit of either the Kamigata (western) or the Edo (eastern) stage. Instead it continued to progress step by step as it prepared for the future.

*Jidai-mono* and *sewa-mono* written for the doll theater by the Kamigata playwrights—notably Tominaga Heibei, Chikamatsu Monzaemon, and Mizushima Shirobei—were adapted for the Kabuki stage. Prior to this time, the two representative theaters had gone their separate ways. Adaptations from the puppet theater offered the Kabuki patrons more complex and interesting dramas, for puppet scripts had now reached the stage of *sammaku* or *mimaku* (*san* or *mi,* three; *maku,* act, curtain)—that is, of three-act plays.

The ballad singing of the *jōruri* was an indispensable element of the puppet theater and became the accepted accompaniment for all Kabuki *maruhommono:* plays originating in the doll theater. Before that, Kabuki had been composed chiefly of dialogue plays, although the *geza* or music and sound effects room was already in use.

The mid-eighteenth century was a time of marked improvement in Kabuki both in costumes and in stage settings. It must be acknowledged that the Kabuki not only patterned its costumes after those of the puppet theater but also copied the style of acting of that theater.

During Hōreki, Kabuki introduced many interesting actors, some of whose descendants are carrying on the family names and the *kata* (acting format) in twentieth-century Tokyo and Kansai Kabuki. Among these Hōreki actors were Ichikawa Danjūrō II, Ichikawa Danjūrō III, Ichikawa Danjūrō IV (known earlier as Matsumoto Kōshirō II), Sawamura

Sōjūrō I, Ichikawa Danzō I, Onoe Kikugorō I, Ōtani Hiroji I, Bandō Hikosaburō I, Anegawa Shinshirō I, Arashi Sangorō I, Sadogashima Chōgorō I, Nakamura Jūzō I, Segawa Kikunojō I, Nakamura Karoku I, and Sanokawa Ichimatsu I.

Among the above, Ōtani Hiroji I is remembered for originating the *hikinuki* or quick change of costume on stage. Sadogashima Chōgorō I was famous for his dancing, but his acting family survived for only one generation, as did the acting family of Anegawa Shinshirō I. Sanokawa Ichimatsu I reached stardom in Edo, although he came from Kamigata.

Probably the greatest single inspiration to improve costumes and acting was generated by the competitive maneuvering of the various Kabuki managements in presenting identical plays. *Kanadehon Chūshingura* (The Noble Precept Set by the Loyal Retainers or, less literally, The Revenge of the Forty-seven Faithful Rōnin) was first staged in 1748. *Chūshingura* became the foremost play in the Kabuki repertoire as well as an excellent vehicle for the versatility of Kabuki actors in designing costumes.

The basic story of *Chūshingura* is that of the Daimyō of Akō, Enya Hangan. Tried beyond endurance by the insults of a high official, Kō no Moronao, Hangan draws his sword and attacks Moronao in a room of the palace—an offense punishable by death. On orders from the shogunate, Hangan commits *seppuku,* and his staunch retainers vow revenge upon Moronao. The play revolves around the accomplishment of this revenge by the forty-seven masterless samurai and their eventual mass suicide at the order of the government.

Descriptions of the costumes worn by three prominent actors in the role of Yuranosuke, leader of the *rōnin,* in Hangan's *seppuku* scene are found in the *Hachimonji-ya Jishōhen* (Self-Criticism by Hachimonji-ya) and the *Kokon Iroha Hyōron* (Old and New Criticism of *Chūshingura*), the "iroha" of the latter title being the 47-symbol Japanese syllabary, here used metaphorically for the 47 *rōnin* of the play. The *Kokon Iroha Hyōron* was the first complete dissertation covering all plays produced on the theme of *Chūshingura,* from the appearance of the first one in 1748 to 1785.

The actors whose costumes for the role of Yuranosuke are described in these two books were Sawamura Sōjūrō I, Onoe Kikugorō I, and Bandō Hikosaburō I.

Sōjūrō dressed in a black *kosode* (small-sleeved kimono) over which he wore a brown *kamishimo* with white polka dots. He had presented *Ōyakazu Shijūshichi-hon,* another play about the incident of the Akō *rōnin,* the year before the initial appearance of *Chūshingura* in 1748. In the former play, he was a hit as Ōyakazu, but *Chūshingura,* since its first presentation, has been unsurpassed in popularity.

Onoe Kikugorō I chose a dark-green *kamishimo* with white polka dots and wore it over a *kosode* of the type known as *koshigawari noshime* (*koshi,* hips; *kawari,* change; *noshime,* a style of weaving). On the stage, a kimono having a different pattern across the midriff is called *noshime.* The pattern also extends across the lower part of the sleeves, so that when the arms are outstretched the pattern will appear in a continuous straight line. In everyday life, the *noshime* is a pattern woven with silk thread previously dyed by the tie-and-dye method.

Bandō Hikosaburō I appeared in a *kamishimo* of the type known as *Kembō komon,* the color of which is not recorded. The name Kembō was that of a famous master of fencing, Yoshioka Kembō, who is said to have originated the technique of dyeing *komon*—that is, a small over-all design somewhat difficult to differentiate from a solid color when seen from a distance.

Hikosaburō wore two swords, one long and one short. His *hakama* were tucked up at the sides, showing his bare legs from the thighs down and thereby displaying his *sanri-ate* (knee pads). To disclose the fact that Yuranosuke had traveled hurriedly on horseback, a horsewhip was pushed through the right side of the back of the obi. Today the actor taking the role of Yuranosuke does not wear swords during the scene of Hangan's suicide, and the horsewhip has also been discarded.

Throughout the Hōreki period and onward during the most popular years of Kabuki, actors exerted great influence on the choice of colors and textile patterns, as well as on styles worn by commoners. Moreover, styles worn by the people were appropriated and adapted by the actors. This exchange of ideas in clothing was made freely, though the stage versions were ordinarily not the exact facsimile of those of the everyday man.

The Sōjūrō *zukin,* a hood made popular by the actor Sawamura Sōjūrō I, however, was worn by samurai in everyday life, as well as by actors on the stage. It was conceived and worn by Sōjūrō when he played the role of Ume no Yoshibei, an *otokodate* (chivalrous commoner) of Edo. As a rule, today's Sōjūrō *zukin* is black, although Sōjūrō introduced it in purple. The same style of *zukin* is worn in other plays—for example, the Sōjūrō *zukin* is worn by Nippon Daemon in the "Hamamatsuya" scene of *Benten Kozō* or *Shiranami Gonin Otoko* (The Story of the Five Notorious Thieves).

Modern Kabuki owes much to one of the outstanding *onnagata* of Edo, Segawa Kikunojō I (1691–1749), who wrote many detailed notes on the techniques of make-up, wardrobe, and histrionics for the female impersonator. Among them one finds the suggestion that an *onnagata* representing a ghost, a demoness, or a wicked woman should not try to create the part by make-up but by acting and should accentuate the unearthly or ugly natures of these characters by such devices as long, flowing hair and somber-colored clothes or by wearing the kimono in a special manner. Kikunojō felt strongly that actors taking men's roles might change their make-up, but not the *onnagata,* for he believed that the female impersonator must, superficially at least, appear to be a graceful, charming woman at all times, and any change of make-up even for wicked roles would break the illusion of femininity and reveal the *onnagata* as a man.

It can be assumed that the *onnagata* did not shave their eyebrows, for Kikunojō wrote, "If you have heavy eyebrows do not paint over them because it would be very unnatural-looking." In order to look like a woman, he suggested that the actor pad his hips, since women were broader than men. He also recommended that *beni* (red coloring) be heated over a direct flame, then applied to face and lips to prevent wrinkles and assure the maintenance of a beautiful complexion.

"An *onnagata*," Kikunojō said, "should not be 'liked' by women in the audience. Let it not be said, 'I wish I were his wife.' Rather, an *onnagata* should evoke from men the words, 'I wish I were her lover.' On the stage you must make the women of the audience think you are of the same sex as they. If you can make them copy your kimono, your obi, your *katsura*, or any article of apparel you wear, you will be successful."

The field of dancing was dominated by *onnagata* from the outset. This was probably a tradition carried forward from the time of Okuni Kabuki, when most dancing was the accepted accomplishment of women. Another reason for this predominance might have been the fact that the "women" always had to be in the background in dramas; thus, dancing afforded the early *onnagata* his only opportunity for a stellar role. The *shosagoto* or dance-drama sought mainly to please the eye of the avid public; consequently, costumes for the dancers became increasingly extravagant, diversified, and detailed (Figs. 11–13).

It was during Hōreki that *shosagoto* such as *Kyō-Ganoko Musume Dōjōji* (The Gay Scene of the Maiden in Kanoko Kimono at Dōjō Temple) and *Sagi Musume* (The White Heron Maiden) were first introduced. Kikunojō was the first to appear in the ethereally lovely white costume with black obi in *Sagi Musume*. Nakayama Tomijūrō I entered via the *hanamichi* in a heavily embroidered red silk kimono, wearing a gold *eboshi* in *Dōjōji*. The costumes for these dance plays are essentially the same today, but Onoe Kikugorō VI, father of the present-day *onnagata* Onoe Baikō VII and himself a noted *onnagata*, changed the order of the costumes in *Dōjōji*. He appeared on the *hanamichi* in a black costume and changed swiftly to a red kimono (Fig. 12) on the stage by the quick-change technique of *hikinuki*.

Kabuki often used the *kata* or format of the puppet theater. Some of the more famous costumes taken over from that theater are noted here. From the historical drama *Sugawara Denju Tenarai Kagami* (The Teaching of the Secrets of Sugawara's Calligraphy), the Kabuki adapted the costumes for the triplet brothers Matsuō-maru, Umeō-maru, and Sakuramaru. These were wadded costumes differentiated from each other only by the designs on the material: the pine, the bamboo, and the cherry taken from the names of the respective brothers. Also taken from a historical play was the black satin garment worn by Tadanobu in *Yoshitsune Sembon-Zakura* (Yoshitsune under the Blossoming Cherry Trees at Yoshino, or Yoshitsune and One Thousand Cherry Trees). The garment was embroidered in gold with a wheel pattern called *Genji-guruma* (Genji cart wheels).

From a *sewa-mono,* a play about the lives of the commoners, the Kabuki copied the white-and-rust checkered costume worn by Danshichi Kurobei in *Natsu Matsuri Naniwa no Kagami* (The Summer Festival of Osaka).

Though the Kabuki has been accused of flagrantly duplicating anything and everything valuable that the Bunraku (puppet theater) had to offer, it must be kept in mind that this imitation was reciprocal and that Bunraku borrowed quite as freely from Kabuki *kata.* One of the best known instances of the latter was Bunraku's *Kanadehon Chūshingura,* in which the puppeteers emulated Sōjūrō's entire *kata* for the seventh act, including the famed purple kimono. This costume, incidentally, was readapted for the Kabuki at a later period.

Anything unexpected stimulated the interest of the audiences to a high degree. It is little wonder that *hayagawari* (*haya,* quick; *kawari,* change)—the technique of going off-stage hurriedly to make a complete change of costume, wig, and make-up and of returning in an entirely different role in the same scene—created such a sensation. When it was introduced, *hayagawari* was executed deftly by Nakamura Shinkurō in playing the two roles of Sadakurō and Yoichibei in *Kanadehon Chūshingura* and by Ichikawa Danjūrō II as Kagekiyo and Hatakeyama Shigetada in *Daibutsu Kuyō* (The Memorial Service at the Great Statue of Buddha). In the next era during 1783, Nakamura Utaemon III took the three roles of Sadakurō, Yoichibei, and Kampei in *Chūshingura.* In classical plays, this technique is resorted to quite often.

Disobedience to government regulations on costumes was no less characteristic of Hōreki than of other eras under the Tokugawa shogunate. In fact, the whole of the Edo period was one long struggle between sovereigns and people. The sovereigns, uncertain of their power and ever watchful for uprisings against themselves, contended with people yearning for release from the oppressions of past years, yearning the more fervently because of new-found pleasures: beautiful clothing, interesting women, objects of art, new activities, luxurious possessions. Hōreki, coming as it did at the zenith of an extremely rich century with the cessation of wars at home and abroad, felt this growing struggle acutely.

The *chōnin* (merchants), who were becoming wealthy and leisured, chose deliberately to ignore the restrictions imposed on their growing love of indulgence. But the shogunate was firm and again and again renewed repressive edicts and restrictions in order to keep the lower classes subjugated. In 1755 a new proscription against elaborate costumes both on and off stage was promulgated.

Nakajima Mihoemon, an actor who appeared in the role of a *kuge-aku* (court villain), was one of those to feel the teeth of the law when he was arrested for his disregard of one of the restrictions. He not only had appeared in a stylized hat known as a *kammuri,* usually worn by civil officials or nobles, but also had unwisely outdone himself in indulging his imagination to excess, for to make his costume interesting, he had had his hat covered with thin sheets of gold foil, and he shone in splendor as he wore it.

A few years later, in 1763, handsome Segawa Kikunojō II came close to a like mishap when he appeared in *Sagi Musume* in a kimono of white *rinzu,* a small-figured cloth resembling damask, with a black *rinzu* obi— this in a day when plain-woven cloth was almost *de rigueur.* Since he was an exceedingly famous actor, he escaped with only a public warning, but this near disaster served as a fearful deterrent to others who were abusing the law, and Hōreki ended, sedate and subdued, the following year.

11. *Shosagoto* costume: *Fuji Musume*. The dance-drama known as *shosagoto* sought mainly to please the eyes of the avid public; consequently the costumes became increasingly extravagant, diversified, and detailed, as exemplified in *Fuji Musume* (The Wisteria Maiden).

12. *Shosagoto* costume: *Kyō-Ganoko Musume Dōjōji*. The entrance costume of the *shirabyōshi* Hanako in *Dōjōji* —a heavily embroidered red silk kimono and a gold *eboshi*—remains essentially the same today as it was when Nakayama Tomijūrō I first performed this *shosagoto* two centuries ago.

13. *Shosagoto* costume: *Kagamijishi*. This is the costume of the maidservant Yayoi as she begins her dance with the lion mask in *Kagamijishi*. The kimono is the long-sleeved *furisode*.

CHAPTER 4

# Kansei Kabuki

The Kansei Kabuki period also includes the three eras prior to Kansei (1789–1800)—that is, Meiwa (1764–71), An'ei (1772–80), and Temmei (1781–88).

Kamigata was rapidly losing its position as the vital center of all the arts. It was only natural that cultural and political activities should be combined in the eastern city of Edo, where the shogunate had established its headquarters. Influences that had formerly flowed in all directions from the capital now stemmed from Edo, where the most energetic people of the fast-growing metropolis, known as Edokko—offspring or children of Edo—soon formulated a typical culture that left a vivid imprint on the whole of Japanese life as the Edokko spirit.

Along with the rest of the arts, the pivotal center of Kabuki moved to Edo, where new playwrights came to the fore to vie in craftsmanship with their Kamigata counterparts on an equal level. Both *jidai-mono* and *sewa-mono* were in demand. Dramas in the latter genre by two of the more prominent writers, Sakurada Jisuke I and Namiki Gohei, are still being produced regularly, so much are they loved. Many of the plays of this period were based on stories of the Yoshiwara, after that former "field of reeds" had become the official gay quarters of the now teeming city of Edo. Today those plays are all that remain to give modern man a picture of the heartbreak and the violence that went with the gaiety of Yoshiwara, which had been taken as a matter of course for over three centuries.

The use of appropriate *ōdōgu* (*ō*, big; *dōgu,* tool, instrument, material—in this case scenery) for Kabuki became extremely important about this time, and the Kansei period saw its rapid development on the stages of both eastern and western Japan under the inspired guidance of Hasegawa Kambei I, the first of a long line of outstanding stage designers. It is perhaps because of this new and colorful innovation that in Edo the performances of Nakamura Nakazō I, Ichikawa Danjūrō V, Ichikawa Danzō

IV, Iwai Hanshirō IV, and Nakamura Utaemon I so brilliantly outshone those of their forebears; it is certain that the old western capital found in Arashi Sangorō II and Arashi Hinasuke II more charm, more grace, more artfulness than could be hoped for in their predecessors who performed in the dry riverbed.

Costume regulations during Kansei brought upon the scene Matsu-daira Sadanobu, a *rōjū*—that is, an official of the highest rank—of the shogunate government. Matsudaira, in a new effort to stifle any semblance of luxury among the populace, was adamant in proscribing every ex-travagance. He was instrumental in issuing new restrictions banning the use of luxurious clothing by all classes, but especially by Kabuki actors, who were of no accepted class and were held in great contempt socially. The four classes of approved society were, in order of precedence, the samurai, the farmers, the artisans (including carpenters, potters, utensil makers, and the like), and merchants.

The inability of officials to enforce the bans led to repeated re-enact-ment of regulations and eventually to the first *ishō-kembun,* an official ex-amination of all Kabuki costumes which operated in the following manner.

At the beginning of each new program, the government dispatched an officer to a designated place in the theater where the costumer or the theater manager would produce for *shita-kembun* (preliminary inspection) all costumes to be used in a new production. The officer determined which costumes and materials were admissible. Later, higher government officials attended the opening performances armed with the list of approved cos-tumes. During the program, they verified that more luxurious costumes had not been substituted. It is difficult to imagine the possibility of altering or forging the lists, so rigid was the inspection procedure.

The regular inspectors were two *yoriki* (high-ranking police officers) and two *dōshin* (ordinary policemen) from the two police headquarters of south and north Edo; two regular *nanushi* (ward bosses) from the districts in which the theaters were located; and two other *nanushi* from a different ward who alternately acted as inspectors each month.

If these inspections had been carried out in the spirit in which they were instituted, rather than according to the exact letter of the law, the Kabuki could well have closed down, for the costuming would have been so unimaginative and lacking in variety that the plays would have lost their appeal. However, the Kabuki managements, forced to extremes in order to survive, looked for and cleverly found loopholes in the regulations. Since satin cloth was specifically prohibited, other materials were used and these were exquisitely hand-embroidered in picturesque designs—all with-in the law, since the present bans made no mention of embroidery. Theater management could in this way face opening-day inspection with easy consciences, and inspecting officials who arrived with their families to attend the Kabuki could, without so much as a misgiving, blissfully enjoy the performances, their responsibilities at an end. It was not theirs to question the unparalleled richness and splendor of the stage wardrobe so long as none of it was specifically outlawed.

In 1789, the use of fabrics was limited for the common man as well as for the actor. All that was permitted was the use of hemp cloth and two types of rough plain silk: *tsumugi*, closely woven from heavy yarn of the cocoon of double silkworms (normally the cocoon is filled with only one worm), or *mawata*, spun from the heavy thread from imperfect filament or silk waste taken from the contents of a cocoon broken through by a butterfly before the cocoon has been heated.

On frequent occasions, basically simple material was artfully disguised and made into magnificent apparel, thus circumventing all government edicts. The general trend to camouflage was clearly defined as early as 1782, when the Ichimura-za produced the play *Ise Heishi Eiga no Koyomi* (The Calendar Record of the Prosperity of the Heike of Ise) with Naka-mura Nakazō I in the role of Endō Musha. Nakazō's costume was made from striped cotton cloth of black *santome* or *tōzan* over which white Kaga-silk patterns were appliquéd and outlined with gold paper thread.

These fabrics are of sufficient interest to deserve a few words of description. *Santome* took its name from St. Thomas, or St. Tome, the then Indian port located on the western coast, from which textiles were exported. *Santome* was a cotton cloth patterned with stripes. To differentiate between the imported *santome* and the imitation made in Japan during the Edo period, the imported cloth was called *tō-santome*, the *tō* meaning Chinese or foreign. For convenience, the name was abbreviated to *tōzan*. Kaga silk, used for the appliquéd patterns in Nakazō's costume, derived its name from the Japanese province of Kaga, which in the old days produced a fine grade of silk.

Since the government officials knew little about materials, other than the textiles used in their own sphere of life, the Kabuki costumer was able to use rare imported (therefore expensive) cottons secured from Dutch and Chinese ships still plying between Japan and the rest of the world.

Danjūrō V, acting the role of Kudō Suketsune in *Kotobuki Soga no Tai-men* (The Confrontation of the Soga Brothers), wore a *katsura* with a par-tially grown out *sakayaki* (shaven part of head) made of dyed cotton in-stead of the forbidden *rasha*, a feltlike material made of wool, or of velvet, which was also proscribed. When hair is used for this purpose, bear fur is utilized. The *katsura* is worn by the daimyō class in *jidai-mono* only.

No longer were the traditional layers of kimono used in Kabuki, but an illusion of them remained in the free display of many edges sewn to-gether on the underneath side of the outer garment so as to appear as multitudinous collars, sleeves, and skirts, a procedure which may have been suggested from the clothing of either the *ningyō-shibai* puppets or ordinary dolls.

During March 1789, Segawa Kikunojō III was intercepted by the police officials when he was walking home from the theater. He was wearing an elaborate silk kimono, and despite his great popularity he was deprived of the garment and was fined. Two years later, the Nakamura-za presented *Sukeroku Yukari no Edo-Zakura* with the major roles taken by Ichikawa Yaozō II as Sukeroku, Iwai Hanshirō IV, major *onnagata* of the period, as Agemaki, and Onoe Matsusuke I as the evil Ikyū. All costumes in this production were confiscated because luxurious materials had been employed in their making. Today, with no bans to denude it of its brilliant trappings, *Sukeroku* is known especially for its elaborately ornate costumes.

No limitation was made on Nō costumes, for the Nō theater was the chosen entertainment of the aristocratic classes, and the most magnificent textiles in Japan have always been utilized to dress Nō actors. Practically no dyed materials, even today, are used to achieve an effect for costumes of the principals. Usually the first quality of silks is employed—silks heavily embroidered in a galaxy of patterns, intricately woven designs in rich brocaded cloth, or cloth imprinted in gold leaf. Only for roles representing lower-class persons do we find hemp cloth in dyed patterns, but it must not be confused with the coarse hemp known to the Western world. It is a kind of ramie, fine and similar to the softest of Irish linen.

One exception other than Nō was made. Costumes used by Kabuki actresses, who performed only at the courts of the shōgun and the daimyō, had no restrictions on material. The restrained elegance of some of the delicate, somber-hued, but beautifully embroidered kimono of these actresses has been preserved. These kimono may be seen at the Tokyo National Museum in Ueno Park.

On the whole, the prohibition regarding luxury in dress was a blessing in no disguise to the theater. The costumes being extremely costly, the prospect of their confiscation made it imperative that the management devise new color combinations and patterns with authorized textiles which could pass the wary eyes of the government officials, yet please the public's demands for elaborate display. The ingenuity thus developed may have been worth the unhappy experiences of the early years.

Kabuki faced another danger in survival. It encountered animosity from another outside source—the conflict between the rapidly growing class of poor samurai and the well-to-do *chōnin* (merchants). The indigent samurai were jealous of the merchants, who could afford regularly to attend the Kabuki and to frequent the Yoshiwara at will—the very activities so appealing to the samurai, but too expensive for their participation.

But times were indeed changing. The shogunate tried vainly to maintain its non-warring military men in the manner to which their status had accustomed them by minimizing the expenditures of other classes. The restrictive laws against lavish display were ignored one by one. It was to the *chōnin* that the samurai were forced to go for monetary help, and in many instances employment, so that they could not afford to oppose the merchants openly.

CHAPTER 5

# Bunka-Bunsei Kabuki

Bunka and Bunsei historically are two eras but are so closely associated that they are usually spoken of as one—namely the Bunka-Bunsei or Kasei period (1804–30). The Kabuki period identified thus also includes a few years before: the Kyōwa era of 1801–4.

Decadence prevailed during the extremely peaceful, mellow years of Bunka-Bunsei under the rule of the eleventh shōgun, Tokugawa Ienari. This rococo period, with its over-all beauty and delicacy, can be likened to the brilliance of a candle just as its flame flickers brightly for the last time, only to die. Ienari, the progenitor of fifty-four acknowledged children, with probably more than fifteen wives and concubines, typified the times and the morals. Ernest Fenollosa has referred to these years as "a real lowering of both the moral and aesthetic standards of the streets. Men and women went to the extravagances of frank vulgarity. It was a sort of Genroku carnival, on a lower plane."

During the high living and spectacular spending of the commoners in these liberal-minded years, Kabuki reached the pinnacle of its popularity and material abundance. Admission to the Kabuki increased to fantastic heights, with management taking full advantage of the greater demand for seats as the *chōnin* rose in monetary power. There were only three licensed theaters in the city of Edo. Those attending the Kabuki dressed sumptuously and frequented the costly teahouses attached to the theaters. *Ichi-ryō ni-bu* (one *ryō* and two *bu*) was the average fee for a day at the theater, including admission, service from the teahouse, and tipping the *dekata* or usher. First-class tickets to the Kabuki were bought through the teahouses, which naturally profited by the connection, but lower-class tickets were purchased at the box office. Some idea of the expense of a day at the theater can be gained from the information that *ichi-ryō ni-bu* was equivalent to the current price of three bales of rice. The *ryō* (four *bu*) was the basic unit of the monetary system represented in gold coins, prior to the advent of which the system was based on units of baled rice.

As a result of the prevailing extravagance, the theaters prospered and the actors benefited by increased salaries. The lush times gave birth to the term *sen-ryō yakusha,* signifying a thousand-*ryō* actor, a complimentary term for a leading artist, used by the theatergoers in calling out in approbation a favorite's stage name when some particular bit of acting struck their fancy.

Kabuki set the vogue for lavish dress—an outgrowth from the increase in actors' pay. Their salaries were also supplemented by regular pecuniary gifts from their patrons. Not a little of the increasing splendor, however, was due to the indifference or indolence of the officers in relaxing the enforcement of edicts prohibiting the use of specified costume materials.

A few examples of lavish expenditures for costumes have been recorded in the annals of *Sukeroku.* Ichikawa Danjūrō VII, considered by many writers to have been the greatest of his family line, appeared for the first time in *Sukeroku* wearing an obi richly embroidered with the two Danjūrō crests: the *mimasu* (three nested grain measures) and the *gyōyō-botan* (peony). About one foot of the embroidery was valued at 58 *momme.* (At this time, white rice cost 65 or 66 *momme* per *koku*—about five bushels—and one *koku* equaled two and a half bales.) The entire obi would have cost the equivalent of 25 bales of rice. A lovely *makie inrō* (gold-lacquer medicine case) picturing a carp in a waterfall, made by the renowned lacquer artist Kajikawa, hung from the obi. This little item cost 30 *ryō,* the equivalent of 27 or 28 *koku* or 70 bales of rice—or five times the yearly income of a lower-class samurai.

As further evidence to emphasize the degree of extravagance in Danjūrō's costume, it can be noted that the daimyō family of Maeda, the richest lord in the country, received an income of one million *koku* yearly, while Asano Takumi no Kami Naganori of Akō, revered as Enya Hangan in *Kanadehon Chūshingura,* received 53,000 *koku* yearly. The lowest-paid samurai of Akō averaged from 20 *koku* and 5 personal food allotments to 5 *ryō* and 3 personal food allotments. The lowest-ranking samurai of all received 4 *ryō* and 1 personal food allotment.

Iwai Hanshirō, as Agemaki in the same production of *Sukeroku,* wore an *uchikake* (ceremonial outer robe) of black velvet embroidered in pure gold thread and an undergarment of *karaori,* the brocaded cloth normally used exclusively for Nō costumes. Hanshirō paid 70 *ryō* for this finery, since this was not provided by the management.

Unlimited spending for costumes continued until 1826, when *Sukeroku* was produced with more dazzling costumes than ever. A 60,000-*koku* daimyō, Matsuura Seizan, author of the popular *Kasshi Yawa* (Night Story of Kasshi, or Essays Begun in the First Year of Bunka), wrote: "This spring *Sukeroku* was performed with Iwai Shikaku II, eldest son of Iwai Hanshirō V, taking the role of Shiratama. His ornate costume, costing 600 *ryō,* included five *uchikake.* The one next to the kimono was made of white satin decorated with clouds and a dragon, painted in *sumie* [black-ink painting] by the famed artist of the day, Sakai Hōitsu Inja [*inja,* honorific term for a retired man], while the four remaining *uchikake,* overlaid with embroidered flowers and lions, were so expertly stitched with gold and silver as to appear like masterpieces of metalwork. Only a few years ago such luxuries were not permitted—only dyed patterns on cotton cloth might be used, causing the actors to be troubled, I hear, but at present matters seem to have changed. How is it that today such extravagant costumes can be used?"

Thriving in an atmosphere of degeneration, society had an insatiable desire for change. Such craving extended to the theater. Management, ever mindful of the source of its income, introduced the *kaidan-mono,* ghost plays of grotesque theme with a ghost as the protagonist instead of as a bit player as had been the custom previously. The realistic domestic plays known as *sewa-mono* normally dealt with domestic problems and double suicides, the main male characters generally being young men and sometimes merchants, laborers, *sumō* wrestlers, *tobi* (firemen), or foppish young men. Love affairs of the young blades, especially those involving *shinjū* (double suicide), also come under this classification, and the dress worn reflects quite accurately that of the commoners. Management now added *kizewa-mono* (*ki,* raw or real; *sewa,* worldly; literally, pure *sewa-mono*) with characters from the lowest strata of society.

The hero and heroine of *kizewa-mono* are not only from the lower classes but are often lawless characters. The *akuba* is the role of a bad woman or villainess. She may be a blackmailer, a thief, a gambler, or a panderer, but she is never a prostitute. She engages in fights and is not a lady in any sense of the word. Usually a well-known *onnagata* appears in the *akuba* role, so it is only proper that there should be something likable about the character. Perhaps she is stealing money to help re-establish her impoverished lord, or she is a bad woman who realizes she is wrong and commits suicide at the end of the play. The *akuba* is the woman *yakuza* (ne'er-do-well, scamp, ruffian). Also seen in the leading roles of *kizewa-mono* are thieves, gamblers, prostitutes, vagabonds, beggars, ne'er-do-wells, and *hinin* (social outcasts).

Genteel poor or common-class people appear in *kizewa-mono* but not in leading roles. Beauty was not the essence of this form; it was the presentation of the ultimate in a realistic style of complete production.

It was at this time that the wig known as *onnagata katsura* made its debut to help enhance the believability of the female impersonator. The copper frame already had been in use since early Genroku, but now the hair, strand by strand, was properly secured to the frame by first attaching it to fine silk by the use of needles. Previously, several strands of hair at a time had been tied across a string which was sewn to the front of the copper base, then combed backward over the frame.

The new type of *katsura* devised by the wigmaker Tomokurō, was worn by Onoe Matsusuke I in the role of Iwafuji in *Kagamiyama Kokyō no Nishikie* (The Maidservant's Revenge) in 1803 at the Ichimura-za. All other actors in the drama wore the old-style *mino* wigs—in which the hair was tied across a string and then sewn to the copper base—with purple *bōshi,* in this instance a decorative piece of cloth placed over the forehead. The *bōshi* was created to envelop the entire head, but it gradually diminished in size, covering only the upper forehead—as now worn by *onnagata*—but it still retains the identical name.

Matsumoto Kōshirō V, celebrated particularly for villainous roles, presented his characters without the usual white make-up, trying the more natural approach. As Shihei in *Sugawara Denju Tenarai Kagami* he appeared almost void of make-up, wearing a more realistic costume than that worn in the play today.

Much to the consternation of the Kamigata inhabitants, Kōshirō V changed the make-up and costume of Gonta in *Yoshitsune Sembon-Zakura* to a typically Edokko style. Though the Kamigata people protested that Gonta was a real man of Yamato (the early name for the central provinces of Japan; Edo did not exist at that time)—in this instance a Kyoto man and not an Edokko—the Kōshirō adaptation of costume and the use of heavier make-up now remain in the *kata* for the play, whether it is given in Kansai or in Tokyo. Gonta's cotton costume is designed in the *Benkei-gōshi* pattern: an oblong checkerboard in black and white, to make the wearer look more slender.

In *Banzuin Chōbei Shōjin Manaita,* better known as *Suzugamori* (The Execution Grounds at Suzugamori)—a *sewa-mono* that tells the story of the gallant commoner Banzuin Chōbei and the young *rōnin* Gompachi—Banzuin Chōbei wears a cotton kimono with a pattern on a white background, an obi tied with a *hako musubi* (square bow) or a *kai-no-kuchi* (shell-mouth-shaped) bow, and a *naga-wakizashi,* the medium-sized sword permitted commoners. Kampei, in Act VI of *Kanadehon Chūshingura,* wears a crested blue kimono called *asagi mompuku,* first worn by Kikugorō III.

Danjūrō VII, after witnessing the poorer class of *rōnin* trying to make a living by putting paper on umbrellas, decided to express the role of a destitute *rōnin* in a real-life manner. His garb was a *kata-ire* (*kata,* shoulder; *ire,* covering) of black cloth, patched over the shoulders to hide the worn spots, over which was tied a cloth *tasuki,* a cord or sash used for tucking up kimono sleeves during manual labor.

In March 1837, when he appeared at the Ichimura-za with Ichikawa Danzō III of Osaka in *Yūsoku Kamakura-Yama* (Kamakura Mountain Man Versed in Ancient Court and Military Practices), Danjūrō VII played the role of Sano Genzaemon Tsuneyo wearing a replica of the true daimyō *asagi* (flax blue) *naga-gamishimo,* a *kamishimo* with long trailing *hakama.* It is interesting to note that the title of the play, while it refers to knowledge of ceremonial matters of the noble class, contains a reference to *yūsoku-*

*moyō,* a textile pattern worn by the nobility. Since the actual theme of the play was political troubles in Edo, the scene was shifted to the Kamakura period to circumvent the ban on stage portrayals of politics. Eventually the *naga-gamishimo* was added to the proscribed list, but Danjūrō VII continued to appear in the costume in Osaka, where there was less chance of his being reported to the government authorities, since the powerful merchant class outweighed the samurai in influence.

Danjūrō's *naga-gamishimo* was made of ramie, replacing satin and other rich-textured cloth previously in popular favor. Today ramie is no longer used, for it is far more expensive than other fabrics and not so lovely as the *ryūmon* silk now available. Chemical dye is occasionally used with results more satisfactory on silk than on ramie.

Although restrictions had been placed on the *naga-gamishimo,* the ordinary *kamishimo* was not affected. In fact, it was worn in real life even by the *chōnin* class. On the stage, any material could be used for it.

Danjūrō, possessed of a curious mind, was an ardent student of history, always eager to adapt his discoveries about the past to the stage, wherever possible. Though some aspects of the Nō had been incorporated into Kabuki, it was Danjūrō VII who modified the pine-tree backdrop (used for Kabuki plays of Nō origin), the costumes, the dialogue, and the acting for the Kabuki theater. Make-up was not introduced from the Nō. Since social intercourse was lacking between Nō and Kabuki actors—Nō being performed exclusively in aristocratic circles, Kabuki in popular ones—it was extremely difficult for a Kabuki actor to gain admittance to any performance of Nō. He had no way to study the costumes carefully enough to imitate the *shōzoku* (costumes) of the older classical theater.

Danjūrō was determined to overcome this social barrier and to study Nō costumes. He called on the Nō costumer Sekioka, but Sekioka refused to see the *kawara kojiki*—the riverbed beggar, as the Kabuki actor was still commonly called. Undaunted, Danjūrō visited Sekioka time and time again until the costumer at last relented and showed him a plain *shiro-ōguchi*—that is, a man's white *hakama* with wide pleats and a stiffened back—a costume worn by the lowliest character on the Nō stage. As a result, even today the *ōguchi* worn by Benkei in *Kanjinchō* (The Subscription List) is white, although it has a pattern in the weave.

Upon seeing *Kanjinchō,* Yamanouchi Yōdō, feudal lord of Tosa and a patron of Danjūrō VII, was so shocked at the poverty of the costumes in comparison with those used on the Nō stage in performing the same story that he presented Danjūrō with his own Nō costume for the role of Benkei. Since then, the costumes for *Kanjinchō* have been made from excellent textiles. This has been especially true since the 1860's, since during Meiji and the following eras restrictive edicts on elaboration of theatrical costume were not enforced, and the field was left wide open for Kabuki in this respect.

Iwai Hanshirō V, an extremely "pretty" actor, was the representative *onnagata* of the Bunka-Bunsei era. The public called him by the pet name of *me-senryō* or thousand-*ryō* eyes, for his eyes were remarkably beautiful and expressive. (Kawarasaki Gonjūrō I was also called *me-senryō*.) Hanshirō was a skillful actor, showing his amazing versatility in a wide range of roles, from *musume-gata* (young women) to *tachi-yaku* (leading male characters). He established the role of the *akuba* (bad woman), and his stylization remains the *kata* for roles of wicked women. He was famous for his portrayal of such *akuba* parts as Mikazuki Osen (Osen of the Crescent Moon), Dote no Oroku (Oroku of the Riverbank), and Kaminari Otsuru (Thunder Otsuru). His stellar *tachi-yaku* parts were Hanaregoma Chōkichi in *Sekitori Senryō Nobori*, a story dealing with *sumō* wrestlers, and Shirai Gompachi in *Suzugamori*. The black costume worn by Gompachi originated with Hanshirō, but the *hiwa* kimono (so named because its chartreuse color resembles that of the small finch called *hiwa* in Japanese) worn by the present-day Baikō VII was introduced by Kikugorō III.

Hanshirō was prolific in contriving fresh ideas for patterns. His *Hanshirō kanoko* (small-spot *shibori* or tie-dyeing resembling the spots on a fawn's hide) in the *asanoha* (hemp-leaf) pattern in blue and red was first used for the costume of Yaoya Oshichi—Oshichi the greengrocer's daughter—in a play given in March 1809 at the Morita-za.

The *Iwai-gushi*, a crescent-shaped comb designed by Hanshirō for use in the role of Mikazuki Osen, was considered very chic and became the rage among style-conscious ladies. It was one of numerous things described as having *iki*, the commoners' word for aplomb, dash, and spruceness. In fact, toward the end of the Edo period, all sorts of things expressed *iki*, for it was a time of debonair activities. Men wore their kimono very narrow, pulled tightly around the body, and open and loose at the top to give a careless dandified effect.

Up to and including the Bunka-Bunsei era all costumes had been paid for by the actors with exception of those for specialized roles and those worn by the lowest-paid actors. It was exceedingly difficult and often embarrassing for even the average-paid actor to maintain proper stage appearance, for his pay was most inadequate. This situation often produced an unbalanced stage effect, for a leading actor might wear a resplendent costume as a *yakko* (samurai's servant or footman) while an underpaid actor who had the misfortune to portray the *yakko's* lord might appear as a minor character because of an uninspired costume necessarily made of inexpensive material.

However, some garments created out of cheaper stuffs turned out to be strikingly original. For example, Ōtani Hiroji II in the play *Koi no Sekifuda* (Strong Love Breaks Every Barrier, or Love Working as an Almighty Passport) lacked the necessary costume for a red-faced villain's role. So he borrowed a woman's everyday kimono patterned with daffodils, which he had made into attractive stage attire.

Nakamura Nakazō III, as Kōmori Yasu in *Yo wa Nasake Ukina no Yoko-*

*gushi* (The Love Story of Yosaburō and Otomi), commonly called *Kirare Yosa* or *Genjidana,* donned his wife's *hanten* with happy results. (The *hanten* is a short outer coat resembling the *haori* but lacking ties to fasten it in front. The collar, occasionally of black satin, is not folded like that of the *haori*.) Ichikawa Omezō I, a popular actor and an accomplished tailor, thought it too costly to have his wardrobe made, so he cut and made his own garments.

The difference between highly paid stars and other actors was as deep as a chasm. The lower-paid actors had great obstacles to overcome, for they had to survive and to keep up appearances without the help of moneyed patrons, yet they remained in the theater to become the sturdy backbone of Kabuki.

CHAPTER 6

# Bakumatsu Kabuki

The Bakumatsu (decline of the shogunate) era includes the eras of Tempō (1830–43), Kōka (1844–47), Kaei (1848–53), Ansei (1854–59), Man'en (1860), Bunkyū (1861–63), Genji (1864), and Keiō (1865–68).

Immediately following Bunka-Bunsei were the unsettled years of Tempō (1830–43), with the shogunate displaying visible signs of weakening. Loyalists who wished to restore the splendor of the court found themselves in the midst of prevailing political disorders. Foreign powers were endeavoring to open Japan to trade, and the differences of opinion for and against isolation added to the restlessness of the masses. Creating even greater hardship, a famine swept the nation.

Wealthy merchants who were closely aligned with corrupt government officials bought up rice, only to deposit it in vast storehouses. The scholar Ōshio Heihachirō, leading a group of students, broke into the warehouses, took the grain, and distributed it to needy people. This precipitated a civil war in 1847. Heihachirō was arrested, took full responsibility for his act, and committed *seppuku*.

During these troubled days, the people began to lose their remaining confidence in the shogunate. Up to that time, Edo Castle, not the Imperial Palace in Kyoto, had been the symbol of the government. The castle was partly destroyed by fire and remained so, for the shaky economic condition of the feudalistic government made repair impossible. To the masses this was indicative of a lost cause.

*Tempō no kaikaku* (the reconstruction of society in the Tempō era) was formulated in 1840 by a resident of Edo, Rōjū Mizuno Takakuni, who was universally known as Echizen no Kami, governor of Echizen Province. Mizuno sought to raise the standard of society which had so thoroughly degenerated during the previous era. However, just as he founded his plans, the Nakamura-za was totally consumed by fire in October 1841, spreading its flames to engulf the Kawarasaki-za, the Ichimura-za, the Yūki-za, and the Satsuma-za, the last two being puppet theaters. Theater managements requested permission to rebuild the theaters, but consent was not granted. Instead government officials decided to call a meeting to determine whether to ban the Kabuki completely, or to allow the theaters to be rebuilt in a remote area of the city. The official stand was that the fire had been caused by carelessness and that the Kabuki was harmful to society. Actually this meeting was only an artifice, for Mizuno had already decided to close the theaters.

Among the *hayashi,* the instrumental musicians of the theater, at this time was Tōyama Saemon no Jō Kagemoto, who was well acquainted with Kabuki. Like many other prodigal sons of the samurai (although never firstborn sons), he had come to the Kabuki, exchanged his sword for a musical instrument, and served with the *hayashi.* As the result of such practice by sons of samurai, this group of musicians received the honorific title of *o-hayashi.* The opinions of members of the *o-hayashi* of samurai origin, being those of the well-born, were heeded.

To the consternation of the officials, particularly Mizuno, Tōyama offered critical opposition to the ban. Here was a freethinker who at least had associated in the past with the common people, as indicated by an elaborate tattoo of cherry blossoms on his back. Tōyama pointed out logically his reasons for opposing the destruction of the Kabuki, for he declared that since a fire could have started anywhere, no one could say definitely that the theater was responsible and was a bad influence on society or vice versa. Since the Kabuki was the greatest form of amusement for the common people, he felt that eliminating it would force the masses again into loose ways. His valid arguments won out, and in December 1841 the theaters were permitted to rebuild in Shōden-chō on the private estate of Koide Shinano no Kami in Asakusa. All land was owned by the government and merely loaned to the daimyō for building purposes, but in this case Koide had left the land unimproved; so it was reclaimed for use by the theaters.

The locality was renamed Saruwaka-chō. The theaters retained their original names, with the Ichimura-za reopening to the public in September 1842, the Nakamura-za in October of the same year, and the Kawarasaki-za in December. The two puppet theaters as well reopened their doors during that year.

Stringent limitations in all walks of life strangled creative efforts as new-found freedom was crushed under the heels of officialdom. Teahouses were not allowed to serve expensive or rare foods. Women of ordinary class, who wore gorgeous dress and displayed tortoise-shell, gold, or silver hair ornaments were arrested. *Sake,* the tasty rice wine, was sold only in limited quantities.

Restrictions were even worse for the Kabuki actor, who was forbidden to fraternize with the common man. By law, when the actor went out, he had to cover his face with an *amigasa* (large umbrella-shaped reed hat) so he would not be recognized. These conditions must have evoked a sense of degradation in the Kabuki actor, who had risen to a high crest of popularity during the Bunka-Bunsei era. Those who study the history of Kabuki are ever mindful of the stern character of these actors who continued to carry forward their talents, many times under the most appalling circumstances.

Punishments were often imposed for infringements of regulations and at times were more severe than can be easily understood now. In 1842, Danjūrō VII, in the Kabuki Jūhachiban (eighteen favorite plays of the Ichikawa family) play *Kagekiyo* (also the name of the hero of the play), wore real *kote* (arm guards) and *sune-ate* (shin guards). This precipitated his arrest in April of the same year. He was imprisoned and handcuffed in his own home: a procedure known as *chōnai-azukari* (house arrest). Officials of his neighborhood *chō* (block) visited Danjūrō VII from time to time to assure themselves that he remained at home. Handcuffs were removed on necessary occasions, for his crime was of a mild nature. Nevertheless, he was kept handcuffed in the confines of his house for two months. He might have been released sooner, but the officials discovered that his way of life resembled too closely that of wealthy daimyō. This broke all the hidebound regulations. Consequently, in June, he was exiled and was forbidden to approach within ten *ri* (about 25 miles) of Edo.

During his enforced absence, Danjūrō VII traveled extensively along the Tōkaidō highway, appearing in theatricals here and there along that road and finally arriving in Osaka in November 1843. For several years the Kamigata citizens took him to their hearts, thrusting plaudits upon Edo's first artist of the Kabuki, until in 1850 he was finally granted leave to end his exile. He returned triumphantly to Edo.

Onoe Kikugorō III, playing the roles of Kampei and Kan Shōjō respectively in *Kanadehon Chūshingura* and *Sugawara Denju Tenarai Kagami* at the Ichimura-za in May 1843, also encountered trouble. The costume for Kan Shōjō was made of expensive *monsha,* a woven silk gauze with pattern, and in the role of Kampei, Kikugorō III used an imitation gun so realistically that at first the officials were completely fooled. Both the costume and the gun were confiscated, and a comprehensive fine of 10 *kammon* (about the same as 10 *ryō*) was levied. (The salary of a footman was about 1 *ryō* and 2 *bu* yearly). Another actor, whose name is unrecorded, was punished for failing to wear an *amigasa* upon leaving the theater.

The levying of frequent penalties made it increasingly difficult to present the Kabuki. With the banishment of Danjūrō VII and the punishment of Kikugorō III within the same year and the depression of the masses on all sides by political and social happenings, the Kabuki lost much of its patronage—a regrettable circumstance when the theater was at the height of its artistic accomplishments. Leading personalities were, and are, the greatest sustaining power of the people's theater.

But Kabuki was to rise again to its former heights. Mizuno, who seemed to revel in the fall from glory that the Kabuki had taken, was relieved of his position, having himself fallen into ill favor for his frustrating limitations on other aspects of everyday life as well. His administration was condemned as unjust, overly severe, and anything but good. It was found that when the government was too strict, the people turned to unlawful means to gain their ends. Bribery was rampant during Mizuno's tenure.

After Mizuno's demotion life became less restrained, and Kabuki regained its former position—this time with added distinction because the great prolific playwright Kawatake Shinshichi II, under the pen name of Kawatake Mokuami, came to the fore, bringing fresh material to the repertoire of a changing theater. Mokuami (1816–93) was the ranking playwright of the Bakumatsu and Meiji eras, accepted by some authorities as surpassing his illustrious predecessors.

Mokuami wrote convincing *kizewa-mono* for the actor Ichikawa Kodanji II, one of the brightest figures of his generation, and this gifted author-actor combination introduced excellent and well-loved realistic plays. Among the most representative are the following, given here with both their formal and their familiar titles: *Sato Moyō Azami no Ironui* or *Izayoi Seishin* (The Tale of Courtesan Izayoi and Priest Seishin), *Sannin Kichisa Kuruwa no Hatsugai* or *Sannin Kichisa* (Three Rogues Called Kichisa at the Licensed Quarter), and *Shiranami Gonin Otoko* or *Benten Kozō* (The Story of the Five Notorious Thieves).

An important event of material and satisfying proportions for the players took place in 1852. No longer were actors required to pay for their own costumes, which were hereafter to be furnished by the owner-managers of the theaters. An Osaka actor, Arashi Rikan III, had come to Edo to perform at the Kawarasaki-za, but it appeared that a satisfactory agreement could not be reached, other than to the disadvantage of the theater. Toward the end of 1851, however, a secret contract was signed whereby the owner-manager would provide costumes for Arashi. Ichikawa Kodanji IV discovered the existence of the document and demanded that his costumes be furnished also. Since the exposure of the agreement with Arashi and the granting of Kodanji IV's demands, all costumes have been furnished by the owner-managers, except for those given directly to the actors by patrons. One of the greatest financial burdens was thus lifted from the actors.

The Kabuki costumes became more and more colorful as regulations were eliminated step by step during the gradual decline of the shogunate. Rich merchants were exceptionally liberal in donating costumes to their favorites, thereby greatly adding to the splendor and harmonious effect of the staging.

A large segment of those frequenting the Kabuki actually had little else of interest, or of romance, in their drab lives. Through the artifice of the stage, they found visions of material elegance, such glimpses assuaging their hunger for the seemingly unobtainable. The Kabuki served their purpose, providing sentimental provender, while the gorgeous costumes added gaiety and imagery to their lives. The Kabuki belonged basically to the commoners, who wholeheartedly accepted its every nuance.

Even samurai, who were indifferent to the shogunate, now began to frequent the theater. Occasionally they would attend the Kabuki wearing an exact replica of the costume of a favorite role being performed that day. They never came dressed as women, however.

Actors went to great lengths to produce striking effects. For example, Bandō Shūka, playing the role of an *onna hinin* (beggar woman), appeared on the stage covered with a *komo* (straw mat sometimes used as a raincape) made of gold threads instead of the usual rice straw.

CHAPTER *7*

# Meiji Kabuki

The Meiji era (1868–1912), born in the throes of vast unrest and civil war, witnessed the defeat of the shogunate forces on the Toba and Fushimi highways near Kyoto in January 1868. The fifteenth Tokugawa shōgun, Yoshinobu, surrendered the reins of government to the Emperor Meiji and was entrusted to the care of the Mito branch of the Tokugawa family.

Though the Kabuki theaters remained open during these unstable months, many seats were empty, for the impending fall of the feudal dynasty, with its uncertainties, had caused unrest among admirers of the Kabuki as well as in all other segments of late Edo and early Meiji society.

It is pertinent here to take a brief look at the background of the social change that marked this period of Japanese history, for it was to have lasting effects on the Kabuki.

There were three main houses or lines of the Tokugawa dynasty, known as the *sanke* (three houses): those of Mito, Owari, and Kii. All of these were in direct line of descent from the first shōgun, Ieyasu, down through the sixth shōgun. The seventh died very young, leaving no heir. In addition, there were three branch families called *sankyō*: Tayasu, Hitotsubashi, and Shimizu—the direct descendants of sons of the shōguns who received their livelihood from the reigning shōgun. The eighth shōgun, without male heir, adopted a son from the Kii house of the Tokugawa family and thereby caused strife between the houses of Owari and Kii.

To avoid a repetition of such trouble in future generations, a rule was laid down and obeyed: any shōgun without a son must choose his heir from among his nearest relatives in the *sankyō* or branch families. The fifteenth and last shōgun, Yoshinobu, retired in 1868 as head of the clan, moving his family, including his son and heir, to Shizuoka and leaving the Tokugawa without a head of the family. Consequently, the Meiji government appointed Tokugawa Iesato to take over, although he never became a shōgun. If he had, his distinguished son, the late Tokugawa Iemasa, would have been the seventeenth shōgun.

The fifteen-year-old Emperor Meiji left his secluded life in refined Kyoto to establish his court in the flourishing bourgeois city of Edo in October 1868, where he saw the city's name change to Tokyo the following year (1869). Old systems of the feudal reign were discarded for new ones, giving rise to prosperity. Even the sumptuary laws directly aimed at Kabuki were abolished. Emperor Meiji encouraged the importation of foreign ideas, and these had a marked effect on the Kabuki, although the results, as viewed by some students of Kabuki today, had a greater impact upon Meiji scholars and government officials who wanted to revolutionize the Kabuki than upon the permanent effacement of pure Kabuki.

Until the restoration of the supreme authority of the emperor, the Kabuki attracted chiefly the Edokko, but afterwards it drew individuals from all walks of life as they flowed into the teeming city. Even the previously segregated foreign nationals patronized the Kabuki. This was the beginning of a decided change. To this new audience, the appearance of imaginary rats, toads, goblins, and other apparitions seemed irrational, if not foolish, but the Japanese in turn naively accepted as best any Western importation, regardless of its merit. A play having a thousand-year-old background and using costumes of the Edo period of the eighteenth century was challenged as incredibly fatuous.

Some of the Meiji playwrights and classical scholars, who knew little from actual experience about Kabuki, were unable to accept Kabuki at the *status quo*. This old theater, which had played to packed houses for hundreds of years, was considered too Rabelaisian for the intelligentsia and the foreigners. The devotees of the Kabuki were now to be ignored while the playwright-scholars devised drama for the intellectual minority, though that was not the intended purpose of the playwrights, for they had hoped to appeal to all people. However, they did not substitute more appealing plays—in fact, if the truth is admitted, the plays they produced were, as a whole, deadly bores.

In 1873, the fifth year of Emperor Meiji's reign, the municipal office responsible for theatrical matters called a meeting of city officials, playwrights, and actors. At this meeting it was suggested that the Kabuki be cleaned up, so to speak, to avoid embarrassment to Japan before the foreigners who had now begun to arrive in considerable numbers and to show decided interest in Japanese culture. Specifically, it was suggested that the real spice of the plays be deleted: the *nureba* or erotic scenes, often bordering on obscenity; the *koroshiba* or scenes of murder involving cruelty and slow bloody torture; and vulgar scenes of low life. At the same time, permission was granted to use the names of the emperor and others of the imperial family, although, to preserve the dignity of the court, they were not to be impersonated on the stage. Names of any other individuals could be used, and such persons could be impersonated.

Kabuki, previously held in the grip of strict laws, was now to be invaded by a group of scholars who, though well-meaning, had more of a detrimental effect than the restrictions. Most actors were persistent in resisting the untheatrical, but some proved apt in accepting the advice, right or wrong, of men of intellectual pursuits. This was indeed an interval of trial and error in the history of the Kabuki.

## DANJŪRŌ IX AND THE THEATRICAL REFORMATION

Ichikawa Danjūrō IX (1842–1903) was the fifth son of Danjūrō VII. He was adopted by Kawarasaki Gonnosuke VI, head of the Kawarasaki-za, and took the name of Kawarasaki Gonnosuke VII, later acceding to the name of Danjūrō.

The leaders of the *engeki kairyō*—the theatrical reformation—were three mainstays of the intelligentsia: Matsuda Michiyuki, grand secretary for domestic matters; Komyōji Saburō, former secretary of the French embassy; and Yoda Gakkai, official of the Ministry of Education. Initially, the Tokyo theaters were greatly influenced by the reformation movement. Foremost among those brought under its spell were Morita Kanya XII, the prominent theatrical manager-owner of the Shintomi-za; Danjūrō IX, leading Kabuki actor of the late nineteenth century; and Fukuchi Ōchi, a newspaperman affiliated with the *Tokyo Nichinichi Shimbun* (Tokyo Daily News). Ōchi later became an exclusive playwright for the Kabuki-za, where he collaborated with Danjūrō IX.

Nine years prior to the reformation movement, the famous "penetrating eyes" of Danjūrō IX foretold the change in Kabuki with his production of *Zōho Momoyama Monogatari* (The Revised Story of Momoyama)—popularly known as *Jishin Katō* (Katō's Fidelity in the Fushimi Earthquake)—a historical drama of the Azuchi-Momoyama period (1573–1603). With some revisions of the original plot and some additions to it, using historically accurate costumes, events, and names, the play told the story of the loyalty of Katō Kiyomasa to his master Toyotomi Hideyoshi, Japan's greatest instinctive military tactician. It was therefore not too surprising when *Sakai no Taiko* (The Drum of Sakai) appeared on the boards in 1874, introducing the tale of the bitter defeat of Tokugawa Ieyasu at the hands of Takeda Harunobu Shingen at Mikata-ga-hara in 1572—a subject barred during the previous Edo period.

In 1879, Danjūrō starred at the Shintomi-za in Mokuami's play *Matsu no Sakae Chiyoda no Shintoku* (The Flourishing of the House of Tokugawa under Divine Blessing). Historical facts for this presentation were gathered by Ichikawa Kumao, a former government official, and costume research was done by Matsuoka Okiyoshi. Sekioka, previously formal-dress costumer to the emperor, the daimyō, and the Nō actors, made the costumes, which included the exact likeness of the hawk-hunting attire worn by Ieyasu, the first Tokugawa shōgun.

Danjūrō also took the role of Ieyasu's wife in the play, wearing for this an authentic lightweight unpadded *kouchigi,* the aristocratic woman's coat used for both indoor and outdoor wear. For the *dammari* (scene of mimic action, usually without words and occurring at night), in this case a dream sequence of the younger days of Ieyasu, Danjūrō wore an exact replica of a nobleman's *kurohō-no-sokutai* (formal court apparel with black upper garment). In real life, Ieyasu had the privilege of wearing such clothing, since the emperor had given him the noble title of *chūnagon.*

The *sokutai,* it should be noted here, was the formal apparel of the *kuge* (court nobles) and special classes of military men. The first four ranking classes wore the *sokutai* with the black upper garment known as *kurohō.* The *hō* for the fifth class was dyed in *suō,* the color of red brazil-wood—that is, a rather dark red color taken from a plant. The sixth, seventh, and eighth classes were entitled to wear the *sokutai* with a *hanada hō* (blue).

In October of the same year (1879) that *Matsu no Sakae Chiyoda no Shin-toku* was produced, there appeared the historical drama *Nichō no Yumi Chigusa no Shigetō,* its plot based on the tale of Saitō Sanemori, a valiant warrior who lived during the period of strife between the Genji and the Heike clans (1156–85). For the role of Sanemori, Danjūrō chose to wear a white *suikan* (nobleman's court robe in ancient days) with white *ōguchi-bakama* (*hakama* with large openings at the ankles and extremely broad stiff back) and a *tate-eboshi* (tall hat), but he replaced the customary white *keshō* (make-up) with a long resplendent beard. His feet were bare, since the *tabi* socks of later times were not yet in use during the period depicted by the play. The *shitōzu* or socks of earlier years were worn only by those appearing in *sokutai* or by elderly men or invalids, and then only when given permission by the emperor.

Kanagaki Robun, editor of the newspaper *Kanayomi Shimbun,* criticized the performance of *Nichō no Yumi Chigusa no Shigetō* as "just *katsureki-geki*" —a living-history play. Indeed, it was not drama but a living event reproduced on the stage, offering little to the emotions. In a word, it was dull. Henceforth, the word *katsureki* was used in a serious sense, yet sometimes it was used to ridicule plays falling into this category.

Although Danjūrō's prolific ideas were passed on to Mokuami and later to Fukuchi Ōchi, not even his comprehensive abilities and vast popularity could inject sufficient life into the *katsureki-geki* to make them fully acceptable to the public. But Danjūrō was a stubbornly determined individualist who firmly believed that theatergoers needed plays of historical accuracy, and in 1886 he founded the antiquarian society known as the Kyūko-kai, whose name literally meant "society for seeking the old."

The association's principal members were the classical scholars Kuro-kawa Mayori and Konakamura Kiyonori, the dramatist Kawatake Moku-ami, the historical painter and scholar Kashiwagi Tankō, the Tosa-school painter Kawanobe Mitate, and the theatrical owner-manager Morita

Kanya XII. At the first meeting of the association, the painter Kashiwagi frankly explained that *katsureki* plays were not liked by the public, but even in the face of opposition from the members, Danjūrō said that he would carry on until he performed them for an audience of as few as two people. Only then would he quit. Coming from a superb classical Kabuki actor, this was hardly less than surprising. Nevertheless, confronted by such determination, the members of the Kyūko-kai agreed to assist Danjūrō, thereafter expressing their opinions at monthly meetings. The association continued for four or five years.

The groups's first production was from the pen of Mokuami, a play entitled *Hōjō Kudai Meika no Isaoshi* (The Ninth Shōgun of the Renowned Hōjō Dynasty) and popularly known as *Takatoki* after its chief character. The most popular scene of the play (the only one given today) was the fanciful sequence in which Takatoki is taunted by the beak-nosed goblins known as *tengu* into dancing the Dengaku, an ancient rustic form of dance. The *tengu* masks for the performance were furnished by the eminent doll-maker Yasumoto Kamehachi.

In order to reanimate the correct forms of dancing, music, and dress for *Takatoki,* members of the Kyūko-kai carried out thorough background research. The painter Kawanobe Mitate was permitted to visit the Imperial Household to study court performances of the Dengaku-mai—the humorous dances taken from those performed by peasants in the rice-planting season—and the accompanying *imayō* music, said to derive from ballads sung by professional women dancers of the Heian period. Since class distinction between the *nagauta* musicians (on-stage singers and orchestra of *samisen,* percussion, and wind instruments) of the Kabuki and court musicians precluded intercommunication, it was essential that a member of the Kyūko-kai undertake such a study if the dancing and music for *Takatoki* were to be authentic. As a sidelight, it is interesting to note that the weird mood of the play was enhanced by replacing the three customary *samisen* strings of tightly twisted raw silk with steel wires. In fact, the *harigane-jamisen*—that is, the *samisen* with wire strings—is used in the Kabuki solely for this one dance scene.

Costuming for *Takatoki* was devised after a study of many old picture scrolls. Of particular interest are the details of the costume for the role of the warrior Nitta Yoshisada, which included the type of helmet known as *tatsugashira* (*tatsu,* dragon; *kashira,* head). Previously, it is presumed, no one in theatrical circles had seen a *tatsugashira* helmet at close hand. It was a magnificently designed helmet with laminar folds, decorated in front with very erect *kuwagata* (helmet horns) and a dragon. The type worn even yet in all true Kabuki is not historically authentic. This *tatsugashira* helmet was a costly one and weighed approximately thirty pounds. The armor and helmet combined weighed more than seventy pounds, quite a substantial weight for any performer.

Under the helmet, a *hachimaki* (headband) served as a cushion, preventing head injury by steadying the cumbersome headgear. For wearing with a helmet, the *hachimaki,* about three inches wide and seven to eight feet long, is placed on the forehead with equal sides drawn to the back of the head and tied, then drawn to the front and tied, and again pulled to the back and tied, allowing the ends to fall to the middle of the shoulder blades. *Hachimaki* are generally white, with the exception of those belonging to young warriors, which are light pink.

Tied over the *yoroi* (armor) was a white cotton obi one foot wide and seven to eight feet long, its center placed directly over the stomach while its equal sides were drawn to the back and crossed, then brought to the middle of the front and tied in a bow.

It is a point of interest to learn how seriously the *katsureki-geki* strove for realism even in minute details. This production of *Takatoki* used one hundred *tan* (about 1,200 yards) of white cotton cloth. (One *tan* or about 12 yards is the requirement for the ordinary kimono.)

But with so much minute exactness Kabuki took wing directly into caricature. The writer Kanagaki Robun, criticizing *Takatoki,* poked a revealing finger at *katsureki-geki* by stating that Danjūrō, held under the spell of the *tengu,* had forgotten Kabuki. By way of illustrating his point, he drew a cartoon of Takatoki surrounded by goblins, but the faces of the goblins were those of the scholars belonging to the Kyūko-kai. Robun's message, however, did not register with the usually receptive Danjūrō. Instead, it quickly severed their relationship.

*Katsureki-geki* did attain some acceptance for a time following the successful run of *Takatoki.* Danjūrō headed the casts for *Ise no Saburō* (Saburō of Ise), *Youchi Soga Kariba no Akebono* (The Soga Brothers' Assault at Dawn on a Hunting Field), *Shigemori Kangen* (Shigemori's Admonition), the dance-drama *Ōmori Hikoshichi* (The Warrior Ōmori Hikoshichi), and other historical plays.

All of these plays were well received, but it was primarily Danjūrō IX's personal magnetism that drew the people to the Kabuki. Through his efforts, talent, and acting ability, he did draw large audiences. By remaining so faithful to historical reality, however, he lost the dramatic quality. Onoe Kikugorō V and Ichikawa Sadanji I were not very successful in *katsureki-geki,* nor were the actors who followed Danjūrō. In a word, *katsureki-geki* were vital only so long as the great master himself trod the boards.

Admittedly, Kabuki was influenced by the changing times, and *katsureki-geki* did add a new element. Though it had serious drawbacks, it laid the foundation for the plays written by Tsubouchi Shōyō, Mori Ōgai, Matsui Shōō, and Okamoto Kidō. The last mentioned authored some of the most interestingly earthy plays seen today.

It is sad that the Meiji era's most skilled Kabuki luminary, Ichikawa Danjūrō IX, should have wasted so many of his precious days over a period of twenty years in *katsureki-geki,* for he was a brilliant actor and dancer in classical and *shosagoto* dramas, which are, after all, Kabuki in purest form. His *kata* for *shosagoto* and *matsubame-mono* (plays taken from Nō) have been preserved in *Kagamijishi* (The Lion Dance), *Funa Benkei* (Benkei in the Boat), *Suō Otoshi* (The Dropped Coat), the hilarious farce *Ninin-Bakama* (Two Men with One Pair of Trousers), and *Kyō-Ningyō* (The Kyoto Doll).

Danjūrō IX was an expert painter with an accurate eye for color and design—factors of great importance in creating new ideas for theatrical dress. When he danced the lyrically exquisite *Sagi Musume* (The White Heron Maiden), there were five changes of costume, but for each costume he always ingeniously used a green *eri* (collar) covered with fine transparent white silk gauze. Today the *eri* is replaced to match the costumes, but Danjūrō's costumes matched a single *eri*. A brief outline of these costume effects follows:

FIRST COSTUME: white, *eri* appearing white
SECOND COSTUME: red, *eri* appearing greenish
THIRD COSTUME: reddish purple, *eri* appearing light red by reflection
FOURTH COSTUME: light blue, *eri* appearing light blue by reflection
FIFTH COSTUME: dark purple, *eri* appearing white

Such uncommon devices endeared Danjūrō to his worshipful public, but it is nevertheless true that he had to depend chiefly on his talent, for he was not blessed with handsome features. This lack, however, was not admitted by his admirers. Once on stage, artistry transformed this conspicuous-nosed actor into a bright star, and his ingenuity was often demonstrated. On one occasion, for example, when costumes failed to appear for a production of *Ōmori Hikoshichi* in which he was to dance the title role, he employed the impromptu device of having cloth in the *ichimatsu* checkerboard pattern sewn on a plain-colored *hitatare*—the military garment, based on a Nō ceremonial robe—which covered the midriff of the kimono, the upper portion of the *hakama,* and the lower sections of the sleeves. By thus making use of this chance mishap, he created a costume that was to become standard for the role of Ōmori.

Danjūrō's creativity in costuming was again displayed in *Ise Heishi Eiga no Koyomi,* the drama, as previously noted, that deals with the Heike clan at Ise. It is in this play that the famous story of Kesa Gozen, her husband Watanabe Wataru, and her lover Moritō is related: the tragic love triangle that formed the theme of the celebrated Japanese film *Gate of Hell* (1953). The leading male character, Moritō, having fallen in love with Kesa Gozen and having ostensibly persuaded her to assist him in murdering her husband, steals into the husband's bedroom at night and stabs the person lying there, only to discover that it is the faithful Kesa, who has taken her husband's place for the night.

For this play, Danjūrō, as Moritō, chose to act in a *hitatare* figured with brown and indigo polka dots against a white background. Indigo indicated the warrior's vigor; brown, the impression of loneliness coupled with sadness—colors most conducive in helping to project the unhappy fate of a man who genuinely repented committing a dastardly crime for a purpose which necessarily would have failed.

## ONOE KIKUGORŌ V

Kikugorō V (1855–1903) was a matchless contemporary of Danjūrō IX, and like Danjūrō, he was versatile. His stylized forms of acting, which expressed various degrees of emotion of the common man in the *sewa-mono* in which he first played the lead, are the accepted models for such roles as Kōchiyama in *Kumo ni Magō Ueno no Hatsuhana* (Cloudlike First Blossoms at Ueno or, less literally, Meeting Evil with Evil at Ueno) and Tatsugorō in *Kami no Megumi Wagō no Torikumi* (God's Blessing for the Reconciliation of the Megumi Firemen and the Sumō Wrestlers), commonly known as *Megumi no Kenka*.

Kikugorō V did not rely solely upon the costumer for ideas. He went to various stores and odd places, even to ragpickers, seeking just the right properties and costumes to fit each role. The same was true of his *kodōgu* (hand properties), especially *kiseru* (pipes), *tenugui* (hand towels), and *haki-mono* (footwear).

Kikugorō was famous for his long intermissions. Every minute detail had to be perfect. He would readjust a costume until he felt it was right. The *tenugui* had to be on and tied correctly. Moreover, he scanned the stage for any discrepancies in the setting that had to be corrected. Only then could the curtain be drawn. An unflattering line was not to be tolerated; so when the script called for him to wear a *tōnasu kaburi,* the unattractive pumpkin-shaped *tenugui* head-covering worn by farmers, he promptly improved the stage style by creasing a fold in the center front and slightly folding back the rear, permitting the *mage* (ponytail) to be visible. Even in his personal life, it appears that Kikugorō V was fastidious about the clothes he wore.

The plays known as *zangiri-mono* became the vogue in Tokyo as a result of the adroit natural acting of Kikugorō. These plays, whose name literally means "short-cropped-hair plays"—a reference to the abolition of the topknot and the leveling of social distinctions following the Edo period—represented Kikugorō's efforts to bring more realism into the *sewa-mono,* just as Danjūrō IX had attempted to do for the *jidai-mono* with his *katsureki-geki.* But the *zangiri-mono,* like the *katsureki-geki,* held their position only during their sponsor's lifetime. Although these Western-dress plays reached the Osaka stage prior to their introduction in Tokyo, nothing further was heard of them after the abortive beginning. The credit for their creation goes to Kikugorō and Mokuami, who wrote the plays. Three representative *zangiri-mono* are *Shima Chidori Tsuki no Shiranami* (Island Plovers over Foaming Waves under the Twenty-Day Moon), which deals with the activities of thieves (also known as *shiranami*—there is a play on words in the title); *Fudeya Kōbei* (Kōbei the Writing-Brush Seller or The Writing-Brush Shop's Tax Paid in Rice—a multiple play on words); and *Onna Shosei* (The Housemaid-Student).

Kikugorō V was a man of discernment, always envisioning new horizons of improvement, even to the minor details of stagecraft. He left his imprint on the Onoe-ke plays—that is, plays belonging to the Onoe family of actors —enriching the *kaidan-mono* (mystery or ghost stories) by special inventions and changes in costumes. By broadening the make-up and wig of the heroine Oiwa in *Tōkaidō Yotsuya Kaidan* (The Ghost Story of Yotsuya), who changes into a ghostly figure in the latter part of the drama, Kikugorō instilled an uncanny believability. In *Furudera no Neko* (The Weird Cat of the Old Temple), a cat disguises itself as an elderly woman, but Kikugorō, believing that the character should partially reveal itself, devised a method whereby ears protruding from the old lady's white hair moved, identifying the true character to the audience. He also replaced the wooden horns of the demon in *Ibaraki* with silver-painted steel wires, enabling them to shake like delicate springs when the head was moved.

Kikugorō V delved into the archives of the Imperial Household Museum for a historical likeness of a *jimbaori* (sleeveless coat worn over armor). For the *yoroi* (armor), he copied a set on display at the Yūshūkan Gallery of the Yasukuni Shrine in Tokyo. His *kariginu* for *Momijigari* (The Maple Viewing) was a duplication of a *hana-no-maru* (encircled floral pattern) *kariginu* kept in the Imperial Household Museum. As we have noted in a previous chapter, the *kariginu* was originally an outdoor or hunting costume worn by court nobles in the Heian period. After the Kamakura period, it was used as plain dress for courtiers and warriors but reverted to ceremonial dress during Edo. Used only for noblemen's costume on the stage, it consists of a wide-sleeved kimono and *hakama*.

Kikugorō's methods of acting in the roles of Igami no Gonta and Tadanobu in *Yoshitsune Sembon-Zakura* and of Enya Hangan in Act III and Kampei in Acts V and VI of *Kanadehon Chūshingura* are criteria today, though individual actors have made slight variations.

In competition with the Kabuki Jūhachiban (the eighteen best plays in the repertoire of the Ichikawa family compiled by Danjūrō VII) and the Shin Kabuki Jūhachiban ("new" eighteen best plays in the repertoire of Danjūrō IX), Kikugorō created the Shinko Engeki Jusshu (ten kinds of new and old one-act plays), the "new" referring to plays introduced by Kikugorō himself, the "old" to plays handed down by his predecessors. These plays are *Hitotsuya* (Lonely House), *Modoribashi* (Modori Bridge, or The Bridge on the Way Home), *Hagoromo* (The Robe of Feathers), *Kikujidō* (The Spirit of the Chrysanthemum), *Osakabe-hime* (Princess Osakabe), *Tsuchigumo* (The Ground Spider), *Ibaraki* (Demon Ibaraki), *Migawari Zazen* (The Substitute Meditator), *Furudera no Neko* (The Weird Cat of the Old Temple), and *Rakan* (The Enlightened Disciples of Buddha).

## OTHER MEIJI ACTORS

Although Danjūrō IX and Kikugorō V were considered the greatest of Meiji Kabuki actors, others were famous and became known for their individual styles. Four of these deserve particular mention.

Ichikawa Sadanji I was extremely impressive in active, vigorous roles, especially those entailing the stylized fighting or swordplay scenes known as *tachimawari*. His Togashi in *Kanjinchō* was fully as splendid as that of Kikugorō, although today it is the latter's *kata* for the role that is followed. Sadanji brought lustre to the role of Marubashi Chūya in the play by the same name.

Iwai Hanshirō VIII was the outstanding *onnagata* of his generation, and Nakamura Shikan IV, a *tachi-yaku* actor, excelled in *kataki-yaku* (villain roles) like those of Moronao in *Kanadehon Chūshingura* and Nikki Danjō in *Meiboku Sendai Hagi* (The Disputed Succession of the Date Family, although the title literally refers to a group of loyal persons "fragrant like famous incense wood.")

Sawamura Sōjūrō of Osaka, another leading actor, was proficient in playing the delicate *nimaime* (lover) roles in the gentle romantic dramas called *wagoto*. On occasion he came to Tokyo to perform with Danjūrō IX, primarily in the Soga Kyōgen: plays of the cycle dealing with the Soga brothers. In these he always took the role of the brother Jūrō opposite Danjūrō's Gorō.

## THE ERA OF THE SHINTOMI-ZA

From the seventeenth-century days of Okuni Kabuki until the end of the Edo period, Kabuki actors had been continuously defamed as "riverbed beggars" and "riverbed people" and had been held in the lowest esteem. Their performances were seldom patronized by aristocrats or persons of higher society. But the Meiji Restoration tore down all these barriers. Kabuki was at last accepted as a dramatic art and its actors as accomplished artists. The new status of the Kabuki was acknowledged by the attendance of the emperor at a performance given by Danjūrō's troupe at the garden of the foreign minister, Count Inoue.

Heretofore, foreign state guests had been invited to view only the Nō or the Bunraku. Now dignitaries from abroad were given the opportunity to see the people's theater. In the Kabuki world, the twenty-year period beginning with the eleventh year of Meiji (1879) was referred to as the Shintomi-za era, since it was this theater that dominated the scene, and never had productions been more scintillating or audiences more select. Morita Kanya XII and his Shintomi-za troupe played host to such dignitaries as Albert Wilhelm Heinrich, grandson of the German kaiser; the former United States President Grant, his wife, and their son; and Napoleon III, pretender to the French throne. The Shintomi-za itself, formerly the Morita-za, was located where the main Shōchiku building now stands in Shintomi-chō of the Tsukiji district of Tokyo, a short distance from the present Kabuki-za.

A devastating blow fell upon the Kabuki world in 1903 when death overtook two of the foremost creative actors of Japanese stage history: Onoe Kikugorō V and Ichikawa Danjūrō IX. An indication of the eminence of Danjūrō IX is the fact that not until April 1962 was his name passed on to another actor, except for the posthumous award of the title Danjūrō X to his son-in-law Ichikawa Sanshō in 1955. In April 1962, Ichikawa Ebizō IX, son of Matsumoto Kōshirō VII and adopted son of the above-mentioned Sanshō, became Danjūrō XI.

During Meiji, management was in full control of all costumes. Gradually, however, they came to be designed and made principally by specialists, the *ishō-ya,* who rented the costumes to the management. Leading actors continued to request individual models, although the styles for classical plays remained firmly established. The only new ideas for costumes introduced by the Meiji actors were the Western dress of the *zangiri-mono* and the realistic clothing of past generations for the *katsureki-geki.*

It seems that chemical dyes were introduced to Japan in Kyoto around 1877, although they were not generally used in Tokyo until the end of the nineteenth century, after the Sino-Japanese war. But such dyes were never to make serious inroads on the dyeing of costume materials, and vegetable dyes still remain in common use.

Immediately following the reinstatement of the monarchy, the stage programs became somewhat irregular. Some theaters would present Kabuki six months out of the year, others only two or three months. Beginning in March 1911, the year before the end of the Meiji era, the Teikoku Gekijō (Imperial Theater, often shortened to Teigeki) inaugurated a different show each month of the year. Soon other Kabuki theaters began to follow this precedent. The performance at the Imperial Theater usually opened on the first day of the month and closed on the twenty-fifth.

The Imperial opened its doors for the first time in March 1911. It was the first Western-style theater with chair seats in Japan, but it proved to be inadequate as a Kabuki theater, for it lacked the conventional *hanamichi* on which the actors in many instances depend for their entrances, exits, and vivid theatrical moments. For a number of years, the Imperial was an exclusive theater for Cinemascope films. In 1964 it was demolished to make way for a high-rise building owned by the Tōhō Company which will house a new Teikoku Gekijō or Imperial Theater.

CHAPTER 8

# Taishō and Shōwa Kabuki

Kabuki entered the modern eras of Taishō (1912–26) and Shōwa (1926–present) with many of its aspects in slight but continuous change. The dramas that emerged in Edo times, however, remained the core of the repertoire—in fact, the only pure Kabuki.

Audiences of the present Shōwa era are still witnessing the Kabuki plays, no longer contemporary except in a few particulars, as a showcase for reviewing in detail the events of their history before the Meiji era. Dress similar to that of Edo times, especially as seen in the *sewa-mono,* can still be seen in Japan today along with the prevailing mode of Western dress, and in this respect Kabuki is not a complete revelation to Japanese audiences.

What Kabuki does continue to offer in theory is a strict code of ethics. Some of the elderly among the current generation and, hopefully, a few of the younger have more than a mere nostalgia for an attribute once strongly entrenched but gradually losing its force in modern times—that of loyalty, which is the theme of many popular Kabuki dramas produced today.

The greatest changes are, in effect, in the theaters and the audiences rather than in the dramas. No longer is Kabuki the only popular theater, as it was well into the Meiji era. Even during Meiji, the active Edo San-za (three theaters of Edo; that is, the Nakamura-za, the Ichimura-za, and the Morita-za)—the three flourishing Kabuki theaters of their day—gradually lost their prestige. Since their demise, theaters have come and gone, notably Morita Kanya's debt-ridden Shintomi-za.

By August 1890, the government had recognized in Tokyo ten large (Kabuki) theaters and twenty-two small (comic dance) theaters. Built about this time were two of the important Kabuki theaters existing today: the Kabuki-za, which opened in November 1889, and the Meiji-za, successor to the Kishō-za, which opened in November 1893.

Both the Kabuki-za and the Meiji-za have experienced their personal misfortunes. Each was destroyed, as were other Kabuki theaters, during the devastating earthquake of 1923. Rebuilt, they were again destroyed by the bombings of the last world war. The Meiji-za was completely demolished, while a direct hit left only the façade of the Kabuki-za. The Meiji-za was again destroyed, this time by a four-alarm fire, on April 2, 1957. It was again rebuilt and reopened as a modern fireproof building on March 5, 1958. The reconstructed Kabuki-za observed its grand opening on January 3, 1951, with a program that included the ceremonial dance *Kotobuki Shiki Sambasō* and a one-act play, *Hana Kurabe Kabuki Tanjō* (Gorgeous Birth of Kabuki), by Ihara Seiseien. The first of these was performed by three leading actors who have since died: Bandō Mitsugorō VII, Ichikawa Ennosuke II, and Nakamura Tokizō III. The roles in the second were taken by actors from the combined Kichiemon and Ennosuke troupes of that time.

Today such attractions as *shingeki* (literally: new drama), television, hundreds of motion-picture houses, and thousands of coffee shops offering live or recorded music have drawn the youth of Japan away from the classical Kabuki. It is heartening to note that most of the institutions of higher learning do have Kabuki clubs, but the membership is sufficiently limited to offer little resistance to the inroads made by modern entertainment. The greatest patronage of today's Kabuki comes from large industrial and commercial firms which regularly buy huge lots of tickets to furnish their employees with an outing or to present to their customers in gratitude for their trade.

The present (1965) price of first-class tickets at the Kabuki-za in Tokyo averages ¥1,800 ($5.00) to ¥2,500 ($6.95), with higher fees for special performances—prohibitive prices for the average Japanese when he considers how much entertainment of other types the same amount would purchase. How many Japanese attend the Kabuki of their own volition is debatable. Nevertheless, one day of each month's run of performances is taken over by the individual patrons as opposed to those who arrive en bloc for an outing. This is *shonichi* (opening day), a joyous occasion with a feeling of festivity in the air. The theater is crammed with actors' families, their patrons, regular Kabuki devotees, and occasional tourists who seem out of place.

In Tokyo, Kabuki is presented at the Kabuki-za (probably the most patronized theater in Japan, since it pays the highest entertainment tax), yet it does not present Kabuki exclusively throughout the year. Occasionally, for example, the Kabuki-za offers Shinkoku-geki, which is noted for its vigorous two-handed swordplay and its fine leading men, Tatsumi Ryūtarō and Shimada Shōgo, whose acting compares with the finest to be seen in Japan.

In addition, performances by the younger Kabuki actors, backed by one or two established stars, are given at the attractive Tōyoko Hall in the Tōyoko Department Store in Shibuya and at Tokyo's newest theater, the Nissei, across the street from the Imperial Hotel.

Kansai's newest and largest Kabuki theater is the Osaka Kabuki-za, which opened on October 30, 1958, as a replacement of the previous Kabuki-za. It is a showplace—extremely modern and boasting the only escalators in the realm of Kabuki. The theater has a striking exterior and a beautiful interior décor. Smart-looking Japanese-style tearooms are part of the establishment. Original paintings by Japan's foremost artists decorate the walls, and magnificent brocade-covered furniture (which the public can only look at and not use) graces the main foyer. It is a veritable showcase—something beautiful to observe, but without the conveniences or intimacies so typical of true Kabuki theaters.

The Kado-za, oldest of Osaka's theaters, still retains something of an Edo atmosphere and is distinguished by the *yagura* (drum tower) on the front roof—once the symbol of government license to perform Kabuki. The only active Kabuki theater in Nagoya is the Misono-za.

The old Minami-za in Kyoto does an especially flourishing business when Tokyo stars join the Kansai actors for a month's performance. The *kaomise* program in December is played to full houses.

Individual Kansai actors come to Tokyo to star with the troupes of the capital. These visits are very welcome, for they give Tokyo theater patrons a glimpse of the excellent Kansai style of acting. Ichikawa Jukai III, born in 1886, though not considered a true Kansai actor since he originally came from the Tokyo stage, is the pre-eminent actor of Kansai, who enlivens every performance with which he is associated. He is equally captivating in *wakashu* roles and those of mature adults. Surprisingly, even close at hand, Jukai's face and hands show few traces of his actual age.

Little, if any, change in styling of costumes has been introduced since the advent of the historically accurate costumes for *katsureki-geki* and the Western apparel for *zangiri-mono*. Only when a neo-Kabuki play is to be produced do the costumers create costumes unfamiliar to the Kabuki audience. Research for such costumes must be carried out, and old pictures and scrolls or the playwright's ideas taken from literature set the criteria.

The most memorable display of authentic early clothing was presented to the public in March 1951 at the Tokyo Kabuki-za with the initial production of *Genji Monogatari*. The costumes were those of the Heian period. The *onnagata* were clothed in layers of soft, loose gowns and robes of unsurpassed quality, although the Western observer probably found their plain hair styles (authentic for the period, of course) theatrically unbecoming. Actors in the male roles fared better in this respect, as they always seem to do, for unless they are depicting ruffians or certain odd characters, the men's wigs enhance their features. The masculine attire for *Genji Monogatari* was the aesthetically elegant clothing of the Heian court.

Another display of ancient costumes—this time that of the remote and legendary Kamiyo, the Age of the Gods—was seen in the October 1954 production of *Nippon Kenjō-ki* (The Record of Japan's Surrender), an original play by Naitō Yukimasa. The play was chosen by the Ministry of Education for performance at an art festival given at the Tokyo Kabuki-za and was presented by the Kikugorō Gekidan (Kikugorō Troupe) with Ichikawa Ebizō IX (later Danjūrō XI) as guest star. An adaptation from the *Kojiki* (Record of Ancient Matters), one of Japan's two oldest histories (completed in A.D. 712), it tells of the hostility between two ancient races, Takamagahara and Izumo.

The entire complement of costumes for this drama was based on those of the ancient clay burial images called *haniwa,* dating from the Grave Mound period of A.D. 300–650. The women's costumes had the flattering, free, fluid lines typical of Chinese and Korean dress of the same period, from which, in fact, the Japanese styles had been copied. For the authentic rendering of costumes of the Kamiyo in this play, the production depended upon Maeda Seison, one of Japan's outstanding artists. The stage direction was in charge of the late Kubota Mantarō, president of the Japan Theatrical Association.

The mantle so long expertly held by Danjūrō IX in Tokyo Kabuki was to be shared, after his death in 1903, by two totally different types of actors: Onoe Kikugorō VI (1885–1949) and Nakamura Kichiemon I (1886–1954). Kikugorō VI was the son of Onoe Kikugorō V, the scion of an illustrious Kabuki family, but Kichiemon I reached the heights without that advantage—and an advantage it is in the feudalistic world of the Kabuki.

Kikugorō VI, a favorite pupil of Danjūrō IX, was a specialist in realistic domestic dramas. He is still reverently spoken of as Rokudaime (the Sixth) and is remembered as an ideal dancer and a magnificent *onnagata* without peer in modern times, and his son, Baikō VII, is today's foremost *onnagata.*

Kichiemon I, though always frail and often in poor health, seemed to be revivified on the stage. He was one of the last of the classical actors of the old school who could arouse the audience's emotions to the highest pitch during eloquent scenes in *jidai-mono*. Kichiemon was not a dancer, although the ability to dance is usually a requisite for stardom. His acting was confined to *tachi-yaku* roles.

Today's type of program, divided into matinee and evening performances, was not instituted until 1940. Under this arrangement, time is vastly reduced for actor's rehearsals, for creating and sewing costumes, and for painting scenery. The system limits the personal life of all concerned with the Kabuki. Although the monthly opening date may vary, since 1940 most Kabuki theaters have been running on a 25-day-a-month schedule, thus presenting the theatergoers of Japan with an almost continuous Kabuki season.

During the winter of 1961, Kabuki underwent another change when 37 actors, under the leadership of Matsumoto Kōshirō VIII, severed their connection with the Shōchiku Company, the established management for traditional Kabuki. It has been intimated that the actors were prompted to their decision by a contract system between a new management and employees that afforded them additional pay and more leisure time. The new management is the Tōhō Company, owner of a large movie industry, a chain of theaters, the Takarazuka All-Girl Troupes, and other enterprises. It must be acknowledged that the feudalistic ideas held by the Shōchiku Company had much to do with the defection of these actors.

Changes may come and may go, but Kabuki remains an actor's theater in which the play is secondary. In emphasizing form rather than content, it parallels much of the activity of Japanese life. Kabuki, not giving way to modern innovation, has held unconditionally to the past with dramas of sentiment, sacredness, glory, filial piety, and sacrifice.

Today many in the Western world seriously question these sentiments and are often embarrassed by such emotional manifestations. Side by side with Western patterns of thought and habit, the Japanese live unbrokenly with the past in their private lives. Even in their choice of Kabuki entertainment, the emotion-packed dramas of steadfast loyalty and filial piety remain favored over all others.

These dramas, with the most simple of plots, project themselves for one basic significant reason: to entertain. The theatrical scene is never overlooked. A day's performance seldom consists of a Kabuki play in its entirety but the best scenes or acts from a number of plays, with the program furnishing summaries of the entire plays. Each performance, consisting of two diverse programs daily, gives a royal sampling of dance-dramas; domestic plays of the commoners of the Edo period; aragoto plays; dramas of courtesans, feudal lords, thieves, samurai, firemen, sumō wrestlers; and plays of love and passion.

Kabuki is less like Western theater, where the play is the thing, and more like opera or vaudeville, where the individual performance is judged in terms of the way it repeats what was once done in what seems the best manner. Perfection of technique is most prized.

Though the skill of the actor comes first, it is supplemented by beauty and theatrical quality in costumes, make-up, and staging. These are all so intertwined and set in an established pattern in Kabuki that the play and each role has a known kata (format). The effectiveness of each performance is judged by the critics in terms of the established kata.

Because of the variety of roles, the costumes are multiplied endlessly. The unity of costumes with the accompanying make-up and accessories is part of the fascinating cohesive fabric that is Kabuki.

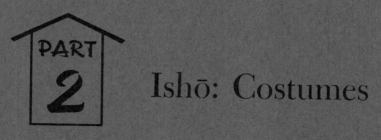

# PART 2

# Ishō: Costumes

CHAPTER *9*

# Costumes: A General View

The Japanese costumer, known as the *ishō-ya,* combines a notable array of colors, at times almost discordant, to produce dazzling costumes of incredible beauty and unexpected vibrancy. Some costumes are startling in their rich hues or in patterns sweeping from neck to heel, while others are beguiling in unadorned simplicity. The *ishō-ya* clothes his comics in costumes that are amazingly original bits of bold comedy in themselves, but it is for the dance-dramas known as *shosagoto* that today's costumer is most articulate. With the masterliness of a Kandinsky, he combines delicately and sensitively as many as thirteen distinctly different colors for a single costume—for example, in an opening-scene kimono worn by Onoe Baikō VII as the famed Wisteria Maiden in *Fuji Musume:* a delightful inspiration of soft pink, light green, canary yellow, orange, purple, leaf green, white, gold, candy-stick red, silver, delicate lavender, shocking pink, and black. Yet, with all the impressive subtle nuances of color to be found in Kabuki costume, it is rather difficult at times for the Westerner to accept the wide use of the combination of red and pink in great masses.

Before we engage in a detailed look at the various elements of Kabuki costume, it is essential to have a general view of the costume picture. For this purpose, we shall glance briefly at four aspects of this picture: the kimono, *onnagata* clothing, the *hakama,* and *otoko* clothing—that is, clothing for actors in male roles.

## THE KIMONO

The woman's kimono (Fig. 14) is one of the unique expressions of Japanese life. It can denote the age and marital status of the wearer, the season of the year, the beginning of a new life, and even death. Youth is represented by the *furisode* (*furi,* swinging or hanging; *sode,* sleeve), the kimono with long swinging sleeves worn by unmarried girls and young wives. After marriage, except for young wives, but strictly after childbirth, the sleeves are shortened. The young wear bright hues, especially red, with the various colors of the kimono becoming gradually less and less vivid by middle age, only to reach the somber state of gray, yellowish tan, and beige in older age, although all retain the loveliness of some of the world's finest fabrics created on the hand looms of Japan.

The kimono is neatly wrapped around the body with the two front pieces overlapping from left to right (the kimono of a dead person is overlapped from right to left) and is held firmly in place not by buttons, hooks and eyes, or zippers—for no such mundane accessories are ever used—but by the most eye-catching accessory: a stiff obi, a foot-wide sash that is wound around the waist and tied in back to form various fascinating shapes, such as that of a butterfly in flight. The obi is symbolic of the vast reservoir of beauty that is an integral part of the Japanese scene.

Some kimono have huge designs splashed across the shoulder or diagonally down the back to produce a vivid effect, while others may have a bold hem pattern only. Symbolism is also carried out in the weaving and designing of the kimono. Sometimes a delightful old turtle is depicted as a symbol of longevity, while a graceful white crane utilized in an allover pattern represents longevity and good luck.

The creation of fabric designs to be woven for the kimono has been given careful attention since the fifteenth or sixteenth century, when the more elaborate designs came into fashion. This meant that the design for the back of the kimono must be woven upside down, since a straight piece of cloth was used, as it is today, without cutting in the manner of Western dress.

The kimono, with its silk damask designs in satin, its brocades of gold and silver with glossy silk threads, its flat crepe in striped, plaid, or geometrically woven designs, its fabulous tie-and-dye patterns—often simulated for Kabuki—and myriads of other types of materials and designs, presents a never-ending panorama of sheer beauty, especially in a theatrical sense.

The kimono is made five or more inches longer than the wearing length; consequently, it must be carefully drawn up so that the hem is level with the wearer's heels. To hold the kimono in this position, a silk cord is tied around the waist, and over it the slack or kimono fold is smoothed down to permit flat winding of the obi.

The actors, for both male and female roles, are padded at the midriff in order to make the kimono look straight up and down, eliminating the curves of the body. The Japanese have always looked on the straight figure as the epitome of beauty.

Kimono is the Japanese word for robe, clothes, garments, clothing, raiment, apparel, dress, and costume, and it is used in some form as a part of every Kabuki costume. It takes different names as it varies in form or is adapted for different characters.

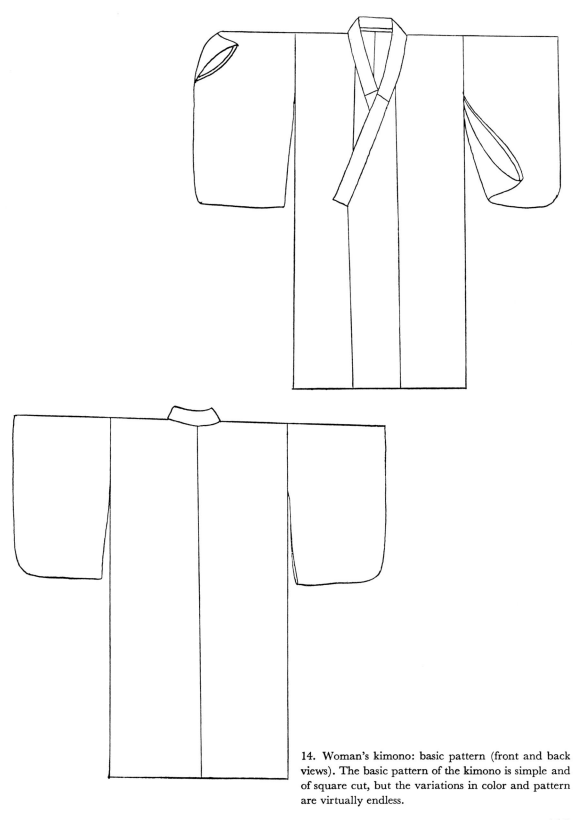

14. Woman's kimono: basic pattern (front and back views). The basic pattern of the kimono is simple and of square cut, but the variations in color and pattern are virtually endless.

## ONNAGATA CLOTHING

The *onnagata*, in addition to wearing one or two basic kimono, is dressed in the garments listed below, with some degree of variance according to the role. Three dressers—sometimes four—are needed to put on the costume, tie the obi, and give other help.

> *shitabaki*: (*shita*, under; *haki*, wear) a type of loincloth worn for the same purpose as undershorts
> *koshimaki*: (*koshi*, loin; *maki*, wound, rolled) a strip of red silk crepe wound around the midriff; literally, "waist wrapper"
> *hada-juban* or *hadagi*: (*hada*, skin; *gi*, from *kiru*, to wear) a tight undershirt, worn next to skin, of white *sarashi* (cotton cloth) with a red edge around the neckline, low-cut back neckline, short red sleeves reaching midway on the upper arm, and a *himo* (belt) to fasten it at the waist
> *fungomi*: (from *fumikomu*, to step into) a kind of trousers, red in color, used for hiding the legs; predecessor of the *hakama*
> *han-juban*: (*han*, half, middle, short) short underwear
> *naga-juban*: (*naga*, long) long underwear
> *hakama*: divided skirt or culottes

## THE HAKAMA

The culotte garment seen throughout Kabuki is the *hakama* (Figs. 19, 22–24), this word being the general designation for the loose skirtlike trousers worn by both men and women. With the kimono, it forms the basis for many costumes. A list of the most frequently worn *hakama* follows.

> *han-bakama* or *hambakama*: (*han*, half) short *hakama* used mostly as part of *han-kamishimo*—that is, *kamishimo* with short *hakama*
> *naga-bakama*: (*naga*, long) long *hakama* used mostly as part of *naga-gamishimo*—that is, *kamishimo* with long *hakama*
> *no-bakama*: (*no*, field) *hakama* for outdoor wear
> *kukuri-bakama*: (from *kukuru*, to fasten, to tie) *hakama* tied at the ankle
> *ue-no-hakama*: (*ue*, top; *no*, of) outer *hakama*, for formal dress of court nobles
> *hari-bakama*: (from *haru*, to spread out, to swell) long red *hakama* worn by court ladies
> *kiri-bakama*: (from *kiru*, to cut) short *hakama* for women, including those of the court
> *tattsuke-bakama*: (from *tachi*, cut or tailored, and *tsuke*, put together) *hakama* with lower part in form of tight leggings

## OTOKO CLOTHING

Men's costumes are more varied, since the male roles are more diverse

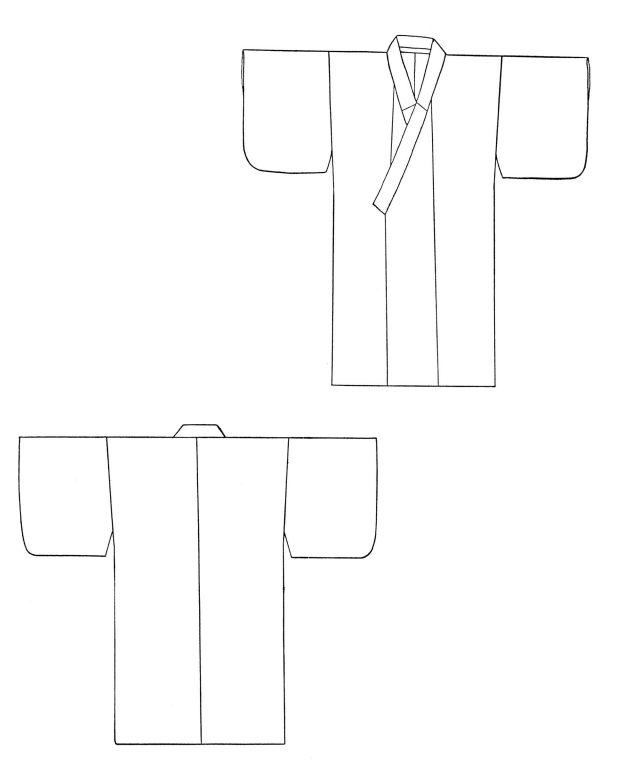

15. Man's kimono: basic pattern (front and back views). Essentially the same in cut as a woman's kimono, a man's kimono shows its chief differences in the sleeves. In Kabuki, although not in real life, it is capable of almost limitless variations.

than those played by the *onnagata,* although the standard kimono (Fig. 15) is usually the basic costume. The number of articles of clothing will range from one outer garment in the *kizewa-mono* dramas of lower-class life to a combination of *han-juban, naga-juban,* one or two kimono, and *haori* for the roles of daimyō and other persons of the more well-to-do classes. The number of undergarments reflects the status of the role.

<br />

CHAPTER **10**

# Men's Costumes for Jidai-mono

Costumes worn exclusively in *jidai-mono* are relatively few, and these plays fall into the *ō-jidai-mono* class: the plays of the old nobility. This condition might have reversed itself, since it was the general trend for a time to try authentic historical styles, but the urge to fall back on the *kata* of old classics, using traditional costumes deliberately made in an unusual manner, was too great to be overcome.

The most elegant men's apparel reflects the Chinese dictates of dress represented in the splendid but modified formal *sokutai* of the gentlemen of the imperial court and in the more realistic robes of Buddhist priests. The *sokutai*—brocaded silk garments of unquestioned grandeur—are designed with supreme artistry, imaginatively mirroring the prevailing aristocratic masculine dress during the years from the middle of the Heian period to the end of the Edo period. They are an intrinsic part of the structural beauty of classic staging. While these costumes, worn only by the leading characters, are distinguished by their foreign (that is, Chinese) origin, the minor characters vary the trend by wearing dress modeled after the traditional Japanese design, clearly defining the two modes of dress of the period.

A more diversified array of clothing may be seen in *jidai-mono* dealing with the lives of the powerful daimyō and samurai (Fig. 18), the great military class that held sway over Japan from the thirteenth century to the middle of the nineteenth century, when the long years of peace of the Edo period finally saw the rise of a moneyed merchant class. It is in these plays that some of the most resplendent (and sometimes most fantastic) masculine costumes appear, quite often in exaggerated versions of their actual historical counterparts. Costumes also cover a wide range in *jidai-sewa-mono,* the historical-domestic plays that represent the commingling of samurai and plebeian families. Only the costumes most widely used in these plays are included in the following divisions of dress.

<br />

119

## DAIMON

The *daimon* (*dai,* large; *mon,* crest), a costume decorated with large family crests (Figs. 16, 17, 19), is worn in Kabuki by the shōgun and his highest retainers, the daimyō. It is worth noting here that during the Edo period the shōgun's existence was held to be inviolable, and therefore the genuine name of a shōgun could not be given to any stage role. In dramatic works after the Meiji Restoration, however, there have been many instances in which actors have taken the role of a shōgun. Ieyasu and his son Hidetada, the first and the second Tokugawa shōgun, are characters in *Kasuga no Tsubone;* the fourth shōgun, Ietsuna, is impersonated in *Sakura no Sōgorō;* and, more recently, the fifth shōgun, Tsunayoshi, has appeared as a character in the final scene of *Atake Maru.*

The *daimon,* worn for very formal occasions, consists of a wide-sleeved top garment with prominent crests and a pair of *naga-bakama,* long trailing trousers in which the feet are hidden. The costume combines regal dignity and grace. Although the last assertion may seem questionable, it can readily be admitted that the wearer must be graceful to move about in such cumbersome trousers as the *naga-bakama.* It is interesting to note, historically, that the wearing of *naga-bakama* at court is said to have had the advantage of hindering a man's movements, thereby preventing him from getting involved in swordplay.

With the *daimon,* the Kabuki daimyō wear the *hikitate eboshi,* a high-crowned hat fastened with white ties to symbolize their class. An exception is Moronao, the evil daimyō of *Kanadehon Chūshingura,* who has purple ties for his hat to distinguish his rank from that of Hangan, who uses white ties. The shōgun may wear a *kin sammi eboshi,* a gold hat with purple or white ties, to signify his exalted position, although this headgear is a stage innovation replacing the traditional black hat, just as the *hikitate eboshi* of the daimyō is a substitute for the *kazaori eboshi,* a rather tall hat with the crown flattened to one side, that the actual daimyō wore with the *daimon.* The suggestion for the *hikitate eboshi* was probably taken from the Nō or from a warrior character in the Kyōgen. Similarly, it should be noted that in real life the *hitatare* and not the *daimon* was worn by the shōgun.

The *daimon* of the stage (Fig. 19) is generally made of solid-color ramie with seven large *mon,* five superimposed on the top garment and two on the *naga-bakama,* and is worn with the kimono called *kitsuke.* This aesthetically well-conceived costume is worn by Shōgun Yukihira in *Rampei Monogurui* (The Mad Rampei) and Shōgun Yoshiie in *Ōshū Adachigahara,* but the most impressive display of *daimon* is paraded in the *daijo,* the prologue to Act I of *Kanadehon Chūshingura*—the play with the widest scope of costumes to be seen in Kabuki drama. The colored *daimon* of three of the principal roles are indicative of their personalities. Moronao's, of black, accentuates a treacherous character and fawning mannerisms,

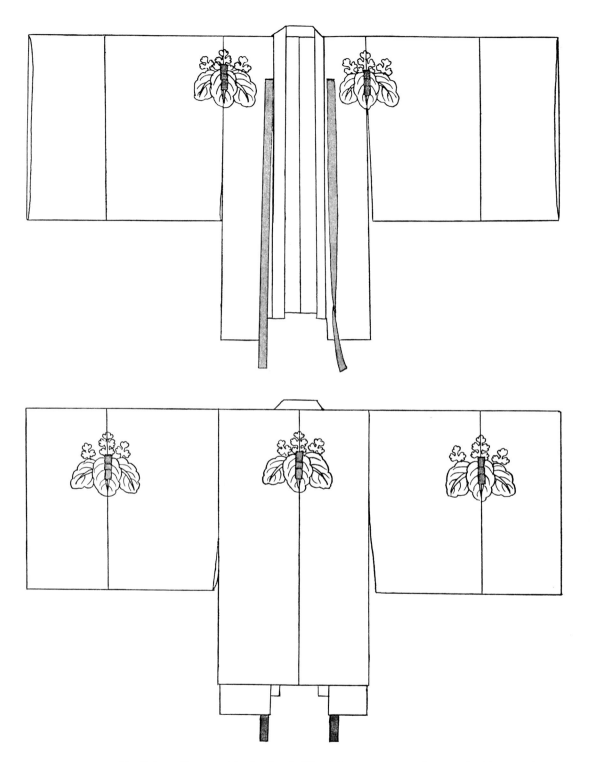

16. *Daimon* (front and back views). The *daimon*, a costume decorated with large family crests, is worn in *jidai-mono* (historical plays) by the shōgun and his highest retainers, the daimyō. The complete costume consists of a wide-sleeved top garment with prominent crests and a pair of the long trailing trousers called *naga-bakama*.

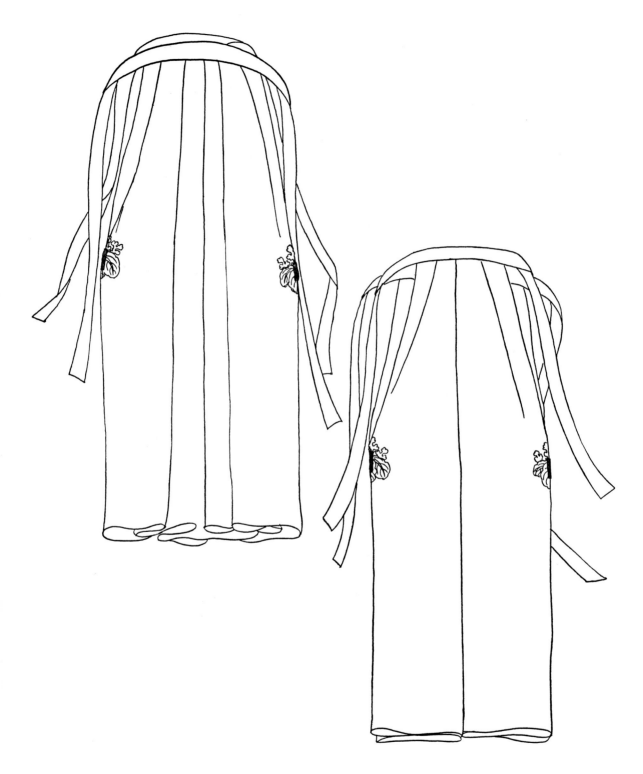

17. *Naga-bakama* for *daimon* (front and back views). It is interesting to note that the wearing of *naga-bakama* at court is said to have had the advantage of hindering a man's movements, thereby preventing him from getting involved in swordplay.

although black does not always denote a villain, since it is also the color for ceremonial dress. Hangan's *daimon* is of the color *ukon,* the soft canary yellow produced by the dye made from the turmeric root or the saffron plant. Yellow fittingly portrays the warm, gentle nature of the quiet Hangan. Wakasanosuke's costume is *sora-iro,* the color of the clear blue sky, expressing with clarity the virility and impulsiveness of his youth. These costumes are comparatively realistic, having been changed from the original non-conforming designs, during the Meiji era, through knowledge garnered from woodblock prints.

## SUŌ

The *suō* looks like the *daimon,* the chief means of differentiation being the particular type of hat worn. Also, with the *daimon* the *naga-bakama* are always a part of the costume, whereas the *hakama* of the *suō* may be either the *han-bakama* or the *naga-bakama.* In the former case, the costume is known as the *ko-suō* (*ko,* small).

The *suō* was the apparel for non-commissioned military men of the Muromachi period. By Edo times, it was generally being used for ceremonial wear by the lower-ranking samurai. The military *suō* had leather *himo* (laces or tie bands) on the collar, but the Kabuki *suō* varies greatly in this respect. The *suō* is made mostly of dyed ramie for *aragoto* characters, villains, and elderly men; purple satin for the gentle characters of *wagoto* plays; and light-blue satin for the roles of good-natured men.

Belonging to the *suō* class is the *ryūjin-maki* (Ryūjin, dragon god of the sea; *maki,* from *maku,* to wind), one of the strange styles of *suō* copied from the Bunraku (although the name itself comes from the Nō). The style (Fig. 20) must have found its way into the puppet theater from the Nō, for the dragon god appearing in the Nō always wears a sleeve in *ryūjin-maki* style rolled at the hip. Unlike the rolled sleeve of the Nō costume, the right sleeve of the *ryūjin-maki suō* of the Kabuki is a stiff-standing style. It does not cover the arm but is wound over a flat wooden board and is borne on the back, forming a point over the left shoulder, with the opposite end inserted into the belt. The lower hanging portion of the sleeve is stretched into a square by the insertion of cloth-covered bamboo splints, giving the appearance of a huge square shield with a relatively large-sized crest blazoned at the center.

The wadded brocade *uwagi*—the garment worn directly under the *suō* in ordinary or in *ryūjin-maki* style—brilliantly contrasts with the subdued coloring of the *suō.* Under the *uwagi* appear the edges of a *juban* of plain bright color. All garments are pulled up from the waist and folded under the belt to make walking easier, for the *ryūjin-maki* is generally worn by messengers attached to the shōgun, to the nobles, or to the government officials. (Exceptions are Yorimitsu in *Tsuchigumo* and Kajiwara Genta in *Hiragana Seisuiki,* who are not messengers.)

The messengers wear flesh-colored tights and *sanri-ate,* round or triangular cloth knee accessories placed just below the kneecaps in the manner of garters. If the stylized *kumadori* make-up is extreme, the knee pads are round; when make-up is plainer, they are triangular. Though some commentators on Kabuki have stated that villains wear the round and other individuals the triangular knee pads, this is not exact. Arajishi Otokonosuke, for example, in Act IV of *Meiboku Sendai Hagi,* wears round knee pads, yet he is a kindhearted man. It is not known if knee pads were ever actually worn by the people, but those seen on the stage are supposed to conceal scars made by moxa cautery or to indicate that the messenger has walked a long distance.

Other accessories to the costume of these characters include *tabi* socks, *zōri* (sandals), a *chūkei* (the spread fan of the Nō), two swords tucked into their proper places, and the written order they are transmitting—a folded paper inscribed with the character 上—slipped into the bosom between the collar of the top garment and the undergarments.

Another important costume accessory, which should not be confused with the folded written order, is the bundle of *hanagami* (tissue paper) often thrust into the bosom in a similar manner. The *hanagami,* because of its importance as a Kabuki accessory, deserves a special note here.

Prior to the Meiji era, foreign-style handkerchiefs were unknown in Japan, and the small towel known as *tenugui* was used instead. Also, neatly folded *hanagami* was used as a handkerchief, as Kleenex tissue is used today. The *hanagami* was carried in a bundle, the sheets being about the size of regular letter paper, folded over once. It was originally intended for toilet purposes. On the stage, the size of the paper varies according to the theatrical effect desired. One of the primary stage uses for *hanagami* is to wipe the blood off a sword after it has been run through the body of an adversary.

Only two kinds of *eboshi* ever appear with the *suō* or the *ryūjin-maki* style of *suō:* the *samurai eboshi* and the *mage-kakushi* (*mage,* topknot; *kakushi,* concealing), an *eboshi* looking very much like the small periwinkle with its short one-valved spiral shell and covering only the topknot.

## NAGA-GAMISHIMO

The term *naga-gamishimo* (literally, long *kamishimo*) describes the *kamishimo*—that is, the combination of the wing-shouldered jumper and *hakama*—worn with long trailing trousers (Fig. 21). It is to be contrasted with the *daimon* and is the less formal attire of daimyō and samurai of almost equal rank—composed of *naga-bakama, kitsuke* (kimono and obi worn under the outer garment), and *kataginu,* the jumper with broad winglike shoulders. The back hem and the lapel streamers of the *kataginu* are placed beneath the belt of the *hakama.*

Separately this shoulder garment or jumper is called the *kataginu,* but

18. Daimyō costume: *haori* and *kitsuke* (kimono). This is the costume of Enya Hangan in Act IV of *Kanadehon Chūshingura* at the beginning of the *seppuku* scene.

19. *Daimon.* The *daimon* of the stage is generally made of solid-color ramie with seven large *mon* (crests), five superimposed on the top garment and two on the *naga-bakama*. With the *daimon*, the Kabuki daimyō usually wears the *hikitate eboshi*.

20. *Suō: ryūjin-maki* style. The left sleeve of the *ryūjin-maki,* decorated with a large crest, is stiffened with bamboo splints to give the appearance of a square shield. The costume, generally worn by messengers attached to the nobility, is seen in *jidai-mono.*

127

21. *Naga-gamishimo* with *noshime* pattern: Nikki Danjō in *Meiboku Sendai Hagi*. The *naga-gamishimo*—wing-shouldered jumper and long trailing trousers worn over kimono—is the less formal attire of daimyō and high-ranking samurai. Here it is seen with the midriff pattern called *noshime*.

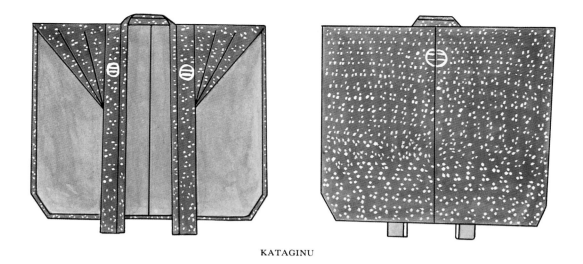

KATAGINU

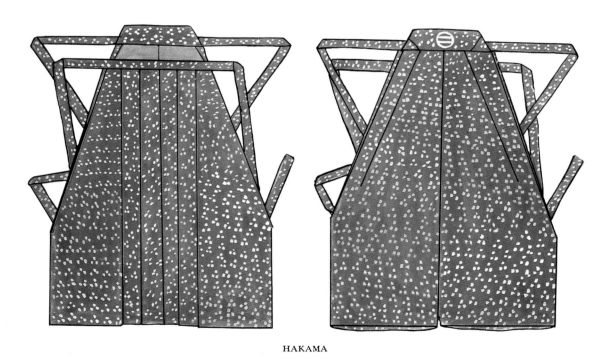

HAKAMA

22. *Kamishimo: kataginu* and *hakama* (front and back views). The costume of all samurai serving the daimyō, regardless of the era in which the play is set, is the *kamishimo*, the most widely used costume in *jidai-mono*. It is composed of ankle-length *hakama, kataginu,* and *kitsuke* (kimono).

**23.** *Tsugi-gamishimo.* If the *kataginu* (jumper) and *hakama* (trousers) are of different pattern and cloth, the combination is known as *tsugi-gamishimo.*

**24.** *Mizu-gamishimo.* This is one version of the *kamishimo,* consisting of solid-color *kataginu* and *hakama* worn over a white kimono. Like other versions of the *kamishimo,* it appears in *jidai-mono.*

25. *Iro-gamishimo:* Jūjirō in Act X of *Ehon Taikō-ki*. Young samurai appear in bright-colored—usually purple or clear light blue—*iro-gamishimo* with large designs on both *kamishimo* and kimono.

26. *Omigoromo:* Yoshitsune in *Yoshitsune Sembon-Zakura*. The *omigoromo,* a floor-brushing brocaded coat with an upstanding tuxedo collar and large open-mouthed sleeves, is the leisure-style indoor attire of a shōgun, a daimyō, or a general. It is worn over a *shiromuku:* a kimono of spotless white silk.

when the *naga-bakama* or *hakama* and the *kataginu* are made of the same pattern and color of cloth, the whole garment is called the *naga-gamishimo* or *kamishimo*, depending upon whether the trousers are long or short. If the *kataginu* and the *hakama* are of different pattern and cloth, the combination is known as *kataginu-hakama* or *tsugi-gamishimo* (*tsugi*, attached together) (Fig. 23).

Satin and brocade are of particular Kabuki usage, but the *asa-gamishimo* (*asa*, ramie) and the *tsugi-gamishimo* were once in practical use among the people. Since a wide variety of designs and colors are represented, depending upon age and type of role, the *naga-gamishimo* has far greater leeway in the use of patterned material than the *daimon*, in which little change is ever made. Wakasanosuke's costume in *Kanadehon Chūshingura* is comparatively true to life, whereas Gorō's in *Kotobuki Soga no Taimen* is not but is merely used for color and effectiveness.

The long trailing trousers are presumed to have been worn only short distances out of doors, but on the stage they are used without regard to distances. To date, studies have not been made to determine whether the *naga-gamishimo* were in fact worn outdoors, but from a practical viewpoint and for the sake of cleanliness it could be assumed that they were not.

## KAMISHIMO

The costume of all samurai serving the daimyō regardless of the era in which the play is set, is the *kamishimo*, the most widely used costume in *jidai-mono* (Figs. 22–25). It is composed of ankle-length *hakama*, the above-described *kataginu*, and *kitsuke*, the kimono worn under the *hakama*, often in *noshime* pattern—that is, with a design across the midriff and the bottom of the sleeves.

Bright colors and elaborate designs were ignored in daily dress, but the actors, challenging the conformity of the times, chose designs and variegated colors to harmonize with the scenery and to dramatize the roles, so that as soon as the playgoers saw an actor they would recognize the type of character he was impersonating. Even today villains are clearly identified by their unmistakable guise of clear, bold patterns on dark-colored materials, often black, pine-needle green, or dark brown. Aggressive warriors wear costumes in richly brocaded patterns overlaid on a strikingly metallic-looking red ground. *Wakashu* (young samurai) appear in bright-colored—usually purple or clear light blue—satin *iro-gamishimo* (*iro*, color) with large designs in the above-noted *noshime* pattern on the kimono (Fig. 25).

Koganosuke in *Imoseyama Onna Teikin* (The Precept of Noble Womanhood) and Jūjirō in *Ehon Taikō-ki* (The Picture Book of the Taikō) wear *kamishimo*. During the Edo period, wealthy merchants wore the *kamishimo* to weddings and other special affairs, but in Kabuki it is a convention that merchants never appear in this costume.

## OMIGOROMO

The *omigoromo* (Fig. 26) is the everyday, indoor, leisure-style attire of a shōgun, a daimyō, or a general, adapted with slight changes from the Bunraku. It is a floor-brushing brocaded coat having a tuxedo collar with a *tachi-eri* or upright pleated neckband and large open-mouthed sleeves. The collar is made with a different pattern and color from that of the body of the robe and is fastened with intricately knotted gold-corded ties with tassels called *keman musubi* (*ke,* flower; *man,* ornament; *musubi,* knot) —in other words, a knot resembling the *keman,* a stylized flower decoration hung before a Buddhist image.

The kimono under the *omigoromo* is the *shiromuku* (*shiro,* white; *muku,* pure, spotless) and is without exception made of silk, as are all of the white undergarments worn with the *omigoromo.* The large round wadded obi, covered with brocade that has the dull but beautiful lustre of old gold, is always tied in the *kata-wana musubi* (*kata,* one of a pair; *wana,* loop): a bow having only one loop.

A smartly fashioned wig is worn with the *omigoromo.* It is known either as the *taishō mage* (*taishō,* military general; *mage,* topknot) or the *bō-chasen* (*bō,* stick; *chasen,* bamboo tea whisk), a wig mainly used throughout Kabuki for the roles of *tonosama* (court lords) and daimyō. The topknot, tightly bound with paper strands called *motoyui,* rests on the scalp with the tea-whisk end facing forward. The *bin* (sidelocks) are slightly inflated and the *tabo* (back hair) is pressed to the head.

If the character dressed in *omigoromo* is a villain or an *aku ōji* (wicked prince) wearing stylized *kumadori* make-up, he appears with long black hair. Iruka in *Imoseyama Onna Teikin* and Shihei in the "Kurumabiki" (Stopping the Carriage) scene of *Sugawara Denju Tenarai Kagami* have such a hair style.

A slight differentiation of the *omigoromo* is made for certain roles in which the *hakama* is worn over the *shiromuku.* The *hakama* is invariably the one called *sashinuki*—that is, baggy trousers resembling a harem skirt, gathered just above the ankles.

## YOTEN COSTUMES

The *yoten ishō* are seen solely on the Kabuki stage. These costumes are thought to have been devised after the apparel of the priests of the Ōbaku sect of Zen Buddhism, although this has not been proved.

There are five distinct types of *yoten* costumes: *nishiki* or gold brocade, *shiro* or white, *kuro* or black, *hana* or flower, and *uroko* or scale (Figs. 29–33). *Yoten* are worn only in scenes where speedy action occurs, such as the stylized fighting scenes known as *tachimawari.* Though the wearers, also referred to as *yoten,* are widely divergent personalities—including courageous warriors, brave men, police chiefs, ordinary policemen, notorious thieves, and sorcerers—the cut of their costumes is essentially alike. The sleeves are always large and have wide openings, and the bottom of the top garment is split at each side. Some writers state that the *yoten ishō* receives its name from the fact that the bottom of the skirt is split into four *(yo)* sections, but this is not accurate, because the split on each side divides the bottom into only three sections: two in front and one in back.

*Nishiki Yoten.* This costume (Fig. 29), sumptuously gold-brocaded in profuse designs and worn by the higher-class *yoten,* is uniquely impressive and the most lavish of the *yoten* types. Along the bottom of the outer robe is attached a *baren,* a heavy ropelike gold fringe whose movement adds a furious look of strength during moments of action. This is especially true during the actor's exit on the *hanamichi* when he executes the *tobi-roppō:* the flaunting with great might of outstretched arms and widely opened hands while taking enormous steps by leaping with utmost concentrated strength, producing a vision of primitive beauty. The *tobi-roppō* is one of the truly superb theatrical moments in Kabuki, especially when executed by a versatile artist like the great Ichikawa Sadanji III.

The large sleeves of the *nishiki yoten* are sewn with a pleat at the shoulders in *chikara-age* (*chikara,* strength; *age,* pushed or pulled up) style. A *shigoki* (soft obi) of silk crepe, usually white, is wound around the waist and tied in a large bow, loosely hanging in front. The actor who appears in the *nishiki yoten* almost always wears *momohiki,* dark blue underpants tightly covering his legs but loosely draped from the waist. Another distinctive feature is the close-fitting black *suami* (net undershirt), which indicates that the wearer is prepared for a fight. Originally this net was of chain mail, but now it is made of silk cording dyed black. In very rare instances gold *suami* are worn by young men, women, or children. The average playgoer, however, has never seen women in *nishiki yoten,* since dramas with such roles are seldom performed.

Actors appearing in *nishiki yoten* may wear either of two types of wigs: the *hyakunichi-no-tare* (Fig. 169) or the *kiku-byakunichi,* literally "hundred-day" wigs, implying that the hair has not been cut for that length of time. The *hyakunichi* (*hyaku,* 100; *nichi,* day) wig has bushy hair covering the top of the head, very much like a huge pompon with long hanging underneath hair tied at the neck with a gold cord. The hair has no fixed length.

The *kiku-byakunichi* (*kiku,* chrysanthemum) is a stunning male coiffure. The hair is of the same length as for an ordinary *katsura,* but it appears shorter because it has been sprayed with lacquer and combed into layers of separate falling strands to give the appearance of chrysanthemum petals, from which the wig acquires its descriptive name.

These particular *yoten* actors always wear only one sword, although the *nishiki yoten* appearing in the mime plays known as *dammari* are often pictured holding an unsheathed sword in addition to their own personal sword. The second sword is sometimes a treasured weapon, the object of strife and the occasion for the stylized fighting scenes called *tachimawari,* in which case the *yoten* has seized it from the sheath of another actor.

In plays presented in Tokyo, the feet of *yoten* are without exception bare, since this is considered attractive and facilitates quick action, but in Kansai *kasane waraji* (*kasane,* layer)—cotton-rope sandals with built-up soles, a heel guard, and laces for tying—are worn.

Famous among roles displaying the *nishiki yoten* are those of Katō Masakiyo in *Ehon Taikō-ki* and Inuyama Dōsetsu in *Hakkenden no Dammari.*

*Shiro Yoten.* This costume (Fig. 30) is of the same cut as the *nishiki yoten,* but all the garments are of white silk, except for the soft crepe *shigoki* sash, which is purple. The coiffure that accompanies the *shiro yoten,* however, is decidedly different. Its name, *honke-no-mizuiri* (*hon,* real; *ke,* hair; *mizu,* water; *iri,* entering), literally means hair that has been dipped into water. Long hanging hair is sprayed all over with lacquer, some of it being hardened with the lacquer to make the strands glossy, thereby indicating that it has become wet from immersion in water. A colored *hachimaki* is tied around the head with a bow in the back or on the side. The *honke-no-mizuiri* coiffure is seen in the "Mizuiri" scene of *Sukeroku Yukari no Edo-Zakura,* and the *mizuiri* wig is often worn, especially in battle scenes.

*Kuro Yoten.* The most simple of *yoten ishō* is only slightly unlike other types. The *kuro yoten* (Fig. 31) is a totally black costume except for the obi, which displays a striped design on a white background. The obi is wrapped around the body three and a half times, with the end tucked under the inside layer. The bow, tied in the *waribasami* or *komageta musubi* (resembling a pair of *geta* or wooden clogs), is a ready-made item with two flat evenly looped pieces sewn side by side (Fig. 248). It is put on underneath the obi and flattened to the back with the loops showing above and below the obi. Over the obi is an *uwa-obi* (band), white or colored, tied in front with the square knot called *hako musubi.*

A *tasuki* (cloth band) is circled around each sleeve to pull it up and is then crisscrossed over the shoulders and tied in back. This prevents soiling of the kimono sleeves and allows freer movement. The function of the *tasuki* is essentially the same as that of the previously noted *chikara-age* of the *nishiki yoten,* which is also used for the *shiro* and *uroko yoten* sleeves.

The *kuro yoten* characters do not carry a sword but have a metal stick called a *jutte* (literally, "ten hands," meaning that it theoretically works like ten hands) with a tassel at the prong handle (Fig. 162). The stick is much smaller in diameter but much like a policeman's billy in the Western world. This implement is the symbol of the *kuro yoten* role: that of a policeman who appears in *jidai-mono* and *sewa-mono.*

*Hana Yoten.* The flower-designed side-split costumes known as *hana yoten* (Fig. 32) are usually employed in the *shosagoto* dance-dramas and in some *jidai-mono* scenes such as the "Michiyuki" in *Chūshingura. Hana yoten* costumes have a solid-colored background, mostly white cotton, with a pattern of opposed serpentine lines enclosing conventionalized flower and leaf motifs. The *tasuki*, the *hachimaki*, and all underneath garments are clear red. Obi and *uwa-obi* are of the same style as those worn with the *kuro* and the *uroko yoten*.

There are two variations exclusive to the *hana yoten*. Red cloth *tekkō* (fingerless mittens), covering the back of the hand only, are held in place by narrow cloth finger straps attached to the back of the mittens. A flower branch or a spear with flowers at the pointed end is carried for use in feigning sword manipulation during the colorful stylized scenes of *tachimawari*, the rhythm of which can be likened to the choreography of a dance.

*Uroko Yoten.* *Uroko yoten* costumes (Fig. 33) have a background of white silk with a triangle pattern done in silver leaf, making an allover triangle diaper of white and silver, symbolizing the scales of a snake. The *uroko yoten* is a combination of the other *yoten* costumes: *chikara-age* (tucked-up) sleeves, bright red undergarments, obi tied in *waribasami* or *komagetamusubi* fashion with *uwa-obi* in *hako-musubi* (square-knot) style, and colored *hachimaki*. The feet are bare.

The *uroko yoten* appear in the last scene of *Kyō-Ganoko Musume Dōjōji* whenever the performance is based more nearly on that of the Nō—that is, when the heroine Kiyohime is transformed into a giant serpent through the tenacity and vindictive fury of her passion for the young priest Anchin of the Dōjō Temple.


## YAKKO COSTUMES

*Yakko* is the costume worn by the lowest order of servants or footmen, who are also known as *yakko* or *chūgen*. These men are attached to the households of military men and for that reason appear in *jidai-mono*. Servants of the same status working for daimyō were called *ashigaru*.

When the *yakko* had no special duty, he cleaned the garden, chopped wood, or accompanied his lord as a footman, and toward evening, when his lord went visiting, the *yakko* was permitted to wear one sword. Though he was considered unqualified to go into battle, he took charge of the horses and cleaned his master's swords within the battle encampment.

Chōbei of Banzuin (the Banzuin Chōbei of Kabuki fame), purported to be the most admired *otokodate,* started his adult life as a *chūgen.* Though these people came from the underprivileged class of the community during Edo, they were treated somewhat as heroes by the public, since some of their members became Kabuki actors. Danjūrō I was a *chūgen,* then an *otokodate* before becoming an actor. The rise of *chūgen* to the status of actors gave the commoners a feeling of intimacy, one of sharing, with the men who had broken from their ranks.

The Kabuki *yakko* or *chūgen* is a handsome, a charming, or a foppish servant referred to as either *iro-yakko* (*iro,* color or sensual passion) or *shusu* (satin) *yakko.* He is played by an outstanding mature actor or a promising young one. In the past, the *yakko* took a rather prominent part in historical plays, but his parts are not so major today. Among present-day *yakko* roles are those of Chienai in the "Kikubatake no Ba" (Chrysanthemum Garden Scene) of *Kiichi Hōgen Sanryaku no Maki* (Kiichi Hōgen's Book of Tactics), Tsumahei in *Shin Usuyuki Monogatari* (The New Tale of Usuyuki), and Rampei in the previously noted *Rampei Monogurui.*

The *iro-yakko* or *shusu-yakko* costume (Fig. 34) is quite decorative. It is styled from clear blue satin and has a *date* (dandy) collar, cut on the bias and displaying either a *tazuna* (horse bridle) design of alternating broad bands of bright colors, often gold and black or gold and green, or a *watsunagi* (chain) design of overlapping circle outlines. The bottom of the costume is more often than not hand-embroidered with three rows of impressionistic iris flowers worked in gold thread.

Always directly underneath the costume is worn a *sagari,* an apron-like garment with heavy gold fringe at the bottom. The length of the fringe may depend upon the preference of the actor, but if the choice is left to the costumer, it is six inches long. Five large gold-embroidered crests appear on the upper part of the outer garment. The crest is usually the first ideograph of the character's name, but an actor may use his own crest if he so desires.

The *iro-yakko* wears black or dark *tabi.* A young *yakko* will occasionally wear purple *tabi* with *sammai-gasane zōri:* three-layer sandals, the thongs for which are by custom twined with two colors. The obi of no set color is designed with the above-described *watsunagi,* or sometimes the *tazuna,* pattern and is tied in the oblong knot known as *karuta musubi* (Fig. 248).

The *iro-yakko* wears a wig in *iro-nonko* (*iro,* sensual pleasure; *nonko,* a type of topknot) style, technically called *aburatsuki-kara-no-bin-no-iro-nonko* and *aburatsuki-naimaze-fukashi-bin-no-iro-nonko. Nonko* refers to the particularly long queue of hair at the back of the wigs, although the origin of the name is unknown today. All *iro-nonko* styles are characterized by back hair that is hardened with pomade, highly polished, and combed upward and flattened to the head. One of the attractive features of the first-mentioned coiffure is the lacquered *omatsuri* at the top of the *bin* or side-locks. These *omatsuri* are hanging petal-like strands of short hair, thoroughly lacquered, resembling the paper decorations at Shinto shrine festivals, from which they take their name. The second type of wig is neatly different. The *bin* are mixed half and half with straight and curly hair and do not have the *omatsuri.*

The body of the *juban* for the *iro-yakko* is always bright red without pattern. In the past, the *juban,* including the loincloth, was red, but today undergarments are white, except those used in the theater. The collar of the *juban* matches the design on the collar of the outer garment. The costume is worn in *azuma-karage* (*azuma,* east or Edo; *karage,* tucked-up) style (Fig. 240). This naturally gives the wearer unrestricted ease of movement and earmarks him as a working man. On each side of the top garment is attached a string with a small ball at the hanging end. The balls, when pulled up and placed out of sight under the obi, leave the garment in a tucked-up position. The make-up of the *iro-yakko* is without exception *shiro-nuri* (*shiro,* white; *nuri,* coating, painting).

The *iro-yakko* costumes are completely stylized, with no intention of being true to life. *Yakko* nearer to the everyday servant style are seen in the bearers in Act III of *Chūshingura.* Here, upon plain navy blue kimono, appears the crest in the shape of a *kuginuki,* a type of carpenter's tool used in the past for pulling out nails. The make-up is more natural, and the wig—one of several variations for *iro-yakko*—is the *aburatsuki-kara-no-shiitake-jiri-no-iro-nonko* (*aburatsuki,* hardened with pomade and polished; *kara,* foreign; *shiitake,* a kind of mushroom; *jiri,* from *shiri,* bottom, end) with a topknot whose end looks like a mushroom. *Iro-nonko,* in addition to being a type of wig, is also another name for *iro-yakko,* the young, handsome, gay servant.

## BŌZU COSTUMES

The raiment of Kabuki *bōzu*—that is, Buddhist priests—is fashioned from the likenesses of the robes and surplices of the sects established in Japan centuries ago (Fig. 35). As these priests moved in the wake of the changes experienced by a rising nation, the plain robes of yesteryear gave way to those unmatched in splendor, and simple garments became translated into the exquisite fabrics of the Momoyama and later periods.

The outstanding vestment of the priest is the *kesa*—the surplice worn over the outer garment—an official symbol of priesthood. This garment is quite often made of many squares of cloth, traditionally symbolizing the ragged vestments worn by Buddha during his mendicant days.

As Buddhism swept over the islands, gaining increased favor from the public, the more powerful denominations added elaborate ritual to their religious rites. For these ceremonies they spiritedly acquired the richest of imported and domestic fabrics for their *kesa* and altar cloths. The avid acquisition of material possessions led the sects to develop individual styles of *kesa* that are now duplicated on the Kabuki stage. The priests' costumes thus include several styles of *kesa.*

The *wa kesa,* used for daily wear, is a surplice made of a single strip of cloth, three to four inches in width, placed around the neck, from which it hangs down in front, looking very similar to a long collar.

The *gojō* (five-strip) *kesa* is composed of five strips of cloth forming a rectangular bag hung over the left side by two shoulder straps, of which one goes over the left side and passes under the right arm while the other ties with it just below the left shoulder.

The *shichijō* (seven-strip) *kesa* is a medium-sized rectangular ceremonial vestment of seven strips of luxurious brocaded material with which is worn the *ōhi,* a single strip of fabric about one foot wide, drawn over the right shoulder, across the chest, and under the left arm.

The *kujō* (nine-strip) *kesa* is a large oblong ceremonial *kesa* made up of nine strips of fabric.

*Bōzu ishō* as described here do not include costumes worn in the *matsu-bame-mono*—plays taken from the Nō. Kabuki priest costumes have always remained in the shade of the rich Nō costumes of *kinran, karaori,* and *nishiki,* which have been considered the supreme achievement of all stage costumes and whose fabrics deserve a special description in the following paragraph. Yet, when a Kabuki actor appears as a Buddhist high priest, his costume seems as refined as that of a Nō priest, though often having the quiet elegance of simplicity rather than the noble symbolism of the cherished Nō priest robes.

Since the above-mentioned Nō-costume fabrics also have their place on the Kabuki stage, it is appropriate to look at them more closely for a moment. *Kinran,* perhaps the least pretentious of the three, is silk brocaded only with gilt-paper strips. *Karaori,* the name of which means Chinese or foreign weaving, usually displays silk thread in large superimposed patterns resembling embroidery, together with a different design brocaded with gilt-paper strips, known as the so-called Chinese-style float weave or embroidery weave. *Nishiki,* the third of these luxurious fabrics, is a silk compound woven or brocaded with colors and gilt or silver paper strips.

There is a greater divergence of dress between the actors taking leading and minor priest roles than among vestments of actual priests. All priests had the privilege of appearing in ornate *kesa,* but this custom is not followed on the Kabuki stage. When a priest has the main role, he will customarily wear a soft silk kimono and a superb *kesa* to which is attached an intricately designed and knotted gold-braided cording, called the *shutara,* which is allowed to hang gracefully over and down the back of the left shoulder.

The minor priests are dressed in unadorned clothing to make them less conspicuous, so that they will not detract from the stellar role (Fig. 36). They appear in plain white silk kimono with a white obi, tied in front in a *hako musubi,* the typical little flat oblong or box bow with loops and knot of equal squared size (Fig. 248). The obi is about three inches wide, slightly narrower than the ordinary obi, which is tied with the *kai-no-kuchi* or shell-mouth bow (Fig. 248). Around the hips is a transparent black *koshi-goromo* (*koshi,* loins; *koromo,* garment): a kind of overskirt that drapes from the waist to a little below the knees. White *tabi* cover the feet.

One of the most memorable priests to appear in the Kabuki repertoire is the felon *bōzu* Kōchiyama, the leading character in *Kumo ni Magō Ueno no Hatsuhana* (Cloudlike First Blossoms at Ueno), a role that became almost legendary with the late actors Nakamura Kichiemon I and Ichikawa Chūsha VII and is today excitingly portrayed with personal interpretation by Ichikawa Danjūrō XI and by his youngest brother, Onoe Shōroku II.

27. *Juzu.* One of a Kabuki priest's most important accessories is his *juzu* or Buddhist rosary. Most *juzu* consist of 108 beads alternating in rows of 7 and 20, although some are shorter.

The costume (Fig. 37) is a high priest's *hi-no-koromo,* a scarlet wide-open-sleeved coat so sheer that one can discern the satin diaper pattern of the white silk kimono underneath. The bottom of the coat has an eighteen-inch flounce with equally spaced sets of eight knife pleats, each set four inches wide and having four pleats facing each other. All the undergarments and the *tabi* are white. In his hands Kōchiyama carries a fan known as a *chūkei,* which has a black lacquered frame, and a crystal *juzu,* a Buddhist rosary of twenty regular beads and one large one to which is attached a pale-blue silk pompon. Kōchiyama has a distinguishing mark: a mole on his left cheekbone, very much like a beauty mark—the means whereby he is unmasked in the course of the story.

A priest always holds a *juzu* (rosary) (Fig. 27) except when he is engaged in preparing food or performing other manual duties. With solemn piety, during prayers, the *juzu* is held between the palms of the hands with the middle fingers in the strand, and the beads are then rubbed back and forth, making a sound that is familiar to all Kabuki audiences. Deeply religious characters, both men and women, also carry *juzu*. In certain scenes, a lay person may carry a *juzu* because of a preceding event, such as a memorial service.

*Juzu* are made of various kinds of material, including wood, crystal, metal, and seeds, but the choicest strands are those made of pearls and red or white coral. The *juzu* used in the Kabuki are made predominantly of crystal, although those carried by *yamabushi,* the mountain priests of the Shugen sect, are of dark-brown wood—the only discernible indication of the difference between Buddhist sects in Kabuki. All Kabuki *juzu* have tassels of exaggerated size to add to the stage effect.

The majority of *juzu* consist of 108 beads, alternating in rows of 7 and 20. The 108 beads represent the evils, temptations, and sins of men. A different type of bead is placed in the strand between the rows of 7 and 20 for convenience in counting, but it is not included in counting the 108 beads. Sometimes the *juzu* is of 54, 27, or 14 beads, each of these being just half the length of the immediately longer strand. The 14-bead *juzu* can occasionally be seen adorning an actor's ear. For example, it was displayed in this fashion by Ichikawa Sadanji III performing the role of old man Sabu in *Natsu Matsuri Naniwa no Kagami* (The Summer Festival of Osaka). The beads of the *irataka juzu* carried by Benkei in *Kanjinchō* are diamond-shaped like those of the Japanese abacus. *Juzu* are made in one or two strands but never more. The longer strands can be doubled to give the appearance of additional strands.

The word *bōzu* has two definitions, priest and bald head, and the term *bōzu-katsura* thus means the priest's wig representing a shaven head. More technically, these wigs are called *maru-bōzu* (*maru,* complete, round). Descriptions of various *bōzu-katsura* will be found in the chapter on wigs.

## SPECIAL COSTUMES

The *kokumochi* (*koku,* black; *mochi,* rice cake) takes its name from the circles that decorate it. It is a single-colored kimono with no other design than the three or five white circles appliquéd on it in substitution for the family crests that common people did not possess. It is worn in *jidai-mono* by farmers or lowly people, both male and female.

*Kata-ire* (*kata,* shoulder; *ire,* inserted, patched on), supposedly affairs of shreds and patches, are kimono for those who have seen better days. Some, however, are made to look gorgeous by patching beautiful fabrics together, often pieces of dazzling brocades. Such is the costume of Kampei in Act V of *Chūshingura* (Fig. 38). When Kampei is portrayed by an actor related to the Onoe Kikugorō family, the sleeves and collar of the *kata-ire* are of the same color and feature the *Kikugorō-goshi,* a check design with crossed lines in the squares. Other actors use *kasuri,* a splash-designed fabric made of pre-dyed threads woven in silk or cotton materials. *Kasuri* differs according to the material used. It can be produced in silk, ramie, or cotton, the last of these being used for the costumes of commoners, while ramie *kasuri* is for a role such as that of Mitsugi in *Ise Ondo Koi no Netaba* (The Dance of Death at Ise) and is sometimes used in costumes for samurai.

The *chōken,* seen exclusively in *jidai-mono,* is the Kabuki version of the *kariginu,* refined dress of a general or a high-ranking samurai as required for not too formal occasions (Figs. 28, 39). It does a splendid job of imitating the real *kariginu,* the informal costume of the noblemen of the Heian period. Another informal masculine costume is the *suikan,* the name of which is taken from the wet-and-dry method of stiffening the garment —without starch. Because the *kariginu,* the *suikan,* and the *chōken* so closely resemble each other, their names are sometimes confused.

With the *chōken* are worn either the Dutch-style pantaloon-like trousers called *sashinuki* or the short trousers called *han-bakama.* Both garments are made from exquisitely patterned or brocaded silks, and their contrasting colors present an appealing picture. To get an impression of its tasteful richness, it is best to examine an illustration of the picturesque *chōken* with its long, wide-mouthed sleeves extending below the finger tips, the lower edges stitched with flat-plaited multicolored silk tapes. The sleeves are attached to the *chōken* only at the back, thereby offering a glimpse of the white silk garment underneath. The front of the *chōken* is pulled up and tied with an obi made of the same material and allowed to blouse.

Accessories for this costume are a *tachi* (a sword suspended from a belt of its own), a fan of the *chūkei* type, a gold *sammi* hat tied under the chin with a tasseled silk cord, and a pair of black-lacquered square-toed clogs known as *kuro-nuri-gutsu.*

The *chōken* is worn in Act I, Scene 1 of *Chūshingura* by Tadayoshi, who, although he is not of the noble class, is of the highest samurai rank.

The *hitatare* is another costume worn exclusively in *jidai-mono.* Developed from the plain garb of the commoners, it was the costume generally worn by warriors in the Kamakura period. In the early Edo period, the *hitatare* was used on ceremonial occasions by the samurai and gradually became dignified in form. The *hitatare* of real life, however, is never used in classical Kabuki because it was the dress of shōgun and daimyō. The Kabuki *hitatare* is based on the Nō costume of ceremonial dress and seems to be a vulgarized form of the original.

As seen on the Kabuki stage, the *hitatare* consists of short pleated *hakama* and a coatlike garment with long wide-opened sleeves that have a short tie attached to the bottom of each sleeve opening. A matching plaited tie is attached to the collar and tied just below the breast. These ties have no functional value but are put on the *hitatare* primarily as attractive details.

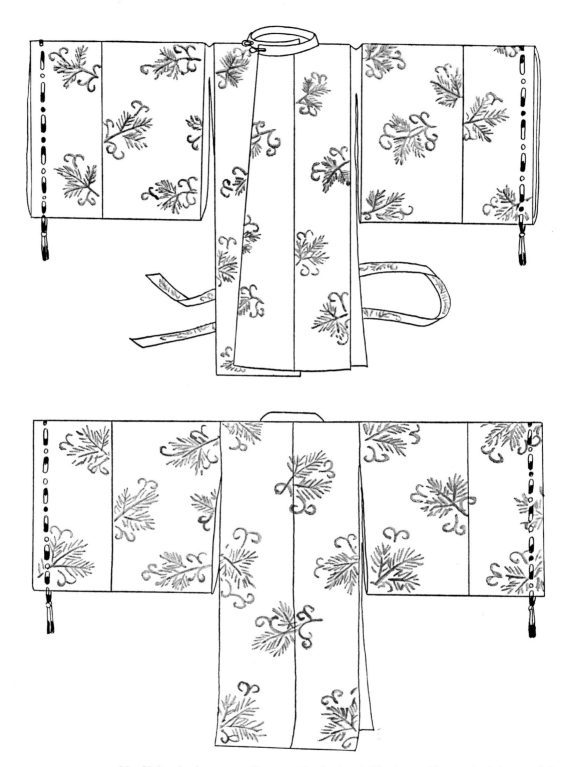

28. *Chōken:* basic pattern (front and back views). The long wide-mouthed sleeves of the *chōken* are attached only at the back, thereby offering a glimpse of the white silk garment underneath. The lower edges, which extend below the finger tips, are stitched with flat-plaited multicolored silk tapes.

29. *Nishiki yoten.* This costume, sumptuously gold-brocaded in profuse designs and worn by the higher-class *yoten*—chiefly warriors and brave men—is the most lavish of the *yoten* types. The costume is worn for such roles as those of Katō Masakiyo in *Ehon Taikō-ki* and Inuyama Dōsetsu in *Hakkenden no Dammari.*

30. *Shiro yoten.* This costume is of the same cut as the *nishiki yoten,* but all of the garments are of white silk except for the purple *shigoki* sash. The wig is also different, in this case being the *honke-no-mizuiri* type, which is often worn in battle scenes.

31. *Kuro yoten.* The *kuro yoten* is a totally black costume except for the obi, which displays a striped design on a white ground. *Kuro yoten* carry a metal stick called a *jutte* which theoretically does the work of ten hands. The implement is the symbol of the *kuro yoten* role: that of a policeman in *jidai-mono* and *sewa-mono.*

146

32. *Hana yoten*. The costumes known as *hana yoten* are usually employed in *shosagoto* (dance-dramas) and in some *jidai-mono* scenes like the "Michiyuki" in *Chūshingura*. They have a solid-colored background, mostly white cotton, with a pattern of opposed serpentine lines enclosing conventionalized flower and leaf motifs.

33. *Uroko yoten*. Costumes classified as *uroko yoten* have a background of white silk with a triangle pattern done in silver leaf, making an allover triangle diaper of white and silver that symbolizes the scales of a snake.

147

**34.** *Iro-yakko.* The Kabuki *yakko,* a footman attached to the household of a military man in *jidai-mono,* is a handsome, charming, or foppish servant referred to as *iro-yakko* (sensual *yakko*) or *shusu-yakko* (satin *yakko*). His costume of blue satin, worn over an apron-like *sagari,* is quite decorative.

35. *Bōzu* costume: Kumagai in *Ichinotani Futaba Gunki*. The raiment of Kabuki priests is fashioned from the likenesses of the robes and surplices of Buddhist sects established in Japan centuries ago. Kumagai appears here in the garb of an itinerant priest.

36. *Bōzu* costume: Kisen in *Kisen*. Minor priests appear in plain white silk kimono, white obi, and *koshi-goromo*, a kind of overskirt draped from the waist to a little below the knees.

149

37. *Bōzu* costume: Kōchiyama in *Kumo ni Magō Ueno no Hatsuhana*. One of the most memorable of Kabuki priests is the felon *bōzu* Kōchiyama. His chief garment is a high priest's *hi-no-koromo*, a scarlet wide-open-sleeved coat sheer enough to let the diaper pattern of his white silk kimono show through.

38. *Kata-ire:* Kampei in Act V of *Chūshingura*. *Kata-ire,* supposedly affairs of shreds and patches, are kimono for those who have seen better days. Some *kata-ire,* however, are made to look gorgeous by patching beautiful fabrics together.

39. *Chōken:* Koremochi in *Momijigari*. The *chōken,* seen exclusively in *jidai-mono* and *shosa-goto,* is the refined dress of a general or a high-ranking samurai as required for not too formal occasions. With it are worn either the pantaloon-like trousers called *sashinuki* or the short trousers called *han-bakama.*

40. *Happi* and *hangire*: Tomomori in *Funa Benkei*. *Hangire* have broad, stiff backs and are made of solid-colored cloth exquisitely patterned in gold.

41. *Sokutai* with *naga-bakama:* Shihei in the "Kurumabiki" scene of *Sugawara Denju Tenarai Kagami*. This is an exaggerated *aragoto* version of the costume as worn by a *kuge-aku* —that is, an evil court gentleman.

42. *Ōguchi:* Benkei in *Kanjinchō*. The expansive *ōguchi,* with its wide leg openings and its extremely broad stiff back, is worn in Kabuki plays adapted from the Nō. It was first used among the military in the **Kamakura** period.

155

43. *Happi* and *ōguchi:* the lion in *Kagamijishi.* In this *shosagoto* costume, the short topcoat known as the *happi* is worn with the *ōguchi.* The sleeves of the *happi* often appear to be short, an illusion produced by folding them up and sewing them with a pleat at the top.

A narrow white obi is knotted in a traditional square bow, while the bare feet are protected by *zōri* (sandals) with white thongs. An *eboshi* rests on the head and is fastened by a cord under the chin. Warriors in *hitatare* costume carry a fan and wear a short sword. The color and design of the *hitatare* are not standard but vary with the role or the taste of the actor.

The *sokutai* (Fig. 41) is a voluminous stiffened silk costume worn by *kuge* or noblemen. It has a flat narrow collar buttoned on the right side— one of the few instances in which a garment is secured by other than just a tie or an obi. The *sashinuki hakama* (Dutch-style pantaloon-like trousers) worn under the *sokutai*—often purple in color—are so full that the feet are rarely visible under the puffed-out legs. The top garment, with a straight flounce of similar material at the hem, is made of rich black silk with a diaper pattern repeated throughout. The sleeves completely envelop the arms and hands. An intricately woven belt, braided with innumerable colored silk threads and known as the *hirao* (*hira,* flat; *o,* belt, cord), suspends the sword and enables the costume to be pulled up and bloused. The wide fringed panels of the belt overlap in front and fall almost to the hem. A red unlined *juban* called the *hitoe* adds a bit of brightness at the neckline and the sleeve openings. Kabuki noblemen in *sokutai* wear a *tachi* (sword) suspended from the belt and a black *kammuri* (hat) with a long cockscomb-like ornament at the back. They also carry a wooden *shaku,* which can probably best be described as a staff: an implement approximately one and a half feet in length, made of wood, ivory, bone, or other materials and carried at court. According to Charlotte M. Salwey in *Fans of Japan,* the *shaku* "had to be held right in front of the holder, pressing against the lower part of his chest and slightly inclined outward to give the body a dignified bearing in the presence of royalty."

White make-up is usual with the *sokutai.* Kan Shōjō, in Act I of *Sugawara Denju Tenarai Kagami,* wears this flattering costume.

Two of the most intriguing costumes worn in Kabuki are seen in the *matsubame-mono,* the plays of Nō origin. These costumes are fascinating because of their impracticality yet of supreme theatrical effect. They are the *ōguchi* (*ō,* big; *kuchi,* mouth) and the *hangire* (*han,* pattern; *kire,* cloth), both of which are types of *hakama* with wide leg openings—that is, the lower part of the trouser legs is neither tied nor long enough to hide the feet but is cut off and wide open at the ankle.

There are two forms of *ōguchi:* the one worn under the *ue-no-hakama* (outer *hakama*) in the formal dress of court gentlemen and the other seen in both Nō and Kabuki in exaggerated Nō style with a wide, stiff back (Figs. 42, 43). The *ōguchi* was first used among the military in the Kamakura period. It was sometimes worn underneath the top *hakama* in order to inflate or stretch this outer garment and sometimes worn over it to create a similar impression of breadth. The Kabuki *ōguchi* has an extremely broad stiff back extending the full length of the trousers and thus impeding the natural gait of the wearer.

The difference between the *hangire* and the *ōguchi* lies in the cloth used to make the *hakama*. The *hangire* (Fig. 40) is made mostly of colored cloth with a pattern in gold, while the *ōguchi* is made of cloth of a single color without design, such as white, gray, red, green, blue, or purple. Any color may be used for the *ōguchi* in Kabuki, but Nō accepts only five colors: white, red, green, brown, and purple.

The *hangire,* both in the Nō and in the Kabuki, has a matting called *goza* between the cloth and the lining at the back as a stiffener. The back of the *ōguchi* is made of *seigo,* a tightly woven cloth with a thick weft similar to Ottoman cord silk, which gives the *hakama* a natural stiffness.

In the Kabuki, the short topcoat known as the *happi* is worn over the *kitsuke* (kimono) with either the *hangire* or the *ōguchi,* but in the Nō it is worn only with the *hangire.* The sleeves of the *happi* often appear to be short, an illusion produced by pulling them up and sewing them with a pleat at the top in *chikara-age* style. Only white tabi are worn with the costume.

The *ōguchi* is worn in such plays as *Kanjinchō* (Fig. 42) and *Kagamijishi* (Fig. 43) and the *hangire* in *Funa Benkei* (Fig. 40).

CHAPTER **11**

# Onnagata Costumes for Jidai-mono

The charm of *onnagata* costumes for *jidai-mono* lies mostly in their richness of color and the sumptuousness of their textile patterns, since their cut is quite limited in comparison with the great variety of styles for male costumes. This fact, of course, can be attributed to the men's many activities as contrasted with those of the women, who remained sheltered within their homes and gardens. *Onnagata* costumes used solely for *jidai-mono* are singularly few, but the range widens in the *jidai-sewa-mono* and the *sewa-mono*. Courtesans, adult women, and young girls from all walks of life wear individually styled kimono with complex color harmonies.

The kimono has varied little in style or class since the introduction of the radical change in the kimono sleeve during the Muromachi period: the change from the long flowing sleeve of the preceding periods to the *kosode* or small sleeve. The shorter sleeve became the distinguishing feature after which many stage kimono are patterned. Before we look more closely at the short-sleeved kimono, however, a description of a costume infrequently seen in classical Kabuki may prove interesting.

## JŪNI-HITOE

The stage version of the Heian woman's court dress of numerous layers of kimono, the *jūni-hitoe* (*jūni,* twelve; *hitoe,* any unlined kimono), is unquestionably one of the most fascinating costumes seen in Kabuki (Fig. 44). *Jūni-hitoe,* which can be translated as twelve-layered robe, is the popular name for the *mo-karaginu-shōzoku.* Where or when the term *jūni-hitoe* came into being is unknown, but today we know with certainty that its meaning does not refer to only twelve layers of kimono, as the name states, for the court ladies wore as many as twenty garments at one time. They vied with one another for the much-sought-after effect of many shades of color at the neck, sleeves, and hemline. This was acquired by subtle grada-

159

tions of faultless color schemes, selected according to season, in the wearing of plain solid-colored kimono one on top of the other. The *jūni-hitoe,* with its beautiful, long, flowing lines, combines dignity and splendor with a feeling of serenity.

The outside garment, the *karaginu,* is a loose short jacket with abbreviated sleeves. The exquisite lining is of a fabric different from that of the jacket itself, and the neck is folded back to form a tuxedo collar, which produces a pleasant contrast with the outer material.

The *mo,* another essential part of the costume, is best described as an apron train. It is tied on at the waistline. Up to the Nara period—that is, until about the year 710—the *mo* fitted entirely around the body, but it gradually decreased in size until it covered the back half of the body only. The prevailing color of the *mo* is white, with a diaper pattern in *monsha* (*mon,* pattern; *sha,* gauze) weave for summer wear and *mon-aya* (*aya,* twill) weave for other seasons. Occasionally a colored motif will appear in the pattern of the *mo,* but the stage *mo,* for the most part, are made of gauze-woven fabric. Only when the *karaginu* and the *mo* are worn is the *jūni-hitoe* regarded as formal dress.

Next to the *karaginu* is worn the *uwagi* or overcoat. In actual life, under the *uwagi* the ladies wore the *uchiginu* (*uchi,* from *utsu,* to strike; *kinu,* silk cloth), which took its name from the fact that in ancient times in Japan, as in Korea today, cloth was struck or pounded to make a kimono soft and give it a sheen. But the *uchiginu* is not worn today in Kabuki.

Underneath the *uwagi,* this long cloak that trails gracefully several feet behind the wearer, are five *kasane uchiki* commonly called *itsutsu-ginu,* or kimono with widely opened sleeves, the number of which became standard during the Kamakura period. Originally, eight to twenty *uchiki* had been worn at one time. In Kabuki, five edges of colored silk material sewn to the under edge of the *uwagi* substitute for the five kimono of real life. The edges are padded with silk floss to give the impression that the garments have been lined with batting. Underneath is worn the unlined kimono known as *hitoe.* All other garments are lined.

The *shiro kosode* (short-sleeved white undergarment) is put on under the *hitoe.* The *kosode* style, it should be noted, later became the accepted shape of the present-day kimono. The final garment, worn over the *shiro kosode,* is known as the *hari-bakama* (noted in Chapter 9) or the *uchi-bakama* (literally *hakama* that have been ironed out long). The long *hari-bakama,* always red in color, spread out three feet beyond the heel of the foot. Since the *hakama* have an attached belt and since narrow *himo* (strings or ties) are used to tie the undergarments, an obi is not worn with the *jūni-hitoe.* It is worth noting that in real life the *hakama* for young people were of dark colors like wine red or purple and that, with advancing age, the color gradually passed through the purples to white, representing old age.

With the gorgeous *jūni-hitoe* the hair styling is always the very simple *sagegami* coiffure: long hair hanging down the back. Court ladies often wore their hair ankle length to two or three feet on the floor. It is recorded that false hair was tied to the owner's to give greater length. Since this practice developed during the Muromachi period, it appears that additional hair was not tied on before this time.

To denote maturity (thirteen or fourteen years of age), a ceremony called *bin-sogi* (*bin,* temple or sidelocks; *sogi,* cut) is held, and the hair around the temple is cut to about one foot in length. This coiffure is limited to the upper classes. In some roles the *gin hanagushi,* a hair ornament fashioned of three to five rows of thin silvered metal flowers—for the most part plum blossoms—and butterflies provides added beauty to the unsophisticated headdress.

A very curious bit of make-up is applied over the basic white make-up of the face. This is the *kurai-boshi* (*kurai,* class, court rank; *hoshi,* star, dot, spot), an extra pair of dotted eyebrows put on above the natural ones. Only in Kabuki, however, are both sets of eyebrows allowed to appear at the same time. In the past, the natural eyebrows of the nobility were shaved off. Those on the Nō masks were obliterated, as they are today. In actual life, the artificial eyebrows were called *tsukuri-mayu* (*tsukuri,* made; *mayu,* eyebrows) and were worn by persons of higher classes and attendants at court and in the homes of the Kyoto nobility.

As a final touch, the lady clad in *jūni-hitoe* carries an *akome ōgi,* or *hi ōgi,* an ornamental many-staved folding fan with long twisted-silk-thread streamers (Fig. 159).

## KAOYO GOZEN COSTUME

This costume, which takes its name from the role of Lady Kaoyo (Kaoyo Gozen) in *Kanadehon Chūshingura* (Fig. 45), is an exclusive property of Kabuki. It is the standard costume for roles referred to as *midai-dokoro*—the wives of feudal lords or court gentlemen—such as those of Lady Kaoyo, Lady Sonou no Mae in *Sugawara Denju Tenarai Kagami,* and Lady Wakaba no Naishi in *Yoshitsune Sembon-Zakura.*

The costume consists of three floor-sweeping garments: *uchikake* (long coat), kimono, and *juban.* The outer garment is the *uchikake,* the coat mentioned before as being worn on formal occasions. This coat, in many cases, has a purple silk background with embroidered circular flower patterns and a wadded hemline. The kimono worn under the *uchikake* is plain red, and the *juban* under the kimono is pure white. A narrow brocade obi is tied in the familiar small *bunko* bow with even loops curved slightly downward.

The wig belongs to the *mino-shikoro-no-sagegami* group—that is, coiffures with long hair hanging down the back—and has a purple *bōshi* (silk cloth) covering the forehead. The long, hanging back hair is covered with purple silk crepe and tied at shoulder length with three pieces of starched white paper. The *hanagushi* or ornamental hairpin, consisting of three rows of silver flowers, is placed directly in back of the *bōshi*. Make-up and *tabi* are white.

## KATAHAZUSHI COSTUME

The costume of the upper-class samurai wife and the *goten jochū* (ranking lady-in-waiting) at the courts of the shōgun and the daimyō—but not at the imperial court—is referred to as the *katahazushi ishō* (Fig. 46) because these women wear the wig with the asymmetrical topknot known as *katahazushi mage* (*kata,* one side; *hazushi,* unfastened, disconnected; *mage,* topknot).

The *uchikake,* kimono, and *juban* are very like those of the above-described *Kaoyo Gozen* costume. The *uchikake* are made with backgrounds of white, black, blue, or purple, according to the age of the character portrayed. Iwafuji in *Kagamiyama Kokyō no Nishikie* wears an *uchikake* whose ground color is black.

The *shiitake-tabo-no-katahazushi-mage* (*shiitake-tabo* means back hair in mushroom shape) wig, with its prominent hairline and asymmetrical knot, is decidedly striking (Fig. 222). One side of the divided *mage* or ponytail passes over, and the other side under, a *kōgai*—a polished or lacquered wood or tortoise-shell hairpin in the shape of a bar—to form a figure-of-eight knot.

When the ceremonial *uchikake* is not worn, the samurai wives appear in crested kimono, mostly of plain material but sometimes with a design. The choice is left to the individual actor. Ladies-in-waiting sometimes have crests on their kimono, but this is not standard. The *juban, tabi,* and make-up are white.

Some of the *onnagata* roles of samurai wives are those of Kumagai's wife Sagami in the "Kumagai Jinya" (Kumagai's Camp) scene of *Ichinotani Futaba Gunki* (The Chronicle of the Battle of Ichinotani), Kakogawa Honzō's wife Tonase in *Kanadehon Chūshingura,* Moritsuna's wife Hayase in the "Moritsuna Jinya" (Moritsuna's Camp) scene of *Ōmi Genji Senjin Yakata* (The Strife at Uji), Lady Iwafuji and Lady Onoe in *Kagamiyama Kokyō no Nishikie,* and Lady Shigenoi in the "Shigenoi Kowakare" (Shigenoi's Parting from Her Child) scene of *Koi Nyōbō Somewake Tazuna* (The Pack-Horse Driver's Beloved Wife).

## KOSHIMOTO COSTUME

The *koshimoto* (Fig. 47) is the kimono for daughters of samurai who serve at court, ladies-in-waiting (but not princesses), and wealthy merchants' daughters—all customarily young. In this instance, as in many others, the role and the costume have the same name. The *koshimoto ishō* is worn by Okaru in *Kanadehon Chūshingura,* Ohatsu in *Kagamiyama Kokyō no Nishikie,* and Yayoi in *Kagamijishi.* Yayoi is an example of the *okoshō* or personal maid among the *koshimoto:* a girl between thirteen and seventeen years of age.

The *koshimoto* repeatedly wear the *yagasuri* or arrow-patterned kimono, a rather quiet garment that achieves great dignity when properly worn. The purple-and-white *yagasuri* kimono is traditional for the role of Okaru in the renowned "Michiyuki" scene of *Chūshingura.* It nicely compliments the subdued elegance of the apparel of Okaru's lover Kampei. However, Tokyo audiences were shocked out of their enjoyment of the *mise en scène* when Nakamura Utaemon VI appeared on the *hanamichi* as Okaru in an obtrusively ornate costume, which they felt showed lamentably poor taste. Indeed, costumes can detract from as well as add to the stature of a role.

When not otherwise designated, the *koshimoto* wear the obi tied in the knot called *tate-ya-no-ji musubi,* literally "the standing-character-*ya* knot" (Fig. 247). In other words, the shape of the bow resembles that of the *hiragana* phonetic symbol *ya* (や). The bow is flat, and the loops are almost three times as long as the knot is wide. Presumably to give freedom of movement while the wearer is outdoors, the highest point of the bow is tied in the direction of the left shoulder. For indoor wear, the highest point is toward the right shoulder. Almost all stage daughters of samurai tie their obi in this manner. When the wearer is outdoors, the obi of soft crepe known as the *shigoki* is tied on the left side of the principal obi corresponding to the loop at the highest point at the shoulder. The *shigoki* is never worn in indoor scenes. This custom of the right and the left *ya-no-ji* seems to be followed only on the stage, for in real life the left *ya-no-ji* was frequently worn both indoors and outdoors.

The *koshimoto* wear the *bunkin-taka-shimada* wig with the back hair stiffly pomaded and polished into the mushroom shape called *shiitake-tabo* (Fig. 224). The term *bunkin* is a reference to the Gembun era of 1736–40, an era of extravagance and flamboyance during which a gold coin called the *bunkin* (the *bun* is the same character as the *bun* of Gembun) was minted. It was from this coin that the wig took its name, for the style of the tall topknot was extravagantly gay. Although there were many *shimada* (bouffant) hair styles, the *bunkin-taka-shimada* can still be seen today at many Japanese weddings. Such high coiffures were kept in place by the use of pomade, a practice initiated in Edo times.

Prior to 1688, only vegetable oil was used to dress the hair, and only water was used to wash it. With the introduction of the pomade called *bintsuke,* however, water was inadequate, and women began to use the crushed shells of *mukuroji* (a type of soapberry), while men usually rubbed red clay on their hair and scalp, rinsing with water. Eventually whites of eggs, rice-bran powder, and *funori* (a glue made from seaweed) were also used to shampoo the hair.

Minor *koshimoto* actors wear plain pink or blue silk kimono with a solid black satin obi. These actors are separately identified with the name of *narabi koshimoto* (*narabi,* in a row), since they not only portray secondary roles but also speak and move in a group, somewhat like a chorus line. Individually, their lines are never complete sentences; each speaks only a portion of a sentence, which in turn is finally completed in unison.

*Koshimoto* taking prominent roles wear the kimono called *suso-moyō* (*suso*, bottom of a kimono; *moyō*, pattern): a kimono with a lovely design covering the skirt from about the knees to the hemline. The *suso-moyō* is without design on the shoulders and waist and may have crests.

If a samurai's daughter is not a *koshimoto*, she wears neither the *yagasuri* nor a plain colored kimono but usually dresses in a kimono of the *suso-moyō* or *sō-moyō* (allover pattern) type. The actor playing a lady-in-waiting *koshimoto* or a samurai's wife or daughter always carries a *kaiken* (dagger) in a bag inserted into the upper left side of the obi and generally has a *hakoseko* (a kind of compact) placed in the bosom of the kimono.


## KOKUMOCHI COSTUME

The *sewa nyōbō*, the staunch, loyal, tragic wives—mostly of samurai and *rōnin*—appear in realistic scenes in *jidai-mono* wearing the *kokumochi ishō*: kimono with round white circles resembling crests but without a crest design (Fig. 48). The color of the costumes is always plain *kuri-ume* (*kuri*, chestnut; *ume*, plum), a subdued purple with a bit of yellow and red in the dye. The collar, the lining of the kimono, and the obi are of black satin. The sleeves and collar of the *juban* are lavender.

The style of tying the obi is *sewa musubi*, an uninspired, rather bulbous bow with the ends protruding straight from its sides. The *obijime*, a narrow belt tied over the obi, is white, but it was not used in Kabuki or in real life by the people at large until the last years of Edo, although it came into fashion during the Bunsei era of 1818–30.

The *sewa nyōbō* wear the wig known as *maru-tabo-mino-no-Katsuyama-mage*, which takes its name from that of the seventeenth-century Yoshiwara courtesan Katsuyama, who is credited with devising this hair style. The short, rounded *tabo* or back hair is rolled on a metal frame, and the wig has a rather high puffed topknot. A purple *bōshi* covers the front hair. This style of doing the hair belongs to the same class as the *marumage* coiffure, which in most cases symbolizes married women, although in some instances ladies-in-waiting and maids are seen with their hair dressed in *marumage* style.

The *sewa nyōbō* do not wear *tabi*. A white *tenugui* (hand towel) hanging from the left side of the obi is often used to bite on in scenes of emotional stress to prevent crying out loud, since in the past it was thought shameful to give vent to one's feelings in this manner.

A typical *sewa nyōbō* is Owasa in the "Benkei Joshi" scene of *Gosho-Zakura Horikawa Youchi*, a play dramatizing episodes taken from the *Heike Monogatari* (Tales of the Heike) and the *Gikei-ki* (Accomplishments of Yoshitsune).

The younger *sewa nyōbō*, such as Okaru in Act VI of *Chūshingura*, wear the *maru-tabo-no-tsubushi-shimada* (*tsubushi*, crushed), a flat or low *shimada* as compared with the *taka-shimada* (Fig. 205). This wig is widely used, being worn for numerous roles including certain *koshimoto* and *oiran* (courtesans), but the decorative tying materials differ according to the nature of the roles. The various *shimada* coiffures are believed to have received their names from Shimada, a town facing the Tōkaidō highway in today's Shizuoka Prefecture, since the courtesans of this town first dressed their hair in this puffed-out gay manner. Another viewpoint, however, is given by J. E. DeBecker in his book on the Yoshiwara, *The Nightless City*. He states that the *shimada mage* reportedly originated with a seventeenth-century Kyoto dancing girl named Shimada Jinsuke.

The *kokumochi ishō* for young girls—primarily country maidens—are *suso-moyō* of a green called *moegi* and have profusely embroidered skirts, black satin collars, and scarlet *juban* for undergarments (Fig. 49). The obi worn with this costume is the *shibori* (tie-dyed) obi with the hemp-leaf pattern, *asanoha*. The reverse side of this obi is of black satin, with the two edges turned over to form black borders for the obi. The hemp-leaf pattern is dyed in red on a white ground. The obi is tied in either a pendulous *bunko* or a *furisage* knot (Fig. 247), the latter having pendulous ends but no loops, such as is seen in *Kyō-Ganoko Musume Dōjōji*. It is worn in this style only by young girls. The *obijime*—the previously mentioned band that is tied over the obi—is generally red and sometimes pink.

The wig for the young *kokumochi* is either the *mino-no-yuiwata* or the *habutae-ji-tabo-no-yuiwata* (Fig. 207), both having a topknot that resembles tied silk wadding. The latter wig is not so decorative, but the *habutae* (hair sewn on silk) hairline is far more natural-looking than the old-style *mino* hairline, which shows the white cloth base on which the hair has been tied. Silk crepe or raw silk, often light pink, is smartly knotted around the center of the topknot, and the front locks are decorated with an ornamental comb and colorful knotted cloth.

A hair ornament known as a *kanzashi* is stuck into the top of the right *bin* (side hair), but country girls usually display a red lacquer comb and an ornament of pampas grass on the right side of their hair. Generally the prongs of the *kanzashi* are made to look like silver. The *yuiwata* wigs are also worn by young girls from merchants' families.

Representative of a young *kokumochi* is Omiwa in the "Goten" (Palace) scene of *Imoseyama Onna Teikin*.

## AKAHIME COSTUME

This is the standard red robe of the *akahime* (*aka*, red; *hime*, princess), a word used only in Kabuki. The *akahime ishō* (Fig. 50) is considered by many to be one of the lush costumes for women's roles, but others find it monotonous. The name denotes the costume of a high-ranking princess or the daughter of a shōgun or a daimyō who should appear in a long-sleeved red kimono and *uchikake* with wadded hem, richly embroidered with either clouds and flowers, cherry blossoms, or chrysanthemums, or a pattern of a curving stream and flowers, or sometimes a bird pattern called *onagadori* (long-tailed bird).

Recently, *onnagata* appearing in *hime* roles have departed from the tradition of wearing red kimono by appearing in white, light purple, or pink. This is a misrepresentation, since the *akahime* or "red princess" is invariably associated with the color impression given by the costume.

All *hime* wear the wig with rounded back hair known as the *habutae-maru-tabo-no-fukiwa-katsura* (Fig. 219). In the past, if the role was not pure *hime* but, for instance, that of a daughter of the samurai class, the *takenaga* (long ornamental paper ties) in *inazuma* (lightning) style were not used as hair decoration. Today, however, these decorations are attached to the wig. The ornamental hairpin called *hime hana-kanzashi* is made with four rows of silver plum blossoms and butterflies. Although it is usually referred to as the *hanagushi* (flower comb), it is not actually a comb but a hairpin.

The *shitagi* (underkimono) worn beneath the main *kitsuke* kimono is white, and the *juban* is the usual red. The obi, tied in *furisage* style with extremely long, hanging ends, is made of dazzling gold brocade, contrasting in color with the flaming red of the outer robe. Make-up is properly white, for the upper-class maiden rarely exposed her skin to the glare of the sun. The *tabi* are also white.

Contrary to the strong impression created by the brilliant-hued costume, the *akahime,* with their limited scope of histrionics, are weak in physical attributes. The *akahime* hasn't the vitality to lift her beloved's helmet. She sheds copious tears when confronted with any disagreeable situation. And often she lacks the strength of character to fight for what she wants or what she believes is right. There is, however, one exception to her weakness. This fragile, coy maiden, like clinging vines the world over, is aggressively active in pursuing the man she loves.

CHAPTER **12**

# Men's Costumes for Sewa-mono and Kizewa-mono

The genre plays picturing the everyday life of the townspeople during the Edo period are known as *sewa-mono*. These dramas do not involve the samurai, although *sewa* (domestic) scenes are found within the framework of *jidai-mono* whenever the main character is of the merchant or townsman class known as *chōnin* or is a *rōnin*—a masterless samurai.

If the songlike narrative accompaniment known as *gidayū-jōruri* is sung, the costumes are comparatively elaborate, and the acting is exaggerated and stylized in the manner of the *ningyō-jōruri-shibai*—the puppet theater. Such costumes will be seen in *Kuruwa Bunshō* (Tales of the Licensed Quarter), commonly called *Yūgiri Izaemon* after its heroine and hero; *Soga Moyō Tateshi no Goshozome* (The Story of Gorozō, the Chivalrous Commoner); and *Sonezaki Shinjū* (The Double Suicide at Sonezaki).

It is a mistaken idea that the entire repertoire of *sewa-mono* accurately depicts actual dress. It is only in the *kizewa-mono,* the realistic plays of low life produced toward the end of Edo, that one sees costumes and acting nearer to the true habits of life as they were in those days. At first, *sewa-mono* costumes did not have a fixed style, but as Kabuki gradually attained the prominence of a classical theater, the costumes to some extent took on a format.

The *kizewa-mono* are almost consistently without the *gidayū-jōruri* accompaniment, as may be seen by attending performances of such plays as *Kami no Megumi Wagō no Torikumi, Yo wa Nasake Ukina no Yokogushi* (The Love Affair of Yosaburō and Otomi), *Tōkaidō Yotsuya Kaidan,* and *Edo-sodachi Omatsuri Sashichi* (The Story of Edo-bred Sashichi).

## TOBI OR HIKESHI COSTUMES

Extremely popular characters in many *sewa-mono* are the town firemen, known as *tobi-no-mono* (*tobi* for short) or *hikeshi*. The name *tobi-no-mono* (*tobi*, Siberian black kite; *mono,* person) derives from the fact that the sharp implement used by the firemen to hack down burning buildings had a head shaped like the beak of the kite. *Hikeshi* (*hi,* fire; *keshi,* from *kesu,* to extinguish) is a more literal name for the occupation. Firemen were classified into two separate divisions: those maintained by the *chōnin* and those maintained by the daimyō. The daimyō *hikeshi* appear in the drama *Mekura Nagaya Kaga Tobi* (The Windowless Hovel and the Brave Firemen of Lord Kaga), in this case representing the firemen serving under the influential Maeda family that reigned in Kaga Province.

*Tobi* consistently wear dark-blue cotton *haragake* (*hara,* abdomen; *gake,* from *kakeru,* to put on, to hang). The *haragake* is a sleeveless, backless work shirt or waistcoat held to the body by broad cloth straps crisscrossed in back, brought around the waist, and tied in front.

Drawn snugly over the legs are *momohiki:* long, thick navy-blue cotton drawers, split in the seat but made to flap over so as not to expose the body. They are fastened in front. In actuality, the *momohiki* were so tight that the sheath of the bamboo plant was used in shoehorn fashion to pull them on. Today stiff paper is used in easing an actor into these drawers. The *momohiki* were worn not only by firemen but also by carpenters (Fig. 51), laborers, and sometimes servants in the employ of merchants. In Kabuki, commoners may appear in *momohiki* when they are traveling.

The next part of the costume to be put on is an indigo-and-white-patterned *shita-uma,* an undergarment resembling a cotton *yukata* (summer kimono), or *tsumugi* (coarse pongee) underwear with a black collar. Over this garment is placed a white-and-indigo-colored kimono designed with the *tōban tsunagi* (*tōban,* fireman's staff; *tsunagi,* linked) pattern, symbolizing the *tobi's* occupation.

With the kimono is worn a Hakata obi, named for the city in Kyushu of which it is a famous product. It is tied in a *kai-no-kuchi* (shell-mouth) bow (Fig. 248), sometimes called the *otoko musubi* (*otoko,* man; *musubi,* knot). The typical *ippon-tokko,* the one-row pattern in the center of the dark-blue-and-white-striped Hakata obi, is taken from the shape of the *tokko,* a metal implement with a single claw at each end which can be held in the hand like a dumbbell and is used by Buddhist priests to exorcise evil spirits during religious ceremonies. This implement comes in several forms besides the *tokko* (single claw), such as the *sanko* (three claws) and the *goko* (five claws). The *chōnin* obi worn by the firemen can always be recognized by its *ippon-tokko* pattern, whereas a *nihon-tokko* pattern is standard for the wider samurai obi.

Around the neck is hung a *mameshibori tenugui,* a towel with a tie-dyed pattern resembling rows of beans, or a *matsuba-yamamichi tenugui,* a towel dyed to represent pine needles on a zigzag mountain road or path. Kabuki *tenugui* are usually of white cotton with designs in indigo.

Navy-blue *tabi* with white soles are worn either with *setta,* the sandals used for formal occasions or visiting (Fig. 250), or with *asa-ura* (*asa,* hemp; *ura,* bottom), a wear-and-tear kind of *zōri* (sandals), light in weight and used for everyday purposes (Fig. 250). The sole of the *setta* is made of rawhide, with metal at the heels for durability. *Zōri,* even today, are always worn shorter than the feet, and this places an uneven, heavy weight on the heels. The soles of the *asa-ura* are made of braided hemp cords, although both the *setta* and the *asa-ura* have straw tops. The thongs of the *setta* are of dark-blue velvet, a woolen cloth called *rasha,* or white leather, while those of the *asa-ura* are mostly white cotton.

A simple distinction is made for the formal dress of the chief and the higher-ranking firemen, who can be recognized by the *kawa-baori* (*kawa,* leather; *haori,* short coat) that they wear. The long cords with tassels that hold the coat together are not tied in front in the conventional manner but are swung over the shoulder at the neck to give the casual, debonair appearance of a dandy.

The Kaga *tobi*—firemen of Kaga Province—wear the *fukurotsuki-honke-bin-no-Kaga-masakari* wig, which displays the distinctive topknot in the shape of a broadax *(masakari)* head. The hair styling is very similar to that of the wig worn by the actors of the Ichikawa family and their *kōken* (assistants) at all *kōjō,* the formal stage ceremonies introducing new actors to the public, marking the accession of actors to new names, and the like. The *chōnin tobi,* the firemen maintained by the merchants, wear the *fukuro-tsuki-honke-bin-no-ichō,* a wig with a topknot in the shape of a ginkgo *(ichō)* leaf—always curved a little at the end as though to give a devil-may-care appearance (Figs. 196, 197).

## WAGOTO AND NIMAIME COSTUMES

The word *wagoto* (*wa,* soft; *koto,* matter, affair) originated during the years of Genroku and came to be known in the Kamigata district (western Japan) for roles in which the hero enjoyed himself at the licensed quarters or otherwise engaged himself in love affairs. The style of *wagoto* acting, the movement of the body, the peculiar walk, used solely for this type of role, and the make-up are deliberately effeminate and soft. The gentleness of *wagoto* contrasts sharply with the rhythmic, accented, forceful behavior of *aragoto* and *budōgoto* (duels of revenge among the samurai) and is limited to male roles.

*Wagoto* parts were played by *wagoto-shi,* actors who specialized in such characterizations. Two former actors renowned in this field of acting were Sakata Tōjūrō I of Kamigata, a great matinee idol, and Nakamura Shi-chisaburō I of Edo.

The word *nimaime* (literally, second board) came into being toward the end of the Edo period, originating from the fact that the wooden name plaque of the *wagoto-shi* was customarily hung up outside the theater in second place after that of the troupe's head in the Kabuki version of the billboard. Gradually the words *wagoto* and *nimaime* came to be used inter-changeably, although *nimaime* should rightfully be used only as the name of the role, generally that of a handsome man (Figs. 52–54), whereas *wagoto* is proper when speaking of the style of acting and movement.

Both *wagoto* and *nimaime* are found in *jidai-mono* and *sewa-mono*. In Osaka the *nimaime* were usually main characters, whereas in Edo, in the vast majority of cases, they were not. Edo audiences were reluctant to accept such prominence for the *nimaime,* preferring instead the more robust *aragoto* characters with their great bluster and verve.

To learn to emphasize the gentle behavior of the *wagoto* style of acting, the *nimaime* is taught a body movement for walking, handed down by word of mouth through generations of actors, which takes on the motion made when writing the Japanese *hiragana* character *no* (の). When the *nimaime* is standing still, one foot is straight and the other is placed slightly in front of it, thereby showing that his manner is not fully feminine, since a woman stands pigeon-toed with one foot somewhat in front of the other.

*Wagoto* dramas should have an element of the comic, usually over-emphasized but one that comes naturally. However, these are not comic plays, although from the observer's point of view the efforts of a person hopelessly in love to convince those around him that he is completely indifferent to the person of his choice appear just a little comic and prove to be an agreeable diversion following a sentimental or a tragic scene.

The *wagoto* influence is seen in certain roles in *jidai-mono*. Sakura-maru in the "Seppuku" scene of *Sugawara Denju Tenarai Kagami,* Kajiwara Genta in *Hiragana Seisuiki* (The Alphabetical Chronicle of the Rise and Fall of the Minamoto and the Taira), and Sonobe Saemon in *Shin Usuyuki Mono-gatari* play their major scenes in the subdued and understated *wagoto* style.

These roles have *wagoto* elements, but the more truly *wagoto*-style roles are those of Izaemon in *Kuruwa Bunshō* (perhaps the most purely *wagoto*-style of all), Chūbei (Fig. 54) in *Koi Hikyaku Yamato Ōrai* (Love's Mes-senger on the Yamato Highway), Jihei in *Shinju Ten no Amijima* (The Love Suicide at Amijima), Soga no Jūrō in *Kotobuki Soga no Taimen,* Motome in *Imoseyama Onna Teikin,* Kanōnosuke Naonobu in the "Kinkakuji" (Golden Pavilion) scene of *Gion Sairei Shinkōki* (Traveling to the Gion Festival), Taira no Koremori in the "Sushiya" (Sushi Shop) scene of *Yoshitsune Sembon-Zakura,* and Yosaburō (Fig. 52) in the "Misome" (Fall-ing in Love) scene of *Yo wa Nasake Ukina no Yokogushi.*

*Wakashu* roles which display *wagoto* elements are those of Shirozake-uri Shimbei in *Sukeroku Yukari no Edo-Zakura* and Takechi Jūjirō in *Ehon Taikō-ki.*

In general the *nimaime* is a role setting forth the exploits of a handsome male character. His acting may or may not have *wagoto* features. It must be remembered that all handsome men in Kabuki are not *nimaime*. For instance, Enya Hangan in *Chūshingura* is handsome and quiet, yet he is not a *nimaime* nor does he have *wagoto* traits. Neither by his walk nor by his actions does he approach even slightly the feminine quality considered so inherent in the *wagoto* character. Hangan is a *shimbō tachi-yaku,* a character who even when grossly provoked suppresses intense anger or emotion.

A *nimaime* usually has a sweetheart, although it may appear that he does not. If the action is traced throughout the play, there will always be an amorous sequence. *Nimaime* roles include those of Fukuoka Mitsugi in *Ise Ondo Koi no Netaba,* Tokijirō in *Ake-Garasu Yume no Awayuki* (Dream in the Light Sleep of Dawn or, more freely, Ephemeral Love like Light Snow of the Dawn), Kampei in *Chūshingura,* and Sukeroku in *Sukeroku Yukari no. Edo-Zakura.* With regard to the last of these plays, whose English title we have already noted as *Sukeroku's Affinity for Edo Cherry Blossoms,* it is pertinent to mention that " cherry blossoms " embodies a play on words, since it also means beautiful young women.

Probably the most famous costume for the older or more classical *nimaime* is the *kamiko,* a kimono supposedly made of paper (Fig. 53). It seems incredible, but in real life a paper kimono was actually worn as an at-home dress or as an undergarment during the winter, since paper clothing is exceedingly warm. The Japanese are noted for their ability to produce tough, durable paper that can be waterproofed. Japanese warriors wore a sleeveless paper-coat armor for these reasons.

It is of interest to note what Mock Joya, in his *Quaint Customs and Manners of the Japanese,* has to say of the *kamiko.* He writes: "*Kamiko* is a contraction of *kamikoromo* or paper dress. The making of *kamiko* is not so simple as it might sound. At first pieces of very strong paper are selected. They are pasted together to form the usual shape of woven cloth. The paper is then made stronger and waterproofed by applying to it a starch made of devil's-tongue or the astringent juice of *kaki* or persimmon. When it is treated with the persimmon juice it becomes brown in color. Thus there are two kinds of *kamiko,* the brown and the white. The paper thus prepared is then thoroughly rubbed by hand, so that it will become soft as silk. It is then cut and sewed together to form a kimono." It should be added that there was also another kind of *kamiko,* beautifully patterned in various colors by woodblock printing.

In the more classical *wagoto* plays, the *kamiko* costume is frequently worn. When it is not, the actor will be clothed in either a black, a heavenly blue, or a light-purple satin kimono with a pattern across the bottom embroidered in soft pastels of indescribable delicacy. The costumes are specifically designed to enhance the placid look of the actor and naturally were never worn in real life. As time progressed and the Kabuki costumes became more extravagant, satin and crepe replaced the paper kimono. Consequently, today we never see a real *kamiko* on the stage but only an imitation.

Kabuki characters who wear *kamiko* represent *wagoto* persons who are not strong physically and are weak-willed. They are usually poor because they have spent too much money in the gay quarters or have been disinherited by their families for their dissolute ways. *Kamiko* are also worn by the foppish and by older types of *nimaime*.

The *kamiko* has a Japanese calligraphic design, a pattern peculiar to Kabuki called *fumi-hogo* (*fumi*, letter; *hogo*, waste paper). The *nimaime* is supposed to have saved his paramour's letters and later, under dire financial stress, to have had a kimono made from them. When the *nimaime* appears in a *kamiko*, he wears an *ami-gasa*, a rather large folding hat woven of rushes, pointed in front and back and with narrow streamers attached to the underneath sides. These are tied in a small flat bow on the upper part of the chin. The *ami-gasa* covers the face so that the *nimaime* cannot be recognized on his way to the brothel district.

The back hem of the *kamiko* tends to drag a little, while the front hem is slightly raised. The collar is worn off the back of the neck in the titillating manner of a woman, and the obi is tied in a *kai-no-kuchi* bow. The *nimaime* sometimes does not wear *tabi* but has his feet painted white, the same as his hands and face.

The older *nimaime*—for example, Izaemon in *Kuruwa Bunshō* and Koremori in *Yoshitsune Sembon-Zakura*—wear the wig named *abura-tsuki-honke-bin-no-futatsu-ori-mage*. The back hair is hardened with pomade, pressed to the head, and polished *(aburatsuki)*. The sidelocks are made with real hair *(honke-bin),* and the queue is long and folded or doubled *(futatsu-ori)* and tied at its root.

The *nimaime* whose hair is dressed in *aburatsuki-no-bō-chasen* (pomaded back hair with tea-whisk topknot)—such as Sonobe Saemon in *Shin Usuyuki Monogatari* and Kanōnosuke Naonobu in *Gion Sairei Shinkōki*—wear delicate silk kimono decorated with the *tsuyu-shiba-moyō* (*tsuyu*, dew; *shiba*, lawn; *moyō*, pattern): a hem design of dewdrops on a lawn over a background of black or sometimes blue, pink, or another color of the actor's choice (Fig. 93). Mild *wagoto* characters often wear kimono in a shimmering design called *iyo-zome* which gives the effect of sunlight shining through blinds of split bamboo (Fig. 90).

The costumes for the later *nimaime* roles are completely realistic and were used in Kabuki both in Kamigata and in Edo, having been modeled after the dress of the *chōnin*. The cloth of the kimono was often patterned with narrow stripes, generally in a bluish color to give an impression of softness. Although the *chōnin* wore kimono of cotton or hemp, since they were not permitted the use of silk, the stage versions of these costumes were made of silk to heighten the impression of gentleness conveyed by the characters.

The *nimaime* tie their obi in *kai-no-kuchi* fashion; paint their faces, hands, and feet white; and wear *zōri* with white (or sometimes black or blue) thongs. Their wigs, the *fukurotsuki-no-futatsu-ori-katsura* (Fig. 193), differ from those of the older *nimaime* style by having a bag effect at the back of the neck, a style worn by *nimaime* in *sewa-mono gidayū* dramas—that is, realistic dramas taken from the puppet theater and having *gidayū* accompaniment.

Since the *nimaime* frequently appear in the scenes called *michiyuki*, it is apropos to pause here for a look at this well-known Kabuki convention. Although playgoers often define the *michiyuki* (*michi*, road; *yuki*, going) as a scene sandwiched in between the acts of dramatic plays, there are a number of famous *michiyuki* scenes in the *shosagoto*, notably in *Kyō-Ganoko Musume Dōjōji* and in the dance sequence on the *hanamichi* in *Yasuna*. In this last dance-drama the role of Yasuna, a young man who has been driven mad by the death of his sweetheart, is one of the most plaintive and poignant roles in Kabuki, a role famous with Onoe Kikugorō VI and recently so superbly interpreted by Ichikawa Sadanji III that after witnessing his tender performance applause would be sacrilegious.

*Sewa-mono michiyuki* is a type of Kabuki eroticism picturing a couple who are eloping or who are on their way to commit *shinjū* (double suicide). The man usually covers his head with a bleached cotton *tenugui*, more often tied on the left side than on the right. If it is tied on the right side, it is considered to give an *iki* (dandified) appearance, as in *Ake-Garasu Yume no Awayuki*. Here a man comes to rescue a woman and wears the *tenugui* tied on the right side. In contrast, when a *nimaime* is on his way to commit suicide, the *tenugui* would in all probability be tied on the left side. But the side used depends upon the actor's preference.

The *nimaime* is fond of pulling up the back hem of his kimono and tucking it into his obi, thereby showing his bare white legs, a custom supposed to add a touch of manly attractiveness to the staging. This *hashori* style of tucking up the kimono began in Edo and was later copied by the Kamigata actors. Nevertheless, the Kamigata actors disliked showing their legs, and in many roles the *hashori* style was dispensed with for the more usual modest manner of wearing the kimono.

In 1798, Matsumoto Kōshirō V played the role of Hanshichi in *Sankatsu Hanshichi* (The Love Story of Sankatsu and Hanshichi), a play in which Hanshichi commits suicide with the beautiful geisha Sankatsu. For this role, Kōshirō wore his kimono tucked up, covered his head with a white *tenugui* in *michiyuki-kaburi* (travel or elopement head covering) style, and for the first time introduced white-painted legs. His feet, also painted white, remained completely bare.

Prior to the introduction of Kōshirō's *michiyuki* style of dress, actors in such scenes wore red *himotsuki momohiki* (tight trousers with strings attached for fastening) and over these a kimono. The seat of the kimono was placed under the obi, giving the appearance of *azuma-karage*—that is, of the hem pulled up by attached strings. *Tabi* were not worn. The feet were painted white, and *asa-ura zōri*—the sandals previously noted as part of the fireman's costume—were worn. The head was covered with a purple, blue, or black *tenugui* tied under the chin in *koshō* (page-boy) style. Rikiya, in Act VII of *Kanadehon Chūshingura*, appears in a costume very similar to this older style, except that his kimono is worn in *azuma-karage* style (Fig. 240). Since Rikiya has been traveling the great distance from Yamashina to the Gion in Kyoto, it can be assumed that this is the reason for his style of wearing the kimono.

## MICHIYUKI DUAL-STYLE COSTUMES

If a man and a woman dressed in like kimono in everyday life, the result would be unnatural, but on the stage this intimacy broadens the knowledge of the viewer, for surely only true lovers would proclaim their devotion so blatantly for all to see. Often in the *michiyuki* both lover and lady are attired in *suso-moyō,* the skirt-patterned kimono. No design appears on the shoulders or waist other than the slightly overlapping crests of the *onnagata* and the actor playing the role of the lover. These are placed in traditional formal-kimono style: one pair on each side of the chest, one pair on the outer side of each sleeve near the elbow, and one pair on the back.

These particular crests are spoken of as *hiyoku mon,* the word *hiyoku* from *hiyoku-no-tori* meaning an imaginary pair of male and female birds with one eye and one wing, always flying together as a symbol of eternal love. The reference is to an old Chinese poem written for an emperor who was grieving over the loss of his cherished wife. The poet relates the tale of a husband and wife who died and were transformed into *hiyoku-no-tori.* It is interesting to note that the grave of the real-life Gompachi and Komurasaki, whose tragic love affair formed the basis for the play *Hiyoku no Chō Yume no Yoshiwara* (Love's Nightmare in the Yoshiwara), is called Hiyokuzuka (*tsuka,* grave).

When the *michiyuki* pair wear *tenugui* about their heads, these carry the crests of the actors, but they are not necessarily placed in the same overlapping position as on the kimono. Generally the man ties the *tenugui* on the left, and the woman wears hers in the "streamer" fashion known as *fuki-nagashi,* holding one side or the other between her lips after it has been loosely draped over her head. The man's obi has a *kai-no-kuchi* bow, but the woman's varies according to the type of role. Both wear *asa-ura zōri* (Fig. 250) without *tabi.* Unlike other *nimaime,* the actor never wears his kimono with the hem tucked up, since obviously this would hide its beautiful pattern.

## WAKASHU COSTUMES

There are several different types of *wakashu*—youths between fifteen and seventeen years old—among Kabuki roles, and each has its individual type of costume. The kimono of *wakashu* are patterned either in *kasuri, shibori,* or *komon* fashion. *Kasuri,* as we have noted, is a splashed design produced by weaving cloth with thread previously dyed in a variety of designs and colors—the *ikat* technique. *Shibori* is the tie-dyeing method. *Komon* is a type of small design produced by stenciling and seen, for example, in the white-dot pattern of the *kamishimo*. The Kabuki *komon* is larger and livelier in mood than that actually used by the samurai.

Young men of the merchant class, such as Hisamatsu in *Shimpan Uta-zaimon* (The Love Story of Osome and Hisamatsu) and Chōkichi in *Sumida no Haru Geisha Katagi*—commonly known as *Ume no Yoshibei* (The Story of Yoshibei)—wear *chirimen* (silk crepe) kimono in the pattern of muted stripes called *iyo-zome* or blue-and-white *komon* designs. The *komon* background consists of one color only. With a striped kimono, the *juban* is of blue *chirimen* with a black *hachijō* silk collar, and the obi is of black satin.

*Wakashu* of samurai families and temple *koshō* (apprentice pages) wear the five-crested kimono known as the *montsuki*, generally in black or char-treuse yellow, sometimes in light blue, the last color being for the more active personalities among the roles. *Hakama* in a striped pattern complete the costume for formal occasions (Fig. 55). The collar of the *juban* may be black or one of the wide range of medium to light-blue colors used in Kabuki. It shows slightly above the collar of the kimono. *Wakashu* wear their kimono low on the back of the neck, much as girls do. Among the roles in which this style of costume is worn are those of Gompachi in *Banzuin Chōbei Shōjin Manaita*, Kichisa in *Yaoya Oshichi* (The Love Story of Kichisa and Oshichi), and Motome in *Sato Moyō Azami no Ironui* (The Tale of the Courtesan Izayoi and the Priest Seishin).

A *wakashu* appearing in *jidai-mono* and *sewa-mono* can be recognized by his uncut *maegami* or forelock, which puffs out attractively above his forehead. Usually the *wakashu* wear either the *aburatsuki-wakashu-no-maegami-honke-bin* (Fig. 177) or the *fukurotsuki-wakashu-no-maegami-honke-bin* style of wig (Fig. 202).

A special type of *wakashu katsura* is the *fukurotsuki-wakashu,* a coiffure that looks like a woman's *shimada* from the front but has the topknot dressed in masculine style. Another distinctive styling is worn by the temple pages called *koshō*. It is the *fukurotsuki-tera-goshō* (*tera*, temple; *koshō*, page) or *kamome-zuto-no-wakashu-honke-bin* (*kamome*, seagull; *tsuto*, back hair), which has the back hair stretched out or draped like the tail of a seagull.

The *wakashu,* with his elegant apparel, white make-up, and attractive coiffure, is the epitome of youthful purity and handsomeness.


## KIZEWA-MONO COSTUMES

*Kizewa-mono* roles include those of vagabonds, good-for-nothings, petty thieves, and various other outlaw types. These persons are colloquially referred to as *sanjaku-mono* (three-foot characters) because they wear the *sanjaku* obi, whose length of approximately three feet *(sanjaku)* is much shorter than that of the regular obi, so that it can circle the body only once and is tied at the front or on either side. This obi, one and a half inches wide, is made of cheap cotton material in reddish brown, dark blue, or medium blue, but never black, and displays a white pattern known as *soroban-dama-moyō*—that is, a pattern imitating the beads or counters *(tama)* of the *soroban,* the Japanese abacus.

In summer scenes the *sanjaku-mono* wear the *yukata,* the cotton summer kimono (Fig. 56). A regular *juban* is never worn, the implication being that these people are of too low and poor a class to own one. In winter scenes a *shita-uma*—the undergarment which we have already noted as part of the fireman's costume—and the kimono are folded across the body as one garment so that, in case of a fight, the two garments can be removed as one or so that the characters can show off their tattooed bodies by allowing the garments to hang loosely open. This combination of kimono with *shita-uma* is called *shita-uma-tsuki.*

Since in real life tattooing is very painful and sometimes fatal, the more elaborate it is, the more it represents great courage and physical strength. Thus, among the *sanjaku-mono,* the scurrilous fellows who are not tattooed are considered inferior to those who are, and even though they have to sell all their meager possessions to pay for it, they wish to be tattooed in order to keep up with their comrades. Elaborately tattooed bodies are still occasionally seen today in real life in Japan.

For Kabuki purposes, tattooing is painted or dyed on cotton-knit tights (Fig. 57), but before the Meiji era the painting was done on the actors' bodies. This custom was discarded because the painting soiled the costumes. Firemen were frequently tattooed in real life, but from around the fifteenth year of Meiji up to the present time there has been a law prohibiting this form of embellishment.

Next to his body, the *sanjaku-mono* wears one *tan* (about twelve yards) of *sarashi* (bleached cotton cloth) wrapped around his midriff to keep him warm, to protect him from injury, and to provide a repository for a short dagger. The dagger may be one of two varieties: the *kusun-gobu* (a 9½-inch sheathed knife—the name is taken from the measurements in Japanese) or the *deba-bōchō* (an unsheathed kitchen knife), usually wrapped in a *tenugui.*

The *sanjaku-mono* are barefoot, but their feet and legs are painted white or flesh color. However, they do wear *zōri,* put on in a slipshod, loose manner.

Two styles of wigs set these men off for what they are, and both styles are called *honke-bin-mushiri-no-ichō* (Fig. 195). The *sakayaki*—the shaven part of the head—when partly grown out is called *mushiri* (plucked or pulled out), and this section of the wig is made with bear fur. The topknot in ginkgo-leaf *(ichō)* style is always bent far to the right to give an *iki* (dandified) appearance. The difference between the two styles of wigs lies in the *mushiri,* the one wig having a *tsumuji* or whorl of natural hair on top of the head, the other lacking this feature.

44. *Jūni-hitoe*. The stage version of the *jūni-hitoe*, the Heian woman's court dress of numerous layers of kimono, is unquestionably one of the most fascinating costumes seen in Kabuki. The costume, with its beautiful, long, flowing lines, combines dignity and splendor with a feeling of serenity.

177

45. *Kaoyo Gozen* costume: Lady Kaoyo in Act I of *Chūshingura*. This costume, named for one of the roles in which it is worn, is standard for the *midaidokoro:* wives of feudal lords or court nobles. It consists of three floor-sweeping garments: an embroidered *uchikake* (long coat), a plain red kimono, and a pure white *juban*.

46. *Katahazushi* costume: Lady Iwafuji in *Kagamiyama Kokyō no Nishikie*. The costume of the upper-class samurai wife and ranking lady-in-waiting at the courts of the shōgun and the daimyō takes its name from the *katahazushi mage*, the wig with an asymmetrical top-knot worn for these roles. The *uchikake*, kimono, and *juban* are much like those in the Kaoyo Gozen costume seen in Figure 45.

47. *Koshimoto* costume: Okaru in the "Michiyuki" scene of *Chūshingura*. The *koshimoto*—daughters of samurai who serve at court, ladies-in-waiting, or daughters of wealthy merchants—repeatedly wear the *yagasuri* or arrow-patterned kimono. Okaru traditionally wears this version in purple and white.

48. *Kokumochi* costume: Tonami in the "Terakoya" scene of *Sugawara Denju Tenarai Kagami.* The *sewa-nyōbō,* the staunch, loyal, tragic wives—mostly of samurai and *rōnin*—appear in *jidai-mono* wearing the *kokumochi* costume: a plain subdued purple kimono with round white spots resembling crests but without design.

49. *Moegi-no-kokumochi:* Omiwa in Act II of *Imoseyama Onna Teikin.* The *kokumochi* costume for young girls—primarily country maidens—are *suso-moyō* of a green called *moegi* and have profusely embroidered skirts, black satin collars, and scarlet *juban* for undergarments.

50. *Akahime* costume. *Akahime* (red princess) is a word used only in Kabuki, and it refers to the daughters of shōgun and daimyō as well as to princesses. The standard costume for the role is a long-sleeved red kimono and *uchikake* with wadded hem, richly embroidered with such patterns as clouds and flowers, stream and flowers, cherry blossoms, chrysanthemums, or a long-tailed bird.

51. *Happi* and *momohiki:* carpenter in *sewa-mono*. The short coat known as *happi* and the snug trousers called *momohiki* are the chief items of the *sewa-mono* carpenter's attire. The accessories include an indigo-and-white obi and a *tenugui* dyed in *mameshibori* style.

52. *Nimaime* costume: Yosaburō in Act I of *Yo wa Nasake Ukina no Yokogushi*. In general the *nimaime* is a role setting forth the exploits of a handsome male character. The costumes for the later *nimaime* roles, modeled after the dress of the *chōnin* (merchants) of real life, are often patterned with narrow stripes, generally in blue.

53. *Kamiko*. Probably the most famous costume for the older or more classical *nimaime* in *sewa-mono* is the *kami-ko*, a kimono supposedly made of a woman's love letters and thus patterned with a calligraphic design. Originally actually of paper, the *kamiko* of today's Kabuki is of satin or crepe.

54. *Nimaime michiyuki* costume: Chūbei in *Koi Hikyaku Yamato Ōrai*. *Sewa-mono michiyuki* is a type of Kabuki eroticism picturing a couple who are eloping or who are on their way to commit double love suicide. The *nimaime's* kimono is tucked up in back to add a touch of manly attractiveness. Headgear is either a *tenugu* or a *kasa*, according to the actor's preference.

55. *Wakashu* costume, *sewa-mono* style. *Wakashu* of samurai families and temple pages wear the five-crested kimono known as the *montsuki*. *Hakama* in a striped pattern complete the costume for formal occasions. The collar of the *juban*, which may be black or any shade of blue between medium and light, shows stylishly above the collar of the kimono.

56. *Sanjaku-mono* costume: Yosaburō in Act III of *Yo wa Nasake Ukina no Yokogushi*. The summer apparel of *sanjaku-mono*, the disreputable characters of *kizewa-mono*, is the cotton *yukata* worn with a cheap cotton " three-foot " obi.

57. *Niku-juban* with tattooing: Benten Kozō in the "Hamamatsuya" scene of *Benten Kozō*. For Kabuki purposes, tattooing is painted or dyed on cotton-knit tights. Here the thief Benten Kozō has just thrown off his female disguise and revealed himself in his true character.

58. *Machi-musume* costume: Osome in the "Nozaki-mura" scene of *Shimpan Utazaimon*. This is a standardized costume for the *machi musume* or city girl. The kimono is a *furisode* of *chirimen* crepe decorated by the famous *yūzen* dyeing process. The obi, tied in *furisage-musubi* style, has an underside of black satin and a front side of crepe.

59. Geisha costume: Miyokichi in *Meigetsu Hachiman Matsuri*. The Kabuki geisha is gowned in rather subdued finery, relying on her *maru-obi* for dramatic effect. A formally dressed geisha usually wears the skirt-patterned kimono called *suso-moyō*.

60. *Oiran* costume: Agemaki in *Sukeroku Yukari no Edo-Zakura*. The most flamboyant Edo *oiran* in Kabuki is Agemaki. Her extravagant costume features a richly embroidered *uchikake*, a red *kitsuke*, a gigantic *manaita* obi, foot-high lacquered clogs, and a fantastically complicated *date-hyōgo* wig.

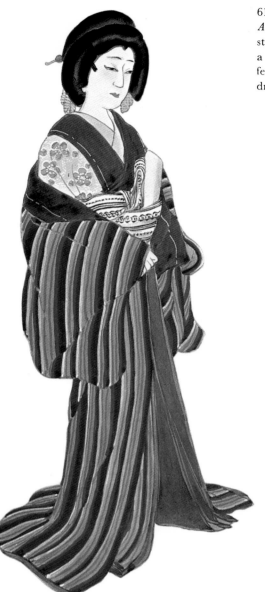

61. *Oiran* costume: Michitose in *Yuki Kurete Iriya no Azemichi*. The *oiran* of Edo appear mostly in the *dōnuki* style of kimono when entertaining their guests. This is a kimono with the upper and lower parts made of different cloth. It is worn with an *uchikake* becomingly draped off the shoulders.

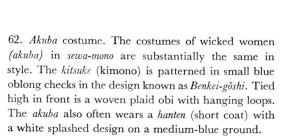

62. *Akuba* costume. The costumes of wicked women *(akuba)* in *sewa-mono* are substantially the same in style. The *kitsuke* (kimono) is patterned in small blue oblong checks in the design known as *Benkei-gōshi*. Tied high in front is a woven plaid obi with hanging loops. The *akuba* also often wears a *hanten* (short coat) with a white splashed design on a medium-blue ground.

CHAPTER 13

# Onnagata Costumes for Sewa-mono

Historical authenticity is found in certain *sewa* or domestic scenes among the commoners in *jidai-mono* and in many pure *sewa-mono* in the personification of *yūjo* or *oiran,* the celebrated courtesans of the Edo period. Eulogizing the women of the demimonde brings to the stage exciting activity, brightness of costume, and absorbing love affairs, the last of which often vindicate the social code by ending in double suicide.

When an *oiran,* accompanied by her retinue, makes an appearance in gala dress, walking on the almost foot-high black-lacquered wooden clogs known as *mitsuba-no-kuro-nuri-geta* (Fig. 249), the complete unexpected lavishness of the scene raises theatrical exhilaration to its zenith. The *oiran* wardrobe and hair styles perpetuate those worn in the licensed quarters and give sparks of brilliance to the otherwise rather ordinary daily-life dramas of the townspeople.

Artistic liberties have improved the dress of commoners appearing in *sewa-mono,* but almost complete realism is seen in *kizewa-mono.* However, these costumes have an appealing curiosity because of their inseparability from the parts so accurately played. At present, to some extent, since Kabuki has attained the status of classical theater, the costumes for *sewa-mono* have formed a *kata* or definite style based on the dress of the *chōnin* class at the end of the Edo period. The representative costumes for *onnagata* have definite classifications, and it is to these that we now turn.

## MACHI-MUSUME COSTUMES

A standardized costume for a *machi musume* (city girl) is worn by Osome (Fig. 58) in the "Nozaki-mura" (Nozaki Village) scene of *Shimpan Uta-zaimon,* which relates the love story of Osome and Hisamatsu. Osome appears in a *furisode* (kimono with long, hanging sleeves) of *chirimen* decorated by the famous resist-dyeing process known as *yūzen-zome*—the

193

late-seventeenth-century invention that revolutionized the craft of hand-painted-dye designing. The collar of the kimono is of black satin. The *juban* and the *yumoji* (loincloth or waistcloth) are of bright red *chirimen*.

The obi for Osome's costume has an underside of black satin and a front side of crepe, often patterned with *kanoko*, the allover pattern of small white dots produced by tie-dyeing—in this case on red. The satin, folded over from back to front, forms a black band along the upper and lower edges. The obi is tied in *furisage-musubi* style (Fig. 247) with long pendant ends, although these are not so long as in the obi worn by the daughters of rich merchants. This type of obi is referred to as a *kujira* (whale) obi because the black satin side resembles the back of a whale while the lighter-colored front is thought of as the belly.

Any type of obi that consists of two different cloths sewn together one on top of the other is referred to as a *kujira* obi. Another name for it is *hara-awase* (*hara*, abdomen; *awase*, put together, confronting), and still others are *chūya* (*chū*, day; *ya*, night—a reference to the light and dark sides) and *katakawa* (one-sided). The opposite of this type of obi is the *maru-obi* (*maru*, whole, round, perfect), which, after tailoring, is about twelve inches wide and made of one piece of woven material. During Edo, the obi was tied without being folded double at the front.

With the *furisage*-style obi, the *machi musume* usually wears one of two types of wigs: the *maru-tabo-no-yuiwata*, which has a *mage* resembling a twisted skein of silk, or the *habutae-maru-tabo-no-oshidori*, with a *mage* whose shape resembles that of a mandarin duck. The most prominent hair decoration is the *kusudama kanzashi* or "medicine-ball" hairpin, a creation of silk cloth with long tassels of various colors—most frequently red—stuck into the upper part of the right *bin* (sidelocks). The decoration takes its name from the balls of medicinal plants, ornamented with flowers, that were formerly hung in the rooms of upper-class homes in the hope of expelling evil influences. The *kusudama* is also the origin of a well-known textile pattern.

The *machi musume's* wig has short *ito-jike* (Fig. 218)—thick silk threads twisted together—hanging on each side under the *bin*. In front of the *mage* is a flowered hairpin with silver dangles. Decorating the *mage* at the root of the ponytail is a *hanagake*, a small scarf of *kanoko*-patterned red cloth, which is tied in a flower knot together with a loop of colored *motoyui*, paper cord used for tying hair. On the opposite side of the paper loop is an attractive hairpin called the *ichi-dome*, which has a plover motif. Four sheets of the starched paper strips known as *takenaga*, folded in lightning design and tied under the *mage*, extend artistically down the sides of the back hair. Depending upon the role, the *takenaga* may be of gold, silver, red, gold-and-silver, or checkered paper.

Like almost all the characters in *sewa-mono*, the *machi musume* does not wear *tabi* but only *zōri*.

A *machi musume* whose costume is very similar to that of Osome is Yaoya

Oshichi in *Sono Mukashi Koi no Edo-Zome* (The Story of Yaoya Oshichi). Her *chirimen furisode* is patterned by the *yūzen-zome* resist-dyeing process with the above-noted *kusudama* design on a light violet ground. The *furisode* has a black satin collar. Underwear and *juban* are of red *chirimen*. The *kujira* obi has a front of red polka-dot *chirimen* and a back of black satin which is folded over to form an upper and lower border for the front. Oshichi's wig is the *bunkin-taka-shimada* (Fig. 224) decorated with red cloth or ribbon.

In addition to these costumes for *machi musume,* there is one which has a *furisode* made of *ki-hachijō* silk, a soft, thin, plain-woven yellow silk checkered with black or brown, specially produced on Hachijō Island. The collar of the *furisode* has a black cover. The obi, in *asanoha* pattern, is tied in *furisage-musubi* style, and the wig is in *yuiwata* style, having a *mage* that resembles a skein of tied silk wadding.

## INAKA-MUSUME COSTUMES

Omitsu, who appears in the same scene with Osome in *Shimpan Utazaimon,* is a typical *inaka musume*—country girl. She wears a *furisode* of dark-blue *tsumugi* (coarse pongee) in *chūgata* pattern: an allover stencil pattern of medium size. Her *juban* has sleeves of red *chirimen,* the only part of the garment made of this crepe. Her *yumoji* (underwear) is of light pink, and her obi of the *kujira* type. Her hair is done in the gay, puffed *shimada-mage* fashion, so characteristic of young ladies, with a red-lacquered comb decorating her front tresses.

## JOCHŪ-MUSUME COSTUMES

The costume of the *jochū musume,* the Kabuki maidservant, is typified by that of Osugi in *Sono Mukashi Koi no Edo-Zome,* the play which we noted above as having Yaoya Oshichi for its heroine. Osugi wears a *kitsuke* of *meisen,* a not so luxurious silk commonly used among the merchant class, with a cross-striped pattern on a dark-blue ground and a black silk cover over the collar. The *yumoji* is of white *chirimen*. The *kujira* obi has a front of *chirimen* with white *kiku tatewaku*—a repeated design of stylized chrysanthemums bordered with serpentine lines on a purple ground—and a back of black satin. A soft purple *obi-age* (cord for maintaining the obi in place) is tied over it. An apron called a *maedare* completes the costume and plainly identifies the character's occupation.

Osugi's wig is the *ji-tabo-no-marumage,* a style worn in all wives' roles in *sewa-mono* and characterized by natural-looking back hair for which no stretcher is used. Other maidservants, however—especially younger girls—wear their hair in the *ji-tabo-no-ichō-gaeshi* style, a headdress in which the shape of the *mage* very much resembles a pair of inverted ginkgo leaves.

## MACHI-NYŌBŌ COSTUMES

The costume of Osan in Act II of *Shinju Ten no Amijima* is characteristically that of the *machi nyōbō* or urban wife. The *kitsuke* is of the short-sleeved type called *tomesode* (*tome,* stopped, cut off; *sode,* sleeve)—that is, the hanging sleeve is short, as in the present-day married woman's kimono. The material for the *kitsuke* is *tsumugi* with a *hakeme* (brush-mark) design on a gray ground. The usual *maru-obi* completes the costume, and the wig is the *ji-tabo-no-marumage.*

## INAKA-NYŌBŌ COSTUMES

A good example of the general classification of the *inaka nyōbō* or country wife is Ohama in *Higashiyama Sakura-Zōshi,* a drama which relates the story of Kiuchi Sōgo of Sakura (Ohama's husband), a public-spirited man who sacrifices his life to save his poor tenants from trouble.

The *inaka nyōbō* wears a *kitsuke* in the above-noted *tomesode* style. It is of *tsumugi* in a *komon* pattern and is artistically patched over the shoulders with cloth in *kasuri* weave with a cross pattern. This garment is known as the *kata-ire* (*kata,* shoulder; *ire,* inserted).

The *juban* is not the usual red but purple. The *kujira* obi has a front dyed in the *chūgata* or *chūgara* (medium-sized) pattern and a back of *kuro-hachijō* silk, a plain-woven black silk with thick warp.

For the first time in this record, we are introduced to the plebeian woman's short coat, the *hanten*. In this case the garment is made of ordinary *meisen,* with black satin covering the collar. The *inaka nyōbō* may also wear a *maekake* (apron).

Ohama's wig is the *habutae-maru-tabo-no-obako,* a very natural-looking coiffure dressed without the use of pomade. Sometimes a piece of cloth is inserted into the *mage*. A tortoise-shell comb is placed in front of the divided looped *mage,* which is tied at the center. A hairpin called a *naka-zashi,* decorated with *makie* (gold-sprinkled lacquer) is thrust through the knot, while another long hairpin of silver, the *mimikaki,* protrudes from beneath the right side of the *mage.*

## KASHA-GATA OR FUKE-OYAMA COSTUMES

Elderly women in Kabuki, known as *kasha-gata* or *fuke-oyama,* often wear *kitsuke* of *meisen* silk with narrow stripes. In winter scenes they wear a wadded coat called the *nenneko* (*nenne,* child's expression for "go to sleep"; *ko,* child or robe), the full-backed garment designed to cover both a mother and the baby on her back. It is made of *ito-ori,* a strong, durable silk woven from previously dyed yarn in a pattern of medium-sized stripes. The *chirimen naga-juban* has a midriff of blue in *chūgata* pattern and sleeves of gray. The lining of the lower part is navy blue. The *yumoji* or underwear is of white *chirimen.* For *kasha-gata* roles the usual obi is the *kujira,* with back of black satin and front of *hattan* (twill).

The wig is the *goma-no-marumage,* worn exclusively by elderly women. *Goma* is sesame, and in this case it stands for *goma-shio*—that is, *goma* and salt or black and white hair mixed. In *jidai-mono* a *babā bōshi* (old woman's decorative headcloth) of brownish-beige *tsumugi* is worn on the front of the wig, but this custom is not followed in *sewa-mono.*

## MEKAKE COSTUMES

For the costumes of *mekake*—concubines or mistresses—the designs principally used are stripes, but the material is very luxurious and soft. A *mekake* such as Otomi, for example, in the "Genyadana" (a place name, called Genjidana in Kabuki) scene of *Yo wa Nasake Ukina no Yokogushi,* usually wears a gray *omeshi* (a flat crepe) with *kasuri* (geometrical design). But in this instance, Otomi wears a kimono with a combination of wide and narrow stripes on a white ground with a *kujira* obi of black satin and the twill silk known as *hattan. Kasuri* designs are formed by the *ikat* method of weaving, meaning to dye thread by tying before weaving. Many different patterns are formed by this method, but generally they are of geometrical design. *Kasuri* weaving in which representational patterns are produced is known as *e-gasuri* or "picture *kasuri.*"

Otomi's wig is the *habutae-no-uma-no-shippo* (*uma,* horse; *shippo,* tail), with the hair in *musubi-gami* style (Fig. 211). The wig takes its name from the fact that the tying of the *mage* resembles a horse's tail tied up or folded over. It is a natural hair style, requiring no pomade or lacquer, and is used mainly for the roles of country girls or wives, although on certain specific occasions it is the coiffure for stylish or smart roles like that of Otomi.

In the "Kisarazu" (Seashore at Kisarazu) scene of the same play, Otomi is dressed in a lovely *kitsuke* of *sukiya,* a fine silk for summer use only, patterned with medium stripes on a dark-blue ground. Her *juban* is of red ramie, with purple *chirimen* covering the collar. Her *kujira* obi is of black satin and *kenjō-hakata,* an excellent-quality silk whose name literally means "dedication Hakata"—that is, silk woven in the Kyushu city of Hakata (also famous for obi weaving) and so superior in quality that it is worthy of being dedicated, for example, to the government, as it was in times past.

The *mekake* wig is the hair-lined *habutae-maru-tabo-no-wari-ganoko* with *kumeza mage*—that is, with the *mage* divided or parted (Fig. 208). The coiffure is decorated with a light-purple scarf in *kanoko* pattern wound around the top of the divided *mage,* a tortoise-shell comb, and a *kanzashi* (hairpin) with a coral ball. *Mekake* may, and in fact quite often do, wear the type of wig known as the *marutabo-no-mitsuwa* (*mitsu,* three; *wa,* circle or loop).

## GEISHA COSTUMES

The talented entertainers known as geisha—women highly educated in the arts of dancing, singing, playing musical instruments, and conversation—should not be confused with the *oiran* or courtesans, although most foreigners have erroneous ideas about the place of geisha in the Japan of the past and the present. They confuse geisha with prostitutes, which they are not. The Kabuki has done little to enhance the stature of the geisha—a group of women who still ply their profession—whereas the courtesan, who no longer exists as she appears in portrayals of the Edo period, has been made the central figure in many of the most compelling dramas.

The Kabuki geisha is gowned in rather subdued finery, relying on her *maru-obi* for dramatic effect (Fig. 59). This type of obi, as we have previously noted, is a broad sash made of a single piece of material, tailored and sewn at the edges and loosely tied, with the ends of the knot hanging quite low. The geisha's ordinary *kitsuke* is made of *chirimen* or of the flat silk crepe called *omeshi* and is decorated with medium-width stripes or a dappled *komon* pattern. Her *naga-juban* is of red *chirimen* and has floral-patterned *chirimen* over the collar.

The wig for the geisha is a hair-lined *habutae-tsubushi-shimada* (Fig. 206) with *ji-tabo* (natural-looking back hair), distinctive because of its flat or low *shimada mage* as contrasted with the higher *taka-shimada*. The *ji-tabo,* made of natural hair only, is dressed without the aid of a stretcher or padding and gives a rather slender, long bag effect. The *tsubushi* or low-puffed *shimada mage* is sometimes made of *kara-ke* (*kara,* foreign; *ke,* hair), in this instance curly or frizzled hair. A tortoise-shell comb and a *kanzashi* with a coral ball are placed in front of the *mage*. The root of the *mage* is tied with white *takenaga,* with two ends on each side of the knot curved gracefully upward. Variations of this hair style and the number of decorations depend upon the age and the type of geisha being portrayed.

A formally dressed geisha usually wears a *suso-moyō* kimono with a skirt patterned in the graphic design called *Edo-zuma*. The upper part of the kimono displays five family crests. The ground color may be plain black, blue, purple, or another color. The obi for formal wear is the Hakata-weave or any other woven *maru-obi*. It is tied in the long-hanging *yanagi* (willow-tree) style. The collar of the kimono may be white, light pink, pale blue, or a similar light color.

Kabuki geisha have a special way of tying their obi when they are called upon to serve guests. It is tied at the back to form a single flat, long loop—an excellent bow to wear under a coat because it is flattened to the body, whereas obi tied in protruding bows tend to make the wearer look hunchbacked when she wears an outer garment over her kimono. One should note, however, that to the Japanese this "disfigurement" presents no aesthetic problem and is an accepted style.

## COURTESAN COSTUMES

The ceremonial or formal dress of the *oiran*—or *yūjo* or *keisei,* as she is otherwise known—is an accurate reflection of the costume of courtesans during the Bunka-Bunsei era of 1804–30, when the kimono were splendid, costly affairs, lushly embroidered and riotous with color. These incredible robes, obtrusively ornate yet strangely regal, are really stunning: a bit of the Japanese past known to us through the ukiyo-e of Moronobu, Utamaro, Kunisada, and others among the woodblock-print artists; through the yearly courtesan procession in Shimabara, Kyoto; and through display on the Kabuki stage.

The dress of the Kabuki *oiran* does not vary between *jidai-mono* and *sewa-mono.* The only difference lies in whether the *onnagata* is appearing in a Kamigata or an Edo play.

The most flamboyant Edo *oiran* in Kabuki repertoire is Agemaki, the heroine of *Sukeroku Yukari no Edo-Zakura,* one of the two most popular plays among the Jūhachiban—the eighteen plays of the Ichikawa family—since it first appeared in 1713. Agemaki is a *tayū,* a courtesan of the top rank.

The Agemaki costume (Fig. 60) has always been elaborate and is certainly one of the most costly. It reached its present stage of extravagant ornateness during the Bunka-Bunsei era and is so voluminous that the *oiran,* when out strolling in a courtesan procession, has to be assisted by a *wakaimono*—a male servant attached to a brothel—on whose shoulder she leans from the height of her foot-high clogs. (In actual Yoshiwara processions, two *wakaimono* assisted each courtesan, one on each side.) J. E. De-Becker, in *The Nightless City,* writes: "The sight of a lovely and bewitching *yūjo* clad in rich silk brocades glittering with gold and polychromatic tints; of her wonderful pyramidal coiffure ornamented with numerous tortoise-shell and coral hairpins so closely thrust together as to suggest a halo of light encircling her head; and her stately graceful movements as she swept slowly and majestically through the Naka-no-chō, must indeed have appeared magnificent and awe-inspiring to the uninitiated."

For her initial appearance, Agemaki is bedizened in a rich red *kitsuke* with a cherry-blossom pattern, worn over white undergarments. Her long, loose coat—the *shikake* or *uchikake*—has a black ground over which the auspicious *shō-chiku-bai* (pine, bamboo, and plum blossoms) combination, the most used design in Japanese history, is embroidered in dark and emerald greens and deep pinks stitched with gold, silver, and varicolored silk threads. The hems of the outer garments are thickly wadded with batting, extra rows being attached to the inside hems to give the impression of additional garments.

Naturally, all Kabuki *oiran* do not wear *uchikake* with the same design. Often striking patterns of a golden dragon and clouds with flashes of lightning, raging lions with peonies and butterflies, landscapes, flying birds, and innumerable other decorations beguile the viewers.

As ornate as the *uchikake* is, it is the unusual spectacularly embroidered satin *manaita* obi worn by the Edo *oiran* that makes this costume stand out beyond all others. This gigantic sash, wider than the normal wide obi, is tied high in front, its folds falling almost to the ground and completely covering the front of the costume. The entire expanse of the obi is covered with fanciful appliqué patterns superimposed with what Helen Gunsaulus, in her *Japanese Textiles,* describes as "untwisted silk threads generally laid in long, soft stitches which are overlaid with weblike filaments crossing one another on the diagonal."

Agemaki's wig is the *habutae-maru-tabo-no-hyōgo-mage* (Fig. 204), popularly called *date-hyōgo* or *date-keisei* (*date,* dandified, gaudy, full-dress; *keisei,* courtesan), the unique feature of which is the enormous *mage* made of yak hair. It is a large, rather flat, globular *mage* with a wide division in the center, particularly referred to as the *shaguma* (literally bear's fur). The *mage* extends high above the head. The Agemaki wig is said to be the heaviest of the *onnagata* wigs. To make it even only a trifle lighter, the *nakazashi,* a long, usually plain-lacquered square-sided bar that passes through the root of the *mage,* is made of paper covered with thin pieces of tortoise shell.

Other hair ornaments adorning Agemaki's wig are twelve tortoiseshell hairpins shaped like the bridge of the *koto* or Japanese harp, six placed at the front and six at the back. Two large *tate-zashi* (*tate,* standing upright; *sashi,* thrust in) hairpins of pine-needle shape are placed in front on the left side and two with red coral balls are inserted in front on the right side. Three combs are overlapped in front of the *mage,* while the above-noted *nakazashi* passes through its root. Completing the coiffure is a gold braided cord tied in what is known as *agemaki* style: a three-loop tie with two tassels looking vaguely like a harness hitch knot. This is attached to the back of the globular-shaped *mage.* Shiratama, another courtesan in *Sukeroku,* wears an identical coiffure except that the thick gold braided cord is tied in a chrysanthemum knot, similar to the loose lanyard knot.

For the courtesan procession, the *oiran* has to raise her skirts and tie them up for easier walking. This allows the audience to see her bare whitepainted feet in tall black-lacquered *geta.* A bundle of white paper, folded once, is slipped under the collar of the *kitsuke* above breast level. This is the previously noted paper that has so many uses on the stage as handkerchiefs, wiping cloths, and the like. A folded bundle of paper is part of the apparel for many Kabuki roles.

The *oiran* of Edo, unlike their Kamigata sisters, appear mostly in the proper *heyagi* (*heya,* room; *ki,* clothes, dress) style of kimono called *dōnuki* (*dō,* trunk; *nuki,* skipping, changed) when entertaining their guests (Fig. 61). *Dōnuki* are specially tailored kimono with upper and lower parts made of different cloth.

Komurasaki, in *Hiyoku no Chō Yume no Yoshiwara,* wears a red *dōnuki*-style *kitsuke* with a brown-striped Hakata-weave obi tied in *hasami-musubi* (*hasami,* inserted between) style: a plain overlooped bow about the same width as the obi with the ends drawn through the inside, barely showing on one side. Over the *kitsuke* is worn an *uchikake* with an allover design of haze and plum trees on a purple ground and a collar of purple satin stitched along the edges with white thread that looks exactly like long basting stitches. Without exception, this type of *uchikake* has a stitched collar. The wig is a *maru-tabo-no-tsubushi-shimada:* stretched back hair with *mage* in low bouffant style and decorated with red cloth (Fig. 205).

It is customary for the *oiran* to turn back the vertical hems of their *uchikake* and *kitsuke,* graduating the opening from the obi to the bottom of the garments to allow a glimpse of their beautiful *naga-juban.*

The *oiran* in Kamigata plays are often confused with geisha because of the similarity of dress of the two professions. Exhibiting the essential characteristics of Kamigata *oiran* dress is the courtesan Kinokuniya Koharu in the "Kamiji" scene of *Shinju Ten no Amijima.* She wears a *suso-moyō kitsuke* of black *chirimen* with a skirt design of a winding stream and sprays of plum blossoms and with the usual five crests on the upper part. The lining of the lower part of the kimono has the same design as the surface, so that when the vertical hem is folded back there is complete harmony of color and design. The underwear is light-pink *chirimen* without pattern, but the *juban* is red *chirimen* with a collar cover of white *habutae* decorated with red chrysanthemums. The *suso-yoke* or outer loincloth is red *chirimen* and the *yumoji* or inner loincloth of the same material in white.

Koharu wears a stunning *maru-obi* worked with woven patterns of cut bamboo, plum blossoms, and chrysanthemums. Her wig is a *maru-tabo-no-tsubushi-shimada-mage*—that is, with low stretched back hair and a *mage* in low bouffant *shimada* style—and has a skein of white silk yarn adorning the *mage.*

The summer costume of a Kamigata *oiran* may be made of *ro,* a silk gauze with vertical or horizontal stripes of open weave, of purple color shading to brownish white toward the lower part and patterned with pink begonias and a flowing stream. The five crests are the *ura-ume:* plum blossoms viewed from the back. The *juban* is quite different, with the middle made of red ramie, the sleeves and the back of the collar of red *chirimen,* and the front of the collar of white *ro.*

The *obi-age* (the cord tied over the obi), as well as the *yumoji,* is of red *chirimen.* The obi itself is a woven *maru-obi* and has a design combining white chrysanthemums with *shikishi,* square colored sheets of paper of the type used for writing poems, against a brownish off-white ground.

During the hours of receiving guests, the Kabuki courtesans have the custom of changing their garments at least once, and the Kamigata-style courtesan may reappear in a white cotton crepe *yukata* with a *chūgata* (medium-sized) pattern. Adding a bit of spice to the costume will be a *shigoki* (soft crepe sash) of light yellowish-green *chirimen.*

## AKUBA COSTUMES

A rather interesting Kabuki role is that of the *akuba* or wicked woman, whose name derives from the words for "bad" *(aku)* and "old woman" *(ba)*. The Kabuki *akuba*, however, is not necessarily an old woman, nor is she a prostitute, but simply a wicked woman of more or less middle age. The costumes of the *akuba* are substantially the same in style (Fig. 62). The *kitsuke* is patterned with small blue oblong checks in the design known as *Benkei-gōshi* and has black satin sewn over the collar. The *yumoji* is of light-blue *chirimen*. Tied high in front is a woven plaid obi with short hanging loops. The *akuba* also often wears the short *hanten* (coat) with a white splashed design on a medium-blue ground and a collar and lining of black satin.

Somewhere on her person, often thrown loosely over one shoulder, the *akuba* carries a *tenugui* in the polka-dot pattern known as *mameshibori*. The wig is the *habutae-no-uma-no-shippo* in *tosaka* or cockscomb style (Fig. 212). The forelocks are cut short and parted in the middle, combed to the side, and curved forward. The *uma-no-shippo mage*, as we have noted earlier, is a *mage* resembling a horse's tied-up tail. As in most roles, the hair style may vary slightly in accordance with the character portrayed.

CHAPTER 14

# Armor and Battle Costumes

Genuine battle armor—*yoroi*—and that of classical Kabuki differ primarily because the use of real armor or copies of it on the stage was forbidden by law. This must have been quite a lucky circumstance for the costumers, since during the century of civil war from about 1490 to about 1600 there were many hasty changes in real-life armor and its appurtenances, with practically every warrior contriving new devices to attract attention and even changing the entire style or form of his armor at will.

During the twelfth century, in the last years of the Heian period, the three fundamental types of *yoroi* had completed their development. These were the *ō-yoroi* (a type of scale armor hanging from the shoulders and coming over the hips) and the *dōmaru* and *haramaki* (types of scale cuirass opening either at the right side or at the back and tied at the waist). In each case, the armor was composed of platelets of lacquered metal or leather called *sane* or *kozane* (small *sane*)—sometimes a combination of both. The color of the lacquered *sane* was generally black, but in the fifteenth century, following the Muromachi period, there appeared armor made of gold or silver or vermilion-lacquered *sane*. It is evident that Kabuki *yoroi* has much more in common with the *yoroi* of these earlier periods than with that of the Edo period, even though the long bow and arrows frequently carried in earlier times by the *bushi* (warriors) are rarely part of the theatrical accouterment of the warrior in *jidai-mono*.

The *hitatare,* which we have already noted among the special costumes described in Chapter 10, was worn directly under the *yoroi.* As a rule, the most luxurious materials—*nishiki,* ramie, plain silk, or damask—went into the making of the *yoroi-hitatare.* Warriors going into battle were attired in their best apparel, since the day of combat might well be their last. For special occasions, it was the custom of gentlemen of the old Kyoto court to whiten their faces and blacken their teeth, since such make-up was thought to enhance their looks, and noblemen going into battle did like-

203

wise, for a lasting impression of refinement and dignity meant much, even in death. In *Ichinotani Futaba Gunki* the playwright speaks of Atsumori's "deeply dyed teeth and slightly whitened face." A similar reference may be found in the original *Heike Monogatari,* from which this drama takes its story, and in *Gempei Seisuiki.*

Women often washed and groomed the severed heads of the dead enemy, combing the hair and painting the teeth black—this last touch for the purpose of making the heads appear to be those of generals. So we are told in the *Okiku Monogatari* (Tale of Okiku), written in early Edo days by an elderly woman named Okiku who had served the defeated lord of Ōmi Province. Such heads, now supposedly those of more important persons, were then presented to the daimyō as the rich spoils of war. Abhorrent as the practice may seem, such gruesome scenes of the washing and grooming of enemy heads are realistically enacted in a few of the historical dramas.

Kabuki *yoroi* (Fig. 63) is a corselet of armor composed of a multiplicity of small metal or leather pieces firmly fastened together with threads of silk or strips of leather. Some seventy or eighty variations of armor have been created, and their splendor lends touches of brilliance to otherwise somber scenes on the stage.

*Yoroi* is the apparel of generals or warriors of high rank, and the color clearly defines the type of role. Young generals are conspicuous in red, although a few individualists like the youthful Yoshitsune may wear armor of purple or red. Purple belongs exclusively to the domain of the generals.

Armor used in Kabuki is rarely made to order but is generally of two ready-made types: adult and juvenile. There may, however, be the exception of a leading actor's having armor made to order, as did the late Matsumoto Kōshirō VII some years ago. Because of his advanced age, he ordered a lightweight *ō-yoroi* in *shiroito odoshi* (white plaited design) for his role as the hero in the dance-drama *Chūsei* (Loyal Spirit).

It is not unusual to see Kabuki *wakashu* in full battle regalia—for instance, Koshirō in *Ōmi Genji Senjin Yakata.* Nor was it uncommon in real life for boys to go into battle at an early age. Minamoto no Yoritomo, elder brother of Yoshitsune, had his first taste of warfare at the age of eleven or twelve.

Although *onnagata* may be arrayed for battle in Kabuki in what appears to be a woman's special war costume, such a costume does not exist on the stage, nor did it exist in history, since fighting women wore the battle dress of men. It is said that during the Kamakura period there were exceptionally strong women, like Tomoe Gozen of Kabuki fame, who did go into battle, but their garb was that of men, although the feminine figure and headdress tended to give the attire a womanly appearance. In the "Moritsuna Jinya" scene of *Ōmi Genji Senjin Yakata,* Koshirō's mother Kagaribi appears ready for battle, but she is actually disguised as a soldier in order to help her son escape from captivity.

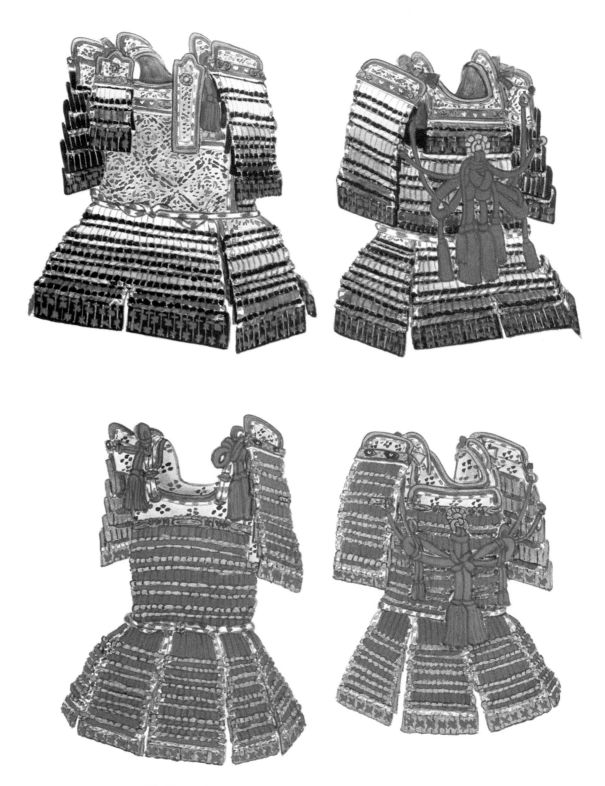

63. Two styles of armor (front and back views). Kabuki *yoroi* (armor) is a skirted corselet composed of a multiplicity of small metal or leather pieces firmly fastened together with silk thread or leather strips. It is the apparel of generals or warriors of high rank.

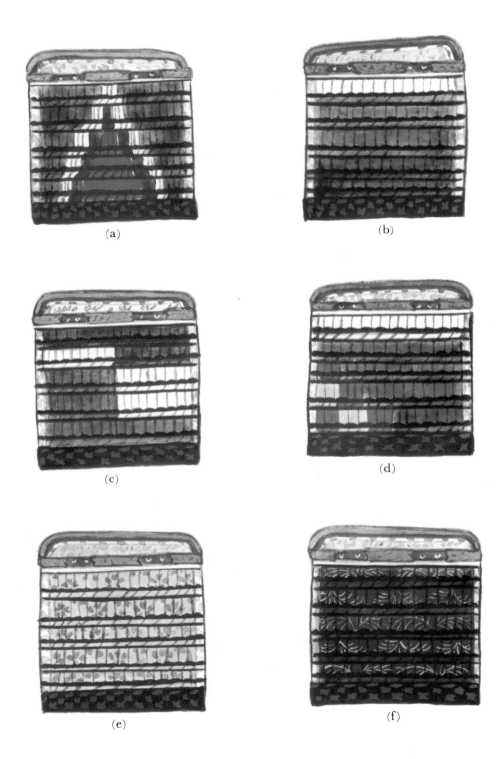

(a)

(b)

(c)

(d)

(e)

(f)

64. *Odoshi:* styles of armor lacing. The decorative patterns of Kabuki armor, formed by the lacing of the small plates, are extremely varied. Six are shown here: (a) *omodaka odoshi*, (b) *unohana odoshi*, (c) *kommurago odoshi*, (d) *tsumadori odoshi*, (e) *kozakura odoshi*, (f) *shidagawa odoshi*.

65. *Yoroi* and *jimbaori:* Yoshitsune in the "Kumagai Jinya" scene of *Ichinotani Futaba Gunki.* Yoshitsune's elaborate battle costume features armor worn over a gorgeously patterned *hitatare* and surmounted by the camp coat known as *jimbaori.* Accessories include *kegutsu* (fur boots), a *hachimaki* (headband with a gold decoration), and a *saihai* (baton of command).

66. *Wakashu yoroi:* Jūjirō in *Ehon Taikō-ki.* Young warriors of high rank usually appear in armor of brilliant red worn over a *hitatare* of luxurious material and flamboyant color and design. Jūjirō's helmet has the typical *kuwagata*, the horn-shaped crest that distinguishes the ranking warrior.

## YOROI DESIGNS

The decorative patterns of Kabuki armor are so varied as to deserve special note. The lacing or braiding of colored silk thread or leather thongs forms *odoshi,* the singular inwrought designs of the armor, depicting plants, vegetables, and other objects. Several of the well-known patterns (Fig. 64) are the *omodaka odoshi,* the *unohana odoshi,* the *kommurago odoshi,* and the *tsumadori odoshi.* Stylizing the arrow-head-shaped leaf of the *omodaka* (water plantain) plant that grows so abundantly in Japanese swamplands, the *omodaka odoshi* has a background of green with the leaf pattern in red and purple outlined in white, the lacing of silk only. The *unohana odoshi* stylizes the white flowers of the deutzia shrub, the upper ranks of the *sane* (platelets) laced with white and the remaining ranks with green. Another variation is the design known as *kommurago odoshi,* which forms a rectilinear pattern in blue and white. *Tsumadori odoshi* employs a design of a half pyramid of several colors against a background of green.

If the pattern is not formed by the lacing process of *odoshi,* it will be formed by *odoshige* or *odoshi-ito* (*ke,* hair; *ito,* thread)—that is, stencil-dyed designs mostly on leather, such as *kozakura odoshi,* a design laced with leather on which are applied stencils of cherry blossoms, and *shidagawa odoshi,* in which the leather is printed with a pattern of fern fronds.

## MODE OF DRESSING FOR BATTLE

The order in which Kabuki generals and high-ranking samurai put on their combat apparel is of interest, as are the various accessories that complete the costumes (Fig. 65). First come the usual undergarments, over which goes either the *yoroi-shita* (garment under the armor) or the *hitatare.* The next item to be donned is the *ōguchi-bakama,* the wide pleated culottes that we have already noted in Chapter 10. The bottom of the battle *ōguchi* is wide, hangs loosely, and is not tied as in the case of the general's ceremonial *sashinuki-bakama* (pantaloon-type trousers). The length of the *ōguchi-bakama* may appear short, but the garment is no shorter than the normal *hakama.* However, when it is put on, the stiff piece at the belt line in back is folded to the inside, giving the *ōguchi* the appearance of being shorter in back.

Next the actor puts on the metal arm guards called *kote* and under them slips the *yugake,* a pair of leather gloves or gauntlets that reach halfway to the elbows and are tied securely at the wrists. To the audience, the *yugake* appear to be made of figured cloth, but this is an illusion projected by stencil dyeing on leather.

The *hiza-yoroi* (*hiza,* knees) follows. This is a belted two-piece armor resembling an apron split in the center, so that each flap extends from waist to knee level. The *yoroi* itself—that is, the corselet or armor cloak— is drawn over the head and fastened at the shoulder. Since buttons are seldom used, the fastener in this case is the combination of *tombo-gashira* (dragonfly head) and *ukeo* (catching loop or string)—in other words the frog that is often seen on Chinese costume. The *yoroi* is composed of four main sections. The first two of these, the *mete-no-sode* (right-arm sleeve) and the *yunde-no-sode* (left-arm sleeve) are worn over the "horse-hand shoulder" and the "bow-hand shoulder" respectively. They are adjusted to permit a view of the elegant sleeves of the *hitatare* puffed out above the arm guards. The *dō* section of the *yoroi*—the corselet proper—covers the trunk. The fourth section, known as the *hachiken kusazuri,* is a skirt of eight plaited sections just long enough to graze the top of high grass as the warrior walks through it.

The top section of the corselet is gold-plated metal. Directly below it are several inches of leather patterned by stencil dyeing and contrasting in color with the remainder of the armor. The back of the *dō* is probably the most resplendent part of the armor, for it is ornamented with an elaborate knot formed by the tying of the long braided silk cords attached to the above-described shoulder pieces and brought around from the front to be caught in a metal ring between the shoulder blades. A white obi of cotton, plain silk, or crepe is fastened around the waist.

A *jimbaori* or sleeveless battle coat is worn over the armor. It is split about halfway up the back to allow the warrior's swords to protrude. Although it is quite a handsome garment, it is not usually worn in the Kabuki during scenes where swift action is necessary. Generals, however, have less cause to move about than do their subordinates; so they frequently appear in *jimbaori*. On real battlefields, it seems, the *jimbaori* was worn not only by generals but also by their subordinates—even their footmen, so that swift or slow action had nothing to do with the matter. There are exceptions, of course, to the rule that the *jimbaori* is not worn in Kabuki battle scenes. For instance, Hayami no Tōta, the cowardly and comical chief of Yoritomo's pursuers of Tadanobu and Shizuka Gozen in the "Michiyuki Hatsune no Tabiji" scene of *Yoshitsune Sembon-Zakura,* wears a *jimbaori,* although this scene can hardly be called a scene of battle.

The *hakimono* or footgear worn with armor is put on over *tabi.* The samurai's feet are covered with leather *tabi* stencil-dyed in such patterns as the *tomoe* (a whirl pattern of circular shape formed of two or three figures resembling large commas), *kozakura* (small cherry blossoms), *kachimushi* (dragonfly), and *arare* (hailstones or dots). Stage warriors always wear *tabi* indoors.

Only generals may wear the *kegutsu,* low boot-shaped shoes of bearskin with eyelets on the sides through which leather thongs or silk cords are drawn to fasten around the ankles (Fig. 250). *Waraji* or straw sandals, however, are standard footgear for all ranks, including generals, since they are considered to accentuate the strength of the portrayal. General Kumagai, for example, wears *waraji*. But stage *waraji* (Fig. 250) are made of cloth rather than straw and are called *kire-waraji* or *nuno-waraji* (both prefixes mean cloth). The cloth is dyed yellow in order to make it look like straw.

Certain accessories—not the least of which are his helmet and his weapons—are part of the warrior's costume. There is, for example, the *saihai* or baton of command, an eleven-inch wooden rod lacquered black or red, to which is attached a long duster made of strips of thick paper slightly less than an inch wide and about a foot long. It is said that there are ninety-eight strips of paper in the duster to represent the ninety-eight thousand gods of war. A *saihai* with a gold duster instead of a white one is wielded only by a daimyō or a general, although a soldier who has excelled in combat may have the privilege of carrying one with a red or a white duster. The chief purpose of the *saihai* is to direct troops in battle, but it is also symbolic of rank, as is another of the warrior's accessories, the *jin-sen* or camp fan. This, in its Kabuki version, has painted outer wooden ribs to make it look like the real-life iron *gun-sen* or battle fan (Fig. 157). Two swords, one long and one short, are always a part of the accouterment of military men, regardless of their rank.

The daimyō's headgear is the *kuwagata-tsuki hikitate eboshi*, the regular tall hat, curved back and downward, with an attached *hachimaki* or headband to which has been added the erect gold *kuwagata*, the horn- or hoe-shaped crest that distinguishes the front of the warrior's headgear.

The *kabuto-no-Hachiman-za* (*kabuto*, helmet; Hachiman, god of war; *za*, seat), the round ornamentation at the very top center of the crown, is considered the seat of the war god Hachiman, and thus sacred. For this reason, one should never put his fingers on this portion of the helmet, nor should the helmet ever be placed upside down on this "seat."

Helmets are rarely worn in Tokyo Kabuki but are carried in the hand, since otherwise they would hide the handsome features of the actors. Atsumori wears a helmet in the "Suma-no-Ura" scene of *Ichinotani Futaba Gunki*, as does Kumagai, but only briefly. However, helmets are worn in plays produced in the Kansai district—for example by Jūjirō in Act X (in the "Amagasaki" scene) of *Ehon Taikō-ki*.

The *hachimaki* for battle wear has a gold decoration called the *hachigane* (*hachi*, crown of the head; *kane*, metal) sewn to the part that covers the forehead to help protect the head. This type of headgear is used mostly by generals.

## WARRIORS' WIGS

The standard wig for wear with armor either has the *mage* in the *bō-chasen* or tea-whisk style or has it untied and disheveled to indicate previous participation in combat. There are varying styles of these warrior wigs, and several of them are distinctive enough for mention here.

The first of these is the *aburatsuki-naimaze-orikake-bin-chūdachi-no-bō-chasen-mage*, with *chirichiri* (curly hair) and a *mage* tied with a lace plaited in *hotaru* (firefly) fashion. The sidelocks, coated with lacquer, are made with mixed curly and straight hair. They are inflated and combed slightly loosely and attached to the root of the *mage*. A *hachimaki* with *hachigane* (as described above) is worn around the head. This is the wig worn by Yoshitsune in the "Jinya" scene of *Ichinotani Futaba Gunki* and the "Tokaiya" scene of *Yoshitsune Sembon-Zakura*.

The wigs worn by the *go-chūshin* or battle messengers are also of interest. Although the role of the *go-chūshin* is a relatively small one, it is usually given to an important actor, since his stage business is quite dramatic. He always makes his entrance on the *hanamichi*, where he begins his lines with the exclamation "Go-chūshin! Go-chūshin!" (equivalent to "Now hear this" or "Hear ye! Hear ye!"). He relates the proceedings of the battle and at the same time tries to prove his faith to his lord by telling of the experiences the latter is having in battle.

The *go-chūshin* wears either the *aburatsuki-naimaze-orikake-bin-no-happō-ware* with *sara-no-matsuri* or the *mizu-iri* wig.

The first of these has the back hair lacquered, pressed to the head, and polished. The lacquered sidelocks are of mixed curly and straight hair, and the *mage* is divided in eight directions *(happō-ware)*. The *sara-no-matsuri*—hanging short hair resembling the paper decorations at Shintō shrine festivals—is put on above the sidelocks in *sara* style, the natural style of washed hair without pomade. A white or reddish-yellow *hachimaki* completes the headdress.

The hair of the *mizu-iri* wig, as we have already noted in Chapter 10, hangs disheveled, an effect produced by spraying the whole wig with lacquer and hardening some of the strands to make them glossy. Although the *mizu-iri* is generally worn to indicate that the actor has been for some reason or other immersed in water, it is also worn by battle messengers to show that they have been in combat. Still, even those messengers who are on their way to battle wear the *mizu-iri*. A wounded battle messenger, incidentally, is very rare in Kabuki.

## DAIMYŌ BATTLE DRESS

The war costume of the daimyō is sufficiently different that his status is readily grasped by the audience. No longer do we see a full coat of armor over the *hitatare*. The daimyō wears a dark-colored *daimon* (described in Chapter 10), usually purple or black, over the *yoroi* to signify his authority, but since merely an illusion of the armor underneath is enough to give the effect of the whole, only parts of it, such as arm guards and breastplate, are evident under the *daimon*. For historical authenticity, the *munahimo* or breast tie of the *daimon* should be knotted in front, but this is not generally done in Kabuki. Instead, it is tucked into the *hakama* belt in the manner of Nō costumes. The wide-mouthed sleeves of the *daimon* are pulled up to permit greater freedom of movement.

The daimyō, as noted earlier in this chapter, wears the *kuwagata-tsuki hikitate eboshi*—the regular tall, down-curved hat with attached *hachimaki* to which has been added the gold horn-shaped *kuwagata*. Over leather *tabi,* he wears a high version of the bearskin boots called *kegutsu,* in this case called *jōmegutsu:* step-in fur boots without ties (Fig. 250). A gold *saihai* and a set of swords complete his costume. He does not wear a *jimbaori.*

## YOUNG WARRIOR BATTLE DRESS

The young warrior of good family wears the red-laced armor called *hi odoshi* or *akaito odoshi,* its vibrant color accentuating his youthfulness (Fig. 66). Under the armor are a magnificently brocaded *hitatare* and *kukuri-bakama,* the culottes that are normally tied at the ankles in harem style. In this case, the culottes are pulled up and tied just below the knees on top of the *sune-ate* or protective greaves. Similarly, the sleeves are pushed up and tightened with their own tasseled ties, which form swinging bowknots just above the *kote* or gauntlets.

The customary accessories are part of this battle garb, except that the *jimbaori* is not usually worn, since it would inhibit the movements of youthful warriors who are always eager to be in the center of the combat. Jū-jirō, however, in one scene of *Ehon Taikō-ki,* does wear a *jimbaori.*

## OTHER BATTLE COSTUMES

Lower-ranking samurai or the *gumpyō* (troops) do not wear a defensive covering for the body but have instead a wadded cotton coat and *tattsuke-bakama,* the trousers with lower parts resembling tight leggings. The color of the coat is persimmon or black. Taking its name from the wearer, this two-piece costume is known as the *gumpyō.*

The common soldier ties a white *mukō hachimaki* (*mukō,* front) or a black *ushiro hachimaki* (*ushiro,* back, rear) at the front of his head with a small flat bow, without the adornment of a *hachigane.* Or he may wear the pyramid-shaped hat called the *jin-gasa.*

CHAPTER 15

# Costume Patterns and Color

Regardless of the genre of the drama, the color, contour, and textile patterns of the costumes customarily have definite significance and generally designate class, various notable traits, or the age of the depicted character. Traditions in design and color were established when an actor made a role famous by wearing a specific costume. The costume was then set for all subsequent actors who essayed the role, especially for those bearing the family name of a great actor. A role might have been played many times in costumes of different colors and designs until the one performance seemed perfect. After that, the entire *kata* for the role was set and followed exactly. Members of the actor's family (also adopted members) reproduced the costumes exactly in color and design. Rival acting families might vary the costumes slightly, but the audiences demanded a minimum of change. The faithfulness of the reproduction of costumes was an important criterion in determining the success of the play.

In principle, the costumes for classical dramas are standard, having become established by late Edo, although those for such plays as *Shibaraku, Sukeroku,* and *Asahina* were set before that time. Even in these three plays, however, in exceptional instances, a leading actor has requested alteration of costumes to accommodate his peculiar physical traits or to heighten his interpretation of a role. Occasionally a leading actor has requested minor players to modify their costumes to harmonize with the changes in his. Minor players, on the other hand, could not make changes in their costumes on their own account. Traditions about costumes remain unchanged today.

After the Meiji Restoration in 1868, the costumes of Kabuki actors had little or no influence on the attire of the people, who were by then more interested in European trends in dress. At this time, many phases of life in Japan were in a state of flux. Even Kabuki was affected. Under the influence of scholars and artists who had traveled abroad, Danjūrō IX was

215

moved to make Kabuki dramas and costumes more realistic. Today noted painters and scholars are still regularly asked for advice about costumes and often make critical studies on costumes and their authenticity.

Kubota Beisai, a versatile painter and a designer of textiles and stage sets, after making a study of the dress of the period in which the play was set, sketched all the costumes for *Kiri Hitoha* (A Paulownia Leaf), a play written by Tsubouchi Shōyō in 1894. Kubota did not let authenticity overshadow audience appeal, nor did he forget the intrinsic beauty of Kabuki.

Torii Kiyotada, a painter and head of the Torii school of painting, collaborated with Sadanji II in reviving old plays and designed from old pictures the entire complement of costumes for such plays as *Kenuki* (Tweezers) and *Narukami*. Torii's costumes were also featured in the revival of *Kagekiyo,* which takes its name from its hero, a valiant Heike general of the thirteenth century.

Seki Yasunosuke, painter and eminent scholar, felt that Kabuki dramas defrauded the public because costumes and hand properties were not true to life. He was prevailed upon to make a historical investigation of the apparel of early Heian days, and on the basis of this study he created the costumes for *Nichiren Tsuji Seppō* (Nichiren Preaching at the Crossroads) and for *Ikutagawa,* a Kabuki *buyō* or dance.

Among contemporary designers of costumes for new plays are Komura Settai, painter and set designer; Maeda Seison, painter and patron of Danjūrō XI; Yasuda Yukihiko, who designed a number of costumes for the late Kichiemon; and Matsuoka Eikyū. All were professional painters of note who specialized in historical paintings before they were called upon by the Kabuki management to try their hand at costume designing.

Despite all these efforts to achieve authenticity, the costumes for new dramas are not standard. The costumes worn on the second day of a performance are not always identical with those worn on opening day, for the actor, management, and playwright are free to improve or change a costume. There is, however, much less originality than might be expected with all this freedom, and costumes tend to remain faithful merely to the apparel of the period in which the play is set.

## STANDARD COSTUME DESIGNS

The middle Edo period found kimono patterns leaning toward "picturesque freedom which culminated in huge designs splashed across the shoulder and diagonally down the back," as Yamanobe Tomoyuki expresses it in his *Textiles* (Arts and Crafts of Japan series). The highly decorated kimono made lively use of sparrows, plum and cherry blossoms, chrysanthemums, and the like. These were followed by patterns of more complicated meaning: those which suggested romantic stories or anything that captured the popular fancy—even comical conceptions—or were related to traditional art motifs. Prime examples of such meaningful

67. *Aragoto* costume: Matsuō-maru in *Sugawara Denju Tenarai Kagami*. The *atsuwata* worn by Matsuō-maru is patterned with pine branches *(matsu)* in reflection of both his name and his stalwart character.

217

68. *Aragoto* costume: Umeō-maru in *Sugawara Denju Tenarai Kagami*. Umeō-maru's *atsuwata*, like that of his brother Matsuō-maru, reflects his name and his bold character. In this case, the design is of plum blossoms *(ume)*, symbolizing courage and hardiness.

69. *Aragoto* costume: Sakura-maru in *Sugawara Denju Tenarai Kagami*. Again, as in the case of the costumes worn by his brothers Matsuō-maru and Umeō-maru, the *atsuwata* worn by Sakura-maru is a reflection of name and character, but the cherry blossoms *(sakura)* in this case suggest a more gentle and somewhat effeminate character.

218

70. *Danshichi-gōshi.* This white-and-rust textile pattern takes its name from the role of Danshichi Kurobei in *Natsu Matsuri Naniwa no Kagami* and from the word *kōshi,* meaning checkered or cross-barred.

71. *Dōji-gōshi.* This checkered pattern, almost identical with *Danshichi-gōshi,* alternates purple and white squares.

patterns are a kimono design depicting the famous eight views along the shores of Lake Biwa (Ōmi Hakkei) and another showing, with subtle humor, a bee stinging a deer's antler.

In every play based on the famous story of how the Soga brothers avenged their father's death, the elder brother Jūrō's costume is patterned with the *chidori* (plover) and the younger brother Gorō's with the *chō* (butterfly). Legend has it that when the brothers succeeded in avenging their father they wore *hitatare* emblazoned with these designs.

*Danshichi-gōshi,* which takes its name from a Kabuki role and from the word *kōshi,* meaning checkered or cross-barred, is a white-and-rust checkered pattern (Fig. 70). It was used in the puppet theater before it was adopted for Kabuki, where it continues to be the pattern of the costume for the role of Danshichi Kurobei in *Natsu Matsuri Naniwa no Kagami.* An almost identical pattern, the *dōji-gōshi* that we have noted in Chapter 2 as used by Danjūrō I, alternates purple and white squares (Fig. 71). *Benkei-gōshi,* a black-and-white checkered pattern introduced by Kōshirō V, closely resembles *Danshichi-gōshi,* but the checks are formed of perpendicular oblongs. Various reasons have been given for the introduction of this new pattern, but it is generally thought that the purpose of using oblongs rather than squares was to make the actor look taller and more sleek. *Benkei-gōshi* is worn by Igami no Gonta in *Yoshitsune Sembon-Zakura.*

Kikugorō III created the pattern known as *Kikugorō-gōshi:* a cross-barred design in which heavier lines form the main squares and lighter

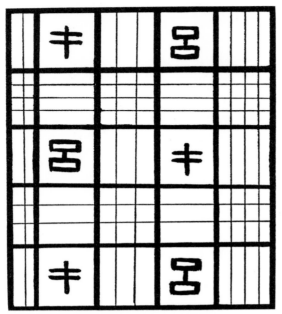

72. *Kikugorō-gōshi*. In this cross-barred pattern, created by Kikugorō III, heavier lines form the main squares and lighter lines run through every other vertical and horizontal stripe bounded by the heavier ones, with the characters *ki* and *ro* (a play on the name Kikugorō) alternating in the center of the plain squares.

73. *Rokuyata-gōshi* or *mimasu tsunagi*. This pattern of linked *mimasu*—the three concentric squares forming the crest of the Ichikawa family of actors—was the favorite of Danjūrō VII for the role of Okabe no Rokuyata in *Ichinotani Mushae no Iezuto*.

lines run through every other vertical and horizontal stripe bounded by the heavier ones, with the characters *ki* and *ro* (a play on the name Kikugorō) alternating in the center of the plain squares (Fig. 72). This pattern was a familiar sight on the streets of Edo during the time of Kikugorō III.

The *rokuyata-gōshi* or *mimasu tsunagi* (Fig. 73), a pattern of linked *mimasu*—the three concentric squares that we noted earlier as the crest of the Ichikawa family of actors—was the favorite of Danjūrō VII for the role of Okabe no Rokuyata in *Ichinotani Mushae no Iezuto* (Souvenir Pictures of Warriors at the Battle of Ichinotani). This handsome, much admired, but very quiet actor deserves a word of mention, for he was the recipient of an uncommon honor for a Kabuki actor. The shogunate, in recognition of his deep filial piety, conferred an award upon him. (The late Ichikawa Danjūrō XI was said to bear a strong likeness to him.) It is also of interest to note that the *rokuyata-gōshi* pattern was frequently seen on the cotton *yukata* and sometimes on the kimono of Edo women of the time. Today it appears on the *kamishimo* of Arajishi Otokonosuke in *Meiboku Sendai Hagi*.

Among Danjūrō VII's finest portrayals was that of Yosaburō in *Yo wa Nasake Ukina no Yokogushi*. For this role he was attired in a kimono pat-

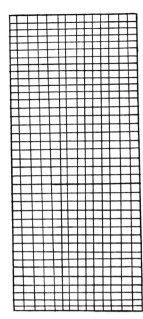

74. *Ai-mijin* or *mijin-jima*. Among Danjūrō VII's finest portrayals was that of Yosaburō in *Yo wa Nasake Ukina no Yokogushi,* for which he was attired in a kimono patterned with the small blue-and-white check called *ai-mijin.*

75. *Hikosaburō-gōshi* or *hikoza-gōshi.* The late-Edo actor Bandō Hikosaburō IV formulated this design from his own name. The *sabu* (from *san,* three)— actually three-line stripes—cross on the diagonal to form large diamond-shaped spaces which enclose the interlocking *katakana* characters for *hi* and *ko.*

terned with a small blue-and-white check—a style immediately appropriated by the younger set for daily dress. Though the Yosaburō costume is essentially the same today, the size of the checks was enlarged by Ichimura Uzaemon XV, presumably for the same reason that the squares of the above noted *Benkei-gōshi* were elongated. The Uzaemon kimono is referred to as *ai-Benkei* (*ai,* indigo; Benkei, name of role), since it was adapted from the *Benkei-gōshi* costume worn by Benkei in *Kanjinchō.* Danjūrō VII's pattern (Fig. 74) was known as the *ai-mijin* (*ai,* indigo; *mijin,* small, fine).

The *Hikosaburō-gōshi* (often abbreviated to *hikoza-gōshi*) pattern was conceived by the universally admired late-Edo actor Bandō Hikosaburō IV. *Kōshi* usually means squares formed by cross bars or horizontal and vertical stripes, but Hikosaburō very astutely formulated this design from his own name. The *sabu* (from *san,* three) lines—actually three-line stripes —cross on the diagonal to form large diamond-shaped spaces which enclose the interlocked *katakana* characters for *hi* and *ko,* creating a bold but neat allover pattern (Fig. 75).

The *yoki-koto-kiku,* another original design of Kikugorō III and one of Kabuki's most typical designs, evokes an amusing play on words. The design consists of vertical stripes in which the figure of a *yoki* (hatchet), the character for *koto* (Japanese harp), and a stylized *kiku* (chrysanthemum) are repeated in rows, each row divided from the next by plain-colored stripes (Fig. 76). The three words *yoki, koto,* and *kiku* can also mean (although the characters would be different in this case) good, thing, and hear, respectively. In combination, then, the meaning is "good thing to hear" or "good news."

The *yoki-koto-kiku* continues to be a design especially favored by the Onoe Kikugorō family. The late Kikugorō VI wore a costume in this pattern in the "Kōshisaki" scene of *Soga Moyō Tateshi no Goshozome,* and his son, Baikō VII, selects the same pattern for the roles of Otomi in *Yo wa Nasake Ukina no Yokogushi* and Okaji in *Kisen* (The Poet-Priest Kisen).

*Kumo-ni-inazuma* (*kumo,* clouds; *ni,* in; *inazuma,* lightning) is a pattern of clouds interspersed with a diagonal flash of conventionalized lightning used in the costumes of forceful characters or those who have supernatural powers (Fig. 79). It appears in the costume of the *kijo* or she-devil in the dance-drama *Modoribashi* (Modori Bridge) and that of Fuwa Banzaemon, an *aragoto* role, in *Ukiyozuka Hiyoku no Inazuma* (commonly called *Nagoya Sanza,* after its hero). The lightning design also appears on the *happi* coat of the demon in the dance-drama *Ibaraki*. Again, in a slightly altered form, it is employed for the *happi* of the female demon in *Momijigari* (The Maple Viewing). Here the design is composed of floating clouds outlined with gold, the glittering gold symbolizing the lightning.

In the above-mentioned *Nagoya Sanza,* the *ame-ni-nure-tsubame* or rain-and-wet-swallow design (Fig. 78) decorates the kimono of Nagoya Sanza in contrast with the *kumo-ni-inazuma* pattern of Fuwa Banzaemon's costume. The symbolism reflects the characters of the two men and figures importantly in their famous dialogue in the third act of the play.

The design called *unryū* or *kumo-ni-ryū* (*un, kumo,* clouds; *ryū,* dragon), with its drifting clouds and masculine dragon (Fig. 77), is reserved for roles of great strength, for, as Helen C. Gunsaulus explains in her *Japanese Textiles,* "the dragon is the most exalted symbol of the Buddhists, the operating force of nature typifying the underlying cause and the dominant power which permeates all things." It should be noted, however, that the dragon also symbolized the emperor in China. The *kumo-ni-ryū* design appears on the *yoten* costume of the hero in *dammari* (mime dramas) and on the *kamishimo* of Wada Byoe Hidemori in *Ōmi Genji Senjin Yakata*. In the latter instance, it is woven in brilliant gold on a bright red background, so that it is almost completely submerged in its own metallic radiance.

One of the earliest patterns to attain prominence was *Kodayū kanoko,* a simple allover umbrella-shaped polka-dot design produced by the tie-and-dye method called *shibori* (Fig. 80). Itō Kodayū, a mid-seventeenth-century *onnagata* of Kyoto, wore a purple *shibori* pattern for a stage appearance in Edo and made it more popular than it was in his native city, with the result that it was renamed *Edo kanoko*.

*Ichimatsu-zome* (Ichimatsu, name of an actor; *zome,* from *someru,* to dye) was originally a checkerboard *hakama* pattern of red on a white ground known as *ishidatami* (tile flooring) or *arare* (hail). In 1714, at the Nakamura-

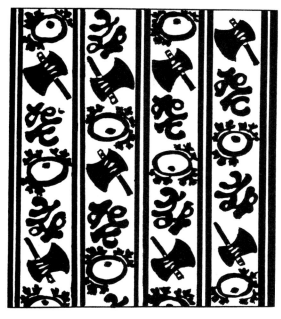

76. *Yoki-koto-kiku.* This design, another originated by Kikugorō III, evokes an amusing play on words. The vertical stripes enclose the figure of a *yoki* (hatchet), the character for *koto* (Japanese harp), and a stylized *kiku* (chrysanthemum) repeated in rows. The three words *yoki, koto,* and *kiku* also combine to mean "good thing to hear" or "good news."

77. *Unryū* or *kumo-ni-ryū.* This design, with its drifting clouds and masculine dragon, is reserved for roles of great strength. It appears on the costume of the hero in *dammari* (mime dramas) and on the *kamishimo* of Wada Byoe Hidemori in *Ōmi Genji Senjin Yakata.*

78. *Ame-ni-nure-tsubame.* In the play *Nagoya Sanza* the rain-and-wet-swallow design decorates the kimono of Nagoya Sanza and serves as a reflection of his character.

79. *Kumo-ni-inazuma.* This pattern of clouds interspersed with a diagonal flash of lightning is used in the costumes of forceful characters or those who have supernatural powers like the demon in *Modoribashi.*

80. *Kodayū kanoko* or *Edo kanoko*. One of the earliest patterns to attain prominence in Kabuki was this simple allover design produced by the tie-and-dye method called *shibori*. Originally named for Kyoto actor Itō Kodayū, who made it popular in Edo, it was later renamed *Edo kanoko*.

81. *Ichimatsu-zome*. Originally a checkerboard *hakama* pattern known as *ishidatami* (tile flooring) or *arare* (hail). This pattern takes its present name from actor Sadokawa Ichimatsu I, who used it for a kimono in one of his roles. It is seen today in various contrasting color combinations.

za in Edo, Sadokawa Ichimatsu I wore it for the part of Okoshō Kumeno-suke (the *wakashu* role of a *koshō* or page) in *Kōyasan Shinjū,* one of Chika-matsu's double-suicide plays. Today the *Ichimatsu-zome* pattern (Fig 81) may be seen in numerous contrasting color combinations, quite frequently in blue and white, purple and silver, purple and white, and black and silver.

In *Kanjinchō, Gojōbashi* (Gojō Bridge), and the "Benkei Joshi" (Benkei the Envoy) scene of *Gosho-Zakura Horikawa Youchi* (Night Attack under Cherry Blossoms at the Horikawa Imperial Palace), the hero Benkei appears in costumes patterned with the *rimbō,* a circular frame with spokes extending beyond the outer rim (Fig. 87). The design is taken from the Buddhist *rimbō,* a symbolic weapon used in rites of the Shingon sect to ward off evil spirits and beasts. The *rimbō* pattern usually appears on kimono and sometimes on *happi* but never on *hakama* in Kabuki.

Expressively designed *juban* are part of the costumes worn by Gorō and Asahina in *Kongen Kusazuri-Biki,* the earliest of a cycle of plays dealing with the Soga brothers. Both *juban* reflect the rebus designs that were popular in kimono decoration for a time during Edo. Gorō's design (Fig. 82 left), originated by Ichikawa Danjūrō VII, is composed of a *kama* (sickle), a *wa* (circle), and the *hiragana* syllable *nu,* which together make up the word *kamawanu* (I don't care). Asahina's (Fig. 82 right), originally

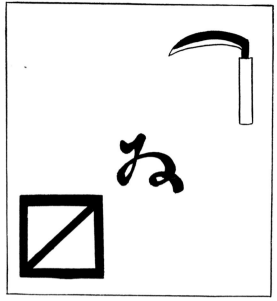

82. Two rebus designs: *kamawanu* (left) and *kamaimasu* (right). These designs, displayed on the *juban* of Gorō and Asahina in *Kongen Kusazuri-Biki*, reflect the speeches of the two characters at a climactic moment in the play. Gorō's design—a sickle *(kama)*, a circle *(wa)*, and the *hiragana* character *nu*—reads "Kamawanu" (I don't care). Asahina's—a sickle *(kama)*, the *hiragana* character *i*, and a rice measure *(masu)*—reads "Kamaimasu" (I do care).

worn by Danjūrō's disciple Ichikawa Omezō I, has a *kama,* the *hiragana* character *i,* and a *masu* (rice measure), which together read *kamaimasu* (I do care).

In the dance for which these costumes are worn, Gorō is eager to go and help his beleaguered brother Jūrō. His faithful friend Asahina tries to stop him, but Gorō exclaims: "Don't try to stop me, for I don't care what happens to me." To this, Asahina replies: "I do care." Their *juban* are revealed to the audience through the device of *hadanugi:* slipping off the upper part of the kimono and tucking it into the obi.

The *Shikan-jima* (Shikan, name of an actor; *shima,* stripe) or *kan tsunagi* is a pattern with sets of four stripes, each set separated by a row of linked drawer pulls such as those used on Japanese chests of drawers (Fig. 83). The pattern was devised by Nakamura Shikan (later Utaemon III) for actors taking male roles and wearing either *yukata* or regular kimono. Today Utaemon VI uses the *Shikan-jima* pattern for *onnagata* roles such as those of the teahouse waitress Okaji in *Kisen.*

Shikan's rival, Bandō Mitsugorō III, introduced the pattern known as *mitsu-dai-jima,* which takes its name from its use of a stylization of the character *dai* (big) in groups of three *(mitsu)* placed between rows of three closely spaced vertical stripes (Fig. 84). This pattern and the above-described *Shikan-jima* were created almost simultaneously.

83. *Shikan-jima* or *kan tsunagi*. Sets of four stripes, each set separated by a row of linked drawer pulls, compose this pattern devised by Nakamura Shikan (later Utaemon III) for actors taking male roles and wearing either *yukata* or regular kimono. Today Utaemon VI uses it for *onnagata* roles.

84. *Mitsu-dai-jima*. Introduced by Bandō Mitsugorō III, this design takes its name from its use of a stylization of the character *dai* (big) in groups of three *(mitsu)* placed between rows of three closely spaced vertical stripes.

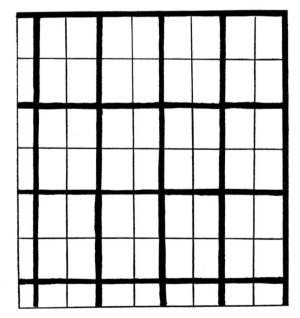

85. *Kōraiya-gōshi*, *kōraiya-jima*, or *okina-gōshi*. This pattern became a favorite following its introduction by Kōshirō V. It consists of white stripes forming squares on a rust ground, with alternate stripes twice the width of the other stripes.

86. *Koroku-zome* or *tazuna-zome*. Earlier known as *tazuna-zome*, this pattern of red and white oblique stripes takes its present name from the Kyoto *onnagata* Arashi Koroku, who brought it to the stage.

87

88

89

87. *Rimbō*. In *Kanjinchō, Gojōbashi*, and the "Benkei Joshi" scene of *Gosho-Ẕakura Horikawa Yōuchi*, the hero Benkei appears in costumes patterned with this circular frame of spokes extending beyond the outer rim. The design is taken from a symbolic Buddhist weapon used to ward off evil spirits and beasts.

88. *Hōshu*. The "flaming gem" or fire-rimmed circle is the pattern seen on the costume of the supernatural fox in Kabuki.

89. *Sasa-rindō*. This pattern, a symmetrical arrangement of *sasa* (bamboo grass) and *rindō* (gentian-like mountain flower), is adapted from the floral crest believed to have been the actual insignia of the Minamoto brothers, Yoshitsune and Yoritomo. It is used on their costumes in the many plays of the Genji-Heike cycle.

The pattern called *okina-gōshi* or more popularly *kōraiya-gōshi* or *kōraiya-jima* became a favorite following its introduction by Kōshirō V. It consists of white stripes forming squares on a rust ground, with alternate stripes twice the width of the other stripes (Fig. 85).

*Koroku-zome,* a pattern of red and white oblique stripes (Fig. 86), takes its name from the Kyoto *onnagata* Arashi Koroku, who brought it to the stage. Earlier, it had been known as *tazuna-zome,* since the oblique stripe pattern was one of the standard designs for *tazuna* or bridle reins.

*Hōshu* (*hō,* treasure; *shu,* gem) is the "flaming-gem" or fire-rimmed circle pattern (Fig. 88) seen on the costume of the supernatural fox in Kabuki. Its remarkable brilliance and play of colors symbolize the essential elements of a gem, which the fox was believed to possess.

The *sasa-rindō,* a pattern adapted from the floral crest believed to have been the actual insignia of Yoshitsune and his elder brother Yoritomo, is used for the roles of the brothers on the stage in the many plays of the Genji-Heike cycle. It is a symmetrical arrangement of *sasa* (bamboo grass) leaves with the *rindō,* a gentian-like mountain flower (Fig. 89).

The *iyo-zome* pattern (Fig. 90) takes its name from the province of Iyo, now Ehime Prefecture, in Shikoku. As we have already noted in Chapter 12, this pattern, which suggests light shining through split-bamboo blinds, is worn by mild or *wagoto* male characters. It appears, for example, in the costume of Yasuke in the "Sushiya" scene of *Yoshitsune Sembon-Ẕakura.*

90. *Iyo-zome.* The *iyo-zome* pattern, which suggests light shining through split-bamboo blinds, is seen in the costume of such *wagoto* characters as Yasuke in the "Sushiya" scene of *Yoshitsune Sembon-Zakura.*

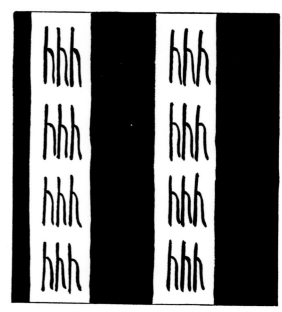

91. *Genji-kō* or *Nakazō-jima.* Named for the actor Nakazō I, who used the design for his crest, this pattern is said to have featured a stylization of the character *hito* (man) in groups of three.

Two outstanding creative artists, Danjūrō IX and his pupil Kikugorō VI, had an instinctive skill for improving traditional costumes in a manner most pleasing to the public as well as satisfying to themselves. Evidence of their ingenuity may be seen in the costumes for two famous roles.

The costume worn by the girl Omiwa in *Imoseyama Onna Teikin* was originally patterned with the *shinobugusa* or hare's-foot fern, but this pattern was changed by Danjūrō to that of the *jūroku-musashi* (a game played on a board with round disks) against a background of *moegi-iro* (Kelly green). The pattern—white zigzag lines intersected by white circles, with an occasional black one—covered the lower part of the green kimono skirt.

In the second instance, Kikugorō altered the costume for Sakura-maru in *Sugawara Denju Tenarai Kagami* by discarding the original *kata-eri* (padded collar or neckband), which bore the *ga-no-iwai* pattern of cherry blossoms on a light purple ground, in favor of a *kata-eri* with the *yare-gōri* (*yare,* broken; *kōri,* ice), a pattern of cracked-ice tracery.

On top of an unbelievably keen sensitivity to the subtle as well as the obvious beauty in nature, Japanese designers seem to be blessed with the ability to adapt with skill and ingenuity whatever they see in nature for use in the theater. There is hardly a better example of this ability than the adaptation of the steel blue and the narrow black stripes of the bonito (in Japanese, *katsuo*) for the very interesting *katsuo-jima* design used chiefly for *hakama.* In the "Hamamatsuya" (Hamamatsu Cloth Shop) scene of *Benten*

92. *Araiso*. The *araiso* (wave-beaten shore) is a pattern of waves and carp. This very old, adroit design was greatly favored by Danjūrō IX.

*Kozō* (Benten the Rascal), this design, with its suggestion of shimmering bonito scales, appears on Nangō's *hakama*.

Along the hem of the costume of Sekibei in *Tsumoru Koi Yuki no Seki no To* (The Love Story at the Snow-covered Barrier Gate) there appears a design called the *Genji-kō* (Fig. 91). In the Kabuki world this design is said to be composed of the character for *hito* (man, human being) in groups of three. A legend relates that the actor Nakazō I believed he could gain courage by writing the character *hito* on his palm three times and then licking off the writing. The *hito* or *Genji-kō,* as it came to be called, eventually became Nakazō's crest, and the kimono pattern is known as *Nakazō-jima*. The *Genji-kō* was originally one of the 54 signs or symbols which, according to the various combinations of incense woods used in the incense-guessing game, represented the 54 chapters of *Genji Monogatari*.

Nakazō I had a very short neck, and for this reason he styled the costume for the role of Sekibei with a wadded collar so that it would appear heavy. Since that time, actors taking this role have worn a wadded collar, which gives them the appearance of having short necks.

Auspicious designs of crane, tortoise, and *shō-chiku-bai* (pine, bamboo, and plum) appear regularly on strikingly lovely hand-embroidered kimono used in dance numbers. The crane and the tortoise symbolize longevity, while the combination of pine, bamboo, and plum represents strength, uprightness, and fidelity. These designs may be seen on the costumes in the New Year's felicitation dance called *Sambasō* and on Togashi's *suō* (both on the *uwagi* and on the *naga-bakama*) in *Kanjinchō*.

*Araiso* (wind-swept and wave-beaten shore) is a pattern representing a carp swimming in waves rolling one after another against the shore of a river and bringing in their wake a spray represented by scattered dots (Fig. 92). This very old, adroit design was greatly favored by the master craftsman Danjūrō IX.

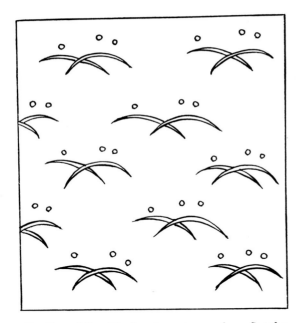

93. *Tsuyu-shiba*. *Nimaime* characters such as Sonobe Saemon in *Shin Usuyuki Monogatari* and Kanōnosuke Naonobu in *Gion Sairei Shinkōki* wear delicate silk kimono decorated with the *tsuyu-shiba-moyō*: a hem design of dewdrops on a lawn.

94. *Ikarizuna*. Among designs derived from or related to significant characteristics of the roles for which they are worn is the *ikarizuna* (anchor rope) pattern on the costume of Watōnai in the "Beninagashi" scene of *Kokusenya Kassen*. It serves to indicate his fisherman origin.

Also to be mentioned among these patterns is the *tsuyu-shiba* (Fig. 93), which we have already noted in Chapter 12 as the hem design of dewdrops on a lawn used in *nimaime* kimono.

### DESIGNS RELATED TO ROLES

There are a number of costume designs derived from or related to significant characteristics of the roles for which they are worn. Watōnai, for example, in the "Beninagashi" scene of *Kokusenya Kassen* (The Battles of Coxinga), wears the *ikarizuna* (anchor rope) design on a purple background to indicate his fisherman origin (Fig. 94). The Watōnai style and design are also used in the type of *aragoto* role known as *oshimodoshi* (pushing back), but the reason for this is not clear, since the role has no relationship with a fisherman. It must be admitted, however, that the stuffed-out costume is perfect for any *aragoto* role.

In the "Inasegawa" (Inase River) scene of *Benten Kozō*, the five leading characters, all thieves, present themselves on the *hanamichi* wearing sensationally splash-designed costumes and carrying umbrellas which each in sequence opens with a great flourish. Each costume has a symbolic meaning.

Nippon Daemon, leader of the thieves, is in a costume patterned with the design known as *shiranami:* anchor, rope, and whitecapped waves. A play on words is indicated, for *shiranami* means white waves as well as thief or brigand, and the word *ikari* means both anchor and leader.

Benten Kozō Kikunosuke's costume is decorated with the *biwa* (lute), the *shirohebi* or *hakuja* (white snake), and the *kiku* (chrysanthemum)—all related to his name. Benten is the goddess of music, who is properly depicted holding a lute, and the white snake is her messenger. *Kiku* has a double significance, for it is not only the chrysanthemum but also a reminder that the role was first performed by Kikugorō V (then Kikunosuke), for whom the play was written.

Tadanobu Rihei's costume is handsomely patterned with cherry blossoms *(sakura)* and hand drums *(tsuzumi)* for the reason that his name is taken from that of another Kabuki figure: that of Tadanobu in *Yoshitsune Sembon-Zakura,* who appears under blossoming cherry trees with Yoshitsune's mistress Shizuka, who carries a hand drum.

The costume of Akaboshi Jūzaburō, whose surname means red star, is decorated with a design combining "stars" and the *onagadori,* an imaginative long-tailed bird. The "stars" or *hoshi* are actually not stars at all but circles circumscribing the upper and lower points of a jagged row of pyramidal lines drawn on a solid-colored background.

Nangō Rikimaru wears a kimono boldly patterned with the *raijū* or thunder beast who supposedly causes thunder and lightning—an apt analogy, since Rikimaru is a pirate who strikes like lightning.

Several excellent examples of characters who are easily recognizable because of the designs on their costumes were described by the noted Kabuki-drama critic and author Toita Yasuji during a 1958 international broadcast:

"The three brothers in the long play *Sugawara Denju Tenarai Kagami,* originally written for the doll theater, are named respectively for three trees: Matsu (the pine), Ume (the plum), and Sakura (the cherry); and these identities are often used during the course of the play in an effective symbolism. The stalwart pine, the hardy plum, the delicate cherry—each suggests the character of the respective brothers. Both Matsuō-maru (the pine) and Umeō-maru (the plum) are bold and masculine, depicting their roles in a strong, exaggerated manner and speaking in a special intonation to bring out this masculine nature; while Sakura-maru (the cherry) is gentle and effeminate.

"The brothers appear first in identical garments to emphasize their identity as triplet brothers; but as the scene progresses, each slips the outer garment off his shoulders to reveal a brighter garment beneath, bearing the design representing the tree of his name, the pine in green, the plum and cherry in pink, thereby creating a vivid color contrast on the stage." (Figs. 67–69).

Many colors have become symbolic and standard for certain costumes and identify the age or social position of the individual roles. Princess red is for royalty or the nobility; tan or gray represents older people. *Moegi-no-kokumochi,* a bright green version of the *kokumochi* costume described in Chapter 11, is the name of the costume for *inaka musume* (country girls), its color symbolizing the verdant countryside. Omitsu in the "Nozaki-mura" scene of *Shimpan Utazaimon,* Omiwa in the "Goten" scene of *Imoseyama Onna Teikin,* and Okane in the dance-drama *Ōmi no Okane* are such country girls.

*Asagi-no-kokumochi,* a blue costume symbolizing the sea, identifies the wives and daughters of fishermen, such as Chidori in *Heike Nyogo ga Shima* (commonly known as *Shunkan* and dealing with the exile of the priest Shunkan by the Heike to a desolate island) and Matsukaze and Murasame, the two sisters in *Suma no Utsushie* (A Picture of Suma), a dance-drama.

Nikki Danjō, the villain of *Meiboku Sendai Hagi,* appears in the "Yuka-shita" scene in *nezumi-iro* (mouse gray) *naga-bakama* and *kataginu,* with a *kitsuke* in *noshime* style—that is, a midriff of different color and pattern (Fig. 21). Although costumes of other colors had been the accepted apparel for this role, the gray costume adopted by Kōshirō V became the favorite, probably because of the immense distinction that he gave this role. It is also true that gray would seem most appropriate, since Nikki Danjō, through sorcery, transforms himself into a rat during one of the more exciting moments of the play, appearing in this guise on the trap lift of the *hanamichi.*

The commoners in *sewa-mono* customarily wear blue-striped kimono, although the stripes can be of other colors. Blue became the usual choice because indigo was a practical dye of strong color and was at the same time inexpensive, and cotton and hemp took the blue dye well.

As men and women grow progressively older, their kimono are toned down to less conspicuous colors, but such details of everyday life are often ignored by the Kabuki. Consequently, what would appear coarse or inappropriate in real life is often accepted as natural on the stage.

CHAPTER 16

# Mon: Crests

The clan or family crests known as *mon* made their appearance during the Kamakura period at the height of an age of nationalistic development and soon became widely accepted. The *mon* at first was only a mark conspicuously placed on a diversity of possessions, including battle flags, helmets, traveling chests, lacquer ware, household articles, palanquins, carts, and *fusuma,* the sliding paper doors used to partition off rooms in a house. Not until the middle of the Muromachi period was the *mon* generally put on clothing, and then only by the elite *bushi,* the military caste. This early association with the *bushi* gave the *mon* a suggestion of strength.

The *kuge* or court nobles never used the *mon* on any costume except when dressed in the manner of samurai. At this period, such *kuge mon* were used by servants and dealers who serviced the *kuge,* but the *mon* of *bushi* were never so used.

It took several centuries before the general public placed *mon* on their garments, following the custom of their idols the Kabuki actors, who had made the exhibit of *mon* familiar during the eighteenth century by the display of individual crests on theater signboards and lanterns. In addition, the playgoers had a pertinent reminder of the *mon* in the *mombanzuke* or theater programs, which always indicated the actor's *mon.*

Today the privilege of having a crest is not confined to one class. Institutions, business or banking houses, department stores, as well as each Kabuki theater and, of course, private families—all display their individual crests.

With reference to the family crests, Isao Honda in his *Monshō* writes: "These crests are entirely different in nature from the modern day emblems that are sported by business firms and municipalities. Also, these crests cannot be protected by law from arbitrary use as in the manner of registered trade marks."

On the formal crested kimono, called the *montsuki,* the *mon* appears in five places on the upper part of the outer kimono and on the *haori:* on the back (centered between the shoulders), on each sleeve, and on the right and left breast (Fig. 95). For more informal occasions, three *mon* are proper: one on the back and one on each sleeve.

The size of the *mon* is not standard. It ranges in diameter from three-fourths of an inch to one inch for women and from one inch to one and a half inches for men, with a few exceptions favoring larger sizes. Nor is the *mon* of a fixed color, although principally a white pattern is used on a black background, embroidered or dyed by the resist method.

Vast numbers of *mon* exist today, showing varied stylizations of basic subjects, which include cherry and plum blossoms, bamboo, peonies, hollyhocks, morning-glories, chrysanthemums, and other flowers, many species of birds, butterflies, fans, helmets, vegetables, leaves, geometrical figures, ideographs—in fact, any object that may have caught the designer's fancy. By tradition the sixteen-petaled-chrysanthemum crest is reserved for the exclusive use of the emperor and certain other members of the imperial family. Also, custom does not sanction the wearing of *mon* of noted families by persons who are not members of those families, although in the past the retainers of a lord were given the privilege of wearing their master's *mon.*

Actors' *mon* (Fig. 96) have been deliberately designed for a dual capacity: retaining their identity and being flexible enough to be used as textile patterns for *ishō.* For instance, Ichimura Uzaemon's crest, the *uzumaki*—a spiral design reminiscent of the coil of incense burned to repel insects during hot summer evenings—makes an attractive free, casual pattern. The *uzumaki* is Uzaemon's *kaemon* or alternative crest for less formal wear, whereas his *jo* or *omote mon,* his main crest, is the *tachibana:* the leaves and fruit of the Japanese orange tree. Actors may have several *kaemon* but only one *omote mon.* In cases where the *mon* of a family is considered too masculine for women, it is presented in a slightly changed version, also known as the *kaemon.*

Kabuki *mon* are larger in size than those used in daily life, ranging from two inches in diameter to seventeen inches square for those worn by Kamakura no Gongorō Kagemasa in *Shibaraku.* The number of *mon* for formal wear is not limited to five, as in real life. In *jidai-mono* the highest-ranking samurai dressed in *naga-gamishimo* have six *mon.* The additional crest is centered on the stiffened upper piece at the back beltline of the *hakama.*

Though most *mon* can be effective patterns for costumes, there are some which are not considered suitable for fabric decoration. Among these is the crest of Sawamura Sōjūrō, the *maru-ni-i,* which consists of the hiragana character *i* (い) in the center of a double circle. It is presumed to have been influenced by the *futatsu-domoe* (two large comma shapes inverted clockwise to form a slightly disjointed circle) belonging to the seventeenth-century samurai impersonated as Yuranosuke in *Kanadehon Chūshingura.*

95. *Montsuki:* crested kimono. The formal crested kimono, shown here as worn by a *rōnin* in *jidai-mono* or *sewa-mono,* displays the *mon* (crests) in five places: on each sleeve, on right and left breast, and on the back. Kabuki *mon* are larger than those on real-life kimono.

MIMASU     GYŌYŌ BOTAN     HIYOKU     UZUMAKI

TACHIBANA     MARU-NI-I     FUTATSU-DOMOE     KASANE ŌGI

MITSU-ICHŌ     YOTSU-HANABISHI     MATSUKAWABISHI-NI-TSUTA     MARU-NI-FŪJI-BUMI

MIMASU (Sadanji)     GION-MAMORI     YUIWATA     MITSUBIKIRYŌ

TSURU-NO-MARU     MARU-NI-CHIGAI-TAKANOHA     YOTSUME-YUI     YOTSUME-YUI

MUKAIBATO    HANA-GIRI    GENJI-GURUMA    KANGIKU

KICHIBISHI    SUMIKIRIKAKU-NI-
HON-NO-JI    SUMIKIRIKAKU-NI-
HEI-NO-JI    TORA

96. *Mon:* family crests. (See Chapter 16 for detailed descriptions.)

Since Sōjūrō could not copy the *futatsu-domoe* exactly, he redesigned it as it is seen today.

A second example of *mon* considered unsuitable for fabric decoration is the attractive *kasane ōgi*—two overlapping fans—chosen by Onoe Kikugorō I as his family crest. It is related that Kikugorō attended a gathering of nobles at which he was presented with *kashiwa mochi*, rice cakes wrapped in oak leaves, on two overlapping opened fans. Presumably, this gave him the idea for his *mon*, although the *kashiwa mochi* do not appear in it. And although the original fans were fully opened, Kikugorō designed his *mon* with two half-opened overlapping fans, since he felt that he was not fully "upright" in his acting—that he was like a half-opened fan—at least until such time as he reached maturity. Whether this is true or not is uncertain, but it is thought in some quarters that Kikugorō merely used this as an excuse because the initial arrangement was considered too sturdy for a *mon* design.

Since both the *futatsu-domoe* and the *kasane ōgi* are rather strong motifs, they cannot possibly be changed for use as a decorative pattern. Moreover, their history is thought to be too illustrious for adaptations suitable for this purpose.

The family *mon* of actors are often applied to their costumes. This is especially noticeable in roles where the actors' particular interpretations have become the accepted *kata*. In the role of Nikki Danjō in the "Yukashita" scene of *Meiboku Sendai Hagi*, Matsumoto Kōshirō V wore his *omote mon*, the *mitsu-ichō* (three ginkgo leaves), on his *kataginu* and his *kaemon*, the *yotsu-hanabishi* (a diamond shape made up of four four-petaled flowers) in *noshime* or midriff design on his kimono. This became the rule for the Nikki Danjō costume, and today's dynamic Kōshirō VIII upholds the tradition of his forebears when he plays the role.

Kōshirō V again introduced his *yotsu-hanabishi* crest for the costume of Banzuin Chōbei in *Banzuin Chōbei Shōjin Manaita*. A dark-blue kimono was decorated with the crest from hem to obi, around the neck, and down the shoulders—a bold adaptation admired during the years of Genroku. This costume is still favored by the Matsumoto family, but the Ichikawa family prefer the *matsukawabishi-ni-tsuta* pattern initiated by Danjūrō II. *Matsukawa* is the bark of the pine; *tsuta*, ivy or an ivy leaf; while *bishi* (from *hishi*, diamond shape) refers to the shape of the *mon*. But the idea for the *matsukawabishi* appears to have originated from several possible sources: from the figures seen in the sand as the tide ebbs, from a cloud formation with rounded "corners," or from the appearance of *kuchiki*, the wood of a decayed tree. The design did not have the name *matsukawa* attached to it until long after it had been in use, and today the "corners" are pointed.

Ichikawa Sadanji I was given the *matsukawabishi-ni-tsuta* crest by Danjūrō IX, and it became his formal crest, but today Sadanji III uses the *mimasu* crest of three concentric squares with the ideogram for the *sa* of Sadanji in the center as his main crest, perhaps because he feels it improper to use the formal *mon* of a family in which he is not a direct descendant. This would be characteristic of Sadanji III the man, for he is a charming, lovable, self-effacing individual.

The *mon* of the *onnagata* Arashi Kiyosaburō I is traditionally used for the costume of Yaoya Oshichi in the drama of that name—a mark of appreciation for his notable performance of the role. The same *mon* appears on the costume of Ojō Kichisa in *Sannin Kichisa Kuruwa no Hatsugai* (The Three Rogues Called Kichisa at the Licensed Quarter), since the role was written with the assumption that Ojō, in one of his disguises, would be dressed like Oshichi. The *mon* is the *maru-ni-fūjibumi*: tied letter paper in a circle, symbolizing a love letter of the sort that dilettantes would have written during the Fujiwara, the Kamakura, or the Muromachi period. In this connection, it is interesting to note the comment of Ema Tsutomu in his *Historical Sketch of Japanese Customs and Costumes*: "Even letter writing was a fine art in which the letters were written in the elegant *tanka* form of poetry on beautiful paper scented with various kinds of incense. And that was not all, for the letters had to be delivered properly: they were finally hung on branches of flowering cherry or plum, or on willows at times, and delivered by a private messenger."

The *gion-mamori* crest of the Nakamura Utaemon line of actors—a two-circle frame intersected by two horizontal lines, with the inside circle crossed by two rolls of Japanese song scripts—is seen on the costume of the leading actor in the dance *Tomoyakko* (A Retinue of Servants), first performed with great success by the *tachi-yaku* Utaemon III.

The costume of the courtesan Umegae in *Hiragana Seisuiki* still retains the *mon* of Segawa Kikunojō I, who popularized the role. This is the *yui-wata* crest: a tied skein of silk thread inside a circle.

The stage character Asahina, a man of great strength and a devoted friend of the Soga brothers, first appeared with the real-life Asahina's crest, the *mitsubikiryō* (*mitsu*, three; *hiki*, line; *ryō*, round): three horizontal equally spaced bars in a circle of the same width. For this role, however, Nakamura Denkurō I preferred his own *tsuru-no-maru* (*tsuru*, crane; *maru*, circle, round) crest: an impressionistic crane with wings outstretched above his head, forming a circular figure. This is now accepted as standard for the Asahina costume, and the *mitsubikiryō* is rarely used.

The costumes of certain Kabuki characters traditionally carry the *mon* associated with the character itself rather than the *mon* of the actor currently playing the part. For example, as we have noted above, the *mon* of Ōboshi Yuranosuke in *Chūshingura* is the *futatsu-domoe*—the two large commas inverted clockwise to form a slightly disjointed circle. Similarly, in the same play, Enya Hangan wears the *maru-ni-chigai-takanoha* crest of hawk feathers crossed in a circle. Wakasanosuke (also in *Chūshingura*) and Moritsuna (in *Ōmi Genji Senjin Yakata*) use the *yotsume-yui* crest: a large square divided into four equal units by two crossed lines, with a small square in the center of each. Kumagai, in *Ichinotani Futaba Gunki,* appears in a costume displaying the *mukaibato* (*mukai*, facing; *hato*, pigeon), a crest that shows two stylized pigeons facing each other. The symbolism here is of interest, for the pigeon was believed to be the messenger of the war god Hachiman, and the stylized pigeons in the crest are made to resemble the ideograph *hachi,* the first component of the war god's name. Again, in *Kajiwara Heiza Homare no Ishikiri* (The Celebrated Stonecutting Feat of Kajiwara Heiza), Kajiwara Heiza wears the *mon* called *yahazu* (*ya*, arrow; *hazu*, notched end of an arrow) with two—no more, no less—arrows side by side in a circle.

Other *mon* are of interest in Kabuki. Kōno Moronao, in *Chūshingura,* is recognized by his paulownia *(kiri)* crest in present-day performances, although in earlier years his *mon* was the *kō-no-ji* or "character-for-*kō*" design. Another crest known as the *maru-ni-i,* different from the one described earlier in this chapter, is worn by the hero Shirai Gompachi in *Hiyoku no Chō Yume no Yoshiwara.* In this case it is composed of a circle with the character *i* (井, a well) in the center.

Of particular interest is the *Genji-guruma* or Genji wheel, a motif inspired by the wheels of the oxcarts used by the nobility during the Fujiwara period. It appears in a number of variations but is basically a design of two circles crossed by spokes radiating from the center. The *Genji-guruma* crest of the *gidayū* singer Toyotake Masatayū III was used for the costume of Tadanobu in *Yoshitsune Sembon-Zakura* when this play first appeared on the boards of the puppet theater in Osaka in 1747, and ever since has been a favorite costume design in both the Bunraku and the Kabuki.

The *kangiku* (*kan,* ring; *kiku,* chrysanthemum), a creation of Sawamura Tanosuke III, was widely accepted for the decoration of hair ornaments as well as other womanly gadgets. The crest is a stylized chrysanthemum with the stem split in half and brought up to the blossom in circular shape.

We have already noted several *mon* which employ either an ideograph or a *kana* character as a component. Among others of this type, three or four are worth noting. The *mon* of the three villain-brothers in *Sannin Kichisa Kuruwa no Hatsugai* is the *kichibishi,* a diamond shape representing a caricature or stylization of the ideograph for *kichi* (good luck), which forms the first part of the name Kichisa. In Act VII of *Chūshingura,* Hei-emon's costume displays the *sumikirikaku-ni-hei-no-ji* crest—that is, the character *hei* from his name in a square with its corners cut off. A similar *mon,* the *sumikirikaku-ni-hon-no-ji,* is worn by Honzō in Act IX of the same play, the ideograph in this case being the *hon* of his name. In the "Kiku-batake" scene of *Kiichi Hōgen Sanryaku no Maki,* Torazō (in reality Ushi-waka-maru) wears the ideograph for *tora* (tiger) in a *daimon,* again an example of the use of a name component in a crest.

A close look at the clothing worn by farmers and lesser characters, including women, in *jidai-mono* will reveal that these people are not wear-ing *mon,* although they appear to have them on their costumes. Actually, these decorations are merely plain white circles appliquéd on their outer garments, since these lower-class people were not permitted to wear *mon.*

To the devotees of Kabuki, the knowledge of the various *mon* and their significance becomes almost second nature, and it is a great factor in understanding the history of families—not only those of the characters in the plays but also those of the actors. In the theater, as in real life, there is a deep-rooted attachment to the *mon,* for it represents family continuity and family honor as it is handed down from generation to generation.

CHAPTER **17**

# Hachimaki: Headbands

The *hachimaki* is a folded cloth worn around the head as a band to keep the hair out of the eyes and to absorb sweat when the wearer is working or engaging in vigorous exertion of any sort. Its use was furthered by a superstitious belief that the act of tying was sacred and brought good luck. In ancient days in Japan it was thought that tying two ends together produced a whole. In this respect, since the head was considered the most vital part of the human body, it is probable that the *hachimaki* was originally tied around the head in the belief that it would keep the head free of evil influences, cure a headache, or prevent head ailments.

Most *hachimaki* styles that we see in Kabuki were used in real life as well as on the stage, but the theater took the liberty of stylizing them and adding colors. Unlike the *tenugui,* which is normally used to form the *hachimaki* in real life, the stage *hachimaki* does not have a standard length or width, although when it is wound around the head it is neatly folded to a width of approximately two inches.

## MEN'S HACHIMAKI

The *mukō hachimaki* (*mukō,* front) is found in two varieties: the *samurai-no-mukō* and the *chōnin-no-mukō* (Figs. 97, 98, 105). Both styles are tied in the same way. The cloth is brought around the head from the rear and tied in a flat bow at the center of the upper forehead. The difference between the *samurai-no-mukō* and the *chōnin-no-mukō* is in the cloth used. The samurai usually has a special cloth for the purpose made of cotton or sometimes silk. The color is generally white, but it may be orange or even red. The *chōnin,* however, forms his *hachimaki* from a *tenugui* that he happens to have at hand. Most of these *tenugui* are of medium-blue cotton, some are tie-dyed in the bean-shaped polka-dot pattern called *mameshibori,* and a few are of miscellaneous types.

97. *Samurai-no-mukō hachimaki.* For his headband the samurai usually has a special cloth—cotton or sometimes silk. The color is generally white, but it may be orange or even red.

98. *Chōnin-no-mukō hachimaki.* The *chōnin* (merchant) forms his *hachimaki* from a *tenugui* (hand towel) that he happens to have at hand. Most of these *tenugui* are of medium-blue cotton, some are tie-dyed in a bean-shaped polka-dot pattern *(mameshibori)*, and some are of miscellaneous types.

The *yamai hachimaki* (*yamai*, illness), by its color and the manner in which it is tied, identifies a Kabuki character who is ill or insane (Figs. 99, 103, 106). It is always tied on the left side of the head. Normally the color is purple, since there is a superstition that this color is beneficial for a headache, but an elderly man's *yamai hachimaki* is black. These *hachimaki* are made either of *chirimen* or of *shioze*, a thick silk resembling taffeta. Matsuō, in the "Terakoya" scene of *Sugawara Denju Tenarai Kagami,* wears a *yamai hachimaki* tied in an oblong bow for his pretended illness. Yasuna, in the dance that bears his name, wears this type of *hachimaki* to symbolize the insanity brought on by the death of his lady.

Gonta, in *Yoshitsune Sembon-Zakura,* wears a headband used exclusively for this role and named for it: the *Gonta hachimaki* (Fig. 100). This special style, with the tied ends standing very upright in front, is highly starched to keep the ends in this position. In this case, the *hachimaki* is a *tenugui* of white cotton patterned in navy blue with *mameshibori.*

The *date hachimaki* is tied a little to the left of the center of the forehead. Sometimes pure white with a navy-blue pattern is selected for the roles of dandies like the *otokodate,* of *tobi* (firemen), of *kagoya* (urban palanquin bearers), and now and then of such artisans as carpenters. The word *date* is said to have sprung from the name of the feudal lord Date, although later research points to a different origin. One explanation states that it first came into colloquial use during the time of Toyotomi Hideyoshi

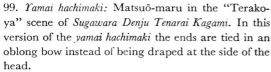

99. *Yamai hachimaki:* Matsuō-maru in the "Terako-ya" scene of *Sugawara Denju Tenarai Kagami*. In this version of the *yamai hachimaki* the ends are tied in an oblong bow instead of being draped at the side of the head.

100. *Gonta hachimaki:* Gonta in *Yoshitsune Sembon-Zakura*. The headband used exclusively for the role of Gonta is a special style with starched upright ends: a *tenugui* of white cotton patterned in navy blue with *mameshibori*.

when he invited the emperor to his Jurakudai Palace in Kyoto in 1584. Hideyoshi requested the feudal lords to keep careful watch over the emperor's retinue, and among the numerous guards were Lord Date's men, whose costumes were gayer and more resplendent than those of all the others. From that time on, the story goes, the word *date* was used to describe any gorgeous style. Gradually the word also acquired the meaning of chic or smart, we are told. Recently, however, Professor Ōno, a philologist at Gakushūin University in Tokyo, pointed out that the word *date* actually came from the verb *tateru,* one meaning of which is to uphold, and that therefore it meant to uphold or maintain one's name and fame.

As its name indicates, the *kuwagata hachimaki* is tied to resemble the *kuwagata,* the upright horn decoration that we have previously noted as part of the warrior's helmet. An ordinary *tenugui* serves the purpose, although this form of *hachimaki* is very stylized for the stage. It is usually worn by palanquin bearers such as the *kumosuke* in *Suzugamori*.

In view of the relative frequency with which palanquin bearers appear on the Kabuki stage, it is of interest to digress for a moment to have a closer look at them. They are actually of three types: the *kagoya* mentioned in the preceding paragraph (actually street porters in Edo, Osaka, and Kyoto), the *kumosuke* or highway porters (sometimes vagabonds), and the *rokushaku* who carry the daimyō's and noble's palanquin. The term *kumosuke* applies, as it did in history, to highway porters in general. In

101. *Usagi hachimaki.* For such roles as that of the rabbit in *Tamausagi* the *hachimaki* is a long white cotton cloth, stiffly starched and tied so that the upstanding ends resemble a rabbit's ears.

Edo days, when a traveler appeared, the *kumosuke* surrounded him like a cloud, taking from him his luggage and his parcels. They also carried people on their backs across rivers—a flourishing trade because the daimyō refused to build bridges, considering them a help to the enemy in time of war. The *kumosuke* asked for greater tips on these river crossings, often waiting until they reached the middle of the river before doing so. This proved to be a workable form of coercion, particularly when the traveler was faced with being dropped unceremoniously into the water. Today, interestingly, the Japanese refer to bad taxi drivers as *kumosuke.*

In real life, women also served as palanquin bearers on occasion, but this is not seen in Kabuki. Since male bearers were not permitted to enter the residences of the wives and daughters of the shōgun and the daimyō, women bearers took over at the entrance to the residential compound.

To return now to the types of *hachimaki,* we note the *usagi hachimaki* (Fig. 101), which takes its name from the Japanese word for hare or rabbit and is used only in such roles as that of the rabbit in the *shosagoto* called *Tamausagi* (The Rabbit Boy), a dance-drama in which the Rabbit Boy appears from the full moon and performs one of Japan's old folk dances. (The Japanese see a rabbit rather than a man in the moon.) The *hachimaki* for this role is a long white cotton cloth that has been stiffly starched and is tied so that the ends resemble the ears of a rabbit.

Perhaps most interesting of all among the Kabuki headbands is the *Sukeroku hachimaki* (Fig. 107), which is worn exclusively by the gallant commoner Sukeroku in the famous play that is named for him. It is made of purple *chirimen* and is tied on the extreme right side to distinguish it from the previously described *yamai hachimaki* worn to indicate illness or insanity. It is wrapped around the head, and the ends are twisted and tied into a stiff standing loop—held up by the insertion of wire—with its streamers falling to the collarbone.

102            103            104

102. *Omiwa hachimaki:* Omiwa in *Imoseyama Onna Teikin.* As another example of a head-band used exclusively for one role, the *Omiwa hachimaki* is worn only by the character for whom it is named. It is the type of *hachimaki* made with a *tenugui.*

103. *Yamai hachimaki:* woman's style. Like the man's *yamai hachimaki* seen in Figure 106, the woman's version of this "illness" headband is tied at the left side of the head, and the ends are allowed to hang loose.

104. *Buke-onna-no-mukō hachimaki.* Women of the samurai class *(buke-onna)* wear a head-band of plain silk—for the most part white—in situations of dramatic tension.

The *Sukeroku hachimaki* is a variation of the smart-looking *date hachimaki,* although it has been said that the style developed because Agemaki —perhaps in an earlier version of the play—tied a bandage around Suke-roku's head after he had been involved in a fight. This account of the *Sukeroku hachimaki* is discounted today, even though credence had been given to it because an old picture by one of the Torii school of painters showed Sukeroku's headband tied on the left as if he were ill or wounded.

In the beginning, the drama of *Sukeroku* contained many *aragoto* ele-ments, and Sukeroku himself wore a *hachimaki* of the reddish brown known as *kaki-iro.* But as the acting gradually changed to *wagoto* style, Danjūrō II replaced this strong-colored *aragoto hachimaki* with one of the softer *murasaki* (purple), and the color has remained unchanged since that time.

It is interesting to note that during Edo it was the custom for fish-market proprietors to present this type of purple *hachimaki* to the actors. This intimate custom is no longer in effect today—another instance of the com-mon man's having drifted away from intimacy with the Kabuki.

## WOMEN'S HACHIMAKI

The styles for women's *hachimaki* are limited. Many playgoers would probably say "amen" if women's *hachimaki* were dispensed with altogether, for they detract from the personal charm of the *onnagata*. Possibly the style of a man's wig lends itself to the wearing of a *hachimaki,* since it gives the man an air of irrepressibly easy unconcern, but a *hachimaki* only makes an *onnagata* look homely.

The *Omiwa hachimaki* (Fig. 102) is worn only during one dance sequence for the role of Omiwa in *Imoseyama Onna Teikin.* It is the type of *hachimaki* made with a *tenugui.*

The *mukō hachimaki* mentioned among the men's headbands described above are also worn by *onnagata*—customarily in comic roles of maid-servants. In this instance, the *mukō-hachimaki* is made with a *tenugui.* The *buke-onna-no-mukō hachimaki* (Fig. 104), worn by women of the samurai class, is made of the plain silk known as *habutae* and is for the most part white, although occasionally it may be pink or *kaki* (reddish brown). It is worn exclusively by women of the samurai class in situations of dramatic tension: scenes of swordplay, fire, and the like. There is also a feminine version of the above-mentioned *yamai hachimaki* (Fig. 103).

At first the *hachimaki* may be an unnoticed part of the costume, yet its material, color, pattern, manner of tying, and position of the knot can tell the observant Kabuki audience much about the role, for the *hachimaki* is a definite part of the *kata* of many roles.

CHAPTER 18

# Kaburi-mono: Headgear

*Kaburi-mono*—that is, things to be put on the head—include Japanese hats, scarfs, and headbands but not *tenugui* used as headbands. Unlike their Western counterparts, these could not all be worn at will by all persons in real life, for each class had its specific types of headgear. In Kabuki there are five general kinds of *kaburi-mono: kammuri, eboshi, zukin, kasa,* and *bōshi*. Other types may appear as very rare exceptions.

## KAMMURI

*Kammuri* (Fig. 109) are the headgear of court gentlemen in classical plays. They can be worn in either indoor or outdoor scenes. Real *kammuri,* which may be seen in neo-Kabuki, copy the proper contours of those of the emperor, nobles, both young and old civil officials, and military officers. The stage *kammuri* of classical Kabuki, however, differ perceptibly in form and sometimes in color and material from real *kammuri,* although they retain the long cockscomb-like ornamental strip that projects from the back of the hat. Kabuki took great liberties in exaggerating the real styles. Although in real life the cords used by the nobles to fasten the hat to the head were made of paper, worn once, and then discarded, the cords of the Kabuki *kammuri,* like those used by the shōgun or the feudal lords, are of heavy silk and are worn throughout the month's run of the play. The gold *kammuri* (Fig. 108), unknown in real life, makes its appearance only on the stage, where it adds lustre to the already intricately beautiful costumes of the actors.

## EBOSHI

The *eboshi* is a black (or infrequently gold) hat shaped from paper and lacquered stiff. The tall type known as *tate eboshi* is sometimes made of gauze, sometimes of paper—both lacquered. *Eboshi* are the headgear of samurai and *kuge* (court nobles) but never of the *chōnin* or other plebeian classes. The *eboshi* is worn during both outdoor and indoor scenes.

Among the *eboshi* worn in classical Kabuki is the *kin tate eboshi* (Fig. 110), the tall gold hat used only by *onnagata* in dance-plays. It is made of either paper or gauze. If of paper, it is covered with gold leaf; if of gauze, it is gold-lacquered. A gold brocade *hachimaki* borders the rim of the hat, and the back rim is curved like a crescent moon instead of being straight as in the real-life *tate eboshi*. Beautiful examples of the *kin tate eboshi* may be seen in *Kyō-Ganoko Musume Dōjōji* and *Shiokumi*.

The *sammi eboshi* (Fig. 111) is a hat lacquered black—sometimes gold—and worn by samurai of the highest class. It is probably the most attractive man's *kaburi-mono*—one about which women would say that "it does something" for the wearer. Tadayoshi wears a *sammi eboshi* in the first scene of *Chūshingura*. Terutora appears in this lacquered hat in *Shinshū Kawanakajima* (The Battle of Kawanakajima in Shinshū), and Okina wears it in *Sambasō*.

There are several types of *samurai eboshi* worn in classical Kabuki, always lacquered in black and decorated with tasseled cords for tying them on. The cords are generally pure white or a combination of purple and white, although they may appear in various other color combinations. The hat itself, which is an ordinary *eboshi* turned down from the crown into a three-cornered shape, resembles the figure of a black crow (Fig. 112). The distinctive triangular design formed on top by the turning-down process is called the *maneki*. The back of the hat forms a point from which extends the decorative *komusubi* or *koyui*, the six-tailed knot formed by the three ends of the ties. This type of *samurai eboshi* is worn by Watanabe no Tsuna in *Ibaraki*, by the lower-class samurai (called *zōshiki*) who carry the helmet box in Act I of *Chūshingura*, and by the daimyō in *Bōshibari* (Tied to a Pole). The musicians in *Kanjinchō* may wear *samurai eboshi* when they wish to appear more ceremonious.

The second type of *samurai eboshi* is of the same color and material as the other; the difference is in the protruding back, which is rounded instead of pointed, and in the ties, which are more often green than white or two-colored and are tied on top of the back of the hat (Fig. 113). This type of *samurai eboshi* is worn by Asahina in *Kotobuki Soga no Taimen* and *Kongen Kusazuri-biki* (The Seized Armor).

The *hanakazari-tsuki samurai eboshi* (*hanakazari-tsuki*, decorated with flowers) is a most attractive hat ornamented with red and white plum blossoms (Fig. 115). The flowers on the right side are usually white; those on the left, red. This is done merely to make the design standard; otherwise there is no particular significance. In the old days, it was a custom among court nobles to decorate their *kammuri* with flowers of the season on ceremonial occasions. Possibly there is some connection between this custom and the Kabuki *hanakazari-tsuki samurai eboshi*. This type of *eboshi*

105. *Samurai-no-mukō hachimaki.* In this style of *hachimaki* the cloth is brought around the head from the rear and tied in a flat bow near the center of the upper forehead.

106. *Yamai hachimaki.* This headband, by its color and the way in which it is tied, identifies a Kabuki character who is ill or insane. It is always tied on the left side of the head, and the color is usually purple.

107. *Sukeroku hachimaki:* Sukeroku in *Sukeroku Yukari no Edo-Zakura.* This headband of purple *chirimen* is used exclusively for the role of Sukeroku. The ends are twisted and tied into a stiff standing loop—held up by the insertion of wire—with the streamers falling to the shoulder.

249

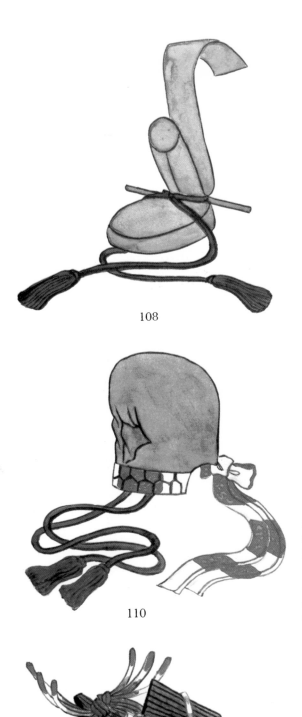

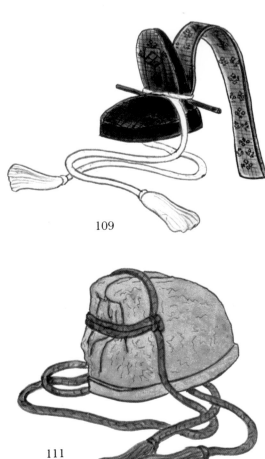

108

109

110

111

112

108. Gold *kammuri*. The gold *kammuri*, seen only on the stage, is sometimes used to add lustre to already intricately beautiful costumes.

109. *Kammuri*. The headgear of court gentlemen in classical plays are of several types, one of which is the *kammuri*. The version shown here is worn by older civil officials.

110. *Kin tate eboshi*. Among the *eboshi* worn in classical Kabuki is the *kin tate eboshi*, the tall gold hat used only by *onnagata* in dance-plays—for example, *Dōjōji* and *Shiokumi*.

111. *Sammi eboshi*. Usually lacquered black but sometimes gold, as seen here, the *sammi eboshi* is worn by samurai of the highest class. Tadayoshi wears this type of hat in Act I of *Chūshingura*.

112. *Samurai eboshi*. There are several types of black-lacquered *eboshi* worn by Kabuki samurai. This version features a six-tailed knot formed by the ends of the colorful ties. Among its wearers is Watanabe no Tsuna in *Ibaraki*.

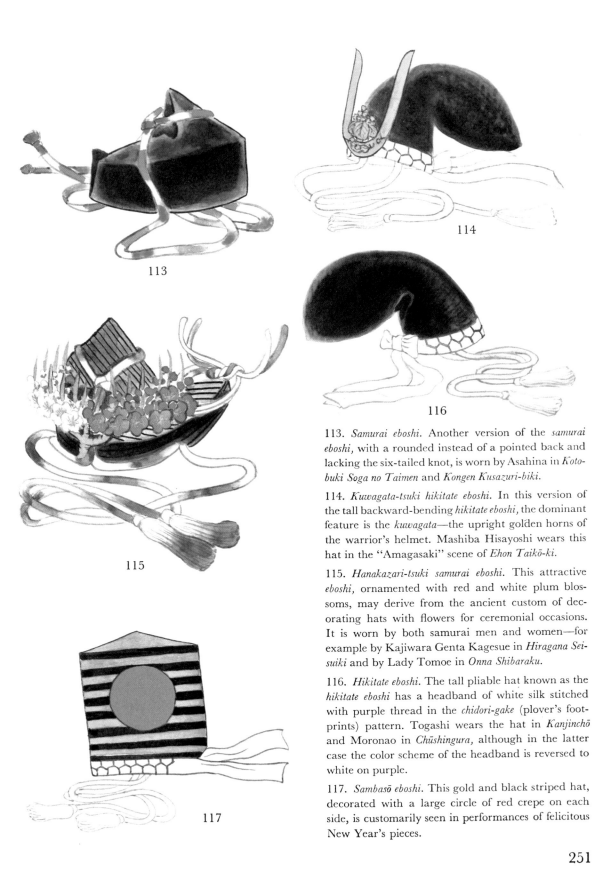

113. *Samurai eboshi*. Another version of the *samurai eboshi*, with a rounded instead of a pointed back and lacking the six-tailed knot, is worn by Asahina in *Koto-buki Soga no Taimen* and *Kongen Kusazuri-biki*.

114. *Kuwagata-tsuki hikitate eboshi*. In this version of the tall backward-bending *hikitate eboshi*, the dominant feature is the *kuwagata*—the upright golden horns of the warrior's helmet. Mashiba Hisayoshi wears this hat in the "Amagasaki" scene of *Ehon Taikō-ki*.

115. *Hanakazari-tsuki samurai eboshi*. This attractive *eboshi*, ornamented with red and white plum blossoms, may derive from the ancient custom of decorating hats with flowers for ceremonial occasions. It is worn by both samurai men and women—for example by Kajiwara Genta Kagesue in *Hiragana Sei-suiki* and by Lady Tomoe in *Onna Shibaraku*.

116. *Hikitate eboshi*. The tall pliable hat known as the *hikitate eboshi* has a headband of white silk stitched with purple thread in the *chidori-gake* (plover's footprints) pattern. Togashi wears the hat in *Kanjinchō* and Moronao in *Chūshingura*, although in the latter case the color scheme of the headband is reversed to white on purple.

117. *Sambasō eboshi*. This gold and black striped hat, decorated with a large circle of red crepe on each side, is customarily seen in performances of felicitous New Year's pieces.

251

118

119

120

121

122

118. *Sōjūrō zukin.* Probably the best known of Kabuki *zukin* is this one designed by Sawamura Sōjūrō I and named for him. It is worn by such characters as Nippon Daemon in *Benten Kozō* when he disguises himself as Tamajima Ittō, by Magoemon in *Shinju Ten no Amijima,* and by Obō Kichisa in *Sannin Kichisa Kuruwa no Hatsugai.*

119. *Kaki-iro zukin.* This *zukin,* which takes its name from the reddish-brown color of persimmon juice, is worn only by strong characters such as Jirōsaku in *Modori Kago Iro ni Aikata* and Sekibei in *Tsumoru Koi Yuki no Seki no To.*

120. *Asagi zukin.* The *asagi zukin* is a blue headcloth worn by more gentle characters—those with "white faces"—including Mashiba Hisayoshi in *Sammon Gosan no Kiri* and Yoshirō in *Modori Kago Iro ni Aikata.*

121. *Sōshō zukin.* The *sōshō zukin* primarily identifies masters of poetry and the tea ceremony such as Byakuren in *Sato Moyō Azami no Ironui* and Kikaku in the neo-Kabuki play *Tsuchiya Chikara.*

122. *Okoso zukin.* In the *okoso zukin,* which is worn only in female roles, the cloth covers the entire head and is pulled down along the cheeks and crossed under the chin, the ends being draped over the shoulders and left to hang down the back. The hood is part of the costume of Mitsugi's aunt Fukuoka Omine in *Ise Ondo Koi no Netaba.*

is worn mostly by handsome, gentle samurai and women. It is used for the *onnagata* roles of Lady Tomoe, the heroine of *Onna Shibaraku;* of Maizuru, the younger sister of Asahina in the dance *Kongen Kusazuri-biki;* and of Yūshide in *Karukaya Dōshin Tsukushi no Iezuto* (A Story of a Priest from Kōyasan). The *hanakazari-tsuki samurai eboshi* is worn for the male roles of Kajiwara Genta Kagesue in *Hiragana Seisuiki* and Senzai in the dance *Kotobuki-Shiki Samba* (A Ceremonial Prelude).

The *kuwagata-tsuki hikitate eboshi* (Fig. 114) is found only in Kabuki. It is a combination of the *kuwagata* or upright golden horns that we have earlier noted as part of the warrior's helmet and a tall *eboshi* with the high crown bent backward and then downward. The *kuwagata* decoration is usually of gold but occasionally of silver, and the ties, tassels, and *hachimaki* are plain white. Mashiba Hisayoshi wears this hat in the "Amagasaki" scene of *Ehon Taikō-ki.*

The tall pliable hat known as the *hikitate eboshi* (*eboshi* pulled upright) has a *hachimaki* of white silk stitched with purple thread in the style known as *chidori-gake,* which represents the zigzag footprints of the *chidori* or beach plover (Fig. 116). In *Chūshingura,* Moronao's *hikitate eboshi* reverses the color scheme and has the *chidori-gake* stitched in white on purple. The silk cords of the hat are also purple. The cords of Togashi's *hikitate eboshi* in *Kanjinchō* are traditionally white, although sometimes purple cords are substituted—a variation instituted by Ichikawa Sadanji I.

Another hat used exclusively in Kabuki is the *mage-kakushi* (literally, "queue concealer"), a small black lacquered hat of cornucopia shape that fits over the queue or topknot only. It is generally reserved for the roles of forceful samurai who primarily wear the *suō* in *ryūjin-maki* style—that is, the large crested garment worn by messengers of the shōgun, of court nobles, and of high government officials—and whose faces are painted red. Gemba, in the "Terakoya" scene of *Sugawara Denju Tenarai Kagami,* wears the *mage-kakushi,* and it seems a particularly appropriate headgear for Watanabe no Tsuna in *Modoribashi.* Seno-o Tarō also appears in this hat in *Heike Nyogo-ga-Shima,* frequently called *Shunkan.*

The *sambasō eboshi* (Fig. 117) is customarily seen in New Year's performances of the felicitous pieces of the season. When it is not being worn, this hat collapses and is very similar to the flat paper hats seen at New Year's Eve parties in the West. The *sambasō eboshi* is made of gold paper. The tall triangular-pointed crown is patterned with equal-sized horizontal stripes of black satin on the gold background and a large circle of red silk crepe at the center of each side. A white *chidori-gake hachimaki* and white cords with tassels are attached in the same manner as they are for the *kin tate eboshi.*

Several types of *eboshi* worn in neo-Kabuki and in the "living-history dramas" known as *katsureki-geki* (see Chapter 7) are worthy of attention. One of these is the *ori eboshi* or folded *eboshi,* which is typically black-lacquered. It is made of paper so that it can be easily folded into the various shapes required for the samurai roles in which it is worn, then stiffened with lacquer. A variant of this style has cords for tying. These hats go by the alternative name of *gosannen,* since the picture scroll *Gosan-nen Kassen Ekotoba* (Battle of Gosannen Scroll) shows many samurai wearing one of the two styles—either with cords or without. It should be noted that the differing styles of *ori eboshi* do not have great significance in distinguishing the separate classes of samurai, although commoners do not wear this headgear.

*Momi eboshi* (literally, "kneaded or crushed *eboshi*") are made of paper in the same manner as *ori eboshi* but are rather untidy-looking crushed hats worn by commoners.

The *samurai eboshi* worn in neo-Kabuki is a real-life *eboshi* with the *maneki* or triangular-shaped part of the crown placed in front. The ties are sewn on the top at the back and are tied around the *mage.* In battle or other action scenes, however, the ties are pulled down and tied under the chin.

The *kazaori eboshi* (literally, "wind-bent *eboshi*") is a rather tall *eboshi* with the crown flattened over to one side. The hat is tied on by cords that are crossed over the top, brought down and knotted under the chin.

## ZUKIN

The *zukin* (*zu,* head; *kin,* cloth or bag) is a cloth head covering or hood used to ward off dust, to help keep warm during cold weather, or to prevent recognition. It is never just an attractive accessory; it always has a justifiable practical use, if not always an honest one. A *zukin* may cover the entire head, including the neck—sometimes even the shoulders—although some cover only the hair. Colors for *zukin* vary: they may be purple, navy blue, black, or rust. The material is plain silk, *chirimen* crepe, or cotton. On stage, the *zukin* can be observed in both indoor and outdoor scenes.

The *Sōjūrō zukin* (Fig. 118), worn by *tachi-yaku* and probably the best known of Kabuki *zukin,* was designed by Sawamura Sōjūrō I. He first wore it for his *otokodate* role of Ume no Yoshibei in *Sumida no Haru Geisha Katagi,* generally known as *Ume no Yoshibei.* Only in this one role is the purple *zukin* substituted for the habitually black *Sōjūrō zukin.* The *Sōjūrō zukin* found favor in real life offstage and was soon copied by ordinary people as well as samurai. On the stage it is worn by Nippon Daemon in *Benten Kozō* when he appears in disguise as Tamajima Ittō, by Magoemon in *Shinju Ten no Amijima,* and by Obō Kichisa in *Sannin Kichisa Kuruwa no Hatsugai.*

The *asagi zukin* (Fig. 120) is a blue headcloth worn by more gentle characters—those with "white faces"—including Shirozake-uri in *Suke-roku Yukari no Edo-Zakura,* Mashiba Hisayoshi in *Sammon Gosan no Kiri,* and Yoshirō in *Modori Kago Iro ni Aikata.*

The *kaki-iro zukin* (Fig. 119), which takes its name from the reddish-brown color of persimmon juice, is worn only by strong characters such as Jirōsaku in *Modori Kago Iro ni Aikata* and Sekibei in *Tsumoru Koi Yuki no Seki no to.*

The *sōshō zukin* (Fig. 121) primarily identifies the masters of poetry and the tea ceremony *(sōshō or sōjō)* as exemplified by Byakuren in *Sato Moyō Azami no Ironui,* Nezumi Kozō in *Nezumi Kozō Haru no Shingata* when he is disguised as a wealthy man, and Kikaku in the new Kabuki play *Tsuchiya Chikara.*

Another type of *zukin,* known as *okoso* (Fig. 122), is worn only in female roles. The cloth covers the entire head and forehead and is pulled down along the sides of the cheeks and crossed under the chin, the ends being draped over the shoulders and left to hang down the back. The *okoso zukin* is part of the costume of Mitsugi's aunt Fukuoka Omine in *Ise Ondo Koi no Netaba.*


## KASA

*Kasa* or umbrella-shaped reed hats are used exclusively outdoors to guard against the elements and at times to conceal the wearers' identities. The ties for men's *kasa* are black, white, or dark blue; for women's, red, pink, light blue, light green, or white. The brim may take a variety of shapes, but the inside portion which sits on or down over the head is confined to two styles: either a pad that sits on the crown of the head or a frame that fits down over the head. The padded *kasa* has two wadded-cloth loops which fit around the ears and is tied on with a double cord attached to the left loop, the cord being drawn through the right loop and then tied under and over the chin into a small flat bow. A variation has double cords attached to both loops and tied in like manner.

The *dōchū-gasa* *(dōchū,* traveling) is a hat worn by young and old women of the samurai class—and by some commoners—when traveling (Fig. 123). It is made of dried *suge* (sedge) and rests on a padded crown. The cords, which are tied under the chin, are usually red but may be pink, white, blue, or light green. The *dōchū-gasa* can be seen in the "Michiyuki" scene of *Kanadehon Chūshingura,* worn by Konami and her mother Tonase.

Another type of *kasa* is the *takenoko-gasa* *(takenoko,* bamboo shoot), nicknamed (for its shape) the *manjū-gasa* or bean-jam-bun *kasa* (Fig. 125). It is made of the dried outer skin of new shoots of bamboo and has an inside frame. It is worn by samurai, their servants or *chūgen,* common people, and farmers.

In Kabuki battle scenes, one frequently sees the *jin-gasa* or battle *kasa,* usually worn by lower-ranking samurai (Fig. 126). Although the real-life battle *kasa* was made of steel, the Kabuki version—rounded at the base and tapered to a point at the tip of the crown—is made of paper, lacquered black and decorated with a solid red circle at the center front. It sits on an inner pad with attached cords for tying.

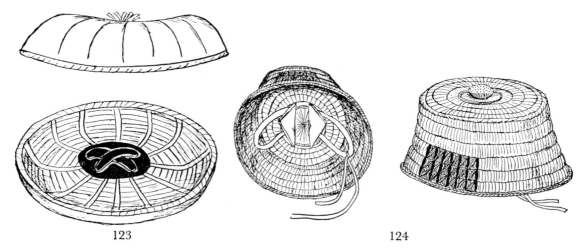

123                                    124

123. *Dōchū-gasa.* The *dōchū-gasa* is a sedge traveling hat worn by young and old women of the samurai class and by some commoners. It appears as part of the costume of Konami and her mother Tonase in the "Michiyuki" scene of *Chūshingura.*

124. *Fuka-ami-gasa.* The *fuka-ami-gasa,* woven of a kind of pampas grass, has the purpose of completely concealing the head and face. The latticework "window" in front permits the wearer to see. In the "Kurumabiki" scene of *Sugawara Denju Tenarai Kagami,* Sakura-maru and Umeō-maru appear in this type of *kasa.*

The *fuka-ami-gasa* (*fuka,* deep; *ami,* woven) is a large, deep woven hat, with inner pad, completely covering the head and face (Fig. 124). At the lower front the woven latticework is loosely interlaced, forming a kind of window and thereby permitting the wearer to see without being recognized, for the main purpose of the *fuka-ami-gasa* is to conceal the face. It is made of the dried leaves and stems of *susuki,* a type of pampas grass known in the West as *miscanthus sinensis.* The *fuka-ami-gasa* is worn by samurai or *rōnin.* In the "Kurumabiki" scene of *Sugawara Denju Tenarai Kagami,* Sakura-maru and Umeō-maru appear in this type of *kasa.*

A variant of the sedge hat is the *ichimonji suge-gasa* (Fig. 127) or *ichimonji-gasa* (*ichimonji* literally means the character for the number one in Japanese but also means a straight line). Under the hat, with its inner pad, the face is clearly revealed. This type of *suge-gasa* is worn by samurai when traveling or accompanying daimyō. It is not worn by *rōnin,* however.

The *futatsu-ori ami-gasa* (*futatsu-ori,* double fold) is used for *wagoto* roles and is worn by men, principally when they are on their way to visit pleasure houses, just as it was worn in real life (Fig. 128). The cords are pulled through the weave on the outside at the top of the hat and then drawn inside again, leaving a small crossed section on the outside.

Still another sedge hat is the *ichime-gasa* (*ichi,* market; *me,* woman), originally worn by women who sold sundries at the market place (Fig.

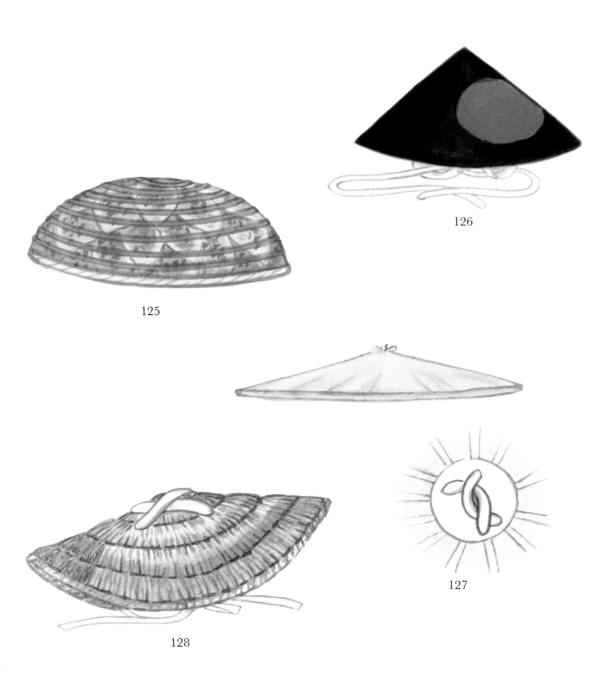

125

126

127

128

125. *Takenoko-gasa* or *manjū-gasa*. This hat, worn by a wide variety of Kabuki characters, is made out of the dried outer skin of bamboo shoots *(takenoko)*. The nickname *manjū* (bean-jam bun) comes from its shape.

126. *Jin-gasa*. In Kabuki battle scenes, one frequently sees the *jin-gasa* (battle hat), usually worn by lower-ranking samurai. In real life it was mostly of steel, but the Kabuki version is of lacquered paper.

127. *Ichimonji-suge-gasa* or *ichimonji-gasa*. A variant of the sedge hat *(suge-gasa)*, the *ichimonji* (straight line) is worn by samurai when traveling or when accompanying daimyō.

128. *Futatsu-ori ami-gasa*. This folding variant of the sedge hat is used for *wagoto* roles and is worn principally by men on their way to visit pleasure houses.

257

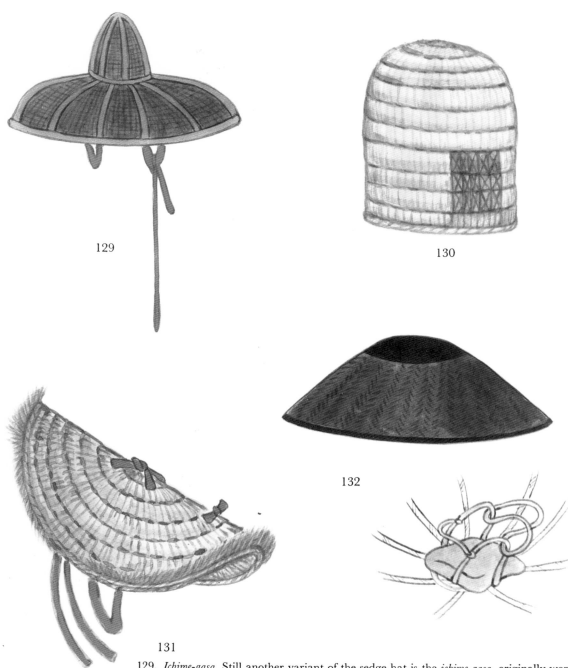

129                 130

132

131

129. *Ichime-gasa.* Still another variant of the sedge hat is the *ichime-gasa,* originally worn by women of the market place and now used in Kabuki for *shosagoto* roles.

130. *Tengai.* The head-enveloping *tengai,* like the *fuka-ami-gasa* of Figure 124, is convenient for concealing the identity of the wearer. It is worn both in Kabuki and in real life by the mendicant monks called *komusō* or by characters who wish to disguise themselves.

131. *Torioi-gasa.* One form of *kasa* seldom seen in Kabuki is the *torioi.* It is worn by strolling female musicians in New Year's scenes and can be seen in the dance *Onnadayū.*

132. *Ajiro-gasa. Ajiro* is a specific type of basket weave: an irregular crisscross wickerwork pattern. *Ajiro-gasa* are made of green bamboo, frequently lacquered black.

133. *Hirari bōshi* or *Okumi bōshi*. A headband folded into a flat oblong and daintily pinned to the wig above the forehead, the *hirari bōshi* is displayed in such *onnagata* roles as those of Okumi in *Hōkaibō* and the dancing girl Hanako in *Dōjōji*.

134. *Wata bōshi*. This *bōshi*, named for the *wata* silk of which it is made, is usually pure white but is sometimes seen in red or yellow.

135. *Okifukusa*. This smart-looking purple *bōshi*, is worn exclusively by the Kabuki *tono-sama* (lord) when he goes to the gay quarters or on a flower-viewing expedition.

136. *Murasaki bōshi*. This style of purple *bōshi*, placed on the upper forehead (actually attached to the wig), is used by some *onnagata* when they wear men's wigs in the *kōjō* or announcement ceremony on the Kabuki stage.

137

138

139

137. *Murasaki bōshi*. The *murasaki bōshi* (see Figure 136) is also worn for some *onnagata* roles in *jidai-mono*.

138. *Babā bōshi*. In wigs for elderly women, the crown of the head is often covered with a *babā bōshi*—that is, an old woman's *bōshi*—which is tied to the root of the queue.

139. *Tsunokakushi*. In real life the *tsunokakushi* is a cloth draped over the headdress of a bride in traditional wedding attire. In Act IX of *Chūshingura* it is part of the costume of Konami.

129). In Kabuki dances, the *ichime-gasa,* which rests on an inside frame, is covered with a gauzelike cloth called *sha,* generally dyed a Kelly green. The edge of the brim and the ribs of the outer frame are colored gold. In the dance-drama *Munekiyo,* however, the *ichime-gasa* is a black-lacquered paper hat. *Ichime-gasa* appear in *shōsagoto* only.

The *tengai* is a deep tub-shaped hat resembling an inverted wide-mouthed wastepaper basket which reaches down to the wearer's jaw (Fig. 130). This *kasa* is one and a half feet deep and one foot and two or three inches wide. It is worn by *komusō,* the mendicant monks of one sect of Zen Buddhism founded by the high priest Fuke Zenji. Such a head-enveloping hat is convenient for concealing one's identity while searching for an enemy against whom one seeks revenge, and it commonly serves this purpose in Kabuki. Like the above-described *fuka-ami-gasa,* the *tengai* has a loose-mesh "window" in front.

The *tengai* is made either with *suge* (sedge) that has been treated with hot water and then dried or with the rush known as *i*—the same plant used in making *tatami.* There are no cords for tying the *tengai,* since it rests firmly on the head without the help of a fastening.

According to strict observance handed down by the *komusō,* the *tengai* is never placed upside down when it is removed from the head, for it is believed that a Buddha is sheltered under it. Nor should it ever be placed on the floor. A more realistic reason for not placing the *tengai* upside down is that the inside, soiled from pomaded hair, should not be shown, since this would be impolite.

Both men and women wear *tengai,* as may be seen in the costume of Kakogawa Honzō in Act IX of *Chūshingura* and of Osono, the heroine, in *Hikosan Gongen Chikai no Sukedachi* (The Vow to the God Hikosan to Aid Revenge), commonly called *Keyamura Rokusuke.*

The *rokubu-gasa* (*rokubu,* Buddhist pilgrim) is made of dried *i,* the reed which we have already noted as being used for *tatami* and sometimes for the *tengai.* The *kasa* is about eight to nine inches deep and two feet wide and is lacquered black—sometimes with the center top and lower edge lacquered chocolate brown. The usual white ties are attached. The correct name for this *kasa* is *rokujūrokubu,* which signifies a Buddhist pil-grim, but for daily use the word has been shortened to *rokubu.* This deep hat conceals the face; so it can be worn for the same purposes as the *tengai.* The *rokubu* has been adapted for stage wear by all classes.

The *ajiro-gasa* takes its name from the specific type of basket weave in which it is made: an irregular crisscross wickerwork pattern (Fig. 132). There are various types of *ajiro-gasa* ranging in diameter from twenty-four to about twenty-seven inches. The usual depth is one foot. *Ajiro-gasa* are made of green bamboo, frequently lacquered black.

In old scrolls, the *gōriki,* who carried baggage and other burdens for travelers in mountain areas, are shown wearing *ajiro-gasa,* and it is this type of *kasa* that Yoshitsune wears in *Kanjinchō* in his disguise as a *gōriki.*

Yoshitsune's *ajiro-gasa,* however, has been made more presentable than the one that would actually have been worn by the low-class *gōriki* that he pretends to be. Its shape is based on that of Mt. Fuji, a symmetrical cone. It is lacquered in brown, with the center of the crown and the edge of the frame lacquered in black. The cords are of black *hachijō* silk.

Kumagai, in *Ichinotani Futaba Gunki,* after he decides to become a priest, wears an *ajiro-gasa.* Normally, the *ajiro-gasa* is worn by stage priests or those impersonating priests, just as priests in real life once did.

One form of *kasa* seldom seen in Kabuki is the *torioi-gasa* (Fig. 131). *Torioi* are strolling female musicians who sport this hat only around New Year's. During other parts of the year the *fuki-nagashi tenugui*—a hand towel worn loosely over the head—or the *suge-gasa* is the approved headgear. The *torioi-gasa* is woven either of the pampas grasses *obana* or *susuki,* or of the reed *i.* The arrangement of the ties is only slightly different from that of the *futatsu-ori ami-gasa.* The ties form the same crosspiece at the crown but are pulled outside to make a flat bow, usually just below the last ridge of weaving, where the ends of the reed are tufted around the brim. The *torioi-gasa* can be seen in the dance *Onnadayū* (The Woman Singer).

The *Fujiyama-gasa,* which has a shape of the outline of Mt. Fuji, is seldom if ever seen in Kabuki today. It was worn in real life only by samurai or by *machi yakko*—that is, *otokodate,* the chivalrous commoners of Edo. It was most popular in civil life during the Genroku era.

## BŌSHI

A *bōshi* is a soft cloth hat, cap, or headcloth developed to enhance the looks of the actors during the days of Yarō Kabuki, when all actors were required by law to shave their forelocks. Essentially, the *bōshi* is a piece of cloth placed over the forehead or just above for decorative purposes, although by a stretch of the imagination it might be considered a protection from dust. *Bōshi* are made of *chirimen* crepe or of *shioze,* a thick silk somewhat like taffeta. The colors are principally white, blue, light blue, or purple. *Bōshi* are worn at any time and in any setting. There are, of course, a number of variations, as noted in the following paragraphs.

The *yarō bōshi* is a man's *bōshi* made of *chirimen* or plain-woven silk, occasionally light blue but usually purple.

The *hirari bōshi* or *Okumi bōshi* is a headband folded into a flat oblong and daintily pinned to the wig above the forehead (Fig. 133). It is displayed by the dancing girl Hanako in *Kyō-Ganoko Musume Dōjōji* and by Okumi in *Hōkaibō* (The Dance of the Wicked Priest Hōkaibō).

The *wata bōshi,* used only by *onnagata,* is made of pure-white *wata* silk, sometimes dyed red or yellow (Fig. 134).

The *okifukusa,* a very smart-looking purple *bōshi,* is worn exclusively by a *tonosama* (lord) when he goes to the gay quarters or on a flower-viewing expedition (Fig. 135).

The *murasaki bōshi* is a small flat purple *bōshi* placed on the upper forehead—actually attached to the wig (Figs. 136, 137). This type of *bōshi* is used by some *onnagata* when they wear men's wigs in the *kōjō*, the formal face-showing or announcement ceremony presented on the Kabuki stage, and in some roles in *jidai-mono*, such as that of Kagaribi in *Ōmi Genji Senjin Yakata*. It is of interest to note that the *onnagata*, when wearing the *murasaki bōshi*, wears the collar of his kimono off the back of his neck in feminine style—an arrangement known as *tsuki-eri* (Fig. 136).

In wigs for elderly women, the crown of the head is often covered with a *babā bōshi*—that is, an old woman's *bōshi* (Fig. 138). This crepe *bōshi* is tied to the root of the *mage*.

The *tsunokakushi* (Fig. 139) is perhaps best listed with the *bōshi*, although it is a distinctive type of headgear. In real life it is the cloth draped over the headdress of a bride in traditional Japanese wedding attire, the purpose ostensibly being to conceal her "horns of jealousy," and the literal meaning of *tsunokakushi* is horn concealer. In Act IX of *Chūshingura* the *tsunokakushi* is the soft head covering worn by Konami.

Headgear in Kabuki does not display the variety of color and pattern seen in the kimono and the obi and often seems to evade classification by role. There is, nevertheless, a strong affinity of role, costume, and head covering—an affinity that is distinctly felt by the Kabuki audience, even though it is not always easy to define.

CHAPTER **19**

# Tenugui: The Small Hand Towel

A small hand towel in the Western hemisphere is nothing more than the words imply, but it is not so in the islands of the Rising Sun, where it is spoken of as a *tenugui* and extends its utility and convenience. Its diversification reaches its apex on the Kabuki stage, where the actors, following personal preference, not only employ the *tenugui* for various utilitarian services but also tie it around their heads in different fashions to lend dash and spruceness to their appearance.

The *tenugui* is an oblong piece of cloth having the standard lengths of slightly more than twelve and a half, thirteen and a half, or fourteen and a half inches and the width of a trifle more than twelve and a half inches —measurements fixed by the standard sizes of the weaving machines.

Regardless of the insignificant size of the *tenugui*, its practical value is amazing. It is principally seen in *sewa-mono* and *kizewa-mono*, where humble folk habitually have *tenugui* tucked into their obi or thrown carelessly over their shoulders, ready for use. On the stage, the *tenugui* accompanies an individual to the public or private bath to serve as both washcloth and towel, doing the mundane job of the turkish towel in the Western bath— how well is questionable, for it seems so inadequate.

The *onnagata* weeps into the folds of the *tenugui* and often clasps it tightly between his lips to prevent the indignity of a loud cry, an admirable trait which the audience compliments by its applause. Workmen, during their day's labor, can be seen using the *tenugui* to wipe the perspiration from their faces and necks. The *tenugui* can revert to an impromptu *hachimaki,* when a headband is unavailable, to prevent the hair from falling into the eyes during work or some other form of physical exertion. It reaches its ultimate glory as an accessory—although of larger than ordinary size— in the *shosagoto* or finds itself serving as a *hōkamuri*—a hood, but not a *zukin* —the actor devising methods for the modest *tenugui* to appear handsome and debonair as a head covering.

*Tenugui*, along with *tabi, shita-obi,* and *hachimaki,* belong to the *kogire* (*ko,* small; *kire,* cloth) section of the costume department. Long ago actors furnished their personal *tenugui,* but in the main today the actors borrow them from the *kogire* section, with the exception of those upon which the actors' crests are dyed. These belong to the actors.

## MATERIALS USED FOR TENUGUI

The vast majority of *tenugui* are made of cotton or hemp, although a soft *chirimen tenugui* with a dyed crest is displayed by actors in dance numbers. Occasionally a *yakko*—the swashbuckling, dandified servant or footman of a samurai—will have a gold-striped satin *tenugui* pushed into the right side at the back of his obi, but only to enhance his costume and not for actual use. This particular type of *tenugui* is named *date-basami* (*date,* chic; *hasamu,* to put between) or *hasami-tenugui.*

## COLOR AND DESIGN OF TENUGUI

Ordinarily the background color of the *tenugui* is *ai* or *aizome* (indigo or indigo-dyed), ranging from light blue to midnight blue. The palest, dipped only once in the dye, is called *kame-nozoki* (*kame,* large earthen jar; *nozoku,* a glance). A slightly darker blue is named *usugake* (*usui,* light, *thin*; *kakeru,* to put on color), followed by a darker shade known as *kon*. As the number of times the cloth is immersed in the dye increases, the shade becomes darker. *Kame-nozoki, usugake,* and *kon* are the three shades of blue commonly seen both on and off the stage. The gradation of coloring is more varied for the *chirimen tenugui,* having a range of eight distinct tones. The cotton or hemp *tenugui* has what is spoken of as six shades, but in reality only five, for the use of the number four has been dispensed with (as is often the custom) because four in the Japanese language is *shi,* also meaning death.

A *tenugui* with a one-color pattern is known as *ippon-zome*—that is, dyed once—while patterns of more than one color are referred to as *kake-awase* —put together. When an actor orders his crest dyed on his *tenugui,* he has several choices, for he may use his main crest or any of several secondary ones. Although rarely used by society at large, the white *chirimen tenugui* is without a doubt the most attractive of the wide assortment of these small towels. One has the tendency to think of it as vying with the Western scarf rather than as a towel.

Patterned *tenugui* are an essential part of costumes for roles displaying *iki*—that quality of freshness or dash seen in persons full of life and self-assurance and those of neat and dapper and perhaps slightly flashy appearance. The roles of *tobi* (firemen) and of *asobinin* (playboys) like Yosaburō in *Yo wa Nasake Ukina no Yokogushi* use the *mameshibori* (*mame,* beans; *shibori,* tie-dye) *tenugui,* generally having a small blue polka-dot design evenly spaced on a white background. The *matsuba-yamamichi* (*matsu*, pine; *ha*, leaves; *yamamichi*, mountain road or zigzag design) *tenugui* is also used by these same characters, but which of the two is carried depends upon habitual practice or tradition. Tatsugorō wears the *matsuba-yamamichi tenugui* in *Kami no Megumi Wagō no Torikumi*. These *tenugui* are never a part of the dress of a samurai.

There is a *tenugui* merely called *yamamichi* used in plays characterized by *sugomi*—a background of horror, weirdness, or ghastliness. *Yamamichi* are worn by villainous persons who have a slight touch of the dashing color known as *iki*. In *Yo wa Nasake Ukina no Yokogushi*, Kōmori Yasu, famed for the bat tattoo on his cheek, is such a character. The *yamamichi* can sometimes be carried by other characters when not worn to cover the head. It is then held as a hand property, as Gonshirō, the old man in the *jidai-mono*, *Hiragana Seisuiki*, holds it. All three *tenugui*—the *mameshibori*, the *matsuba-yamamichi*, and the *yamamichi*—are light blue with white patterns.

Dark-blue *tenugui* are used for *yabo*-type roles: the hickish or countrified persons hailing from the rural areas, who are supposedly not too clever. The *yabo* roles include those of farmers, stubborn elderly men, and boorish people.

White *tenugui* are used by samurai, by *nimaime* in *wagoto* roles, and in *jidai-mono* by such characters as Rokusuke in the play *Hikosan Gongen Chikai no Sukedachi* (The Vow of Rokusuke). *Onnagata* in *jidai-mono* are partial to white *tenugui*, but these may also be seen in *sewa-mono*, sometimes with a small inconspicuous pattern. Dark blue, however, is the preference of elderly women in these daily-life dramas.

A maiden with a lover makes use of her *tenugui* for a variety of gestures. One frequently witnessed occurs on the *hanamichi* during a *michiyuki*, when the maiden caressingly brushes the dust off her companion's garments. Lacking a container, a stage character will dip his *tenugui* into a stream in order to carry water to a wounded person or to one who has fainted. With deference to his acting partner, the *onnagata* carries a *tenugui* with the crest of his regular acting partner when appearing in the same play.

## MASCULINE STYLES OF WEARING THE TENUGUI

Descriptions of the *tenugui* styles for masculine roles will be brief, since the illustrative sketches are self-revealing.

Comical, rather stupid, or naive characters wear the *tenugui* as a pumpkin-shaped headgear which goes by the varying names of *suttoko kaburi*, *kabocha kaburi*, or *tōnasu kaburi* (Fig. 140). *Suttoko* is a colloquial expression for somewhat comical or frivolous action; *kabocha* and *tōnasu* both mean pumpkin. In the main, however, this type of headgear is slightly changed for more serious roles, such as those of Benten Kozō and Naozamurai. It is worn somewhat more deeply, with a crease at the front and with the back partially folded over the *mage*.

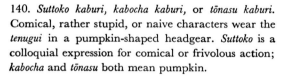

140. *Suttoko kaburi, kabocha kaburi,* or *tōnasu kaburi.* Comical, rather stupid, or naive characters wear the *tenugui* in a pumpkin-shaped headgear. *Suttoko* is a colloquial expression for comical or frivolous action; *kabocha* and *tōnasu* both mean pumpkin.

141. *Michiyuki kaburi.* The *michiyuki tenugui* generally used by the *nimaime* is tied on either the right or the left side of the head. It is seen in such roles as those of Tokijirō in *Ake-Garasu Yume no Awayuki* and Jihei in *Shinju Ten no Amijima.*

The *michiyuki tenugui* generally used by the *nimaime* is tied either on the right or the left side of the head (Fig. 141). The *michiyuki* style was first worn by Matsumoto Kōshirō V. It is seen in such roles as those of Toki-jirō in *Ake-Garasu Yume no Awayuki* and Jihei in *Shinju Ten no Amijima.*

The headgear known as *dōchū* (journey, travel) *kaburi* is made from a *tenugui* and is worn, as the name signifies, when a person is traveling (Fig. 142). Jūbei covers his head with a *dōchū kaburi* in *Iga-goe Dōchū Sugoroku* (Revenge Sought Across the Path of Iga).

Another type of *tenugui* headgear is the *Yoshiwara kaburi,* which takes its name from the celebrated licensed quarters of Edo (Fig. 143). It was worn by such entertainers as strolling musicians when they visited the Yoshiwara. Other people who entered the area, even as customers, imitat-ed the *Yoshiwara kaburi,* and it was eventually adopted by ordinary people for traveling or going on a picnic.

The *komeya* (rice dealer) *kaburi* (Fig. 144), similar to the *dōchū kaburi,* was a *tenugui* first worn by rice dealers to keep rice dust out of their hair, but eventually the style was adopted by salesmen and travelers.

Loafers and other indolent characters favor the *oki* (*oku,* to put) *tenugui,* which is the *tenugui* folded oblong and merely laid on top of the head (Fig. 145). Infrequently it is folded neatly and placed on the top of the head by ordinary men.

The *kenka* (fight, quarrel) *kaburi* (Fig. 146) is always a *mameshibori* (polka-

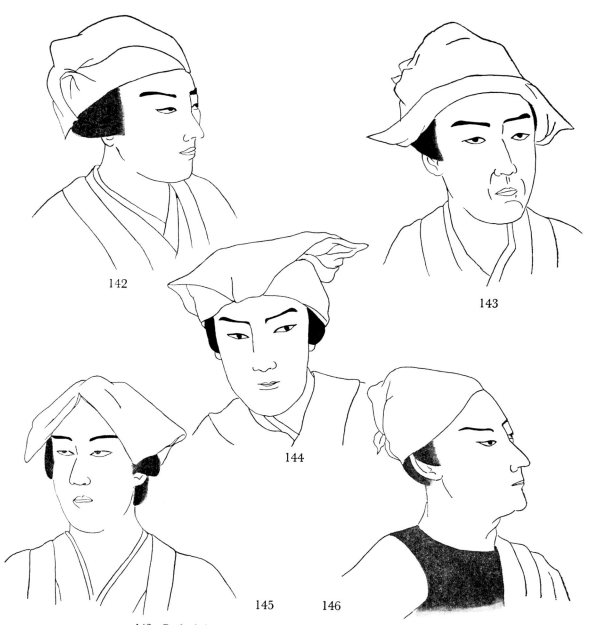

142 143 144 145 146

142. *Dōchū kaburi*. The *dōchū* or travel style of wearing the *tenugui* is displayed in various roles—for example, that of Jūbei in *Iga-goe Dōchū Sugoroku*.

143. *Yoshiwara kaburi*. Named for the celebrated licensed quarters of Edo, the *Yoshiwara kaburi* is a *tenugui* headgear style originally worn by entertainers and musicians performing there and later adopted by visitors to the quarters.

144. *Komeya kaburi*. The *komeya* (rice dealer) *kaburi* was first worn by rice dealers to keep rice dust out of their hair, but eventually the style was adopted by salesmen and travelers.

145. *Oki tenugui*. Loafers and other indolent characters favor the casual style of merely folding the *tenugui* into oblong shape and placing it on top of the head.

146. *Kenka kaburi*. The *kenka* (fight, quarrel) *kaburi* is worn in the fashion of a dandy. It can be seen on the heads of Omatsuri Sashichi in *Edo-sodachi Omatsuri Sashichi* and the firemen in *Kioi-jishi*.

147. *Tekka kaburi*. The *tekka kaburi* is tied under the nose, the purpose being to conceal the identity of the wearer, although enough of the face is left uncovered to allow the actor's expression to be seen.

148. *Dote-tekka kaburi*. To conceal their identity, Kabuki travelers may wear the *dote-tekka kaburi* along with an umbrella-shaped hat.

dot patterned) *tenugui* worn in dandy fashion. It can be seen on the heads of Omatsuri Sashichi in *Edo-sodachi Omatsuri Sashichi* and the *tobi* in *Kioi-jishi,* a very gay dance scene featuring two young men and geisha.

*Tekka* (*tetsu,* iron; *ka,* fire) *kaburi* employ the *tenugui* in three styles: *tekka, yazō-tekka,* and *dote-tekka*—each tied under the nose to conceal identity. In real life, more of the face was hidden to prevent definite identification, but in Kabuki, if the face were covered too completely, the actor's expressions would be obscured. Unlike some other forms of *kaburi,* the *tekka* may be removed during the action of a play.

The evenly spaced small polka-dot pattern known as *mameshibori* is generally the one for the *tekka kaburi,* but now and then white (Fig. 147) or *matsuba-yamamichi*—the pattern we have noted as depicting pine needles on a mountain path—is substituted. The last-mentioned pattern is worn by Kōmori Yasu in *Yo wa Nasake Ukina no Yokogushi.* In the same play, Yosaburō wears the *tekka kaburi.*

The *yazō-tekka* is displayed by Tatsugorō in *Kami no Megumi Wagō no Torikumi* and by Naojirō in *Kumo ni Magō Ueno no Hatsuhana.*

The *dote-tekka* (Fig. 148) is usually worn by travelers who also wear the *kasa,* or umbrella-shaped reed hat, to conceal their identity. It is the only *tekka* style that covers the face under the nose. It is folded across the face with the ends drawn to the back and pushed under the folds without

149. *Hyottoko kaburi*. This style of forming a headgear from a *tenugui* takes its name from the men who formerly tended the community fires. The name has connotations of clownishness.

150. *Shinobi kaburi*. Thieves and murderers in Kabuki are often seen wearing the *shinobi kaburi*, formed from a *tenugui* of black cotton or coarse hemp cloth.

being knotted. The *dote-tekka* is worn with the *kasa* because the knots of the other two *tekka* types would interfere with the tying of the cords of the *kasa*. When *yakuza* (idlers or gamblers) wear a *kasa,* they likewise wear a *tenugui* in *dote-tekka* fashion. The *tekka kaburi* are never worn by samurai, *otokodate,* or serious-minded *chōnin* (merchants or townsmen).

The *hyottoko* (from *hiotoko: hi,* fire; *otoko,* man—literally meaning a distorted mask, an ugly face, or a clown) *kaburi* was a style in which *tenugui* were worn by men who tended the village fireplaces (Fig. 149). In early days, fire was a most precious commodity, widely in use yet difficult to rekindle. Rather than maintain fires in every household, each family took its turn keeping a community fire burning at all hours. The men who threw on the kindling were rather humorous or slow-witted people who could do little else but tend a fire. Such men were eventually called *hyottoko.*

The *shinobi* (*shinobu,* to walk or creep stealthily) *kaburi,* sometimes called *nusubito* (thief) *kaburi,* is made of a black cotton or coarse hemp cloth *tenugui* and is tied under the chin, generally on the left side with the bow along the cheek (Fig. 150). The *shinobi kaburi* is never removed from the head during the sequence of the play. It is a style used by a character who comes to steal from another or to kill. Since the action customarily takes place at night, the cloth is black. The *shinobi kaburi* covers the head of Motoemon in *Katakiuchi Tenkajaya* (The Revenge at Tenkajaya).

TENUGUI: SMALL HAND TOWEL  271

151. *Koshō kaburi*. A cloth between six and seven feet in length, usually of purple *chirimen*, is used to form the young-page style of *kaburi*. It is worn by young men like Rikiya, Yuranosuke's son, in *Chūshingura* and Sonobe Saemon in *Shin Usuyuki Monogatari*.

152. *Gorō kaburi*. A type of *koshō kaburi* (Fig. 151) known as the *Gorō kaburi* also employs a cloth of purple *chirimen*, but it is tied in bow fashion under the chin, and the forelock is not covered. It may be seen in the *shosagoto*, *Ame no Gorō*.

The *koshō* (young page) *kaburi* is a *tenugui* between six and seven feet in length, usually made of purple *chirimen*, tied under the chin so that all ends of the ties hang evenly (Fig. 151). Sometimes, to assure evenness, the ends are held together by a stitch or two. *Koshō kaburi* are worn by young men like Rikiya, Yuranosuke's son, in *Kanadehon Chūshingura* and Sonobe Saemon in *Shin Usuyuki Monogatari*.

A type of *koshō kaburi* known as the *Gorō kaburi* also employs a *tenugui* of purple *chirimen*, but it is tied in bow fashion under the chin, and the forelock is not covered but revealed (Fig. 152). The *Gorō kaburi* is worn by young men in *jidai-mono* and may be seen in the *shosagoto*, *Ame no Gorō* (Gorō in the Rain) and in *Yoshitsune Koshigoe-jō* (Yoshitsune Driven from Koshigoe), in which it is part of the costume of Kamei Rokurō.

## ONNAGATA STYLES OF WEARING THE TENUGUI

The *fuki-nagashi* (streamer) *kaburi* is for the most part made of white cotton (Fig. 153). If it is patterned at all, the design is very faint. The *tenugui* is placed loosely over the head, and sometimes an edge nearest the face, at one side or the other, is held between the lips. The Kabuki courtesans and strolling entertainers resort to a *tenugui* in this fashion, but seldom does a samurai's wife or daughter.

The *anesan* (girl, young woman) *kaburi* is made of the same cloth as the

153. *Fuki-nagashi kaburi.* In this form of *onnagata kaburi* the *tenugui* is placed loosely over the head. It is worn chiefly by courtesans and strolling entertainers.

154. *Anesan kaburi.* This type of *onnagata kaburi,* put on in *anesan* (young girl) style, uses the *tenugui* to envelop the head completely.

*fuki-nagashi kaburi* and can be worn by Kabuki characters when traveling or working around the house (Fig. 154). This type of *kaburi,* put on in young girl's fashion, uses the *tenugui* to envelop the head completely. The middle part of one edge is placed on the front of the head; then both ends are wrapped around the head in such fashion as to form something of a point on each side, with one corner of the *tenugui* drawn from the back over the head and generally tucked under the front edge at the center of the forehead. The *anesan kaburi* is one style of *tenugui* that appears more like a *zukin* (hood) than a *tenugui.* Today in everyday life the *anesan kaburi* is generally worn by women on farms and in fishing villages.

Today, as in the past, avid Kabuki fans carry home souvenirs of the actors and the theater which they buy from the irresistible displays at the theater stands and shops. However, the most treasured are the crested *tenugui* thrown into the audience by the leading actors during performances of such plays as *Kyō-Ganoko Musume Dōjōji.* But also, commercialization has stretched out its fingers, and no longer is the tossing out of *tenugui* limited to the stars, since business firms furnish *tenugui* advertising themselves and their products. Still, little meaning is attached to the catching of commercial *tenugui* as far as the playgoer is concerned.

The *tenugui* is the most versatile of all hand props. As we have noted, it may be used as a towel, duster, headdress, general-utility cloth, and as a souvenir. It is also one of the least expensive parts of Kabuki costume.

CHAPTER **20**

# Ōgi: Fans

The friendly association between China and Japan that had developed during the T'ang dynasty came to an abrupt end when the Japanese government ceased sending official delegates to China about A.D. 894. This was independence taking shape—an independence that gave birth to the development of an insular and unusual culture. During previous centuries, Korean and Chinese influences had dominated all phases of Japanese life, even to such a small item as the flat, rigid Chinese fan known as the *sensu* or "hand screen."

This breeze-maker eventually lost its position in the lives of the aristocrats of Japan during the reign of the Emperor Tenchi (600–71), for Japanese artisans devised the *ōgi,* the graceful, lovely, practical folding ribbed fan, which, as Charlotte M. Salwey says in her *Fans of Japan,* " became an indispensable adjunct of the national costume. From the Mikado, who sat in solemn and silent state upon his throne, swathed in silken robes, to the workman in his holiday attire, each bore about him—almost as a stamp of his nationality—his fan. Each class, no matter howsoever engaged—men and women, court officials, soldiers, sages, priests, princes and noblemen, dancing girls and children—procured a fan, or fans, as a birthright, of particular design, according to their rank, position or profession, not only for agitating the air for the sake of coolness, but to be at hand when required for other uses. A strict code concerning the individual use of each fan was established, which etiquette was handed down from one generation to another."

The *ōgi* had attained such popularity by the year 957 that an *ōgi-awase,* a contest to determine the best-designed fan, was held before the emperor. Though we do not know the complete details of the fans displayed, we do know that poems were inscribed upon them, as well as picturesque designs. Both the poems and the hand-painted features were taken into consideration in judging the contest.

275

In the eleventh century, during the Heian period, folding court fans made their appearance. *Hi ōgi*—fans made for the use of the nobility in formal dress—were fashioned of thin staves of *hinoki* (cypress) held together at the spread end by twisted silk cords and at the bottom by a rivet. For ordinary dress, the nobility carried *ōgi* which had folded paper pasted to the ribs. The first folding paper fans had only five ribs, all of the same length and thickness, including the outer or parent ribs, and durable, pliable paper was pasted on only one side of the frame.

Around the fourteenth century, during the Muromachi period (1392–1573), Japan reopened trade with China. One of her first exports to that country was the five-ribbed folding fan. Chinese craftsmen increased the number of ribs to about three times the original number—that is, to fifteen or more. These fans were in turn imported by Japan, where initially all attempts to produce a better fan were unsuccessful because the fan-makers were not as yet sufficiently skilled. Therefore the top or paper portion of the fan remained too large and bulky. These awkward fans were called *suehiro* (*sue,* end; *hiro,* from *hirogeru,* to spread).

The evolution of the *suehiro* developed several fans in the same category, but with some deviation in the number of ribs and with more flexibility. The original model was revised to a twelve-ribbed fan (including the outer ribs). Later the *suehiro* was called the *chūkei,* the fan borrowed by Kabuki from the Nō and so often displayed on the Kabuki stage in classical historical dramas (Fig. 155).

Another version, the seven-ribbed fan known as *bombori* or *kawahori,* passed through several processes before it reached an acceptable state. The ribs of these fans are slightly bent at the middle, from which point they extend outward, giving an appearance of being slightly opened at all times. Other modifications of the *suehiro,* including the *shizumeori* (from *shizumeru,* to quiet; *oru,* to fold) and the *ukiori* (*uki,* floating; *ori,* fold) followed.

The frames of the *ōgi* are usually made of light, silky bamboo covered or mounted with paper faces, but certain fans are faced only on one side, with the bamboo ribs left exposed on the other side. The face of the fan, as a rule, covers little more than half the length of the frame.

"The *ōgi* are composed of ribs varying in number," writes Charlotte Salwey. "The inside limbs seldom reach to the top of the fan faces, so as to enable the whole to adhere firmly when closed; and the outer frame sticks are purposely made to incurve slightly. This is a marked peculiarity of Japanese folding fans, and it is the means of particularizing them among the productions of other nations." Not all Japanese fans, however, are constructed on this principle.

Today the younger generation takes the fan for granted, but in the past, says Mrs. Salwey, "the fan was an emblem of life. The rivet-end was regarded as the starting point, and as the rays of the fan expanded so the road of life widened out toward a prosperous future."

# KABUKI ŌGI

The *ōgi,* besides being a most attractive, charming accessory, serves the Kabuki audience as a practical implement. The fan helps define an actor's role as to social position and class and sometimes profession or work. As practiced in the past, etiquette is often carried out minutely on the stage, with people of lower status handing objects on a fan to those of upper classes—and sometimes vice versa.

During a play it is not unusual to see an actor write a poem or a message on the face of a fan, just as the nobility did in the leisurely ancient days when the court nobles were dilettantes leading lives of luxury and over-refinement. A fan is an accepted property belonging to all types of roles, though it reaches its greatest artistic merit in the dance numbers.

Kabuki *ōgi* are separated into various classifications with distinctly different types of frames derived from the number, length, and size of the ribs. The range of design and color in fans cannot be estimated. But it is their movement, with their "beautiful designs drawn from nature's endless encyclopaedia," as Mrs. Salwey describes them, that expresses most clearly the common language of the great artists of the Kabuki stage.

The technical names used by the hand-properties department for Kabuki *ōgi* employed in classical drama and *shosagoto* are listed below in alphabetical order, although the same order will not be followed in discussing the fans. The number of ribs noted for each includes the inner or "child" ribs and the outer or "parent" ribs.

| NAME OF FAN | NUMBER OF RIBS | LENGTH OF RIBS |
|---|---|---|
| *akome ōgi* | 40 | 14 3/8 in. (1 1/2 in. wide) |
| *chūkei* | 14 | 13 3/4 in. |
| *hachiken ōgi* | 10 | 11 7/8 in. |
| *haku-sen* | 10 | 10 5/8 in. |
| *hi ōgi* (see *akome ōgi*) | — | — |
| *jin-sen* | 11 | 13 1/8 in. (parent ribs 1 1/2 in. wide) |
| *mai ōgi* (see *shiratake-no-ōgi*) | — | — |
| *matsuri ōgi* | 9 | 11 1/4 in. |
| *ō-jikken* (see *haku-sen*) | — | — |
| *onna ōgi* | 18 | 9 1/2 in. |
| *rokkotsu* | 8 | 12 1/2 in. |
| *shibu-sen* | 30 | 10 3/16 in. |
| *shirahone* (see *chūkei*) | — | — |
| *shiratake mai ōgi* | 30 | 8 3/8 in. |
| *shiratake-no-ōgi* | 10 | 12 1/2 in. |
| *tenchikin* (see *haku-sen*) | — | — |
| *tessen* (see *jin-sen*) | — | — |
| *tetsu-sen* (see *jin-sen*) | — | — |
| *tō-sen* | 25 | 12 in. |

Kabuki fans are used for only one month's performances. Normally there are two copies made of each fan used in a production—one for actual use and one for spare. The fans are always rented to the Shōchiku Company by the hand-properties department. The Fujinami family retains copies of the fans for posterity—neatly arranged and classified in chests of drawers specially constructed for housing fans.

## TACHI-YAKU ŌGI

The *chūkei* (Fig. 155), a fan copied from the Nō, is used by leading actors portraying *tachi-yaku* roles such as those of daimyō, court nobles (*kuge*), and samurai—and always by those wearing *eboshi* and *suō*. It is carried by such luminaries as Togashi in *Kanjinchō;* Moronao, Tadayoshi, Enya Hangan, and Wakasanosuke in the prologue of *Kanadehon Chūshingura;* Kamakura no Gongorō Kagemasa in *Shibaraku;* and Lady Tomoe in *Onna Shibaraku.*

When the actor wears either the *kamishimo* or the *naga-gamishimo,* the *chūkei* is not used. Instead, he carries the ten-ribbed all-white *haku-sen* (*haku,* white; *sen,* fan).

The white fan with a gold band along the top and lower edges of the face was given the separate name of *tenchikin* (*ten,* heaven—i.e., top; *chi,* earth—i.e., bottom; *kin,* gold) (Fig. 156), although it belongs to the *haku-sen* family. For strict formal wear, the *haku-sen* is supposed to be carried, not the *tenchikin.* Regardless of this, the gold-banded fan is carried by actors when impersonating Sanemori in *Gempei Nunobiki no Taki* (Sanemori's Narrative), Kumedera Danjō in *Kenuki,* and Kajiwara Kagetoki in *Kajiwara Heiza Homare no Ishikiri.* Perhaps in these instances the *tenchikin* is used to match the colorful brocade *kamishimo,* which, though sometimes worn on the stage as formal dress, is in reality a semiformal costume for a samurai not of equal rank with a daimyō.

Another *ōgi* used with *kamishimo* is the ten-ribbed (not counting the two main ribs) *ō-jikken* (*ō,* large; *jū,* ten; *ken,* affix for "ribs"), a fan belonging to the *haku-sen* family. The *ō-jikken* is either white or white with gold-banded edges in the above-noted *tenchikin* style. In dramas the *chōnin* use the plain *haku-sen* only, but in dance numbers they may carry the *tenchikin.*

The *jin-sen* or battle fan (Fig. 157) is used for lusty samurai roles such as those of Mitsukuni Ōya no Tarō in the dance-play *Shinobiyoru Koi wa Kusemono* (The Witch Princess) and Yoshioka Kijirō in the drama *Kiichi Hōgen Sanryaku no Maki.* However, the *jin-sen* originally imported from China in the seventh century was not a battle fan but a camp fan constructed of either pheasant or peacock feathers. In Kabuki, the twelfth-century-style *tetsu-sen* or *tessen* (*tetsu,* iron; *sen,* fan), with its ten-ribbed frame of metal—usually wrought iron—is referred to as the *jin-sen* and has lacquered staves to simulate metal ribs. Feathers are not used.

Ordinarily, one side of the battle fan is decorated with seven silver discs against a black ground—representing, for good luck, the seven stars of the Big Dipper. The reverse side, also having a black ground, carries a symbol known as *bonji,* supposedly taken from Sanskrit and varying in design. The weight of the real-life war fan reached several pounds, making it a handy instrument in defense against an enemy.

Two of Kabuki's favorite characters, Kumagai and Yoshitsune, use a *jin-sen* with a red disc—representing the sun—on a gold background for the front side and on a silver background for the reverse side. The *jin-sen* carried by Yoshitsune in the "Kumagai Jinya" scene of *Ichinotani Futaba Gunki* has a tassel attached to it to signify that he is of high birth.

Much in Kabuki has been transplanted wholly from the puppet theater, but there is one noticeable difference in the *kata* or the movements of the *ōgi.* A puppet is unable to hold a fan, and consequently its movements are not as illustrative or delicate as those of the Kabuki actor. In the puppet theater, the manipulation of the fan is not always the same, since the puppeteer is of necessity somewhat handicapped in movement because his hands have to reach from behind the puppet. On the Kabuki stage, however, the action of the fan can be likened to dance steps, always fully the same.

When the characters exhibit dual personalities, the puppet theater clearly states the difference through the *monogatari*—the story related by the *jōruri* or musical narrative that replaces the dialogue of the live theater —and never through action. In Kabuki, on the other hand, even a small movement on the part of the actor—often that of his fan—imparts to the audience the true character of the role. For example, Ichijō Ōkura-kyō in *Kiichi Hōgen Sanryaku no Maki* offers for view the silver side of his fan when he wishes to appear stupid and the gold side when he acts his true self.

Sometimes the function of the *ōgi* is quite meaningful in a bold manner, as in a scene in *Toki wa Ima Kikyō no Hata-age* (The Standard of Revolt). General Akechi Mitsuhide, just before raising the standard of revolt, hands a fan to one of his enemy's aides. The poem written on its folds, "Toki wa ima ame ga shita shiru satsuki ka na," conveys a double meaning that can be translated into English as "The time is now to rain (reign)." The poem is read aloud while nearby on the *hanamichi* Mitsuhide's retainers grasp the significance of its intended meaning. They know at last that their liege lord will raise his standard and conquer the land.

The criminal priest Kōchiyama Sōshun in *Kumo ni Magō Ueno no Hatsuhana* and the priest Sōjō Henjō in one of the dances of *Rokkasen Sugata no Irodori* (The Colorful Styles of the Six Great Poets) both use *chūkei* with ribs lacquered in vermilion. Benkei, in *Kanjinchō,* disguised as a *yamabushi* or itinerant priest, carries a fan emblematic of the profession: a *shirahone* (*shira,* white; *hone,* ribs, bones) with unpainted ribs. Other priests carry different *ōgi* according to their costume or station in the Buddhist hierarchy, but ordinarily the fan they use is the *chūkei* with either painted or unpainted ribs.

In *katsureki-geki,* the living-history plays described in Chapter 7, the fan most prominently used is one of five ribs (including the parent ribs) known by three different names: *gohon-bone* (five ribs), *musa ōgi* (warrior fan), and *kawahori* (bat). The last of these names, an old word for bat, was supposedly given to this fan because, when opened, it looked like the wing of a bat, although some authorities refute this theory.

## ONNAGATA ŌGI

The fans used by *onnagata* are smaller in size and more dainty in appearance than those for actors in masculine roles. Characters like the "red princesses" Yaegaki-hime in the "Jusshukō no Ba" (Incense-Burning Scene) of *Honchō Nijūshi-kō* (The Twenty-four Paragons of Filial Piety) and Sarashina-hime in *Momijigari* hold a designless fan, gold on one side and silver on the other, with black-lacquered ribs and an orange-red tassel—a fan that has been given the name of *onna ōgi* or woman's fan (Fig. 158). Ladies-in-waiting carry the same fan, minus the tassel to denote lower rank.

Ladies of the imperial court, like those in the "Goten-no-Ba" (Mikasa-yama Palace Scene) of *Imoseyama Onna Teikin,* carry the *akome ōgi.* In real life, this ornamental fan was used demurely to hide ladies' faces, since it would have been bold indeed to expose their features indiscriminately. The Kabuki *akome ōgi* or *hi ōgi* (Fig. 159), an adaptation of the original style, has forty *kyō* or slats, including the parent ribs, made of Japanese cypress. Five corded silk streamers of purple, white, yellow, green, and orange-red, each two and a half feet long, have the upper seven inches braided and caught together in two sections. The streamers are sewn to a two-and-a-half-inch double yellow silk cord attached near the top of each main rib, which is held firmly by decorated metal bolts. The front and back faces of the fan are traditionally painted with water colors, but the designs vary widely. The *akome ōgi* are seen in *jidai-mono.*

The *oiran* (courtesans) do not use fans, since they are paid to entertain, and to fan themselves before their patrons would be a distinct rudeness. The *uchiwa,* the round fan with stationary bamboo frame and handle (Fig. 160), may be used occasionally in summer scenes because the courtesan can use it to fan someone other than herself. However, this is an incidental appearance of the *uchiwa.*

The utility of the year-round *uchiwa* finds its proper sphere in the daily events of *sewa-mono* and *kizewa-mono,* where it has a matter-of-fact existence. Not only is it the best of breeze-makers on torrid days; it is also applied as a bellows to accelerate charcoal fires for cooking daily meals or heating water for that wonderful Japanese institution, the *furo* or wooden bathtub.

*Yukata*-clad men strolling in the summer sun or in the warmth of the early summer evening shove an *uchiwa* into the rear of their obi.

## NŌ AND KYŌGEN ŌGI

Most fans used in the Nō and its comic interludes, the Kyōgen, made their first appearance in the fourteenth century. They are employed in Kabuki in the *matsubame-mono*—plays of Nō origin.

In many dance-dramas taken from the Kyōgen, Tarō Kaja and Jirō Kaja are the chief comical characters—stereotypes who can be identified by their particular costumes and fans, which often have similar designs. The fans have been given the name of *Kyōgen ōgi*.

More diversification is approached in Nō in its five main-role classifications, though the fans are stereotyped. These roles are *shin* (god), *bu* (warrior), *jo* (woman), *kyō* (madwoman—only women are mad in Nō), and *ki* (demoness). The designs on the fans differ according to these five categories, and the pictures painted on the faces of the fans are appropriate to the roles.

No specific names are given to fans used for god roles, but they are individualized by their design of the paulownia flower and the phoenix, the latter the emblem of immortality. According to Chinese legend, the phoenix is a deathless bird that lives on the boughs of the paulownia tree and eats bamboo seeds only.

Three different fans are used in warrior roles. The *kachishura* (*kachi*, victory; *shura*, battle) has pictured on its folds the rising sun and an old pine tree: *nichirin to oimatsu*. The *makeshura* (*make*, defeat; *shura*, battle) displays the sun—perhaps the setting sun—and ocean waves: *nichirin to nami*. The *kindachi* shows the sun, waves, and seaweed: *nichirin to nami to kaisō*. The last of these three derives its name from that of a noble class which was partial to the use of this particular fan. At a later date, sons of prominent samurai were also called *kindachi*. Usually the young heroes in the warrior roles meet tragedy, as typified by the Nō drama *Atsumori*, in which the youthful Atsumori, having been killed in battle by Kumagai, appears as a ghost. (The story of Atsumori and Kumagai also forms an important part of the Kabuki drama *Ichinotani Futaba Gunki*.)

For women's roles, a fan interestingly named the *katsura ōgi* is used. *Katsura* is the Japanese Judas tree, and the fan takes its name from the heroines who wear a wig with the headband known as *katsura obi*. Although *katsura* also means wig, in this case the headband is named for the garlands of vine that women once wore around their heads. Thus the *katsura obi* is a small band that decorates a woman's head, although admittedly in an incongruous manner that does not increase the beauty of the wearer.

The decoration on the *katsura ōgi* may be one of two designs: that of the *hana-guruma* (*hana*, flower; *kuruma*, cart wheel) or, if the heroine is a *tennyo* (celestial nymph), that of *sakura* (cherry blossoms) on a golden background.

The fans for *kyō* or madwomen are always without red, since this color represents a bright, youthful mood. For this reason they are given the name *iro-nashi* ((*iro*, color—specifically, red; *nashi*, without) *ōgi*. The fans usually have dark-blue backgrounds with autumn leaves as decoration.

*Ki* (demoness) characters handle the *oni ōgi* (*oni*, demon, demoness), a fan with a red background on which one large peony flower is painted at the center.

Nō priests avail themselves of the *ungetsu-sen* (**un**, clouds; *getsu*, moon; *sen*, fan), which takes its name from its design of clouds and moon. The *rōjo ōgi* (*rōjo*, old woman), handled by elderly women, pictures a golden bridge with a river flowing underneath, while above a graceful white heron is on the wing.

In *Kanjinchō*, the Kabuki adaptation of the Nō play *Ataka*, the actors appearing in Nō-style costume carry *chūkei*, while those dressed in Kyōgen-style costume are seen with *Kyōgen ōgi*.


## SHOSAGOTO ŌGI

Dance fans, the versatile ten-rib folding fans, made their debut in Japan at the beginning of the seventeenth century. The *shiratake-no-ōgi* (Fig. 161), also called *mai ōgi* (dance fan), is the dancer's greatest adjunct in expressing the fullest intent of the dance. The dance fan may be exquisitely designed, or it may appear with little ornamentation. Though its beauty is an attraction, it is the use made of the *mai ōgi* that is everlastingly memorable. Dance fans, usually one foot in length, are invariably larger in size than those in common usage, but the size will vary according to the height and physique of the dancer.

A small piece of lead is embedded into the base of each parent rib of the *mai ōgi*. This is done so that the fan can be flipped over and caught easily during the performance—or purposely dropped to the floor. The weighted handle permits its graceful flight, preventing it from landing on end in an unsightly position. The flipping over of a fan is often a tense yet exciting moment for the playgoers, and one that shows the timing and dexterity of the dancer.

The dancer, however, must never be engrossed with the progress of the fan. If the fan fails to reach its intended destination and instead drops to the floor, although this is a mistake, it is not of real import if the dancing itself is superbly done. The *kōken* (dancer's assistant) never rushes to retrieve the fallen fan. Instead he awaits the proper moment and places a new one in the dancer's hand, and the latter, like the great artist he is, continues his dance without giving the slightest indication that a substitution has been made.

If two dancers should be performing in identical roles and one drops his fan, yet is the more notable dancer, he will still be considered a better dancer than the other, who catches his fan, for the execution of the steps and movements is the foremost criterion in judging a dancer.

To the lay person, the manipulation of the fans by Kabuki dancers seems most intricate, if not a little frightening, but the dancer himself will admit that the *te-odori*—dancing with the hands alone—is the most difficult phase in the choreography of the Japanese dance. Meaning of movement is more easily conveyed when manipulating an *ōgi* or even some other hand property.

The fan comes alive in the hands of a competent dancer, for it can suggest an endless number of objects and actions. The closed fan can mimic, among many other things, a sword, a bow or an arrow, a spear, an oar, or a rope used to rescue a drowning person.

Sugiyama Makoto and Fujima Kanjūrō (the latter, master of the Fujima school of dancing, is admittedly the most renowned choreographer and Kabuki dance instructor in present-day Japan), in *An Outline History of the Japanese Dance,* give a pictured demonstration of the fan used as an umbrella. Initially, Kanjūrō is seen opening the fan as an umbrella, shouldering it, now braving a driving storm, then reaching from under the protective umbrella to see if the rain has stopped, and finally closing it and shaking off the raindrops. If one grasps even such rudimentary meanings in the execution of the dance, the whole is purely satisfying, and one will be consumed with inner as well as visual excitement. It is here that the fan shows its profound resourcefulness.

The partially opened *ōgi* has a curious likeness in shape to the *bachi,* the plectrum or pick used with the *samisen,* and can thus be used to pluck an imaginary version of this musical instrument, or it may represent a rowboat, a broom, a rock, or a stick. One of the hilarious uses of the partially opened *ōgi* is demonstrated in the *sake*-drinking scenes of Kyōgen. Here we see the fan used as a wine bottle, either to drink from or to pour *sake* ceremoniously in three successive draughts—in fact, to pour it so often that the results are seen in the dancer's reeling steps as he cleverly imitates a drunken man.

The completely opened fan is held above the head to represent a *kasa* (umbrella-shaped hat), or it can be a softly falling petal or suggestively represent the movement of water, either as a stream or as a cascading waterfall. It can be used as a sliding paper door or a window. A completely opened fan becomes a hood, pine branches, even a long letter—read and then folded. Upside down, it represents a mountain.

Two fans may be used together. The one, wide open, becomes a stationary mirror; the other, partially opened and held at the back of the head, becomes a hand mirror, permitting reflection in the front mirror. Again, two fully opened fans held slightly separated on top of each other can be made to portray brilliantly the undulating movements of a gently rolling wave in the sea.

During a dance at the water's edge, a closed fan becomes a fishing rod from which a line is imaginatively unwound and thrown into the water. The morning mist is brought near with the movements of a fan—first closed and then gently opened to its fullest extent—to give the feeling that the mist has indeed covered the scene. Or the fan is expertly revolved to suggest the rolling up of *sudare*, the reed blinds used to keep out the glare of the summer sun.

Acquiring a knowledge of the manifold uses of the dance fan opens a glorious avenue to greater perception and appreciation of the full theatrical glow of the Japanese dance.

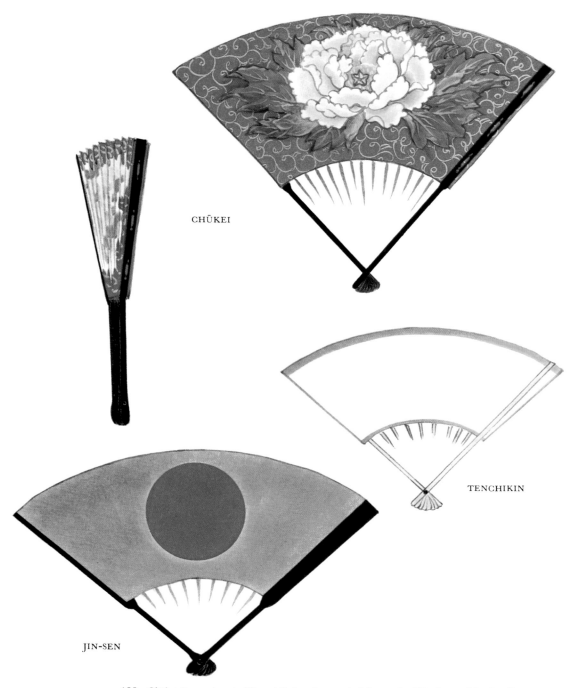

CHŪKEI

TENCHIKIN

JIN-SEN

155. *Chūkei* (two views). The *chūkei,* a fan copied from the Nō, is used by leading actors portraying such roles as those of daimyō, court nobles, and samurai—and always by those wearing *eboshi* and *suō*.

156. *Tenchikin.* The ten-ribbed white fan with a gold band along the upper and lower edges, is carried by male characters attired in *kamishimo*.

157. *Jin-sen.* The *jin-sen* or battle fan is used for the roles of lusty warriors. Two of Kabuki's favorite characters, Kumagai and Yoshitsune—both in *Ichinotani Futaba Gunki* —use a *jin-sen* with a red disc representing the sun.

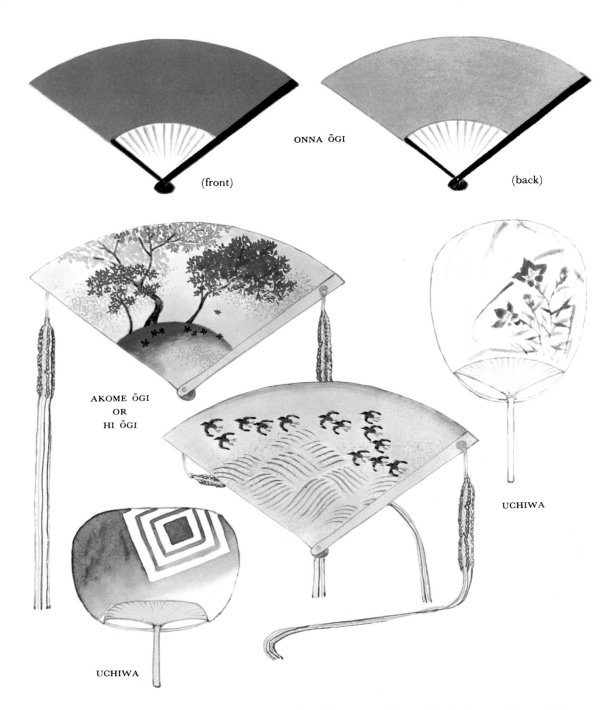

ONNA ŌGI

(front)

(back)

AKOME ŌGI
OR
HI ŌGI

UCHIWA

UCHIWA

158. *Onna ōgi* (front and back views). Characters like the "red princesses" Yaegaki-hime in *Honchō Nijūshi-kō* and Sarashina-hime in *Momijigari* hold a designless fan—gold on one side and silver on the other—that has been given the name of *onna ōgi* or woman's fan.

159. *Akome ōgi* or *hi ōgi* (front and back views). Ladies of the imperial court—for example, those in the "Mikasayama Palace" scene of *Imoseyama Onna Teikin*—carry the *akome ōgi*, a fan decorated with water-color paintings and long colored streamers.

160. *Uchiwa* (two styles). The *uchiwa*, the round fan with a rigid frame, is seen in *sewa-mono* and *kizewa-mono*, where its function is utilitarian rather than decorative.

The *hyōgo gusari-no-obitori* is made of tiny linked chain *(kusari)*, sometimes silver- or gilt-washed. This *obitori* is worn with the *hyōgo-gusari tachi*—that is, the curved-bladed sword hung from a belt and used only for cere-monial occasions, from Heian times to the present day.

The *taikogawa (taiko,* drum; *kawa,* leather) or *taikogane-no-obitori* is made of leather or metal and is shaped quite differently from the other two types. It is a shorter *obitori* with the lower portion cut in a round figure repre-senting a *taiko* or drum. Its only metal ornamentation, somewhat like a star-shaped button, appears in the center of both sides of this section of the strap. The *taikogawa-no-obitori* is made of deerskin, sometimes dyed or decorated. It was in general use during the latter part of Kamakura and into Muromachi times.

All three types of *tachi* were worn by samurai and high-ranking govern-ment officials. In Kabuki, *tachi* are primarily worn with armor or the *shōzoku* (costumes) of court nobles. The swords are always long, although the length is not permanently fixed in Kabuki. In the Edo period, the length was limited, but prior to that time the swords were three to five feet long. When the *tachi* is worn, the sharp edge faces downward toward the ground.

*Tachi* are worn by Ōmori Hikoshichi in the play of the same name, Takatoki in *Hōjō Kudai Meika no Isaoshi,* Watanabe no Tsuna in *Modori-bashi,* Uke in *Shibaraku,* Fujiwara Tokihira (Shihei) in the "Kurumabiki" scene of *Sugawara Denju Tenarai Kagami,* Mitsuhide in *Ehon Taikō-ki,* and Yoshitsune in the "Kumagai Jinya" scene of *Ichinotani Futaba Gunki.* The *tachi* is held by the *tachimochi* (sword-bearer) for Koremochi in *Momijigari* and for Togashi in *Kanjinchō.*

The *kenuki-gata-no-tachi* is one style of *tachi* carried during the Heian period, around the tenth century. Specimens of this type of *tachi* are ex-tremely scarce. The *tsuka* (hilt) and the *ha* (blade) are made of the same metal but with an odd feature: a split cut completely through the center of the *tsuka.* One of the few examples of the *kenuki-gata-no-tachi* seen on the Kabuki stage appears in *Genji Monogatari.*

The *kenuki-gata-no-tachi* was the basis of the *Kamakura-tachi*—that is the *tachi* made during the Kamakura period—and of the *kokushitsu* or black-lacquered sword. After the Kamakura period, two other swords—the *itomaki (ito,* thread; *maki,* winding or wrapping) and the *kawazutsumi (kawa,* leather; *tsutsumi,* wrapping)—with sturdily reinforced sheaths made their appearance.

The main reason for these various changes in the sword was that of sheer necessity resulting from the development of battle techniques after the Kamakura period that differed appreciably from those of previous periods. Though still wearing heavy armor, the warriors no longer rode into battle. They became foot soldiers who entered bush and forest to fer-ret out their enemies or to escape from them. Brushing against such ob-jects as rocks or trees required that the sheaths be firmly reinforced to protect the blades. Also coming into existence at this time was the longer-handled *tsuka* or hilt.

*No-dachi* (*no,* field; *tachi,* long sword) are paired swords, identical except in length and worn in *kannuki* or lock fashion—that is, in a style resembling bolting of Japanese gates. The smaller sword is the size of the longer samurai sword, the *daitō* (described later in this chapter). The larger of the pair (Fig. 162) is an exaggeratedly long curved sword with a *nurumi* (painted red groove) blade. Customarily, when paired swords are worn, the short sword is put on first between the layers of the obi, whereas the long sword, whatever its length, is worn under the obi nearest the body.

Such enormous swords in Kabuki are a reflection of those prominent in the fourteenth and fifteenth centuries, when swords became increasingly longer, necessitating the help of a retainer to carry them. Sometimes there was even a little wheel at the end of the *saya* (sheath) so that it could be trundled along. At times the *no-dachi* were carried over the shoulders of the warriors, and this style of carrying the sword was often depicted by artists in the picture scrolls known as *emaki.* Some of the swords were so huge that they could not be carried into a house.

The model of the famous sword in *Shibaraku* was probably taken from this period, but it has been said that the family of Danjūrō I—the actor who introduced *Shibaraku* to the stage—were samurai attached to the celebrated Takeda family and that the figuration of the *Shibaraku* sword was taken from one of three swords handed down within the family. This, however, is somewhat questionable, since Danjūrō I is said to have been a *chūgen* (samurai servant or footman) before he became an actor.

The larger of the two swords worn by Kamakura no Gongorō Kagemasa, the principal character in *Shibaraku,* is the longest sword in Kabuki. The length of the blade is sixty-four inches and that of the hilt twenty-two inches. Kumedera Danjō, in *Kenuki,* wields a pair of *no-dachi,* but they are not quite so spectacular as Gongorō's.

## THE KATANA

The *katana*—that is, swords of specific type carrying this name, rather than swords in general—are of varying kinds. In the descriptions given below, it will be helpful to remember the following table of Japanese measurements:

$$1 \; bu = 0.119305 \text{ inch}$$
$$1 \; sun = 1.193054 \text{ inches}$$
$$1 \; shaku = 11.930542 \text{ inches or } 0.99421 \text{ foot}$$

The *koshi-gatana* (*koshi,* loins, hips; *katana,* sword) has a short blade with a maximum length of one *shaku,* eight *sun*—a trifle less than one-half the length of the *uchi-gatana,* the longer of a dissimilar pair of swords described below. The *koshi-gatana* (Fig. 162) is interchangeable with the *mete,* an equal-sized sword with a very small *tsuba*(guard). Either of these is used to form a pair with the *tachi* or the *uchi-gatana*. Although they are worn as a pair, they are not identical. During the Edo period, the *koshi-gatana* became the *shōtō,* the shorter of the two swords worn by samurai.

The *uchi-gatana* (*uchi*, from *uchi-awaseru*, to strike or attack) is the longer of a dissimilar pair of swords, its curved blade being two *shaku*, eight or nine *sun* (slightly less than three feet) in length (Fig. 162). The sword is worn thrust through the obi, its blade curving upward, then down, so that, if unsheathed, the sharp edge will face upward. It should be noted that around the twelfth or thirteenth century the *uchi-gatana* was worn singly.

*Daishō* (*dai,* large; *shō,* small)—paired swords identical except in length—make their wearers easily distinguishable in Kabuki, for the samurai is the only person permitted their use. If the sword mountings are not the same, the smaller sword is replaced by the *wakizashi,* a medium-length sword slightly less than two *shaku* (about two feet) long. The two swords, regardless of length, are inserted into the obi in the prescribed manner. The cutting edges of both swords face upward.

The manner of wearing the *daishō* is slightly different for the samurai and the masterless samurai or *rōnin.* The samurai wears his swords in a more or less horizontal position but somewhat apart—a position referred to as *maehan* (*mae,* front; *han,* half). The *rōnin* maintains the same position for the *shōtō* (short sword) as the samurai but inserts the *daitō* (long sword) into the obi so that the hilt projects upward at breast level. The *rōnin's* swords are closer together than the samurai's—a fashion called *otoshizashi* (*otoshi,* dropped; *sashi,* worn, as a sword). Samurai and *rōnin* always appear with two swords.

It is considered most elegant and appropriate if the length of the short sword equals the distance between the point of the long sword and the mounting where the *sageo* (suspending cord) is attached to it. Also, in Kabuki, the hilt is one-quarter the length of the sword.

The *otokodate* in Kabuki wears a *naga-wakizashi,* a long sword that resembles the *daitō* of the samurai but is under no circumstances referred to as a *daitō,* for the obvious reason that the *otokodate* is not a samurai and is therefore forbidden to wear a *daitō.* The wealthy merchants of the *chōnin* class are allowed to wear only one sword: the medium-length *wakizashi.*

## BLADES

Blades of swords are also differentiated in Kabuki. They are made either of metal or of wood, although the former has preference. Even in the days when Kabuki swords were supposed to be made of substitutes for metal, there were numerous blades made of metal, since the sword has always had a very important role on the stage.

Imitation blades were originally made of bamboo, a fact that accounts for the survival of one sword name that is something of a misnomer in today's theater. This is the name *takemitsu katana,* which employs the words *take* (bamboo) and *mitsu,* the suffix of many swordsmiths' names—for example, Kanemitsu, a leading swordsmith of Bizen Province. Today, these blades are never made of bamboo because, when cut thin, it readily breaks. Instead, they are made only of *kashi* (oak).

After the blades have been shaped, black lacquer is applied and, over this, a foil made of a mixture of tin and lead is pasted to give the blades a silver sheen. The lacquer is put on first to insure the durability of the wood and also because, as a base, it has a tendency to give a brighter luster to the foil. Swords with blades of this type are the ones most commonly used in classic plays, both *jidai-mono* and *sewa-mono.*

A sword of plain wood with a *tsuba* is given the name of *bokutō*—literally, wooden sword. Normally *bokutō* are used for practice only, but swords of this type are wielded by the *chūgen* (samurai servants) in the third scene of *Chūshingura.* Since the *chūgen* are persons of inferior social status, their swords are on the same footing. In this instance, the costumes are quite realistic, differing noticeably from the unrealistic wooden swords.

Simply made swords handled by mass groups, such as the many men who appear in a *tachimawari* or fight scene, are called *samma katana* because their shape suggests that of the *samma,* a mackerel with a sharp-pointed head. The blades, made of *sugi,* the wood of the cryptomeria tree, are covered with silver foil pasted directly on the unlacquered wood base. Generally, these swords do not have *tsuba* (guards), and the *tsuka* or hilts are wound with plain black cotton cloth. Certainly they are not objects of art, nor do the blades glisten like silver.

Swords for general plays have unsharpened blades of iron called *hommi* (*hon,* genuine; *mi,* body)—blades of sufficient weight to give the illusion of reality. However, a softer metal blade is substituted whenever the sword must be bent during the action of the play. In dramas in which the action takes place in darkness, the sword has a metal blade when it is required to strike a stone and flick off a spark. An example of the *hommi katana* may be seen in the closing scene of *Iga-goe Dōchū Sugoroku.* The *hommi katana* is also carried by Sano Jirōzaemon in *Kago-Tsurube Sato no Eizame* (The Sword Kago-Tsurube Avenges Its Owner) and by Chijimiya Shinsuke in *Hachiman Matsuri Yomiya no Nigiwai* (Merrymaking on the Eve of the Hachiman Festival).

In *jidai-mono* the *hommi katana* is a perfect implement for Kajiwara Kagetoki, in *Kajiwara Heiza Homare no Ishikiri,* when he proves the excellence of a sword—an heirloom of the Minamoto family—by cleaving a stone water trough in two with one clean blow. The sword used is almost a genuine one, except that the blade is not sharpened.

The distinctive feature of the *nari-tsuba katana* is its guard, which is composed of three unconnected metal discs—two large ones in the form of a regular sword guard, with a smaller disc in the center—purposely put together loosely so that a movement of the sword will bring the discs together with a clang and give emphasis to the action. The sharp ringing sound of the metal as a fight becomes more vigorous or as the blades are snapped into the sheaths resounds throughout the theater with complete realism, even though the movements of the fighting are stylized to the utmost degree.

The blades of the *nari-tsuba katana* must be heavier in order to permit them to make a natural sound and to be thrust into the stage floor, as they frequently are. These swords may be seen notably in plays that call for impressive posing with a sword—for example, the *dammari* and *koroshiba* (murder) scenes as enacted by such characters as Tombei in *Shinrei Yaguchi no Watashi* (The Yaguchi Ferry), Sadakurō in *Chūshingura,* and Danshichi Kurobei in *Natsu Matsuri Naniwa no Kagami.*

*Nurimi* (*nuri,* painted, lacquered; *mi,* body) are black-lacquered wooden blades designed with a red lacquer groove called *chimizo* (*chi,* blood; *mizo,* furrow) slightly below the top edge. The lacquering is a process followed only in Kabuki. In the case of real-life swords, it was commonly said that the groove was made to permit blood to run freely, but according to swordsmiths, it was cut to give balance to the blade. John M. Yumoto, in his handbook *The Samurai Sword,* states that "originally grooves were made to prevent the sword from bending and to lessen weight." The *nurimi katana* are used only in *aragoto*—the bombastic plays described in Chapter 2—and then only by the more powerful characters.

## MOUNTINGS AND DECORATIONS

A basic rule regarding the *sageo*—the heavy cord of silk from which the sword is suspended—although not hung from the waist, as we shall see—is that it should be of the same color as the *tsuka* or hilt. In *jidai-mono,* if the *tsuka* decorations are black, the *sageo* should also be black, and so on, but throughout Kabuki we find such numerous exceptions that the rule seems not to apply. Although both *sageo* and *tsuka* are light blue in the "Michiyuki" scene of *Chūshingura,* and both are dark blue for the role of Mitsukuni in the dance-drama *Takiyasha* (The Witch Princess)—otherwise known as *Masakado* or as *Shinobiyoru Koi wa Kusemono* (The Love That Stole Near Was Villainous and Wicked)—Motome, in the "Michiyuki Koi no Odamaki" (Spindle of Love) scene of *Imoseyama Onna Teikin,* has a sword with a *sageo* differing from the *tsuka* in color. The daimyō prefer all white, yet in the third scene of *Chūshingura* black is worn for formal wear when the daimyō is dressed in *kamishimo,* conforming to actual practice of the period. Occasionally, leading actors display their own preferences, as did Nakamura Utaemon VI when he chose swords with white *tsuka* and black *sageo* for his appearance as Enya Hangan in *Chūshingura* in 1958—a choice that would have appeared uncouth in previous generations. Colors may vary according to the whim of the actor or for the purpose of creating harmony with the costume.

The more gentle *nimaime* and *wakashu* wear swords decorated with light blue, but the more manly *nimaime* use dark blue. The divergence in colors is thought to express the difference in personalities. Impressive characters in the gentle category include Koremochi in *Momijigari,* Kampei in the "Michiyuki" scene of *Chūshingura,* and Shirai Gompachi in *Suzugamori.* There are, however, some gentle male characters in *jidai-mono*—like Motome in *Imoseyama Onna Teikin*—who carry swords with *sageo* and *tsuka* of different colors. The *sageo* may be either red, blue, green, or purple, while the *tsuka* is white. In contrast with the brighter-colored *sageo* and *tsuka* of swords worn by youths, those of middle-aged or older characters run to dark blue, gray, and black.

The length of the *sageo* for swords worn by the younger men of the type noted above is around six *shaku* (about six feet). This long *sageo* is called the *naga-sageo* (*naga,* long). Quite the opposite is the shorter *sageo* on swords of wicked or comical characters.

The *sageo* has several practical uses besides being just a decorative cord drawn through the *kuri-gata* or cord knobs of the scabbard and wound around the scabbard of the sword. It is not worn as a belt around the body, but it can be substituted for a *tasuki*—that is, a band to hold back the kimono sleeves and free the arms for action—or a *hachimaki* or can be used to bind two swords together, enabling the warrior to carry them on his back. It can also be secured tightly around the scabbards in order to prevent the swords from moving.

Several of the gentler characters, including Motome in *Imoseyama Onna Teikin,* Yoshimine in *Yaguchi no Watashi,* and Jūrō in *Kotobuki Soga no Taimen,* carry identically styled swords with *tsuka* of five *sun* (about five inches) and *saya* (sheaths) of one *shaku* (about one foot, four and three-tenths inches) in length. The *saya* is decorated in *makie*—lacquer sprinkled with gold dust—and the *tsuba* or guard is generally round.

Daimyō swords, like those of the younger men noted above, have *naga-sageo* (Fig. 162) running to about six *shaku,* two *sun* in length—that is, approximately six feet. The pattern on the *saya* is the daimyō's personal crest. The *tsuka* is covered with imitation sharkskin.

The decorations of the swords carried by the *aragoto* characters known as *oshimodoshi* (Fig. 162) are appropriately bold, as we shall see, but a word about the role itself will be enlightening at this point.

The virile *oshimodoshi* appears in the final scenes of such plays as *Kyō-Ganoko Musume Dōjōji* and *Onna Narukami* to "push back" (this is the literal meaning of the word) the evil spirits into which the leading characters have turned. He enters the scene by way of the *hanamichi,* whence he physically forces the evil spirit back to the stage proper as it is on the verge of escaping. Having subdued the demon, and with all the characters on stage, he speaks a few lines before the curtain is drawn. He is on stage for the short interval of only one and a half minutes at most. It is of interest to note that the *oshimodoshi* appears only in plays in which the chief character is a woman. It is also pertinent to note that the *onnagata* who is to perform the leading role requests that his regular stage partner take the role of the *oshimodoshi*. When Baikō VII, for example, is to play the leading role in *Kyō-Ganoko Musume Dōjōji* based on the Nō version, he requests that Danjūrō XI appear as the *oshimodoshi*.

The *oshimodoshi* usually carries a sword decorated in black with a large green *fusa* or tassel at the end of the *sageo*. Both *fusa* and *sageo* are green for most *aragoto* roles, although Chōbei, in *Suzugamori*, has a sword with a black *tsuka*, a scabbard covered with imitation sharkskin, and a red *fusa*. The strong green-colored *tsuka* are considered the exclusive property of *aragoto* characters. Frequently, however, such roles as those of the *namazu-bōzu* or comic priests in *Shibaraku*, of *yakko* or samurai footmen, of villains, and of comic persons make use of the same color. The swords in these cases generally have black or salmon-red scabbards with *dōgane* (*dō*, body; *kane*, metal)—that is, three fancy metal adornments in a spaced arrangement on the scabbard. If a tassel is attached to the *sageo*, the length of the *sageo* is shortened to about three feet, and the cord has the name of *fusatsuki sageo*: a *sageo* with a tassel. In *Tomoyakko* (Retinue of Servants), a dance play, the *yakko* do not always wear the prescribed color of green but may change to red or white.

The *saya* or scabbard of the Kabuki sword, made of wood and lacquered or highly embellished with inlaid ornamentation, has only one service: to protect the blade, but its distinctive designs are engaging even to the lay person. Three types of these scabbards are classified as *guri-zaya*, *dōgane-iri saya*, and *kizami-zaya*.

*Guri-zaya* is a Kabuki term; outside the theater this type of scabbard is known as the *ebi-zaya* (*ebi*, shrimp) and derives this name from the regularly carved notches, about one inch apart, throughout its entire length, which resemble those in the shell of a shrimp. The usual color is dark red (lacquered), but in Kabuki a brighter red is common. Occasionally, black is used. The *guri-zaya* is the property of stalwart samurai or *rōnin*.

The *dōgane-iri saya*—that is, a scabbard decorated with *dōgane* (see above)—is recognizable by its metal ring decorations generally found in three positions proportionately spaced on a salmon-red or black-lacquered background. This type of *saya* is used for the swords of forceful samurai, *rōnin*, and *yakko*.

The *kizami-zaya* (*kizamu*, to chop or cut) also has carved notches like those of the *guri-zaya*, but they are neither so deep nor so far apart. The *kizami* or notched pattern frequently decorates sheaths for any size of sword or dagger.

The point or end of the scabbard—that is, the chape—is known as the *kojiri*. Three examples have been chosen for description here because of their diversity of appearance.

The first of these, the *maru* (round) *kojiri*, is lacquered black or red or is covered with sharkskin or *makie* (gold-patterned lacquer). This type of chape is found on the scabbard for the single sword of the *chōnin*. It can be seen in *jidai-mono*, in *sewa-mono*, and in *wagoto* plays, but it is seldom used.

The second type of *kojiri* is cut straight across the end of the scabbard and for this reason is known as the *ichimonji* (straight-line) *kojiri* or the *kiri* (cut) *kojiri*. The scabbards for the *denchū-zashi* (sword worn in a castle) and the *chiisa-gatana* (small sword) display this particular shape of *kojiri*. A scabbard with the *ichimonji kojiri* is part of the costume of daimyō and samurai of almost equal rank when they wear *naga-gamishimo* with *kitsuke*—for example, Wakasanosuke and Enya Hangan in Act III of *Chūshingura*.

The third type of *kojiri,* the metal chape known as *toppei,* derives its name from its similarity to a cone-shaped sea shell of the same name. The scabbard with the *toppei* chape is lacquered either black or red. It houses the swords wielded by men of strong character such as Matsuō in the "Terakoya" scene of *Sugawara Denju Tenarai Kagami* and Ōya no Tarō Mitsukuni in *Shinobiyoru Koi wa Kusemono.*

The *tsuba* or sword guard is usually a flat plate of round, square, oblong, or other shape. The shape is determined by the taste of the individual actor and not by the role.

*Yakko* swords (Fig. 162) have specific scabbards interchangeably called *yakkozashi-no-saya, tazuna,* or *dandara,* but there is no formal name for the sword or for the *kojiri* of the scabbard. The sword carried by the *yakko* is for use only by these individuals or by persons who, like them, have little use of it as a symbol. Consequently, little confusion results from the lack of an established nomenclature. The *yakko* sword has a two-striped scabbard—black and red, white and red, black and silver, or, on exceptional occasions, red and gold. The entire length of the sword, including its *tsuka* and *kakutsuba* (square guard), is about two feet, four inches—the *tsuka* being six *sun* and the scabbard one *shaku,* seven *sun,* and five *bu.*

## OTHER ASPECTS OF THE SWORD IN KABUKI

Women in Kabuki are not without their means of protection, for they quite often have to defend their husbands', their lords', or their own honor. Their principal mode of protection is a dagger called the *kaiken* (*kai,* pocket; *ken,* sword). It is of the same length and style as the *koshi-gatana* but does not have a guard. Women carry the *kaiken* enclosed in a bag, usually brocaded, which they place in their obi. In Kabuki, warriors' wives and daughters carry *kaiken* even on ordinary occasions, but in real life women carried the dagger only for emergencies or on trips that took them fairly far from home.

Other than the *kaiken,* women may use the *kodachi,* a small sword, or the *naginata,* a kind of halberd whose full length, including handle and blade, averages more than six feet, although it varies according to the height of the actor (Fig. 162). The *naginata*, similar in use to the battle-ax, is resorted to for defense by both women and men. It is held with both hands and is wielded with either a thrusting or a cutting motion.

The *aikuchi* (Fig. 162) is a dagger with a maximum blade length of a little less than one foot and without a *tsuba*. It is housed in either a plain wooden scabbard or a lacquered one. The *aikuchi* is the property of ordinary people, including some low individuals such as highwaymen.

Vagabonds and their ilk who appear in *kizewa-mono* thrust one of two daggers into their *sarashi-nuno*, the bleached cotton cloth wrapped around their midriff to assure warmth. This is either the *kyūsun-gobu* (sometimes *kusun-gobu*—literally "nine *sun*, five *bu*"), a nine-and-a-half-inch dagger, or the *deba-bōchō*, a kitchen knife, wrapped in a *tenugui*.

The *kozuka* is a small dagger inserted into a special pocket in the sheath of the *shōtō*, the samurai's short sword. It is used in battle to kill special enemies and is thrust into the neck or head of the corpse to signify that the warrior has killed that particular foe. Not all *shōtō* scabbards have a place for the *kozuka*, however, and in later years in history the *kozuka* served for any purpose for which a knife might be used.

Many Kabuki dramas feature swords with individual names, always ending in the suffix *maru*—for example, the sword Tomokiri-maru, which is the object of search in *Sukeroku* and *Kotobuki Soga no Taimen*. The suffix itself has something of the meaning of "spirit" or "power." When attached to a name—that of a ship, a sword, a hunting dog, a hawk, and so on—it is thought to add fresh spirit or power.

There are certain conventions in the use of swords. A pair of swords is an indispensable part of a samurai's dress in Kabuki, as it was in real life. On the stage, whether in indoor or outdoor scenes, the warrior's trusty blades are at his side. When he pays a visit, after seating himself in Japanese style, he removes the *daitō* and places it at his right side to show friendliness, an action making it evident that he has no intention of drawing his weapon. If he places it at his left side, the hilt to the front, he infers that there might be an attack, for in this position he can easily grasp it in self-defense.

The placing of the sword is different in the presence of his master the daimyō, for then the samurai puts it at his right side but places the *tsuka* toward the back. The warrior who wishes to convey complete obedience to his master ties both swords together with the *sageo*.

On the occasions when a ranking samurai makes a visit, his longer sword is carried by a young *tachimochi* or sword-bearer who sits somewhat to the side or rear of his master throughout the scene.

Swords are stowed in sword racks on the wall or the floor in the sitting rooms of their owners' homes. At night, however, they are removed from the racks and placed within comfortable reach. The only two instances in which the wearer completely relinquishes his blades are when he is in the bath or when he is patronizing a house of assignation, for in the latter all customers, regardless of their station in life, are treated as equals as long as they have funds to pay for the entertainment they seek.

*Kata*—stylized form—more than realistic movement, is essential to Kabuki aesthetics, and this, of course, applies to the use of the sword on the Kabuki stage. Before modern innovations, a most illustrative bit of stage business was the moving of a sword straight up overhead to signify that a warrior had already killed his enemy. Today the *kata* is more natural, even though in combat adversaries never touch each other with the swords. In the "Kurumabiki" scene of *Sugawara Denju Tenarai Kagami,* the three Soga brothers make a movement to draw their swords, but they never really do so. Taking a pose with the suggested intention of doing so imparts the full meaning of the action to the audience.

Swords, like fans, are more than properties. They become an extension of the characters who handle them, and their use is a part of the poetic movement in Kabuki.

CHAPTER 22

# Katsura: Wigs

Little did the maidens in the Age of the Gods realize that they would be the indirect cause for adding the word for wig—*katsura*—to theater terminology. On festival days these young ladies, dressed in holiday finery, decorated their long tresses with *hana-kazura,* flowering vines of the season. These natural hair decorations developed into such artistic creations that their counterparts, represented by wigs, were adapted by the performers of Sarugaku, the forerunner of the Nō drama. Before this, there were many innovations accompanying dramatic dance forms, but wigs had not been introduced.

In the fourteenth and fifteenth centuries, during the Ashikaga-Muromachi period, a primitive wig was already in use for the Nō, in which the actors used white hair for elderly men and women; white or black hair, according to age, under *eboshi* for warriors; and red or black hair for supernatural beings such as mythical lions, divine dragons, and sometimes devils —as in *Momijigari.*

The first known mention of Kabuki wigs occurs in the *Miyako Fūzoku Kagami* (Mirror of Manners and Customs in the Capital), a book dealing with life in Kyoto published in 1680, a little before Genroku. Here it is stated that the *daigane* (*dai,* foundation; *kane,* metal), a copper frame covering the entire head to which hair was attached, was in use. The *daigane* (Figs. 163–166) is an essential part of the present-day wig.

All Kabuki costumes must be complemented by the proper wig, a prime requisite for the completion of the over-all visual picture of the actor. At times, for the sake of harmony, the costume will be made to match the wig.

The wig for pure Kabuki is the fascinating, unique feature of costuming, being almost void of foreign influence. Without a suitable wig, the most stunning costume would lose its instant attraction. The combination of wig and make-up can transform actors into alluring personalities or into disreputable rogues—all easily recognizable to the audience. The wig may also detract—in Western eyes, at least—from the total effect by completely failing to present the embodiment of feminine pulchritude necessary for a female impersonator. This failure may be especially noticeable in a hair style patterned after that of the Nō. The hair is parted in the middle, combed flat at the sides, drawn to the back, and allowed to hang loose after being tied at the nape of the neck or covered with cloth. A slight variation of this coiffure has a *katsura hachimaki* or wig headband wrapped around the head. But male actors impersonating females simply do not have features to offset the austerity of these coiffures.

Many hours of patient and persevering work go into the minute and detailed art of making *katsura*. It is impossible to do complete justice to this subject in the limited space of one chapter, but the introduction offered here will provide a background for further study.


## WIGMAKERS AND COIFFEURS

Two groups of men are essential to the completion of *katsura*: the *katsura-ya,* the wigmakers who cut, shape, fit, and fashion the copper bases, and the *toko-yama,* the coiffeurs who are responsible for dressing and maintaining the wigs during the month's run of Kabuki plays.

Two or three days before the final performance of each month's run, plays are selected and roles are assigned for the next month's program. This is a maddening procedure in the eyes of the Westerner, for there are only five days at most between the end of one month's run and the opening day of the next month's. Immediately after the plays have been selected, the *kyōgen-kata*—the man in charge of production who assumes various duties related to rehearsals and acts as both stage director and prompter —lists in a looseleaf notebook called the *katsura-no-tsukechō* (wig notebook) every scene, act, and role, together with the actor chosen for the role and the type of wig to be worn.

Copies of the *katsura-no-tsukechō* are sent to such interested parties as the costumers, the *toko-yama* or coiffeurs, and the Shōchiku Company's warehouse in Shintomi-chō, where the available *daigane* (copper wig bases) and *habutae* (hair-line silk) are stored. In the case of the Kikugorō Troupe, the men's *toko-yama* receive a complete listing, whereas the listing for the *onnagata toko-yama* is confined to female roles.

The busiest days for the *katsura-ya* and the *toko-yama* have now arrived, for time is of the essence. The *toko-yama* must visit the actors to ask their advice and personal preferences regarding the wigs they will wear. This procedure accomplished, the most fundamental step in making the wig must be taken: the *atama-awase* (*atama,* head; *awase,* fitting)—that is the fitting of the *daigane* to the head.

These are really days of hustle and bustle, for the *katsura-ya* must seize every opportunity when he can find the actor with a free moment. Formerly, the head-fitting was done in a more leisurely manner at the actor's home for starring roles and in the dressing rooms for other actors. Today the entire process must be completed in the theater.

An actor has to be measured for head size and shape for each separate role. The *daigane* (Figs. 163–166) is kept for a lifetime unless an actor's head changes in size (an extremely uncommon occurrence) and is held in storage with the actor's name inside until it is needed for a succeeding time when he performs the same role. Each actor must have a separate *daigane* for each separate role.

The *daigane* fitting is completed through the collaboration of the *katsura-ya* and the *toko-yama*. The former shapes the *daigane* while the latter attends the fitting as a consultant, although at times he may make a specific request.

The *toko-yama* are at present divided into two classes: those who confine their activities to *onnagata* wigs and those who handle only men's wigs. Before the changes in the theater that occurred following the great earthquake of 1923, men's wigs were dressed in the workrooms on the backstage third floor of the Kabuki-za and women's in those on the mezzanine floor—an arrangement that gave birth to the names *sangai* (third floor) and *chūnikai* (mezzanine) for the respective *toko-yama*. Today the backstage mezzanine has completely disappeared, but the traditional names *sangai* and *chūnikai* survive, regardless of the floor on which the workrooms are located. In the Kabuki-za the *sangai* can still be found on the third floor, but the *chūnikai* is on the second.

The *toko-yama* work for the Shōchiku Company, the traditional Kabuki management, but they are assigned exclusively to individual troupes. It requires about ten years' apprenticeship to become a professional hairdresser in this lifetime art. Often the trade is handed down from generation to generation within a family, but outside pupils are accepted. It has always been the custom to hire men for this work, and therefore there are no famous *toko-yama* among women, for they are not accepted as pupils.

Little thought is given to retirement. The venerable Mr. Asai, head of the entire wig department for the Kikugorō Troupe, was eighty years old in 1958 and had then been plying his profession for sixty-seven years. He works personally in the men's department, where ten men are kept busy, depending upon the number of wigs needed for a production.

About three hundred men's wigs are used each month, though there are approximately four hundred male hair styles remaining in Kabuki today. It is regrettable that so many of the old-style wigs—those devised by former actors for use under light radiating through oiled-paper panels or by candlelight—have one after another fallen into disuse through the advent of modern stage lighting, a development that has made the make-up and features of actors appear more distinct and is not suitable to the use of some of the old-fashioned wigs.

A former pupil of the above-mentioned Mr. Asai is Miura Hiro-o, the personable *toko-yama* for *onnagata katsura* of the Kikugorō Troupe. In 1961 he had been in the profession for fifty years. His bright young son, Miura Kikuo, following in his father's footsteps, takes care of the wigs for the lesser *onnagata* roles. With up to three helpers, Mr. Miura dresses from fifty to one hundred wigs a month, around one hundred being the limit for *onnagata* hair styles.

Today new coiffures are fashioned as copies of those in old paintings and scrolls, or an artist may bring in a sketch from which the *toko-yama* attempts to comb the wig according to the desire of the artist and the actor who is to wear it. The actors expect exactness, and it is therefore not always easy to satisfy them. They are quite particular about every detail of clothing, wigs, and staging, as they should be, for without the desire for continued perfection the inward vitality of the Kabuki would cease. This over-all goal of perfection is badly needed in all phases of today's theater, where craving for personal recognition appears to be greater than that for the attainment of perfection in Kabuki as an entity.

### MAKING THE WIG

Before the *atama-awase* the *katsura-ya* has made basic *daigane* for all new wigs in a workshop outside the theater. The *daigane* is initially composed of one main piece and two or three supporting pieces. These the *katsura-ya* bends to size by hand. Then the pieces of the *daigane* are riveted together to form a crude base.

After the basic pieces of the *daigane* have been riveted together, the *katsura-ya* fits the *nedori-no-kane* to the crude base. This is the appendage at the back of the *bin-no-mono daigane* (Fig. 163)—that is, a *daigane* composed of two *bin* or side pieces and a suspension bridge—for fashioning *fukurotsuki* (back hair inflated like a bag) styles, to which the *mage* or topknot is attached (Fig. 166).

The *tsuri,* the suspension bridge across the back of the *daigane,* is then placed to connect the *bin.* Sometimes two *tsuri* are needed for men's wigs, and always two for *onnagata* wigs. The lower-placed *tsuri* is called the *naka-no-tsuri* or middle suspension bridge.

The *tabo-no-kane* completes this part of the wig's construction. It is either a separately attached piece or a continuation of the *bin* around the base and serves as the metal bridge at the base of the back of the *daigane* to which the *tabo* or back hair is attached. The styling of the hair depends on the *tabo-no-kane* for combing into the desired contour. With this addition, the basic construction of all *daigane* is completed, though by no means is the work on the *daigane* finished.

Not all of the steps noted below are included for each base. The number depends upon whether the *daigane* is for a man's wig or for an *onnagata* wig and upon the styling.

The *aibiki,* strings made of hemp covered with *kaiki,* a type of taffeta

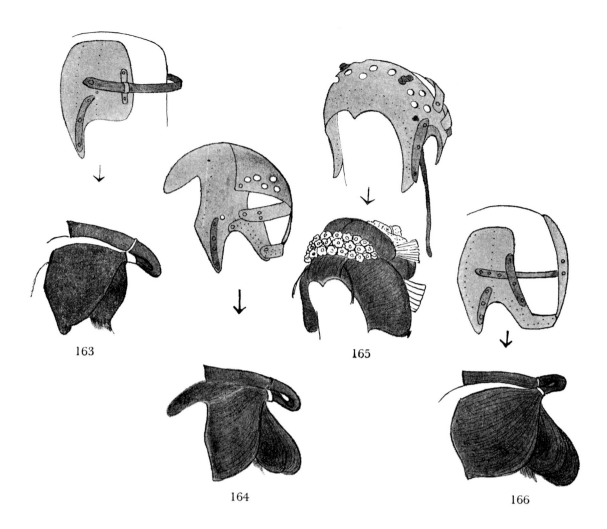

163

165

164

166

163. *Bin-no-mono daigane.* This *daigane,* of two *bin* or side pieces and a suspension bridge and lacking the *kōra* or piece representing the crown of the head, forms the base for the *aburatsuki* (back hair pomaded, polished, and flattened to head) coiffure pictured with it—a style worn by daimyō, *hatamoto,* and samurai in *ō-jidai-mono* and *jidaimono.*

164. *Kōra-mono daigane* with *tabo-no-kane.* This wig base has both the piece representing the crown of the head and the bridge to which the *tabo* or back hair is attached. The wig itself has the back hair in the bag-shaped *fukurotsuki* style. It is worn principally in *sewa-mono* by a variety of characters, including villains *(kataki-yaku),* persons who make final judgments or settle quarrels *(sabaki-yaku),* managers employed in merchants' households, certain *wagoto* characters (to make them appear more sexually attractive), and characters who have some quality of the supernatural or of awesomeness.

165. *Maru-tabo-mono daigane.* This *daigane,* worn mainly for female roles in *jidai-mono,* is shown with a coiffure in which the *tabo* is stretched into a short, roundish puff by the insertion of a *tabo-gane* (stretcher). Actually, this *daigane* is the base for all female coiffures, with slight changes in appendages—such as eliminating the *tabo-gane* in the *ji-tabo* style.

166. *Bin-no-mono daigane* with *tabo-no-kane.* The *daigane* shown here lacks the *kōra* but has the metal bridge at the back for attachment of the *tabo,* which is in *fukurotsuki* style. The accompanying wig is used for a few roles in *jidai-mono* and for practically all *chōnin* and commoner roles in *sewa-mono.*

with thick weft threads, are fixed to all *onnagata* wigs and to some of the more bulky men's wigs so that they may be tied firmly on the head. The *aibiki-no-ana,* the holes back of each temple through which the *aibiki* are drawn and knotted, will be found in all *daigane* except the above noted *bin-no-mono,* a *daigane* with only two side pieces connected by a suspension bridge.

A *bingane* is an extra metal piece inserted by the *toko-yama* in the *bin* (sidelocks) of samurai and court-lady wigs for the purpose of inflating them. It is not used for the *iki* or dandified roles of *sewa-mono,* since such styling does not accord with everyday dress. The *bingane-no-tsubo* is a metal holder attached to the *daigane* for securing the *bingane.*

The *bunko-dome,* medium-size holes cut into the supporting copper pieces connecting the *naka-no-tsuri* (middle suspension bridge) and the *tabo-no-kane* (base bridge), are for the purpose of holding the ornamental back hairpins of certain *onnagata* wigs.

The *chikara-gane* (*chikara,* strength) is a narrow curved strip of metal riveted on each temple of the *daigane* to reinforce it. Wigs are always put on and taken off by handling these parts.

The *ikinuki,* large holes at the back of the forepiece of the *onnagata daigane,* serve to ventilate it and make it lighter in weight. Similarly, a man's wig which has a *kōra,* a copper piece representing the crown of the head, has large ventilation holes at the back called *kazetōshi-no-ana*—literally, holes for letting the wind pass through.

The *mimiwaki* is a metal strip riveted to the *bin* (copper sides of the base) behind the ears to secure the *wagane,* the metal band connecting these sides across the back of the head.

The *nedori-no-ana,* small-sized holes on the upper back of the headpiece to which the *mage* is attached, become the *ne* or root of the *mage.* For *onnagata* wigs, the *nedori-no-ana* are found in the *naka-no-tsuri* (middle suspension bridge).

The *osae-mino* are the small holes along the hairline by means of which *mino-ge*—original type of hair braids or sheets attached directly to the *daigane*—are affixed.

A *tabo-gane,* also known as *tabo-kane,* is a separate piece of metal not riveted to the *daigane* but put into the *tabo* (back hair) at the time of dressing the wig for help in stretching the *tabo* into a short rounded puff. It is not required for the *ji-tabo-mono katsura*—the wig whose *tabo* is dressed without a stretcher and has a natural long, slender contour—and it is never used for *sewa-mono* wigs.

The *tabo-gane-dome* is a metal appliance riveted on both sides of the back of the *daigane* as a holder for the *tabo-gane* or stretcher. It is of the same shape as the above-noted *bingane-no-tsubo* and the *wagane-no-osae* described below.

The *wagane,* which we have already noted as the narrow metal band connecting the *bin* across the center back of the head, is used when a man's *daigane* is composed of only the two *bin* or of two *bin* with a *nedori-no-kane*— that is, a copper appendage at the back of a *daigane* having only two side pieces.

The *wagane-no-osae* are exactly the same shape as the two other metal holders, the *bingane-no-tsubo* and the *tabo-gane-dome*. They are holders near the center edges of the two *bin* through which the *wagane* is inserted. The ends of the *wagane* are then riveted to the *daigane*.

The next step is to mold the crude *daigane* to the shape of the actor's head. An actor must exercise clever judgment as to the shaping of the *bin* and the *kuri-gata* (*kuri*, cutting, scooping; *kata*, shape, mold) or hairline, for one of the most significant means of displaying the character of the role lies in the cutting and shaping of the latter. It was said in the past that an actor could only be called a true actor when he was able to order the most effective *kuri-gata* for his face, since the *kuri-gata* can emphasize the amorousness of the *nimaime* or the strong, forbidding look of the *kataki-yaku* or villain.

The length of the *bin* and the shape of the *kuri-gata* permit the *toko-yama* to dress the wig to enhance the looks of the wearer. A long face can be made shorter, a small face larger, or a short one longer if the proper *bin* and *kuri-gata* have been selected. Consequently, if the actor thoroughly understands his facial traits (and admits their deficiencies), he can have the *katsura-ya* adjust the *bin* and the *kuri-gata* so as to bring out his better features effectively and conceal his weaker ones.

After the *daigane* fitting is over, the *katsura-ya* is responsible for attaching hair to the *daigane* at the sides and back if the wig is a *suppori-no-mono* which completely covers the crown of the head. He also attaches the hair to the *sakaiki-no-mono,* a wig with a *kōra* (Fig. 164) or copper piece attached to the *daigane* representing the crown of the head. The *kōra* (shell) is so named because it resembles the shell of a tortoise.

The *katsura-ya* applies a blue coloring called *seitai* to the *kōra* when it represents the shaven crown of the head. He sews the hair—strand by strand—to *habutae* (plain silk), mostly for *sewa-mono* wigs. He pastes paper on the *daigane* and over this pastes the *habutae* with the hair attached, or he sews on the *mino-ge,* as described below. The *katsura-ya* also molds special removable scars, wounds, and pockmarks and dyes hair to the desired colors.

## MINO-GE AND HABUTAE

The final step—one of the most essential—in constructing a completed wig is that of applying hair to the *daigane*. The use of *mino-ge* (*mino*, straw raincoat; *ke,* hair)—hair flatly braided at one end—is the original method of attaching hair to the *daigane* by hand-sewing and tying through the holes in the *daigane*.

There are two kinds of *mino:* ordinary *mino*, plaited roughly and having the rough appearance of a straw raincoat, is used for the underneath hair, while *keshō-mino,* plaited smoothly, is placed over the ordinary *mino* for finishing the hairline. To relieve the ugliness of the *mino* hairline, the decorative forehead cloth known as a *bōshi* (see Chapter 18) is always worn. *Mino-ge* is still used for wigs in very old pure *jidai-mono,* but the newer method of using *habutae* produces more attractive ones.

The use of the word *habutae* in the following sections may at first seem confusing, for it is the name of three different items. First, *habutae* is plain silk cloth. Second, it is a strip of this cloth on which hair is sewn and then pasted to the base of the wig for dressing in various styles. Third, it is a square piece of the same silk coated with a mixture of wax pomade and castor oil so that actors in male roles can press it evenly over the head prior to putting on certain types of wigs. After being fitted to the head it has the appearance of a skullcap.

The present-day wig made by sewing strands of hair one by one on a strip of *habutae* was introduced in 1803 at the Ichimura-za by the actor Onoe Matsusuke I and was made by the wigmaker Tomokurō. Matsusuke wore the wig in the role of Iwafuji, the evil chief lady-in-waiting in *Kagamiyama Kokyō no Nishikie.* But the *habutae* silk for wigs was so difficult and expensive to make that it was not widely used until the Meiji period, when the hairline *habutae* replaced the *keshō-mino.*

The *habutae,* as we have seen, is a straight piece of silk of the same name on which hair is sewn—a method that produces a more natural-looking hairline. Individual hairs are not sewn one by one to the *habutae.* Up to six needles are threaded, each with a single hair, and drawn simultaneously through the *habutae* and then drawn back through it so that the hair is locked with a loop on the back side. Pasting the *habutae* to the paper on the *daigane* firmly anchors the hair and allows it to be easily combed. It takes an expert at least an entire day to make a *habutae.* The *habutae* wig is used primarily for roles in *sewa-mono.*

Hair is put on two to three inches of the visible part of the *habutae* from the front hairline to the end of the *bin* on each side, and this is then pasted on the *daigane.* The two inches of the *daigane* above the *habutae* are left bare. Then *mino-ge* or hair pieces called *nedori*—the *mage,* for example— are attached. There are four in all: two in the front just back of the hair of the *habutae,* one in back, and one at the top center.


HAIR SUBSTITUTES

The greater percentage of *habutae* wigs are made with human hair, but for unusual wigs and special parts other materials have proved more satisfactory. These materials include yak-tail hair, brought only from Tibet and mainland China at great expense, bear fur, dyed sheep's wool, horse-tail hair, silk threads, velvet or felt for covering the *kōra* for certain roles, wire, and whale teeth—the last referred to by the Japanese as "whiskers."

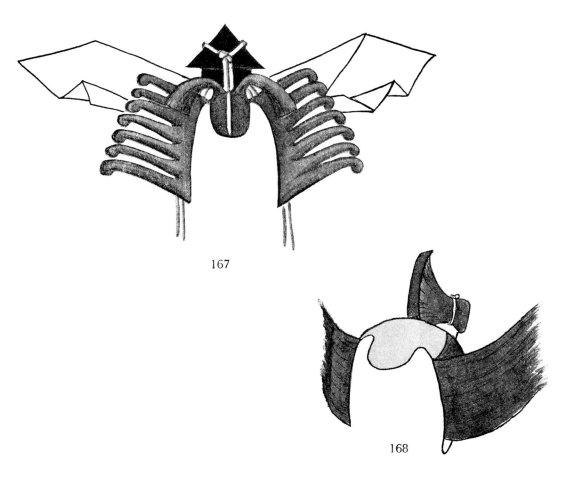

167

168

167. *Aburatsuki-abura-gomi-no-maegami-shichihon-kuruma-bin-mino-no-namajime* with *chikara-gami* and *samurai eboshi*. The formidable name of this wig matches the formidable character who wears it, for it is the spectacular coiffure worn by Gorō in *Yanone*. *Aburatsuki,* of course, signifies that the back hair is stiffly pomaded and polished. Similarly, *abura-gomi-no-maegami* means a forelock thickly treated with pomade. *Shichihon-kuruma-bin,* literally "seven-spoked-wheel sidelocks," refers to the elaborate arrangement of the side hair, and *namajime* is a style of binding the queue high and erect and tying it with a separate strand of hair from the bound lower part. The queue is lacquered stiff and does not touch the crown of the head except at its very end. The style of dividing the forelock is known as *matsu-no-ki* (pine tree), and the part is represented by an ivory or bone *wari-gushi* (dividing comb) attached to the center of the *kōra*. The two accessories are a small *samurai eboshi* and the enormous paper wings *(chikara-gami)*, which are added to the coiffure to give a look of great strength.

168. *Aburatsuki-suppori-yahazu-bin-mino-no-masakari*. This masculine wig is different from the ordinary one, since the *daigane* completely covers the head. The *kōra* is in turn covered with *habutae,* which has been pasted evenly over its surface and then painted blue, varying in shade according to the personality portrayed or the taste of the actor, and finally coated with wax. The tips of the *bin* or sides, which are visible below the sidelocks, are also painted blue. The sidelocks themselves are dressed in the *yahazu* (arrow feather) style, flaring out broadly for strong roles and less extravagantly for minor roles such as those of the attendants in the "Kurumabiki" scene of *Sugawara Denju Tenarai Kagami.* The wig has a *mino* or plaited hairline, and the topknot is done in the *masakari* or broadax style.

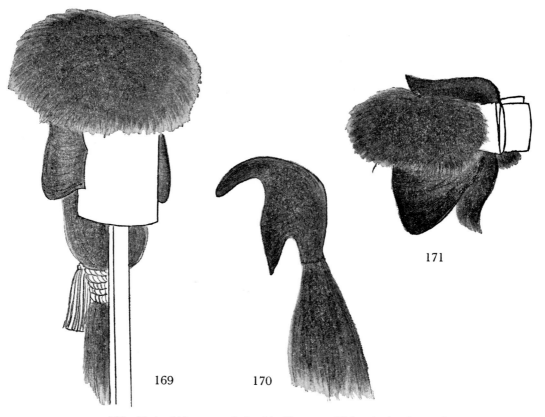

169          170

171

169. *Hyakunichi-no-tare,* tied with *kin nawa.* This wig is often referred to as the "big 100" or *daibyaku* because of the styling of the *sakayaki*—the shaven portion of the head. Here, of course, the *sakayaki* has presumably not been shaven for 100 days—hence the name *hyakunichi-no-tare.* The pompon styling does not have a set length, however. The hanging back hair is bound with the gold rope known as *kin nawa.* The wig is worn for roles expressing moods of dread, weirdness, or horror in *ō-jidai-mono* or *jidai-mono.* It is also seen in *dammari* plays.

170. *Honke-zuzoro-no-nadetsuke.* The *daigane* for this wig covers the entire head and is in turn covered with straight natural hair *(honke),* combed smoothly *(nadetsuke).* Probably in this case *zuzoro* is an expression for looseness, since the smoothly falling hair is not cut evenly at the bottom but left somewhat irregular in a natural-looking state appropriate to the *yamabushi* (mountain priest) roles for which the wig is worn. On the other hand, in Kabuki, when a character announces *ten-ichibō,* or his intention to usurp the powers of a shōgun, a daimyō, or any other person of high authority, the ends of the hair are cut off evenly in a straight line. The back hair is tied lightly at the nape of the neck. The wig is also worn by masters of strategy and tactics and by fortunetellers.

171. *Aburatsuki-gojūnichi-hako-bin-kara-no-mae-chasen* with *yamai hachimaki* and *chikara-gami.* This is a very interesting wig which looks more like a hat than a coiffure. The hair covering the crown is long and bushy, indicating that because of illness it could not be cut for fifty days *(gojūnichi).* The *mae-chasen* topknot is hardened with lacquer and rests on the head. The box-shaped sidelocks *(hako-bin)* are made with naturally curly or "foreign" *(kara)* hair, and the shape is achieved by inserting the stretchers called *bin-gane.* The back hair is hardened with pomade *(aburatsuki),* flattened to the head, and polished. The *yamai hachimaki* worn with this wig is made of thick dark-purple *kohaku* or *chirimen* and is tied in square style on the left side of the forehead. A conservative winglike paper decoration *(chikara-gami)* is tied at the root of the queue.

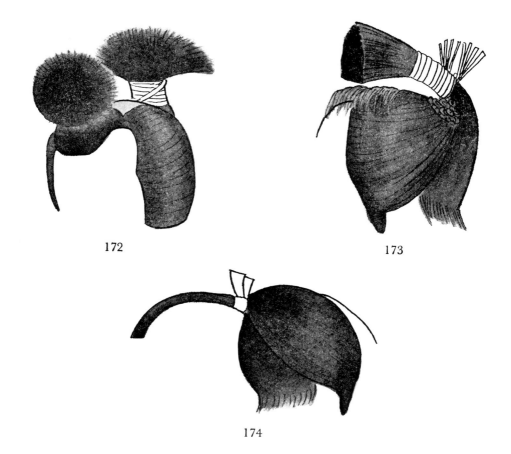

172

173

174

172. *Aburatsuki-kara-no-fukashi-bin-tsukamitate-no-kiriwara.* The *tsukamitate* (grasped erect) forelock in this particular pompon style is used for strong characters and young men. The topknot takes its name from its *kiriwara* (cut bundle of straw) shape and is tied at the root with very thick paper lacing. The inflated sidelocks *(fukashi-bin),* are made of "foreign" *(kara)* hair. This wig is seen chiefly in *ō-jidai-mono* and *jidai-mono.*

173. *Aburatsuki-naimaze-bin-no-issoku-tabane-no-omatsuri-no-chirichiri.* In this wig the *naimaze-bin* (twisted and mixed sidelocks) are made of straight and curly hair equally mixed. The attractive *mage* (topknot)—in the *issoku-tabane* or bundle-of-straw style—is bound with paper lacing, and its front rests on the crown of the head. At the sides of its root are placed bunches of *chirichiri* or tightly curled hair, while on each side, above the sidelocks, are the strands of hair known as *omatsuri* (festival) because of their resemblance to ornamental decorations used at Shinto shrine festivals. The hair of this *omatsuri* is left in its natural state, as it would look after shampooing, and is called *sara-no-matsuri.* This coiffure is for the roles of strong and valiant men in *jidai-mono.*

174. *Kushime-honke-hachi-mai-bin-no-Nō-chasen.* The *kushime* or comb-line style of wig made from real hair *(honke)* was not known in the old days of the drama but was devised later as a somewhat more natural coiffure between the *aburatsuki* and the *fukurotsuki* types. It should, however, be classified as *aburatsuki.* The topknot in this wig is generally referred to as *Nō-chasen* because it is worn by actors taking roles in plays derived from the Nō or the Kyōgen. The *hachi-mai-bin* (eight-sheet sidelocks) are made with eight flat-knitted or braided "sheets" of hair sewn to the *daigane.* The *bin* have a *kobitai* or curved hairline at the temples. This type of wig is worn for the less extravagant roles in *matsubame-mono* plays taken from the Nō and the Kyōgen.

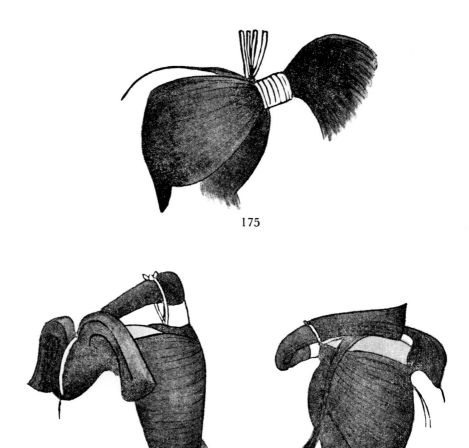

175

176                                                                     177

175. *Aburatsuki-naimaze-komi-no-bin-tachine-no-kiriwara.* The *naimaze-bin,* as previously noted, are sidelocks made of straight and curly hair equally mixed. In the present wig, as the suffix *komi* indicates, they are filled with dried rush to inflate them slightly. The *tachine-no-kiriwara-mage*—that is, the erect-root, cut-bundle-of-straw topknot—is bound tightly in upright position with the paper cord known as *motoyui,* the ends of which stand erect at the front of the topknot. Again, this is a *jidai-mono* coiffure.

176. *Aburatsuki-honke-hako-bin-(mino-)abura-gomi-no-maegami-no-namajime.* In this wig, made of natural hair *(honke),* the sidelocks are inflated by means of a stretcher to give them a box shape *(hako-bin).* They are made of the flat-knitted or braided sheets of hair known as *mino.* The forelock, in *wari-gushi* (dividing comb) style, is stiffened with pomade and highly polished—hence its name, *abura-gomi-no-maegami.* The hair just above the forehead is referred to as *manjū* or bean-jam bun, which it resembles in shape, and this roundish *maegami* is considered quite elegant. The locks curving from the top at each side of the *manjū* are called *matsu-no-ki* (pine tree). In Kabuki parlance the style of the topknot is known as *namajime,* but the origin of the name is unknown. This coiffure is worn for strong *aragoto* and *kataki-yaku* (villain) roles in *jidai-mono.*

177. *Aburatsuki-honke-bin-no-wakashu-mage.* A man's wig with a forelock is generically known as a *wakashu* or young man's style of coiffure. The shaved center of the crown, as seen in this example, is referred to as the *naka-zori* (center shaving). In this wig only real hair is used, and the coiffure appears mostly in *jidai-mono.*

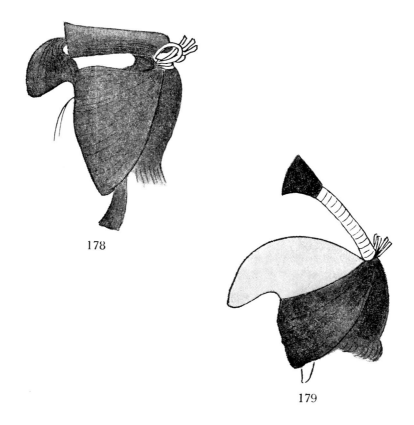

178

179

178. *Aburatsuki-honke-fukashi-bin-wakashu-no-mae-chasen-no-bō-jike.* The distinguishing difference between this coiffure and the one in Figure 177 is the *maegami*, which is combed upward into a smart-looking puff and tied, with the end attached to the root of the *mage*. The inflated sidelocks are called either *fukashi-bin* or *fukashita-bin,* a name probably taken from the verb *fukasu,* meaning to stretch, inflate, or swell. The *mae-chasen mage,* as its name suggests, is combed into the shape of a tea whisk, with the open end resting on the crown at the point where the forelock is tied. A *mae-chasen mage* characterizes wigs used for the roles of romantic or passionate young men. To accentuate the suggestion of amorousness, pomade-hardened strands of hair known as *bō-jike* are placed at the back of each ear. Coiffures of this type usually appear in *ō-jidai-mono* and *jidai-mono.*

179. *Aburatsuki-honke-komi-no-bin-suppori-no-yōji-no-nurigomi-ao-no-warihane.* This is another wig made of real hair, with the sidelocks slightly inflated with dried rush. In this instance, however, the *daigane* is in *suppori* style—that is, it entirely covers the head. In the regular wig, the shaven part of the crown is covered with *habutae* and painted, whereas in the *suppori* wig the crown is attached and covered with either cloth or paper and painted. The word *nurigomi* in the name of this wig refers to the tips of the *bin,* which are painted either blue *(seitai)* or black *(sumi)* and are presumably extensions of the temples, although they are low on the cheekbones. Black is used for strong or villainous roles in *jidai-mono* and blue for the roles of *yakko* and the like. The shade of blue will vary according to the role or the preference of the actor. The term *warihane* (literally, "divided feathers") designates the divided style of the short hair at the back. This styling keeps the hair from being mussed, since the characters wearing this type of wig wear thickly padded costumes with collars that invariably rise above the neckline. The topknot is fashioned like a *yōji,* an old-fashioned Japanese toothbrush made of willow with one end crushed into brush-like shape. This coiffure is used for semicomic roles in *jidai-mono.*

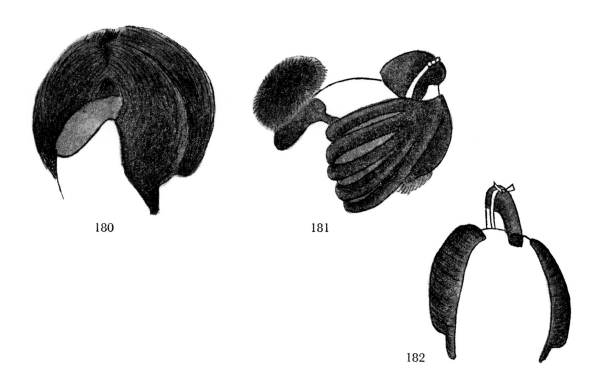

180

181

182

180. *Suppori-no-hishikawa (mino)*. *Suppori,* as previously mentioned, denotes that the *daigane* with its attached *kōra* completely covers the head. The crown is covered with *habutae* or paper and then painted the desired shade of blue, according to the role or the taste of the actor. Occasionally, however, a reddish brown may be used to create what is known as the *aka-bitai* or red forehead. The wig is fashioned of *kara-ke* (curly hair) stiffened with lacquer. It has the *mino* or plaited hairline, and the tuft of hair under each temple is rolled up in *shitchū* style, a shape resembling that of a Japanese comb cleaner. This style of coiffure, known as *hishikawa,* is used primarily for *aragoto* roles such as that of the *oshimodoshi:* the hero who repulses a demon in the concluding scene of a play.

181. *Aburatsuki-tsukamitate-gohon-kuruma-bin-(mino-)no-haritsubu.* In this wig the *maegami* is raised in the upright pompon style known as *tsukamitate* (grasped erect), the lower part in *wari-gushi* (dividing comb) style. This particular style of *maegami* is generally found in wigs for young men or very strong characters. The sidelocks, combed into five "spokes" *(gohon-kuruma-bin),* are hardened with pomade and tied at the root of the topknot with very thick paper strips called *ebiza.* The topknot itself is the attractive *haritsubu,* which takes its name from the words for needle *(hari)* and the top of a small seashell *(tsubu),* the end being cut and combed to resemble a rank of needles. Although the coiffure is primarily used for the roles of minor villains, there is one exception: the *aragoto* role of Umeō-maru in the "Kurumabiki" scene of *Sugawara Denju Tenarai Kagami.*

182. *Aburatsuki-honke-hachi-mai-komi-no-bin-no-namajime.* As noted previously, the origin of the word *namajime* is unknown, but it is the name given to the style of *mage* in this coiffure. The *hachi-mai-komi-no-bin*—that is, the eight-sheet inflated sidelocks—are formed of sheets or strips (four to a side) of *mino-ge* and slightly inflated by the insertion of dried rushes to create a soft, elegant style. The sidelocks are without the *kobitai,* the curved hairline at the temples. This wig is worn for the famous role of Sukeroku with an eight-foot purple crepe *hachimaki* tied on the left side, its plaited loop held upright by wire and its unplaited streamers hanging down to the chin or slightly below. The wig appears in *jidai-mono* or in *sewa-mono.* In the latter case, it is worn for roles characterized by *iroke* or amorousness.

183

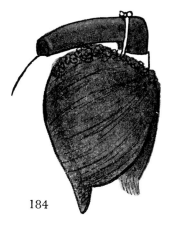

184

185

183. *Aburatsuki-honke-bin-rasha-bari-no-namajime*. This wig looks similar to the one shown in Figure 182, but the *kōra* is covered with a wool flannel cloth known as *rasha* to add an appearance of strength to the character who wears it. The wig is primarily used in *jidai-mono* for the roles known as *sabaki-yaku:* persons who are influential in settling the problems at hand.

184. *Aburatsuki-hachi-mai-naimaze-orikake-bin* with *chirichiri*. *Naimaze-orikake-bin* are sidelocks made of an equal mixture of curly and straight hair and coated with lacquer rather than pomade. *Hachi-mai*, as noted in earlier examples, refers to the eight sheets of hair forming the *bin*. In the present wig the hair around the temples is sprayed with lacquer, and small tight curls known as *chirichiri* are placed around the root of the topknot and along the top of each *bin*. Usually, however, the *chirichiri* are found at only one of these places. The wig is used for strong, elegant male roles in *jidai-mono*.

185. *Aburatsuki-honke-hachi-mai-bin-no-mae-chasen-no-bō-jike*. *Bō-jike*, as noted in a previous instance, are hanging pomade-hardened strands of hair at the back of each ear, and *hachi-mai-bin* are sidelocks composed of eight sheets of hair. In the present example, eighteen strands of *motoyui* (paper cord) are coiled around the root of the topknot to make it stand erect. The end is brought forward to rest on the crown in a briskly opened manner, very much like the bamboo tea whisk from which the topknot takes its name. Although we have noted that a wig with this style of topknot is worn by dandies or amorous characters, the present coiffure is used for the roles of daimyō, *hatamoto,* and samurai in *ō-jidai-mono* and *jidai-mono*.

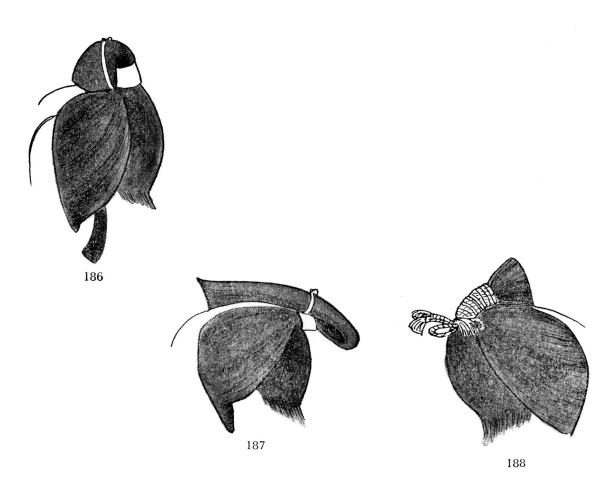

186

187

188

186. *Aburatsuki-honke-hachi-mai-bin-no-hariuchi-no-bō-jike.* The *hariuchi* (literally, "needle-thrust") style of topknot has its end cut and combed to resemble a rank of needles around the front and sides of the root, which has been bound high with thick strands of *motoyui* and then tied with a single strand of this same paper cord. This is one of the infrequent times when the end of the topknot is not actually visible. It will be noted that the sidelocks do not show a curved hairline at the temples. A pomade-hardened strand of hair *(bō-jike)* hangs at the back of each ear. The *hachi-mai-bin* (eight-sheet sidelocks) receive their name from the sheets (four to a side) of flat-plaited *mino-ge* of which they are made. *Honke,* of course, indicates that real hair is used. This particular type of wig is worn by sword carriers in *ō-jidai-mono.* The *hariuchi* topknot, however, is also used in wigs for characters who are in some measure gentle and amorous.

187. *Aburatsuki-honke-hachi-mai-bin-no-daimyō.* All the particulars of this wig have been discussed previously. The only interesting feature not mentioned heretofore is that a daimyō topknot always touches the head. The wig is seen in *jidai-mono.*

188. *Aburatsuki-honke-hachi-mai-bin-chū-dachi-no-bō-chasen. Chū-dachi* designates a style of sidelocks not firmly pressed to the head or pulled tightly back at the root of the *mage* but, instead, loosely flattened. In this instance, as in a number of others previously noted, the sidelocks are composed of eight sheets of hair (four to a side). The *mage* is tied with a cord plaited in "glowworm" fashion, sometimes with light-blue threads with tasseled ends. In tea-ceremony scenes, a purple *cha-bukusa* (tea cloth) is placed over the crown of the head, looking very much like a sunbonnet. The coiffure shown here is seen mostly in *jidai-mono.*

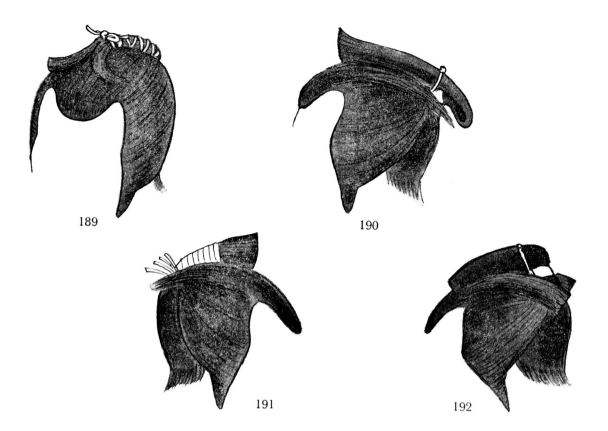

189

190

191

192

189. *Aburatsuki-honke-bin-sōhatsu-Genji-no-kammuri-shita.* The *Genji no kammuri-shita* style of *mage*—that is, a *mage* over which the type of hat known as *kammuri* is worn—is in the *bō-chasen* or "stick tea whisk" class, but the end of the *mage* is quite dissimilar. It is equally divided, and the ends are curved to the sides to touch the crown. The topknot is lace-plaited, usually with old-fashioned dark-purple threads, or is mixed with gold threads in imitation of the glowing or shimmering light of a firefly—that is *hotaru-uchi* or glowworm plaiting. The name Genji, of course, is that of the hero of the celebrated *Tale of Genji.* This wig is worn for such roles as those of *kuge* (court gentlemen) in *ō-jidai-mono.*

190. *Aburatsuki-honke-bin-ende-no-Kichiemon-gatachi.* This wig, made of real hair, takes its name from that of the actor Kichiemon *(Kichiemon-gatachi* means Kichiemon-style) and from the swallow-tail *(ende)* effect of the thick strands of curly hair drawn back on both sides of the *mage.* The remainder of the wig is made of straight hair. A *jidai-mono* style.

191. *Aburatsuki-honke-bin-ende-no-bō-chasen-mage.* The *ende* or swallow tail, as noted in the description of the previous wig, is the effect created by combing back wide strands of curly hair from the forehead and placing them on each side of the *mage.* In this wig, the *mage,* after being coiled with *motoyui,* is brought forward to rest on the crown in "stick tea whisk" style. Wigs of this type are seen in *jidai-mono* and *ō-jidai-mono.* It should be remembered that *aburatsuki* coiffures almost always appear in these classifications of plays.

192. *Aburatsuki-honke-bin-ende-no-namajime.* The combing of this coiffure, except for the topknot, is quite similar to that of the previously described wig. The significant differences are that the curly hair forming the swallow tail is lacquered and that the topknot is in *namajime* style. The wig is used for various roles, including those of *aragoto* and *kataki-yaku* (villain) type, an example of the latter being the role of Nikki Danjō in *Meiboku Sendai Hagi.*

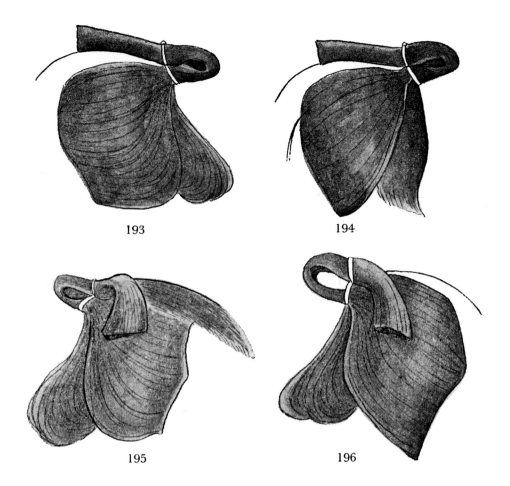

193           194

195           196

193. *Fukurotsuki-futatsu-ori-honke-bin.* The wig illustrated here takes its name from the bag effect of the inflated back hair *(fukurotsuki)* and from the doubled or folded topknot *(futatsu-ori mage)*. The topknot has a long lower loop *(ichi)* which is doubled or folded and then tied at the root. The *ichi* extends from the back of the head while the brush portion of the *mage* rests on the crown. Real hair is always used for the sidelocks—hence the designation *honke-bin*. The coiffure is used for the gentle male characters in *sewa-mono* known as *nimaime*.

194. *Aburatsuki-futatsu-ori-honke-bin.* The only difference between this coiffure and the one in Figure 193 is that the *tabo* or back hair is covered with pomade and flattened to the head. Again the long *futatsu-ori mage* (doubled topknot) signifies that the wig is worn by *nimaime* characters in *sewa-mono*.

195. *Fukurotsuki-honke-bin-mushiri-no-ichō-no-tsumuji.* In this wig the *sakayaki*, the part of the head that is usually shaved, is made of short bear fur and is known as the *mushiri* (partly grown out) *sakayaki*. In this case, of course, the wig base has a *kōra*. A *tsumuji* or whorl of natural hair is part of the *mushiri sakayaki*. The *mage* is done in *ichō* (ginkgo leaf) style and is curved at the end. Ne'er-do-wells and the like in *sewa-mono* and *kizewa-mono* wear this style of coiffure.

196. *Fukurotsuki-honke-bin-no-ichō.* This wig is very similar to the previous *mushiri-no-ichō*, but it does not have the *mushiri sakayaki*. The long *mage* curves to the side—a style considered by the low-class commoners to be very smart *(iki)*. The wig is seen in *sewa-mono* and *kizewa-mono*.

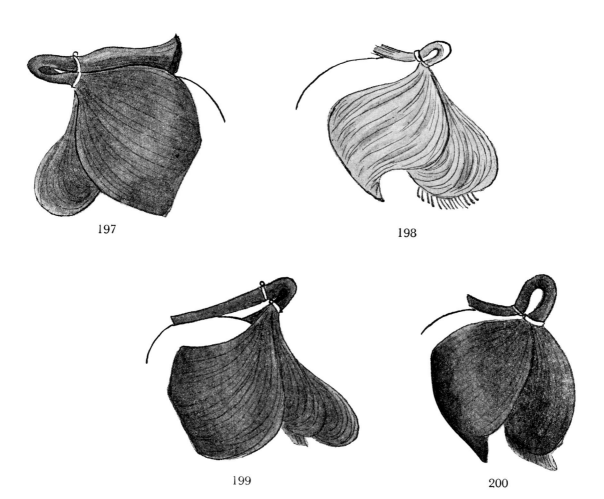

197

198

199

200

197. *Fukurotsuki-honke-bin-no-ichō.* Although this wig has the same name as the one in the previous illustration, there are several differences, the main one being the position of the topknot. Natural hair is always used for the *ichō mage* or ginkgo-leaf topknot. This particular *ichō* style is worn by characters in *sewa-mono* who display traits of gallantry or dandyism.

198. *Goma-no-fukurotsuki.* *Goma* (black sesame seed) and *goma-shio* (black sesame seed and salt) are terms used to designate gray-haired wigs—that is, wigs with black and white hair mixed (pepper-and-salt gray, as English has it). The small size of the *mage* in this wig suggests the thinning hair of old age. The wig is used for elderly roles, usually those of farmers, in *sewa-mono.*

199. *Fukurotsuki-ukine-no-ko-mage.* *Ukine* literally means floating or raised root (of the topknot) and *ko-mage* small topknot. The wig takes its name from the fact that the *ichi* or bound part of the topknot is small and not tied close to the head. It will also be noted that the crown is greatly receded. For all types of *ko-mage* wigs, *honke-bin* (real-hair side-locks) are used. The wig shown here is worn by minor characters in *sewa-mono.*

200. *Fukurotsuki-honke-bin-kado-maru-no-megane.* The appellation *kado-maru* (literally, "corner-round") comes from the fact that the sidelocks have rounded corners. *Megane* means eyeglasses or spectacles, and the bound part of the comical *mage* in this wig is thought to resemble a single eyeglass. The wig is used for *fuke-yaku* (old men's roles) in *sewa-mono.*

201

202

203

201. *Fukurotsuki-honke-bin-nonoko-no-ke-botto.* *Ke-botto* is the short hair placed along the upper part of the *bin* in this wig. *Nonoko,* which designates the style of the topknot, may be a corruption of *nunoko*—that is, clothing *(ko)* made of *nuno* or textile fabrics woven of ramie, cotton, hemp, and other vegetable fibers and worn by the lower classes in olden times. The *nonoko mage* is found in wigs for the roles of farmers, countrymen, hunters, and the like in *sewa-mono.*

202. *Fukurotsuki-honke-bin-no-wakashu-mage.* The distinctive feature of this coiffure is the *maegami* (forelock), which is uncut and is combed into a becoming puff just above the forehead. Usually any wig with a forelock is designated as *wakashu* (youth or young man), The forelock is tied immediately in back of the puff; then the long hair is divided into two equal flat pomaded strands and is drawn over the *naka-zori* (shaved center of crown) and down each side of the root of the *mage* to approximately the center of the inflated back hair. All *wakashu* wigs have sidelocks of real hair. The coiffure shown here is seen in *sewa-mono.*

203. *Fukurotsuki-honke-bin-sakaguma-no-gokenin-mage.* In this wig, *sakaguma*—thatched bear fur—covers the crown of the head. The fur is shorter in length than that used for the previously noted *hyakunichi* and *gojūnichi* wigs. The sidelocks are made of natural straight hair, and the *mage* is slightly curved. In real life, the *gokenin* were the lowest class of samurai under the control of the shōgun; in Kabuki they usually appear as *kataki-yaku* (villains) in *jidai-mono* and *jidai-sewa-mono.*

Silk thread was implanted in the *katsura* around the latter part of Edo, though only in small amounts and for particular functions when real hair was less effective. It is still used today—for instance, for the *ito-jike* (Fig. 218), the long, looped, low-hanging strands of the *kasshiki,* a wig with the front hairline parted in the middle and cloud-shaped, and for the *sagegami katsura* (Fig. 220). Both of these *onnagata* wigs have long hair hanging down the back, either flowing loosely or covered with silk crepe. The back hair is tied once at the nape of the neck or somewhat below with decorative paper lace, silver threads, or the like. The *ito-jike* are made of twisted silk threads that have a clinging quality. Real hair would fly around in an untidy manner, but the silk threads stay in place. The hanging hair or "tail" of all *sagegami* wigs is attached to the wig by a wire hook after the actor is on stage. In a man's wig, the *ito-jike* hang straight down from underneath each sidelock.

Wire produces the desired effect for the short, tightly curled hair known as *chirichiri* (Fig. 173). Fine metal wires are curled, painted with lacquer, and then given a heat treatment to insure that they will stay curled and that the lacquer will be sufficiently hard to prevent chipping. The *chirichiri* is attached to the *daigane* either at the root of the *mage* or at the top of the *bin.*

Only masterful men appear in *chirichiri katsura*—for example, Kumagai in the "Kumagai Jinya" scene of *Ichinotani Futaba Gunki,* who wears a wig with *chirichiri* at the root of the *mage,* and Konoshita Tokichi, a faithful retainer of the shōgun in the "Kinkakuji" (Golden Pavilion) scene of *Gion Sairei Shinkōki,* who wears a wig with *chirichiri* at the sidelocks.

Yak-tail hair (referred to by most Japanese as "bear's tail") is used in the *oiran* (courtesan) *katsura* to produce the large, rather flat, globular *shaguma* or *haguma mage* divided vertically at the center (Fig. 204). The use of yak-tail hair was copied from the courtesans of Edo days, who employed it in their headdresses because it stayed in place better than human hair. After a night with a client, the *oiran* always needed to adjust her coiffure quickly so that her visitor would not see her disheveled. Consequently the *shaguma mage* of yak hair was ideal.

J. E. DeBecker, in his history of the Yoshiwara, *The Nightless City,* states that "at present [that is, the Meiji period] the hair of the red bear *(shaguma)* is used to form the tuft of false hair over which to spread the natural hair in making up a *date-hyōgo* coiffure; sometimes, although very rarely, it is used in dressing the hair in *shimada* style." In Kabuki, however, bear hair is considered too short to fashion an *oiran shaguma mage;* so the longer yak hair is used, although the name *shaguma* is still retained.

## DRESSING THE WIG

After the *katsura-ya* has finished his work, the wigs are rushed to the proper *toko-yama-beya,* the hairdressing rooms in the theater. Usually the *toko-yama's* work begins after the last day's performance of the current month.

The men's wigs are dressed according to either the *aburatsuki* or the *fukurotsuki* classification. For the former, in which the back hair is pomaded, pressed close to the base, and polished, the *mage* is added. For the latter, in which the back hair is combed in bag effect, the already attached *mage* is dressed and tied. The *toko-yama* must be especially careful in selecting the position for knotting the *mage* and inflating the *tabo* or back hair and the *bin* or sidelocks, since he must keep in mind not only the widely varying characters of the roles but also the personal features and tastes of each actor and the ages of both the roles and the actors.

Wigs of the *aburatsuki* type are worn by daimyō, *hatamoto* or direct feudatories of the shōgun, and *gokenin,* the lowest class of samurai, who generally appear in Kabuki as *kataki-yaku* or villains, since in real life their meager pay made them apt to fall into evil ways. Roles employing these wigs are found in *ōchō-mono* (court dramas), *oie-mono* (dramas involving daimyō and other noblemen), and *jidai-mono*—all three in the historical-drama class. Only a few roles in *jidai-mono* employ the *fukurotsuki*-style wigs, but almost all *chōnin* and other commoners in *sewa-mono* wear this style.

*Daigane* for men's wigs are classified as *bin-no-mono* and *kōra-mono* (Figs. 163, 164). The former is without a *kōra;* the latter has a *kōra* attached. The *daigane* may be styled in *aburatsuki* or *fukurotsuki* fashion. Combinations of these features are the basic foundations for hundreds of diversified male-role coiffures.

The *onnagata* wigs are roughly divided into three classifications: *maru-tabo, ji-tabo,* and *shiitake-tabo,* with either *mino* or *habutae* hairline.

The *maru-tabo* (Fig. 165) has a short rounded puff of back hair shaped with the help of a *tabo-gane*—the metal stretcher that we have already noted earlier in this chapter—by rolling the hair over this frame. The *maru-tabo* is used mainly in *jidai-mono* roles.

Unlike the *maru-tabo,* the *ji-tabo* (Figs. 206, 207, 210) is dressed without the help of either a stretcher or padding, the result being a more natural style with a rather long, slender *tabo,* always molded in bag effect with natural hair. *Ji-tabo* coiffures are seen in *sewa-mono* and *kizewa-mono.*

The *shiitake-tabo* (*shiitake,* a kind of mushroom) has a mushroom-shaped *tabo,* highly pomaded and polished, made from hair "knitted" in *mino* style (Fig. 222).

The style of the three finished coiffures and not of the *daigane* is the significant difference in these wigs.

It takes from one to three hours—never less than one—to dress an *onnagata* wig, the *sagegami* wigs taking the least time. *Onnagata* styles will not last the twenty-five days of the run; so they are completely recombed around the tenth or thirteenth of the month. The more intricate male-role wigs, like Gorō's in *Yanone* (Fig. 167), take at least a full day. Because the pomaded *mage* and the *kuruma-bin*—the stiffly lacquered or hard-pomaded sidelocks combed into separate protruding flat strands— are ready-made, the dressing of the wig can usually be completed in one day. Otherwise it might take two or three days. The men's wigs are re-combed during the month's run.

The hair is washed with soda at least once a month to remove the oil. Whenever necessary, a small brush is used to remove accumulated dust. When the production ends, the *habutae* is removed from the *daigane,* combed out, washed, and sent to storage. The *habutae* worn by stars will later be pasted on the *daigane* of lesser actors for use on succeeding occasions. Leading actors always wear fresh *habutae* each month. When the *habutae* turn yellow, they are used in wigs for older roles, but their usefulness is gradually lost, for the hair turns reddish and the *habutae* black.

The tools and supplies necessary for dressing Kabuki wigs are numerous and specialized in use. The tools include at least twenty kinds of boxwood combs, pliers, razors, scissors, irons similar to long-handled cattle-brand-ing irons, two varieties of facial brushes, and nine-inch *magebō* (needles), each with an enormous eye, used to arrange the *aya* or style of the hair, after which the hair is tied in place. The *toko-yama* must also have at hand *tsubaki* (camellia) oil, *mukuro* (pomade) made by mixing together sesame or rapeseed oil, *mizu abura* (an oil used in combing out the hair), and *suki-abura* (a chartreuse-colored soft pomade that gives lustre to the hair). The tools and materials are paid for by the Shōchiku Company but are purchased by the *toko-yama,* often from salesmen who come backstage to sell their products.

The *toko-yama* follows a standard procedure in dressing the wig. First he places it on a *daibōzu* (*dai,* pedestal; *bōzu,* shaven-headed monk or priest), a wooden stand with a head block. On the left side of the block is a metal hook to which the strings of the wig are fastened, thereby firmly securing the wig to allow normal combing of the hair. A string with a *magebō* (one of the previously noted nine-inch needles) is inserted through a hole on the right side for convenient use in arranging and tying the coiffure.

The *toko-yama* first combs out the hair, starting with the *tabo* or back hair and proceeding in order to the *bin* (sidelocks), the *maegami* (forelock), and the *mage* (topknot). Then he irons out the hair to bake away its "habit" or tendency to curl or be unruly. This is just the opposite of giv-ing a permanent wave. The irons, placed in a charcoal brazier, are mod-erately heated to avoid burning the hair. Then the hair is carefully pressed from the base to the ends between consecutive layers of hair.

After the hair has been ironed, the *toko-yama* applies *tsubaki* oil and other oils to straighten it out completely and then applies *suki-abura* (pomade) to give it a living, glossy appearance. He is now ready to start creating the coiffure.

Starting with the *tabo,* he proceeds to the *bin,* the *maegami,* and finally the *mage*. Dressing the separate parts of the wig in a set manner assists in the prescribed styling and allows for tying the parts firmly, one after another, to the *ne* or root of the topknot. The *mage* is properly left till last, for the *ne* must be tied with the *motoyui* (or *mottoi*), a cord made of tightly rolled paper cut into convenient sizes for ready use and often referred to as *Bunshichi motoyui* after the man who first sold it this way. (Formerly it had been rolled into extra-long spiral strands.)

The *motoyui* binds the base of the *mage*. Often the only difference between coiffures is in the mode of winding the *motoyui*. More strands bound around the *ne* result in a higher root and therefore a more upright *mage*. It is the *ne* upon which all parts of the wig depend, and as a result it is under a comparatively heavy tension.

After a man's wig has been dressed, the *mage* is covered with *nihonshi*, very strong thin paper, to prevent it from spreading apart, and remains covered until the wig is ready for use. The covering is removed only after the wig has been placed on the actor's head.

## WIG ORNAMENTS

After the wig has been dressed, the *toko-yama* adds the hair ornaments, some of the most important of which are described here.

The *hanagushi* (*hana*, flower; *kushi*, comb), although referred to as a "flower comb," is really a decorative hairpin with four rows of silver flowers worn by *hime* (princesses or young ladies of high birth) or with two or three rows of such flowers worn by *machi musume* (city girls) (Figs. 219, 220).

Combs of *tsuge* (boxwood) are placed in the sidelocks of *onnagata* wigs done in after-the-bath style.

The *kōgai* (Fig. 205) is basically a stick or a bar, usually made of tortoise shell, metal, or lacquered wood. The classification includes the *hana-kōgai*, a bar with flowers at each end, and the *wari-kōgai*, a divided *kōgai* that can be inserted through the hair and then fastened together. The *kōgai* is sometimes used to conceal a *kozuka* or small knife.

The ornamental hairpins known as *kanzashi* (Fig. 206) are not used in a practical sense but only for decorative purposes. The three types of *kanzashi* used most often in Kabuki wigs deserve brief mention. *Tate-zashi* are large hairpins worn upright. *Sashi-mono* often have a coral ball at one end or a tortoise-shell ornament shaped like the bridge of the *koto*, or Japanese harp. *Hirauchi* are long flat hairpins or two-pronged pins of silver, tortoise shell, or lacquered wood with floral decoration and an earpick-shaped end. The prongs of the *kanzashi* are approximately six and one-half inches long, any decoration at the top adding to the length.

The *nakazashi* (Fig. 208) is a long square-sided bar, usually lacquered, that passes through the root of the *mage*.

The *aida-gire* or *tsurushi-gake* is an ornamental cloth, often with tie-dyed

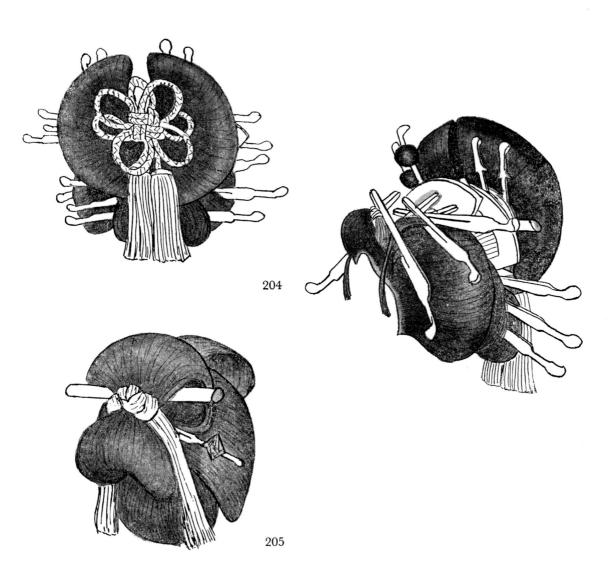

204

205

204. Agemaki wig (back and front views). For full description see page 200.

205. *Habutae-maru-tabo-tsubushi-shimada-no-kara-ke.* The back hair *(tabo)* of this feminine wig is dressed by inserting a *tabo-gane* (metal stretcher) and rolling the hair over it to produce the short and roundish *maru-tabo.* The *habutae* hairline at the front is created by sewing individual strands of hair to *habutae* silk. This is a rather flat *tsubushi* (crushed) *shimada* coiffure. Although the hair ornaments worn with it vary according to the nature of the roles, the three shown here are typical. A *kōgai* or round bar, usually made of tortoise shell, is thrust through the root of the *mage.* Tied around the root is a skein of light-blue and silver threads with the ends hanging down on each side of the *mage.* A silver *hirauchi* (decorative hairpin) is stuck into the right side of the root of the *mage* and protrudes between the *kōgai* and the skein of silk threads.

This wig is widely used for the roles of *musume* (young ladies), *nyōbō* (wives), *koshimoto* (girl servants in the feudal court) and *oiran* (courtesans). The mixture of curly and straight hair called *naimaze* is used mostly for wigs worn by young ladies and wives, whereas *kara-ke* or curly hair is used almost solely for the wigs of courtesans. The wig illustrated here may be seen in *jidai-mono, jidai-sewa-mono,* and *sewa-mono.*

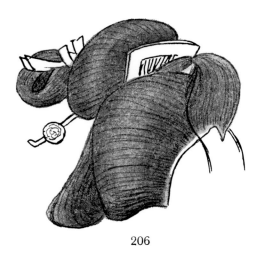

206

207

206. *Habutae-ji-tabo-no-tsubushi-shimada.* The *ji-tabo* (natural back hair) *mage* is for the not-so-young geisha in Kabuki. The back hair is dressed without any stretcher or padding, so that the rather long, slender chignon has a natural look, and the topknot is made of curly hair. The *ichi* or lower loop of the knot is much smaller than the *tsubushi*, the large globular section in front of it. A starched paper band known as a *kuzuhiki* is tied around the root of the *mage* with the ends curving outward and then upward. This low *tsubushi-shimada* coiffure is decorated with a tortoise-shell comb placed in front of the *mage*, a *kanzashi* (decorative hairpin) with a coral ball inserted into the right side of the *ne* (root of the topknot) and sometimes a square-sided tortoise-shell bar *(nakazashi)* that passes through the *ne*. The coiffure is seen in *sewa-mono* and *kizewa-mono*.

207. *Habutae-ji-tabo-no-yuiwata.* Pink silk crepe is tied becomingly around the knot of the *mage* in this wig which then is called *yuiwata* (literally, "tied silk wadding"). The same crepe is folded and pasted over a comb placed in front of the *mage*. A silver flowered *kanzashi* is thrust into the upper right *bin*. The coiffure is worn by young ladies in *sewa-mono*.

208. *Habutae-maru-tabo-no-wari-ganoko.* Taken in order, the terms making up the name of this wig mean that the hairline is produced by sewing individual strands of hair to a base of *habutae* silk, that the back hair is rounded over a stretcher, and that the *mage* is decorated with tie-dyed silk patterned with spots resembling those on the hide of a fawn. The square-sided *nakazashi* passes through the root of the *mage* and is wrapped about with light-purple *kanoko*-patterned cloth that also covers the top of the *mage*. Placed in front of the *mage* is a tortoise-shell comb, while a long silver hairpin ornamented with a coral ball is thrust into the lower part of the *bin* on the right side. *Kuzuhiki* (starched paper bands) are tied at the root of the *mage* under the *nakazashi* and the *kanoko*-patterned cloth. The wig is used for the roles of restaurant and teahouse waitresses and the like in *sewa-mono* and is also worn occasionally by *mekake* (concubines or mistresses). (See facing page.)

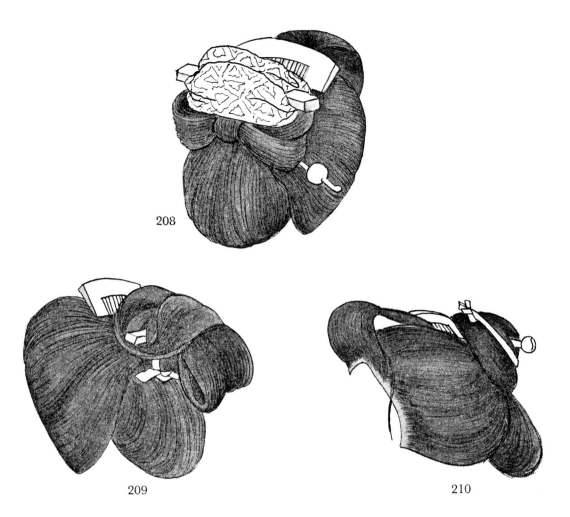

208

209

210

209. *Mino-maru-tabo-no-shimada-kuzushi-no-bōshi.* This coiffure is a newer variety of the *shimada.* (The term *kuzushi* in the name of the wig has the meaning of to break down or simplify.) The *mino* or flat-plaited hairline necessitates the wearing of a *bōshi* or headband (not seen in the illustration) to conceal its unnatural look. The *bōshi* is of purple cloth and is attached to the wig directly above the forehead. A decorative cloth is twined around the square-sided *nakazashi,* concealing the upper part of the *mage.* The lower part of the *mage* is a rather flat, short loop slightly extended from the head, and starched paper bands called *kuzuhiki* are seen tied underneath the *mage* at the root. In the usual place in front of the *mage* is a tortoise-shell comb. *Mino*-style wigs are worn only in *ō-jidai-* or *jidai-mono.*

210. *Habutae-ji-tabo-no-otarai.* The wig shown here is made distinctive by the small tub-shaped *mage* (*otarai* means tub) formed by twining the hair over a tortoise-shell bar with an earpick end. Around the *mage* a band of starched paper is tied with the bow in front. A *binkaki* comb made of spotted tortoise shell is found in the usual place. Small strands of hair called *shike* fall loosely from just in back of the hairline at each side of the forelock. The *shike* are considered quite smart and attractive and are found in various styles of wigs. This headdress is worn chiefly by mistresses and hairdressers in *sewa-mono* and *kizewa-mono.*

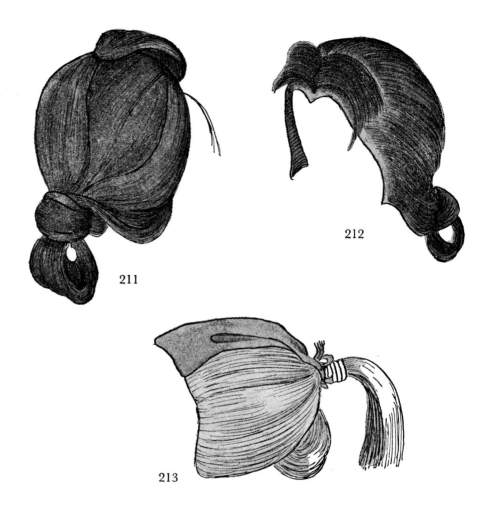

211

212

213

211. *Habutae-uma-no-shippo*. *Uma-no-shippo* means horsetail, and the wig shown here takes its name from the intricately tied *mage*, which closely resembles a horse's tied-up tail. The *mage* is tied with the hair of the whole wig and is not separately attached. The sole ornament is a pin stuck into the lower loop. The forelocks are slightly inflated and are tied close to the head. The small strands of hair known as *shike* fall from just above the hairline at the temples. Although this wig is sometimes worn for stylish or chic roles, it is primarily used for the roles of country girls or wives in *sewa-mono* and *jidai-sewa-mono*.

212. *Habutae-tosaka-no-uma-no-shippo*. *Tosaka* (cockscomb) refers to the style of the *mae-gami*, which is cut short and parted. The only ornament is a boxwood comb stuck into the lower right-hand side of the wig. In certain plays where the hair must be disheveled for murder scenes and the like, the queue is tied in such a manner that a tug at the center of the lower loop loosens the hair. The wig is worn by villainesses in *sewa-mono*.

213. *Habutae-maru-tabo-haku-no-kirikami-no-babā-bōshi*. This simple coiffure is made of *haguma* (curly white hair), and the designation *haku no kirikami* in the name of the wig literally means "white cut hair." The *mage* hangs loose in a ponytail and is bound at the root with gold-and-brown lacing. The crown of the head is covered with a silver-gray crepe *babā bōshi*—that is, an old woman's *bōshi*—tied to the root of the *mage*. To make the round, short chignon, the hair is rolled over a *tabo-gane* (metal stretcher). The wig is worn by elderly women in *ō-jidai-mono*, *jidai-mono*, and *jidai-sewa-mono*.

214

215

214. *Habutae-baren-no-chōchō-mage-maru-tabo.* In this child's wig, the front hair of the fore-lock is cut in bangs *(baren)* while the remainder is tied somewhat upright with silk yarn called *suga-ito* of a light-pink color and divided into two equal parts that are allowed to fall on each side at the temple. The *naka-zori*—the shaven part at the center of the crown—is shaped like the old-time coin known as *koban*. The *mage* is fashioned in but-terfly *(chōchō)* style and tied at the root with red *zanzara* lacing. A red lacquered comb is placed in front of it. The back hair is done in *maru-tabo* style. This is one of the wigs worn for *ko-yaku* (children's roles) in *jidai-mono* and *sewa-mono*.

215. *Habutae-mushiri-no-hariuchi-no-koban. Hariuchi,* as noted in the caption for Figure 186, literally means "needle-thrust" and refers to a style of topknot with the end cut to resemble a rank of needles. But this does not explain even vaguely why the *mage* in the present wig is called *hariuchi,* unless it is because of the extra-high root. The upright *mage* is curved almost to a point and is tied close to the end with silver *motoyui.* Underneath it a red and light-blue *negake* (crepe band) is tied at the root in *hako* (box) style. The hair, with the exception of the *maegami* and the *mage,* is cut in *mushiri* or plucked-out fashion and is actually made of bear fur. The *naka-zori* or center of the shaven crown is in the *koban* shape noted in the previously described wig. Around the inflated forelock a scarf of light-red *chirimen* crepe is tied, with loose ends hanging down at each side. The wig is worn by the *kamuro,* the young girl attendants of the highest-ranking courtesans *(tayū),* and is seen in both *jidai-mono* and *sewa-mono.*

216

219

217          218

216. *Mae-chasen.* Although this child's wig is simply designated as "front tea whisk," it is actually a bit more complicated than the name would suggest. The wig has a round part at the top of the crown, and the hair inside the part is combed upward into a ponytail with its root directly in the center. The root is bound a number of times with purple-braided cord, and the *mage* itself is brought forward to rest on the crown. The *naka-zori* or shaven part of the crown is in the oval *koban* shape noted in the two previous children's wigs. The forward part of the *maegami* is cut in bangs, while the remainder is brought back in upright style. A silk yarn known as *taihaku* is inserted around the front hairline to prevent long hair, which falls from the part to shoulder length, from flying into the face. The wig is seen in *jidai-mono.*

217. *Abu-hachi-tombo. Abu* means horsefly; *hachi,* bee; and *tombo,* dragonfly—and this wig is so named because the *mage, bin,* and *maegami* are tied separately into small knots that resemble these insects. This is the headdress of the *detchi* (apprentice boys or boy servants) in *sewa-mono.*

218. *Ito-jike.* These strands of thick silk yarn twisted together are designed to hang down before each ear in a woman's wig. They are not part of the wig but are attached separately.

219. *Habutae-maru-tabo-no-fukiwa.* The *fukiwa mage* is a wide, rather flat *mage* which is looped over a large ornament in hand-drum shape, ornately decorated and predominantly red in color. The ornaments attached to the root of the *mage* are two silver *takenaga* (starched paper strips); four long *takenaga* with a silver zigzag design on a red ground, each end curled under; and a bow of red crepe. Placed in front of the *mage* is a *hana-gushi* (flower comb) with four rows of silver plum blossoms and butterflies. Smart-looking *shike* (short strands of hair) hang from each side of the forelock. *Ito-jike* (Fig. 218) complete the coiffure. The wig is worn by princesses *(hime)* and young ladies of high birth in *jidai-mono, jidai-sewa-mono,* and *sewa-mono.*

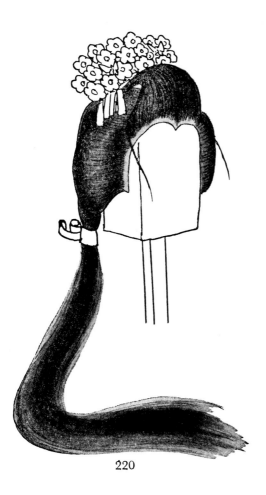

220

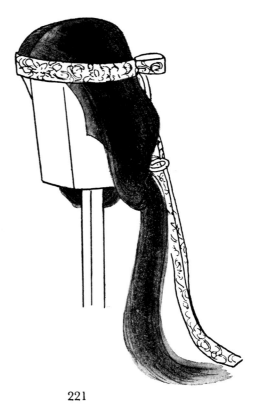

221

220. *Habutae-hana-gushi-tsuki-sagegami.* The only adornment relieving the plainness of this *sagegami* (long hanging hair) coiffure is a *hana-gushi* (flower comb) with three rows of silver flowers. The unbraided hanging hair is tied with three of the starched paper strips called *takenaga.* This coiffure appears in *jidai-mono* and *sewa-mono.*

221. *Habutae-kasshiki* with *hachimaki* in Nō style. This wig of the *sagegami* or hanging-hair class, has the cloud-shaped hairline known as *kasshiki.* The hair is parted in the middle, combed down along the cheeks, and drawn loosely to the back, where it is tied with silk threads in a small bow at the nape of the neck and then allowed to fall loosely down the back. A *katsura obi* (headband) in Nō style is placed around the wig and tied at the back with a square bow, the ends left hanging. The *katsura obi* or Nō *hachimaki,* made of gold brocade, is worn straight across the forehead but is raised slightly at the back. This is not the only *hachimaki* worn with this coiffure, for in many instances the *yamai* (sickness) *hachimaki* replaces the Nō *hachimaki.* The wig is usually seen in *jidai-mono* whenever the cloud-shaped hairline is used.

222

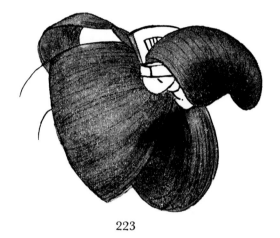

223

222. *Habutae-shiitake-tabo-no-katahazushi-mage*. In this wig the *mage* is not symmetrical—hence its name *katahazushi* (literally, "one side unfastened"). One side of the *mage* loop passes over the *kōgai* (decorative bar) while the other goes under it. The back hair, in *shiitake* (mushroom) shape, is stiffly pomaded and highly polished. Even from a short distance it does not give the appearance of natural hair, although it actually is. Starched paper strips known as *kuzuhiki* are tied around the root of the *mage*. In cases where the wig is worn by villainous women, the hairline is very strong. The *shiitake-tabo* (back hair in mushroom shape) is worn primarily by women of the samurai class in *jidai-mono* and *jidai-sewa-mono*. However, the present wig, with its classical *katahazushi mage,* is used for the roles of daimyō wives and ladies of the feudal court, especially in dramas dealing with trouble among feudal families.

223. *Habutae-maru-tabo-no-marumage*. The rounded topknot—*marumage*—that distinguishes this wig is considered the symbol of a married woman. Hair decorations used with the wig may vary—for example, the comb placed at the front of the rounded topknot may be of tortoise shell or of the gold-sprayed lacquer called *makie*, and the ornamental silver hairpin known as *hirauchi* may or may not be used. The crepe *tegara*—the scarf tied around the root of the topknot over which the top-knot is looped—is not of a set color but may be black, gray, or another color. A square-sided *nakazashi*, usually decorated in *makie*, passes through the root. The coiffure is designed for the roles of daimyō and samurai wives in *jidai-mono* and *jidai-sewa-mono*.

224

225

224. *Habutae-shiitake-no-bunkin. Bunkin* is the name of a gold coin issued during the Gembun era (1736–40) of the Edo period, and it is from this coin that the wig shown here derives its name. The *bunkin* style was one of the most fashionable gay, tall coiffures of the period, and the present wig, with its *shimada mage* and its mushroom-shaped back hair, is commonly known as the *bunkin-taka-shimada.*

Many of the hair ornaments are placed near or through the root of the topknot—for example, the *hana kōgai,* a tortoise-shell hairpin with a floral design; the *nakazashi,* a square-sided bar; and the *hirauchi,* a flat silver hairpin with a floral decoration and an earpick-shaped end. The *ichi* (lower loop of the topknot) is bound several times with string to make the topknot more upright and then is tied with a starched paper strip *(kuzuhiki).* Another paper strip *(takenaga),* silver on one side and either purple or light blue on the other, is tied around the root of the topknot, its loops showing beneath the *ichi.* A *maekozo,* a thick tortoise-shell hairpin, extends from under the front locks. Sometimes a trick pin is passed through the root of the topknot and, during the action of the play, is removed to allow the topknot to become loose or disheveled. The usual *shike*—small strands of hair falling from each side of the forelock—are part of the coiffure, since they were considered quite chic in their time. The wig is worn for the roles of *goshuden-mono* or *goten-mono* ladies of the feudal court.

225. *Habutae-Katsuyama-no-maru-tabo,* also known as *shinobigaeshi.* It is said that this coiffure was designed by Katsuyama, a bathhouse attendant who had previously been a courtesan in the Yoshiwara, and that it became so popular in the early 18th century that it was given the name of *Katsuyama mage.* Its alternate name of *shinobigaeshi,* which means cheval-de-frise, is puzzling, since it is a very regular, smooth hair style.

The wig is free of numerous adornments, and its various sections are quite round in appearance. The *kurigata* or hairline is heart-shaped, and the small strands of hair falling from each side of the forelock add the chic touch. A silver *hirauchi* protrudes from the right side of the *ne* (root of the topknot), which is first tied with its own hair and then with the starched paper strips called *kuzuhiki.* The *Katsuyama-no-maru-tabo* is one of the coiffures for wives in *jidai-mono* and *jidai-sewa-mono.*

patterns, that may be wound in different attractive ways around the *mage* of *onnagata* wigs.

The *hotaru-uchi,* which takes its name from the Japanese word for firefly—*hotaru*—is a colored silk braid, quite often plaited in a glowworm-like pattern, used to ornament the *mage* of certain men's wigs or to bind the root of the *mage* with a given number of consecutive coils (Fig. 188).

The *kin nawa* is a thick gold rope for binding and tying the long loosely hanging hair of special men's wigs (Fig. 169).

## THE HABUTAE AND MEN'S WIGS

Before donning a man's wig, the actor must cover his head with the *habutae,* a square-shaped piece of plain silk coated with a layer of *kata-abura,* a thick pomade composed of wax and castor oil which allows him to press the pliable *habutae* smoothly over his head. At the front corners of the *habutae* are strings or ties—made of black or white silk or satin—which are wrapped around the head to prevent the *habutae* from slipping.

The object of the *habutae* is to give the illusion of the shaven portion of the head (as in men's hair styles of former times) and to pull up the corners of the eyes, a practice considered beneficial in temporarily removing wrinkles. In Edo times it was also considered that slanting eyes were most enchanting (and naturally very Oriental), but in those days the effect was not achieved with *habutae,* since actors, like all other men, still shaved their forelocks. The slanting of the eyes was effected by dressing the hair in the very tight *gakuya-ichō* (*gakuya,* greenroom; *ichō,* ginkgo) style, with the *mage* in the shape of a ginkgo leaf and the sidelocks pulled tightly to the back of the head. This headdress produced the same effect as the present-day *habutae,* which has been in use only since the beginning of Meiji, when men began to wear their hair in Western fashion. The *onnagata,* incidentally, achieves the effect by use of a *me-tsuri,* a type of *hachimaki,* instead of a *habutae.* If ties are attached to the *me-tsuri,* they are always white, since they occasionally become visible under the wig.

All *habutae* are painted to represent the shaven part of the head and must be blended into the make-up. If this is not skillfully done, the *habutae* will look like a headache band and will detract from the reputation of a seasoned actor.

For the young, the *habutae* is painted the shade of blue known as *seitai* (*sei,* blue; *tai,* black inkstick) and for the middle-aged and old the same color but with the coloring extending farther back on the crown and called *oku-seitai. Oku-seitai* is worn by Yuranosuke in *Chūshingura.*

The *sumi-seitai habutae* is mixed with additional black to represent growing hair and is employed mostly for the roles of lower-class men such as vagabonds, palanquin carriers, or farmers who have failed to shave their heads daily. This type of *habutae* is worn by the petty scoundrel Kōmori Yasu in *Yo wa Nasake Ukina no Yokogushi.*

Still another type of *habutae* is worn by Yoichibei in *Chūshingura*. This is the *surihagashi* (*suri*, rubbed or scraped; *hagashi*, peeled off) *habutae*, which is of the same color as his make-up in order to show him as a bald-headed elderly man.

## BŌZU-KATSURA AND OTHER SPECIAL WIGS

Not mentioned among previously discussed types of wigs is the *bōzu-katsura*, a seemingly simple wig denoting the fully shaven head of a Buddhist priest. Actually, it is quite the contrary of simple, and fitting the actor's head for the *daigane* in this case is a difficult task. Although the wigs for priests are mostly without hair, the finished *daigane* is nevertheless called a *katsura*. There are several types of *bōzu-katsura* that are quite distinct from one another.

To create the illusion of a shaven head, paper or silk is pasted on the round surface of the *daigane*, and it calls for skill and dexterity on the part of the *katsura-ya* to prevent wrinkles. According to the age and personality of the stage priests, the *daigane* crowns are painted light blue, tan, or brown. For wicked or robust priests, the painted portion is greatly receded. Finally, the *daigane* is coated with wax to make it appear shiny, as if with the natural oil of the skin.

One particularly inconvenient appendage of the *bōzu-katsura* is the lower back of the *daigane*. It cannot be made of copper, since this would prevent free movement of the head. In order to hide the actor's own hair at the back, a *tare* is attached to the *daigane*—that is, a suspended piece of silk crepe dyed the same color as the wig itself. Recently, in some instances, foam rubber has replaced the silk crepe.

There are different types of *daigane* for priests. The *maru-bōzu* (*maru*, round; *bōzu*, priest) *daigane*, for example, covers the entire head. The *sakayaki* (shaven portion of the head) is painted blue to give the impression of a shaven head, and the blue is not only painted on the copper base but, by means of make-up, is also extended to the upper part of the forehead and rounded to give a somewhat natural hairline.

A *maru-bōzu daigane* is worn by Benkei in the dance-play *Ataka no Seki* (Benkei at the Barrier of Ataka) and by the *namazu bōzu* in *Shibaraku*. The name of the latter, taken from the word for catfish, refers to the long braids made of thick silk thread attached to the bottom of each *bin* of the wig that the *namazu bōzu* wears. These are thought to resemble the whiskers of a catfish, and thus the role derives its name from the headdress. Takatoki, in *Hōjō Kudai Meika no Isaoshi*, also wears a *maru-bōzu daigane* as a base for his wig, as does Kisen, the priest in *Rokkasen Sugata no Irodori*.

The *han-bōzu* (*han*, half) is a *daigane* that covers the back half of the head while a waxed *habutae* covers the front. When compared with the *maru-bōzu daigane*, the hairline of the *han-bōzu* looks more natural, since the *sakayaki* of the former is painted on either paper or silk pasted to the *dai-*

*gane,* whereas that of the latter is painted on the *habutae* without a copper base underneath. The *han-bōzu daigane* are not waxed, and the hairlines vary according to whether they are worn in *jidai-mono* or *sewa-mono.*

The *han-bōzu daigane* is the base for the wig worn by Kumagai in *Ichinotani Futaba Gunki* when he becomes a priest (Fig. 35). It is also worn by Kōchiyama Sōshun in *Kumo ni Magō Ueno no Hatsuhana* (Fig. 37).

The *sumi-fuki* (*sumi,* black ink; *fuki,* sprouted) *maru-bōzu* has black ink sprayed over the blue of the *sakayaki* to represent a slight growth of hair. When seen from a distance it appears somewhat blackish. This wig is for a stronger-than-ordinary priest such as Oshō Kichisa in *Sannin Kichisa Kuruwa no Hatsugai* and Benkei in *Funa Benkei.*

The *suna-zuri* (*suna,* sand; *suri,* rubbed in) *maru-bōzu* is a wig with powdered stone coated on the *sakayaki* to show that the hair has grown a trifle. Originally used in the roles of priests of exceedingly powerful character, it is rarely used today, for it appears flat and ineffectual in the bright glare of modern-day stage lighting.

Spurious priests quite often wear the *igaguri* (*iga,* burr; *kuri,* chestnut) *maru-bōzu,* which represents a close-cropped head. Among the wigs of this type are the *honke-fukige-no-igaguri* (*honke,* real hair; *fukige,* thatched), on which hairs are sewn so sparsely that the "skin" shows through, and the *naimaze-no-igaguri,* which is entirely covered with *naimaze*—that is, straight and imported curly hair mixed together. Still another *igaguri* type is the *sō-habutae-no-igaguri* (*sō,* whole, all), a wig with its entire surface covered with *habutae* to which hairs have been sewn individually.

The Kabuki wig is more than just an essential part of the actor's costume or a means of identifying the type of role that he plays. In its uniqueness as a stage adjunct, it furnishes added proof that Kabuki is an indigenous art form. Nothing comparable to the Japanese wig exists in any other theatrical tradition.

CHAPTER *23*

# Kumadori: Stylized Make-up

Theatrical make-up has consistently been a matter of great interest and curiosity to the playgoer, yet the impact of violent make-up for the more expansive Kabuki roles usually inspires a renewed concern in the staging, for it epitomizes the bold elements of the play demanding exaggerated costumes, exaggerated wigs, and an exaggerated manner. The pomposity of the whole is spellbinding.

This traditionally blatant method of Kabuki make-up is referred to as *kumadori* (*kuma,* lines, wrinkles; *dori*—from *toru,* to take, follow, draw): a multiform make-up denoting the varied emotional countenances belonging to the numerous roles, principally those in *aragoto* dramas or scenes.

*Kumadori* is not the exclusive property of the Kabuki, for it is also used in the Chinese theater. The make-up must be nonrealistic to qualify as *kumadori.* There is, however, a difference between Japanese and Chinese *kumadori.* The Japanese closely follow the bony and muscular structure of the face, whereas the Chinese merely paint a pattern on the face, disregarding the structure. In this respect, Japanese *kumadori,* although essentially symbolic, does in part agree with reality.

The facial muscles are divided into two groups, one depending upon the jaw and the other upon the small bone of the nose. The nose, being the center of the face, is to a great extent the focal point of any expression. This is also quite true in the use of *kumadori.*

Normal stage make-up has a purpose dissimilar to that of *kumadori.* It is applied to emphasize the brow, the eyes, the nose, and the mouth and to differentiate between male and female, young and old, lowborn and highborn, beauty and ugliness. It does not, however, have the added implication of emotion provided by *kumadori.*

*Kage* (shade, shadow) could be called the originating source of *kumadori,* since *kuma* and *kage* are both made by the effects of light. *Kuma* refers to the darkness in the cavities or inner parts of the face and *kage* to the shadow of an object exposed to sun or light.

The aim of using *kumadori* is to show individual emotional responsiveness—most of the time the emotion of anger, with differences in degree. When very angry, some persons turn pale; others blush or distort their eyebrows and mouth, at the same time opening their eyes wide. The frenzied face of anger, filled with mental agitation, is terrible, misshapen, and ugly. Since the plays using *kumadori* pursue a subject of supernatural valor, they respond to the use of a fancifully grotesque and exaggerated make-up.

Not all weird make-up can be classified as *kumadori* merely because it is grotesque. The painted faces depicting a playful mood in the Chinese theater and some of the comical make-up in Kabuki are drawn much like those in the Western theater. The unique quality of *kumadori* lies in the technique of expressing vividly the mental state of stage characters.

Originally, *kumadori* was based only on the changing expressions of the actors' faces. Ultimately it came to follow the shade or shadows made by the muscular delineation or function of the face—but symbolically drawn, becoming in itself an expressively anomalous mask in order to make the character of the role evident. This became necessary because actors specializing in certain roles had difficulty in maintaining a set expression.

Much has been written giving credit to the masks of the ancient Gigaku dance form as the foundation for Kabuki *kumadori,* but present-day authorities discount this. Gigaku, said by some historians to have been introduced to Japan in the Nara period (about the year 612) by a Korean who had learned it from the Chinese, employed elaborate masks. Today this form of art is extinct, having been so completely Japanized as to lose its identity, and the only visual remains of it are some masks housed in the Shōsō-in imperial repository, in some old temples in Nara, and in museums.

*Suji-guma* (*suji,* line; *kuma,* make-up—an abbreviation of *suji-kumadori*), based on the temperament and character shown in the facial features, is the foundation of most forms of *kumadori* (Fig. 226). It is believed by some to have been created from Buddhist sculpture wherein can be found many types of guardian gods, eminent attendants, and followers of Buddha, each with an outraged, indignant physiognomy having a striking resemblance to *suji-guma.* The lines of *suji-guma* are drawn only with a brush, without any touching up; consequently, they appear stiff, strong, and vigorous, and at the same time they produce a magnificent effect.

It was believed that the *kuma*—that is, the lines of the make-up—should not be drawn minutely or painted with artificial elaborateness or intentional delicacy but that the actor must have the feeling conveyed by the verb *toru:* to take, to grasp, or to make. He must possess the reverence of an artist who takes up his brush to paint the greatest masterpiece, for only then can he indicate strength in his make-up.

As we have already noted in Chapter 2, Danjūrō I is credited with

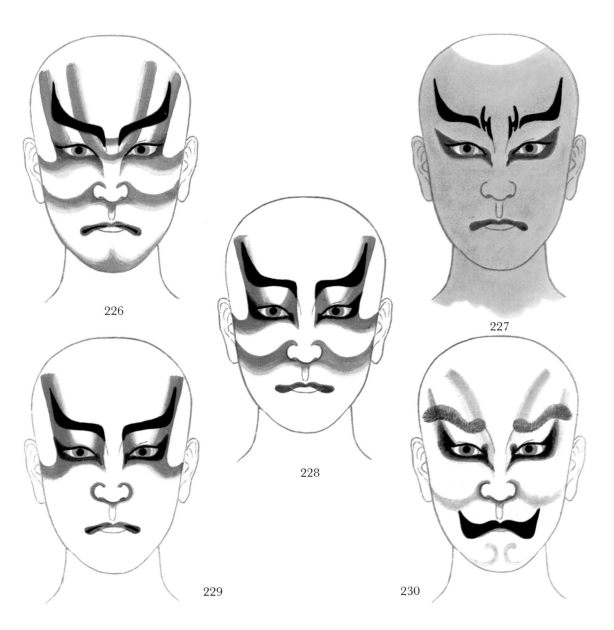

226. *Suji-guma*. The foundation of most forms of *kumadori* make up is *suji-guma* (line make-up), which is based on the temperament and character shown in the facial features.

227. Genroku *Shibaraku kumadori*. This is the make-up devised by Danjūrō I for the role of Kamakura Gongorō Kagemasa in the original Genroku-era *Shibaraku*.

228. *Ryakushi-guma*. A less complicated form of *suji-guma, ryakushi-guma* is surprisingly bold and striking. It was introduced during the late Edo period by Danjūrō VII.

229. *Ippon-guma*. The youthful freshness of *ippon-guma* (one-line make-up) is achieved through the use of single-line *abura-beni-kuma*—that is, red make-up on a white-painted ground.

230. *Hannya-guma* for the demoness in *Momijigari*. The make-up for Kabuki ghosts and demons has been inspired by the masks of the Nō drama, although, as always in its borrowings from the older drama, Kabuki makes its own modifications.

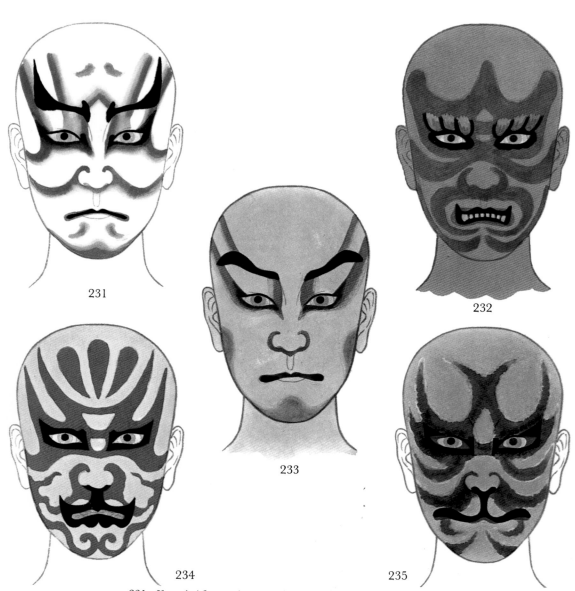

231. *Kumadori* for nonhuman characters. In *kumadori*, indigo is second only to deep red in usage and is particularly associated with the make-up for Buddha, other gods, and the ghosts of villains.

232. *Kumadori* for demon. One of the chief uses of red in *kumadori* is to express anger, indignation, or rage mixed with sullenness and cruelty. Here it is applied in two shades combined with gray and black to achieve the fearful aspect of a Kabuki demon.

233. *Kumadori* for Kumagai in *Ichinotani Futaba Gunki*. This is Kumagai's warrior make-up in the scenes of the play preceding the famous "Kumagai Jinya," in which he renounces the profession of arms and becomes a priest.

234. *Kumadori* for the lion in *Shakkyō*. In the dance-drama *Shakkyō* the lion's face is painted gold with vermilion superimposed and a solid black setting off the eyes and mouth.

235. *Kumadori* for the tiger in *Ryūko*, a *shosagoto*. For the role of Kinko or the golden tiger the make-up is a gold leaf over a gray *sumi* base, the eyes and mouth being peculiarly shaped with pure black paint and slight touches of vivid red.

340

originating *kumadori* for his appearance as Sakata no Kintoki in *Shitennō Osanadachi* in 1673. It was his *suji-guma*, however, worn for the first time in 1702—after he had introduced the exuberant *aragoto* style of drama— that was to become the basic form for most *kumadori*. Although it is said that *suji-guma* was taken from Buddhist sculpture or from a Sanskrit graphic symbol, it is believed that Danjūrō had a more profound intention than that of merely copying from such sources. His *suji-guma* expressed temperament and character by emphasizing facial muscles, veins, and even the facial skeleton. It is remarkable, nevertheless, to note how many points of similarity there are between *suji-guma* and Buddhist sculpture.

In 1712, Danjūrō's son, Danjūrō II, improved the *suji-guma* by using the *bokashi* technique—that is, the shading off or gradation of the painted lines. It has been said that in his quest for new ideas he approached a Nō actor who refused to see him, but he was able to get a look at the actor's *ō-beshimi* mask before leaving. The *ō-beshimi* is a large audacious mask with firmly set mouth and jaw used in the *kirinō-mono* or concluding plays in the regular five-play Nō programs—for example, *Zegai* (The Hobgoblin of China) and *Kurama Tengu* (The Goblin of Mt. Kurama). The protagonist of each of these is a *tengu* or long-beaked goblin. Conceivably this mask was Danjūrō II's inspiration for the make-up of Gongorō in *Shibaraku*. Yet another account would have us believe that he created *bokashi* after looking into the face of a peony in full bloom. This we must discredit as too fictitious.

Danjūrō II was a diminutive man with a small plain face, quite different in physique from his large handsome father. Apparently he gave thorough study to the facial muscles and the physical frame, for with proper gradation of the painted lines he was able to cover his facial deficiencies. This seems to be a more acceptable theory for explaining his use of *bokashi*.

The great Danjūrō VII (1791–1859) completed the *bokashi* method, amplifying the gradation in an attempt to make it more magnificent in showing off an actor's face in all of its perspective. He also introduced the fundamental procedure for making a face appear thinner or larger—a technique favored today—as well as a less complicated *suji-guma* called *ryakushi-guma,* which can be done more hastily (Fig. 228). The simplified form, rather surprisingly bold and striking, is similar in freshness to the youthful *ippon-guma,* a long single-line *abura-beni-kuma*—that is, red make-up on a white-painted ground (Fig. 229).

The *ippon-guma* of the Ichikawa Danjūrō line does not include a line on the chin, possibly because the masters in this line have inherited long faces and because the chin line may be better suited for a short face. To-day, the simplified version of *suji-guma* exists only nominally, but make-up does retain the important parts of the parent *kuma,* enabling the actor to convert his expression easily to the original form by adding comparatively unimportant lines. A line between the eyes may add a grimace or a distortion; a line on the chin or the forehead can change the expression.

*Hannya-guma*—inhuman or unnatural expressions—are seen on the faces of ghosts or demons, the only make-up variation copied from the Nō drama (Fig. 230). Even so, the make-up is only partly taken from the *hannya* mask (worn by the revengeful ghost of a once beautiful woman), since only the lower half of the mask's expression has been adapted for Kabuki use.

*Kumadori* imitating the aspects of nonhuman characters, gods, Buddha, and ghosts from the emotional point of view always conveys rage (Figs. 231, 232). Belonging to the resentment classification are the injured and vindictive spirits of demonesses, the ghosts of court nobles, and other apparitions.

*Kumadori* also expresses emotion by color (Fig. 233). It may be called the ultimate in producing expression, since even a single painted curve vividly shows a nuance of emotion or temperament. The picturesque and symbolical make-up is applied by the actor himself once he has reached his teens, and he becomes more proficient as the years pass.

It is color, rather than lines, that provides an understanding of the close relationship to emotion and temperament implied by *kumadori*. The following list shows the emotions or qualities of temperament indicated by the various colors:

> *beni* (deep red)—anger, indignation, forcefulness, obstinacy
> *beni* (red)—activeness, eagerness, passion, vigor
> *usuaka* (pink or pale red)—cheerfulness, youthfulness, gaiety
> *asagi* (light blue)—calmness, coolness, composure
> *ai* (indigo)—melancholy, gloominess
> *midori* (very light green)—tranquillity
> *murasaki* (purple)—sublimity, nobility, loftiness
> *taisha* (brown or burnt sienna)—selfishness, egoism, dejection
> *usuzumi* (gray, on chin)—dreariness, cheerlessness
> *sumi* (black)—fear, terror, fright, gloom

Deep red on a white base is used more frequently than any other color. It expresses anger, indignation, or rage mixed with sullenness and cruelty or implies bad temper mixed with cruelty. It can also represent characters with forceful personalities who have good qualities. Red make-up is applied after the actor has painted his face all over with *abura-beni:* vermilion mixed with oil.

Pink is restricted to a small number of roles, one being that of the charming or amorous fox.

Indigo is second to deep red in usage and appears on the faces of villains and ghosts.

Brown is worn by villains among court nobles and by gods.

Dark or light black used with *nishoku-guma* (two-colored make-up) of red and blue is reserved exclusively for female roles displaying pertinacity and jealousy—qualities not ascribed to males.

The uses of purple and light green are extremely limited, as is that of gold, the last being seen in the make-up of the lion in the dance-drama *Shakkyō* (The Stone Bridge) and of Kinko, the golden tiger in *Ryūko,* a *shosagoto* (dance-drama) concerning a dragon and a tiger (Figs. 234, 235). The lion's full face is painted a golden color with vermilion superimposed on it and a solid black setting off the eyes and mouth. The tiger's make-up is a gray over a gold-leaf base, the eyes and mouth being peculiarly shaped with pure black paint and slight touches of vivid red.

Throughout the years the actors have gradually modified many orthodox forms of *kumadori*. Often the simplification occurred as an expedient for saving time when an actor had to change rapidly from one role to another in the same scene. Today, about eighty-one forms of *kumadori* remain, though the number fluctuates slightly with the revival of old plays whose scripts have been lying dormant or with the dropping of scenes or plays from the repertoire. The forms still in use include twenty-one belonging to the Ichikawa family as well as those of the Onoe and Nakamura families and some personally conceived forms.

*Kumadori* is a convention in Kabuki and is not thought of as unnatural in the way that it seems unnatural to the Westerner. It is accepted as the red satin dress is accepted as the mark of a prostitute in certain Western plays. Because of the interest that painters and printmakers have shown in picturing actors in *aragoto* roles, the uninitiated may think that *kumadori* is representative of all Kabuki make-up. The restriction of its use to certain roles makes its effectiveness even greater. Stage make-up for all Kabuki roles may seem exaggerated, but *kumadori* goes so far beyond mere exaggeration, both in color and in line, that it adds a new dimension to Kabuki drama.

CHAPTER 24

# Hashori: Pulling up the Kimono Hem

*Hashori* (*hashi,* edge, end; *ori,* folding) is the pulling up of the *suso* or hem of the silk kimono and its summer counterpart, the cotton *yukata,* either by holding it up with the left or right hand or by tucking it into the obi. This action is of particular importance and usefulness in Kabuki roles. In outdoor scenes, characters often pull up the hems of their kimono to prevent their being soiled—particularly in scenes that take place in inclement weather. Ladies of the upper and middle classes, who wear trailing kimono indoors, often pull them up from the hem when they go outdoors. Workmen and travelers do the same in order to achieve greater freedom of movement. Even thieves find the *hashori* habit most helpful in making an easy getaway, and the sometimes obviously exaggerated actions whereby the actor displays his legs in performing the *hashori* on the *hanamichi* draw many a guffaw from the audience.

The custom of *hashori* is not exclusively Kabuki's, although Kabuki has raised it to the level of an art. In everyday life as well, there were strict methods of hoisting the hem. The geisha, for example, always pulled it up with the left hand, while ladies who served feudal lords and the lords' wives and daughters always raised it with the right. The Kabuki actors made an intensive study of the different possible styles of *hashori,* for Kabuki always prefers to project beauty of line, even in cases of utilitarian necessity. A number of these *hashori* styles are discussed in the following paragraphs.

*Ryōbashori* (*ryō,* two, both, double) is the samurai manner of *hashori* (Fig. 238). The hem is pulled up on the two sides of the kimono and tucked into the obi. The samurai is a fastidious man; so he pushes each side of the hem evenly into the obi, permitting the folds of the kimono to fall in equal lengths. Characters who are not of the samurai class may also appear with kimono in *ryōbashori* style, but theirs will not be so precise as the samurai's.

345

236. *Takamomodachi.* If the *hakama* is tucked up high, the style is known as *takamomodachi*. It is shown here as worn in *yoten* costume.

237. *Ryōmomodachi.* The *ryōbashori* (Fig. 238), or samurai style of pulling up the kimono hem, if done with *hakama*, is called *ryōmomodachi*.

This style of *hashori*, if done with *hakama*, is called *ryōmomodachi* (*ryō*, both; *momo*, thighs; *tachi*, opening, exposing) (Fig. 237). *Momodachi* is an abbreviation of *momodachi o toru*, meaning to tuck up the bottom of the side openings of the *hakama* into the belt. (*Hakama* have openings on both sides of the upper part.) If the *hakama* is tucked up high, the style is called *takamomodachi* (*taka*, high) (Fig. 236).

The *bōzu-bashori* style is used by Buddhist priests and young novitiates. The back hem of the kimono is raised up and over the obi and tucked underneath it. This is easily managed because the obi is tied in front, and therefore the bow is not in the way. The *bōzu-bashori* method is used by Seishin in *Sato Moyō Azami no Ironui*, by the priests and novitiates in *Kyō-Ganoko Musume Dōjōji*, and by the poet-priest Kisen in *Rokkasen Sugata no Irodori*.

In the *shichisan-bashori* (*shichi*, seven; *san*, three) style (Fig. 239), the hem is raised higher on one side than on the other, expressing the nonchalance of its wearers, for most of them are the jaunty *yakuza* (gamblers) who play the dandified roles known as *iki-no-yaku*. Among these are Ki-

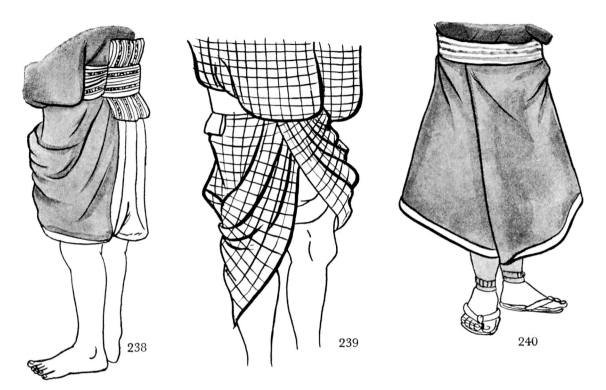

238          239          240

238. *Ryōbashori*. This is the *ronin* and samurai style of pulling up the kimono hem. It is lifted on both sides of the kimono and tucked evenly into the obi.

239. *Shichisan-bashori*. In this style of tucking up the kimono, the hem is raised higher on one side than on the other, expressing the nonchalance of the wearers, most of whom are jaunty gamblers who play dandified roles—for example, Yosaburō in *Yo wa Nasake Ukina no Yokogushi*.

240. *Azuma-karage*. This style of pulling up the hem is achieved with the help of strings attached to the lower hips at each side of the kimono.

rare Yosaburō in *Yo wa Nasake Ukina no Yokogushi* and Benten Kozō in *Shiranami Gonin Otoko*. Benten Kozō's *hashori* is particularly notable in the "Hamamatsuya" scene of this play. Naozamurai, in *Yuki Kurete Iriya no Azemichi* (Evening Snow on the Path Through the Iriya Rice Fields)— commonly known as *Naozamurai*—pulls up the hem of his kimono in *shichisan-bashori* style, as does Megumi no Tatsugorō in *Kami no Megumi Wagō no Torikumi*. A notable exception to the almost exclusive use of the *shichisan-bashori* by *yakuza* is its use by the *otokodate* Gosho no Gorozō in *Soga Moyō Tateshi no Goshozome*. It must be remembered that in the *shichisan-bashori* the kimono is raised high on only one side, and in this respect the style is also called *kata-bashori,* but there is no preference as to which side. This choice is presumably left to the discretion of the actor.

*Azuma-karage* (azuma, east; karage, tucked up) is a style of *hashori* thought to have originated in Edo, since *azuma* means east and Edo was the "eastern capital." The *azuma-karage* (Fig. 240) is achieved with the help of

241. *Yakko-no-nejikiri* (front and back views). The *yakko* style of *hashori* calls for rolling up the entire hem of the kimono and pulling the corners through the obi at the back to suggest the characters for Kabuki's good-luck symbol: *ō-iri* or a full house.

strings attached to the kimono at the lower hips, one on each side. At the end of each a wadded ball is attached. These balls are pulled up under the obi, simultaneously raising the bottom of the hem at the sides and splitting the front open. Kimono are worn in *azuma-karage* style by samurai and other classes, including *yoten* (courageous warriors, notorious thieves, sorcerers, policemen) who take leading roles only. This style is also seen in *aragoto* plays, as illustrated by Soga no Gorō in the dance *Kongen Kusazuri-Biki,* and is worn by Shirai Gompachi in *Banzuin Chōbei Shōjin Manaita,* by Tadanobu in the dance-drama *Yoshinoyama* (Yoshino Mountain), and by Fukashichi in the "Mikasayama Palace" scene of *Imoseyama Onna Teikin.*

*Yakko-no-nejikiri,* often called simply *nejikiri* (wrung out), is theoretically the final squeeze when one is wringing out wet clothes. When applied to *hashori,* it means a style in which the entire hem of the kimono is rolled up (Fig. 241). The corners, from where the hem is split at the front, are brought to the back and pulled together through the obi, forming what looks like an inverted V. This style suggests the ideographs for "large" and "attendance" or "entry," which together form Kabuki's good-luck symbol of *ō-iri*—a full house. The *nejikiri* style of *hashori* allows showing of the *sagari*—originally part of the loincloth—and the *shita-obi* (loincloth). The Kabuki *sagari,* which looks like an apron, is profusely embroidered with gold braid set off by gold fringe around the bottom. This is always a part of the *yakko's* attire.

*Onna-no-tsuma-no-torikata* means the mode in which a woman raises the

242

243

244

242. *Tsuma-tori.* In the *tsuma-tori* style, the vertical hems—where the hem is split at the front of the kimono—are pulled up and held loosely with either the left or the right hand just slightly off center at the front. Kabuki women in general hold their hems in this fashion.

243. *Hidari-zuma-tori.* For this *onnagata* style of lifting the kimono skirt, the hems are held tightly by the left hand with the wrist twisted to the left. Since only geisha hold the hems in this position, the style is frequently called *geisha-no-hidari-zuma-tori.*

244. *Kata-zuma-tori.* For *kata-zuma-tori*, the corner of the left vertical hem is lifted and held in the left hand, or it may be pulled over the obi and pushed underneath. The style is employed by wives and maidens and even geisha when there is a need for rapid movement.

hem of her kimono. Often the social background of an *onnagata* character can be ascertained by watching the use of the hands in holding the hem or by observing the way the hem is folded into the obi.

For the *hidari-zuma-tori* (*hidari,* left; *tsuma,* hem; *tori,* holding) style, the hems are held tightly by the left hand with the wrist twisted to the left (Fig. 243). Only geisha hold the hems in this position, and the style is frequently called *geisha-no-hidari-zuma-tori.*

In the *tsuma-tori* (or *tsuma-dori*) style, the vertical hems—where the hem is split at the front of the kimono—are pulled up and held loosely with either the left or the right hand just slightly off center at the front (Fig. 242). Women in general, both married and unmarried, hold their hems in *tsuma-tori* fashion.

For *kata-zuma-tori* (one-side *tsuma*), the corner of the left vertical hem is lifted and held in the left hand, or it may be pulled over the obi and pushed underneath (Fig. 244). This is done by wives and maidens, even geisha, when there is a need for rapid movement. Princesses and ladies of the court, however, seldom take advantage of the *kata-zuma-tori.*

In the *kaidori-karage* style, usually both kimono and *kaidori* (the Kamigata word for *uchikake* or formal long coat) are lifted upward at the hips and tied with a stitched belt known as the *kuke-himo,* generally white and about two inches wide. This type of belt or a soft crepe sash called *shigoki* is used to hold up the hem of the kimono when both hands are otherwise busy.

For *koshi-age* (up at the hips) *hashori,* the kimono hems are raised up from the lower part of the hips and then pulled to the right under the obi and tied with a *kuke-himo* or a *shigoki.* If the obi is tied in *ya-no-ji* style with the upper loop of the bow over the left shoulder (see Chapter 11), the *shigoki,* which is often a soft yellow crepe sash, is tied on the left; if the bow is over the right shoulder, it is tied on the right. One fold of the obi bow is tied over the left shoulder when traveling and over the right when indoors, although the *shigoki* is not actually intended to be worn indoors.

Not only the pulling up of the hem but also the very manner of the act is part of the actor's performance and is one criterion for judging a production.

CHAPTER **25**

# Hikinuki: The On-Stage Quick Change

Anticipation climaxing in surprise at a display of unexpected splendor and brilliant contrasting color is the powerful dramatic essence of *hikinuki,* an action by which a costume is instantaneously removed, revealing an equally magnificent one, while the actor continues uninterruptedly his rhythmic movement of acting or dancing. In its broadest meaning, *hikinuki* (*hiki,* pulling; *nuki,* taking off) is either a partial or a complete change of outer costume on stage in full view of the audience, whether costume is taken off or put on. To the puppet theater must go the credit for this dramatic device, a practice which later became an integral part of Kabuki, primarily of the dance. Records fail to show, however, in which year it was introduced in the doll theater.

The *hikinuki* costume is rather loosely, but carefully, stitched together (Fig. 245). At the end of each thread, a knot the size of a man's shirt button remains on the outer side of the costume. One or two *kōken* (actors' assistants) must quickly pull out the basting threads, one by one, with the help of these easily grasped knots, so that the timing of the actor's movements does not falter. When the exact moment of revelation arrives, the actor, who may have had his back to the audience (he may also be facing the audience, kneeling or dancing), gracefully turns. In the flash of that moment, his outer garment is gone, and he is revealed in all his new glory to the admiring spectators. The pulling off of the costume is deftly achieved by teamwork. Not the least important is the work of the *kōken,* for if his timing is slow the costume will come off in stages, and thereby a thrilling theatrical moment will be miserably lost.

Another method of quick change is *bukkaeri* (turning over), the pulling out of strings or threads to reveal only the top of a new costume. *Bukkaeri* was first used in the January 1741 performance at the Edo Nakamura-za by Ōtani Hiroji I (1699–1747) when he played the part of the pander Hachibei in *Keisei Fukubiki Nagoya* (Courtesan Lottery in Nagoya). By

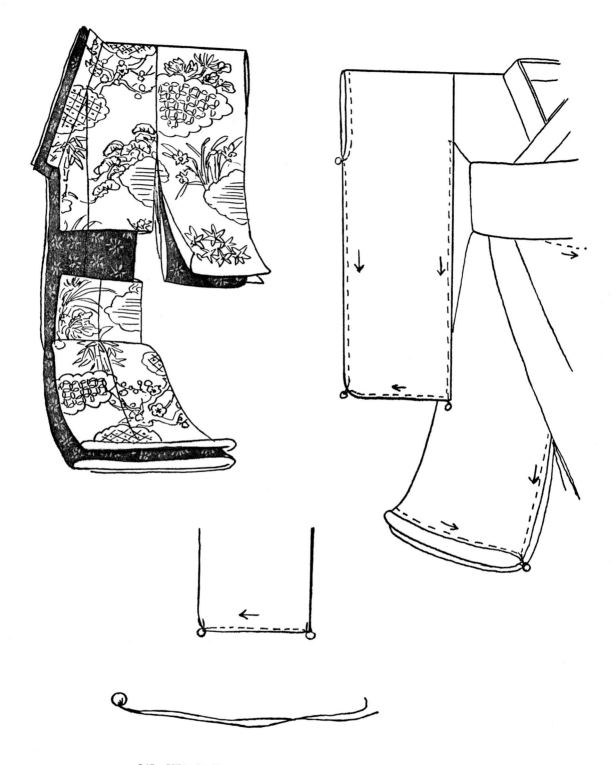

245. *Hikinuki*. For the on-stage quick change of costume called *hikinuki*, each kimono is rather loosely stitched together with basting threads ending in large knots. With the help of these easily grasped knots, the actor's assistant (or assistants) can quickly pull out the threads to permit instant removal of the kimono.

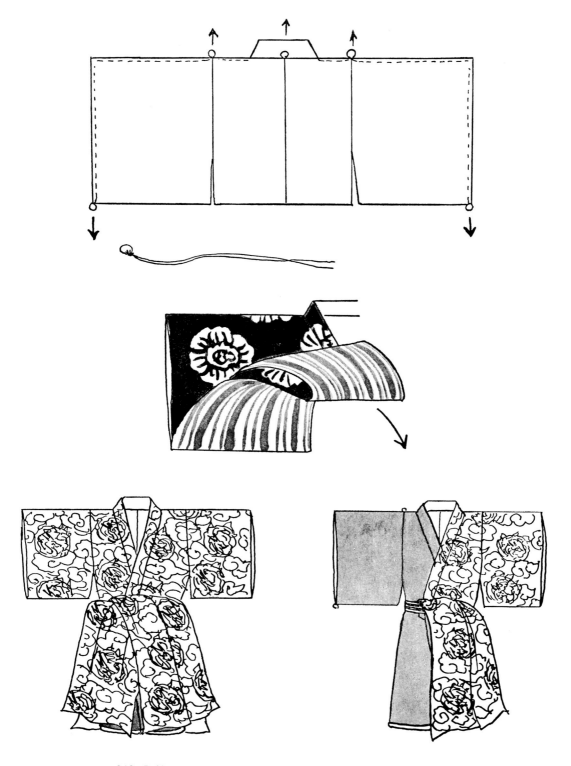

246. *Bukkaeri.* Another method of quick change is *bukkaeri,* the pulling out of threads from the shoulders and the corners of the sleeves to reveal only the top of a new costume. The top of the previous kimono is allowed to fall and cover the obi and the skirt.

means of *bukkaeri* he transformed himself from a *sewa-mono* character into that of the valiant warrior Yuigahana no Chūsetsu. For the latter role, he was clothed in a stunning hand-embroidered robe with designs of intervening spaces formed by a winding stream serving as background for varicolored chrysanthemums. The idea for this costume was taken from a similarly patterned robe owned by the Takeda-za, a puppet theater.

*Bukkaeri* is a different procedure from that of the basic *hikinuki,* in which the top costume is completely removed (Fig. 246). In *bukkaeri* nothing is completely taken off. The execution of *bukkaeri* is skillfully effected by pulling threads from the shoulders and the outer corner of the bottom of each sleeve, allowing the back and the front to fall down separately and cover the obi and the skirt, thereby revealing the lining, while above the obi a new costume is visible, either in startling or subtle color distinction from the first one. Before the actor is dressed, the hanging portions of the sleeves of the underneath kimono are folded flat inside the sleeves of the outer kimono to permit them to fall easily into place when the basting threads are removed. The top of the kimono is so tailored that the upper front sections fall to the opposite lower sides—that is, the upper left side falls over the lower right and the right over the left—but the back falls straight down in one piece.

*Bukkaeri* does not present the beauty of *hikinuki*. It produces an ungainly, awkward costume in which the graceful lines are completely obliterated. In fact, in the bulky folds, the actor looks quite pregnant.

In straight drama, *hikinuki* and *bukkaeri* are resorted to when a character reveals his true identity. These devices are used to good advantage to disclose a different personality or social status in the least possible time, as can be witnessed in the device of *bukkaeri* in the roles of Yokozō in *Honchō Nijūshi-kō,* Ōkura-kyō Ichijō in *Kiichi Hōgen Sanryaku no Maki,* and Sasaki Takatsuna in *Kamakura Sandaiki* (The Kamakura Trilogy). *Hikinuki* is most often seen in female roles in *shosagoto*. Rarely does the male character avail himself of this unusual device.

Kagayama Naozō, in his excellent book *Kabuki no Kata,* explains the use of *hikinuki* as follows: "In the dance drama, it is applied as a bridge from one sequence to another. It does not mean the change of character or psychology." But it does have another true function: that of theatrical surprise, shown so vividly in such pure dance numbers as *Kyō-Ganoko Musume Dōjōji, Sagi Musume,* and *Fuji Musume.*

The opposite of *bukkaeri* is the probably extinct contrivance of *hikiokoshi,* the pulling up of a costume to reveal a new one. The only recorded instance of *hikiokoshi* is that performed by Nakamura Utaemon III (1778–1838) in the role of Ishikawa Goemon, the most notorious of thieves who lived in the Momoyama period, in *Sammon Gosan no Kiri* (The Story of Goemon), a play first produced in 1778. Utaemon, as Goemon, appeared disguised in a priest's gray robe with a *zukin* covering his head. By means of *hikiokoshi,* the costume became a black velvet *yoten* garment—in this case, that of a thief—and removal of the *zukin* revealed a massive wig. This type of manipulation is not known to present-day Kabuki devotees, for only one act of *Sammon Gosan no Kiri* is now given, and this does not include the *hikiokoshi* scene.

The final variety of *hikinuki* is *hadanugi,* the rather simple and commonly used means of showing change in the nature or psychological reaction of a stage character by removing a sleeve from the right shoulder, then the left, or from the right shoulder only. Sometimes this is accomplished with the help of a stage assistant who tucks the loosened waistline into the obi and arranges the sleeves (or sleeve) in the most attractive manner, so that no line of the costume is unsightly, since the foremost thought is to achieve complete fluidity of action, line, and color.

In many instances, *hadanugi* is performed without the help of an assistant, especially if the actor is not wearing a padded *aragoto* costume. The right sleeve is always removed in fighting scenes, allowing for more flexibility in movement, and invariably a man in sudden anger will remove his sleeve. When he cools off, he will slip the sleeve back on his arm.

These old conventions proved appropriate for concepts of theatrical directness. They were retained to hold or renew the interest of the audience. Such conventions, even at present, never fail to arouse the aesthetic pleasure of young and old alike.

CHAPTER 26

# Today's Ishō Department

The rental cost of costumes is one of the inordinately heavy expenses incurred in the production of Kabuki plays. Costumes for all productions given at the traditional Kabuki theaters in Japan are owned and issued by the Shōchiku Ishō Department and the Negishi Company. The former is a separate firm from the Shōchiku Company, the management of traditional Kabuki troupes. For traveling troupes visiting smaller theatrical houses, the costumes are furnished by the Yamano Ishō Company and the Tokyo Ishō Company.

During Meiji, when theaters mushroomed to at least ten in the city of Tokyo alone—creating a sudden shortage of costumes—there sprang into being the costume rental companies, achieved by a number of *ishō-ya* (costumers) who bought *kura-ishō* (warehouse or in-stock costumes) from the managements of the old theaters. To these they added new ones.

The actual prices of Kabuki costumes are never released for publication, for the *ishō-ya* of today are secretive and prefer not to divulge any information. It is known, however, that the more elaborate costumes range from the equivalent of $500 to over $1,500 for a single costume. The most costly Kabuki costumes are those made for *jidai-mono, shosagoto,* and newly produced dramas such as *Genji Monogatari.*

Even so, Nō costumes are comparatively more costly, since all are hand-woven and require the cutting of many paper patterns. Nō textile designs are done mainly by three methods: hand-weaving, embroidery, and gold-leaf imprint. Dyed patterns are used only for the *daimon, suō, kataginu,* and *hakama* of less important roles and for Kyōgen costumes. The method of dyeing these is mostly stencil-resist dyeing. For the principal Nō costumes, including *karaori, atsuita, nuihaku, surihaku, kariginu, hangire, ōguchi, chōken,* and *maiginu,* dyed patterns are not used—only woven, embroidered, gold-leaf imprinted and combinations of embroidery and gold-leaf imprint. Because of the rigid and serious atmosphere of the Nō dramas, the heavy textiles with woven patterns are much more appropriate than the light, gay textiles produced by such processes as *yūzen-zome,* a method of starch-resist dyeing. For weaving textiles for today's Nō costumes, including *karaori* and *atsuita,* hundreds of paper patterns are used, since the materials are woven by the Jacquard loom instead of by the drawloom of the past.

Although the Kabuki *ishō-ya* furnishes the costumes, sometimes an actor, dissatisfied with a rented costume, has one made for which he takes the responsibility of payment—unless he can persuade the Shōchiku Company to foot the bill. One of the most expensive costumes worn in recent years was the one worn by the late Ichikawa Ennosuke II for the role of Iwate in *Kuro-Zuka* (The Black Ogre of the Adachi Plain) for the November 1957 performance at the Tokyo Kabuki-za. Nothing was spared in creating this superb abstract costume. Even the sapanwood dye for it was sent from China, at the request of Ennosuke, by the late celebrated Chinese actor Mei Lan-fang. For this handsome outfit, the cost was reported to have been about ¥800,000 or around $2,200.

Today there are five chief men tailors working for each costume-rental company, with fourteen or more assistants, ten of whom are generally women. Each company has separate staffs of employees in Tokyo and Kansai (Kyoto-Osaka). All handwork is done on the company premises, other than such specialized and intricate details as dyeing, embroidery, and hand-painting, which are contracted to outside establishments known for their skill in these fields.

The *ishō-ya* sends five *ishō-tsuke* (dressers or costume specialists) to each troupe to dress the actors, each having specified actors under his care. Some of these men are attached to the troupe and some to the *ishō-ya,* while a few are free lance. The actors' *otoko-shū* (servants), the *bantō* (clerk), or their pupils assist the specialists, eliminating the need for extra *ishō-tsuke.*

The bit players do not have the comfort of being dressed by the *ishō-tsuke.* They must fend for themselves. They dress themselves personally or assist one another. At the same time, they are responsible for the maintenance of their own wardrobe. Their costumes are often badly in need of a good ironing, and this situation remains one of the laxities of Kabuki staging. A soiled, badly rumpled costume contrasts unfavorably on stage with that of a resplendent lord or a samurai.

During the month's run, the costumes are kept in two places: partly in the actors' dressing rooms and partly in the *ishō-beya* or costume room. An actor playing many roles will not have enough space in his room for all costumes.

The man in charge of the costume room is the *ishō-kata* or theater costumer. His functions are manifold and unending. He has the responsibility for the *ishō-no-tsukechō,* which we have already noted as the loose-leaf notebook in which are listed the names of the roles and the actors who are to portray them. Following the information given in the notebook, the costumer or one of his assistants delivers costumes to all actors, regardless of their rank, prior to each play during the first day's program. This procedure is followed daily except for minor actors or for the costumes remaining in the dressing rooms.

To the expert hands of the theater costumer falls the exacting task of keeping the costumes in immaculate condition, sewing parts that have become unraveled or torn and cleaning the collars—the part invariably soiled by make-up and perspiration—and the long *suso* (hems) that have brushed through the dust on the stage floor. The costumer irons, folds, and puts the costumes in their proper places in preparation for the next day. He must, of course, sew the *hikinuki* (quick-change) costumes back together again. If he should be careless with these, the lightning effect of a rapid change of costume before the audience would be lost. Theater costumers are dedicated artists in their own right, although no applause is offered to stimulate them to a higher level of skill or achievement. Only their devotion to the Kabuki keeps them ever on the alert.

Another assistant in the costuming process is the *kyōgen-sakusha*. The original meaning of the term was "playwright." *Kyōgen* is still used loosely for "drama" or "play," but the term now refers to a man who takes care of odds and ends in the theater. He copies the scripts for the actors (it is still done in longhand), writes bulletin-board notices, and clacks the *hyō-shigi* or *ki*—the wooden clappers that signal the approach of curtain time —beginning at slow intervals and gradually accelerating as the curtain opens. In respect to costumes, it is his duty to inquire about those the actors are going to wear and to list them in the costume notebook for the use of the *ishō-ya* and the *ishō-kata*. If a special artist is to design the costumes, he consults with the artist and makes the proper notations in the costume notebook before giving it to the *ishō-ya*.

A procedure started in the eighteenth century, the *ishō-shirabe* or examination of costumes by actors is followed today. After the costumes have been readied, the *ishō-ya* presents them at the place of rehearsal. There the actors look them over and try them on. Sometimes the costume is not put together in advance in anticipation that the actor may change the design.

A great actor who was very meticulous and eager in his search for perfection was Kikugorō V. His costumes were brought to his home, where one of his pupils modeled them so that he could examine them minutely from all angles. In earlier days there was sufficient time to select or change costumes for a new program because about a month's rehearsal period was provided after the plays had been selected. But today the practice of leisurely and careful examination is virtually impossible because the actual interval between the last performance of one month and the first performance of the following month is only three to five days at the most, with the first day's production taking the place of a full-dress

FURISAGE (city girls)

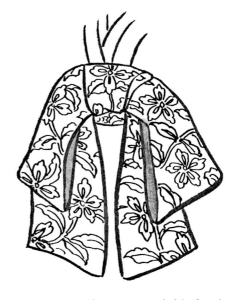

ANKO OBI (courtesans—tied in front)

MANAITA OBI (courtesans—tied in front)

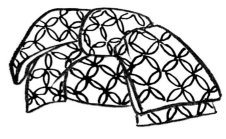

BUNKO (wives of feudal lords
and court gentlemen)

247. Women's styles of tying the obi.

ISHŌ : COSTUMES  360

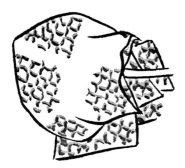

TAIKO MUSUBI (middle-aged wives)

TATE-YA-NO-JI MUSUBI (daughters of samurai or wealthy merchants, younger ladies-in-waiting)

KAI-NO-KUCHI MUSUBI
(commoners' daughters)

YANAGI MUSUBI (geisha)

FUKUSA MUSUBI (commoners' daughters)

HIKKAKE MUSUBI (commoners' wives)

KATABASAMI (merchants)

WARIBASAMI (komageta musubi)
(kuro yoten, uroko yoten)

KARUTA MUSUBI OR HAKO MUSUBI
(yakko, otokodate, minor priests)

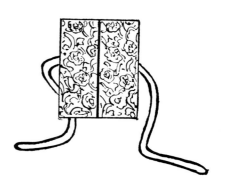

READY-MADE KOMAGETA MUSUBI

KAI-NO-KUCHI MUSUBI
(firemen, nimaime)

TOMBO MUSUBI (aragoto roles)

248. Men's styles of tying the obi.

rehearsal, since there is no other available time. Some time is saved in the case of costumes for plays written before 1868 by playwrights attached to the theater, since these costumes are generally quickly examined and accepted by the actors.

Once the costumes have been delivered to the *ishō-ya* after the examination, they are returned to the theater only in time for any individual costume rehearsal. For the trips to and from the theater, they are carried either in the old-fashioned flexible bamboo trunks known as *kōri* or in *tsuzura*—stiff versions of the *kōri*.

Some stage apparel is in the custody of the *ishō-kata* and includes the following forms of undergarments:

*koshimaki:* the loincloth wrapped around the body below the waist

*hada-juban:* top underwear

*naga-juban:* long underwear for *onnagata,* similar to a slip

*niku-juban:* flesh-colored tights on which tattooing or *kumadori* sometimes appears

*shita-obi:* intimately referred to as the *fundoshi,* worn similarly to an athletic supporter, loincloth, or breechcloth and substituting for Western shorts

*suami:* close-fitting shirt with long sleeves of black net giving the appearance of steel-net or chain-mail armor

Items for outer wear for which the *ishō-kata* is responsible include the following:

*himo:* cloth band or belt worn over kimono before obi is put on

kimono: all types, including *kamishimo* and *jūni-hitoe*

obi: sashes for both men and women

*zukin:* cloth hoods

*sankaku-ate:* white headband with triangular piece in front, worn on forehead of actor taking role of a deceased person

The *ishō-kata* is also responsible for the following items in the *kogire* (small pieces of cloth) classification:

*tenugui:* small hand towel

*hachimaki:* headbands

*tabi:* bifurcated socks

*kyahan:* leggings of the wrap-around type

*tekkō:* protective covering for back of hands, somewhat like mittens

Certain wearing apparel and accessories are the responsibility of the *kodōgu* or hand-properties department. A listing follows:

*hachigane-tsuki hachimaki:* usually a band of white *habutae* to which a golden ornament is attached at the front

*eboshi-no-hachimaki:* a *hachimaki* either attached or tied around the rim of the *eboshi*

MITSUBA NO KURO-NURI GETA
(oiran)

OMOTE-UCHI NO GETA
(oiran)

KYŌ ZŌRI (princesses and
other women)

POKKURI GETA
(young girls)

KYŌ ZŌRI (samurai)

NURI GETA (wives and
daughters of commoners)

AZUMA GETA (wives and
daughters of commoners)

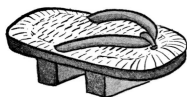

KOMAGETA (women)

UWA ZŌRI (courtesans)

KOMAGETA (men)

249. Footgear: *geta* and *zōri*.

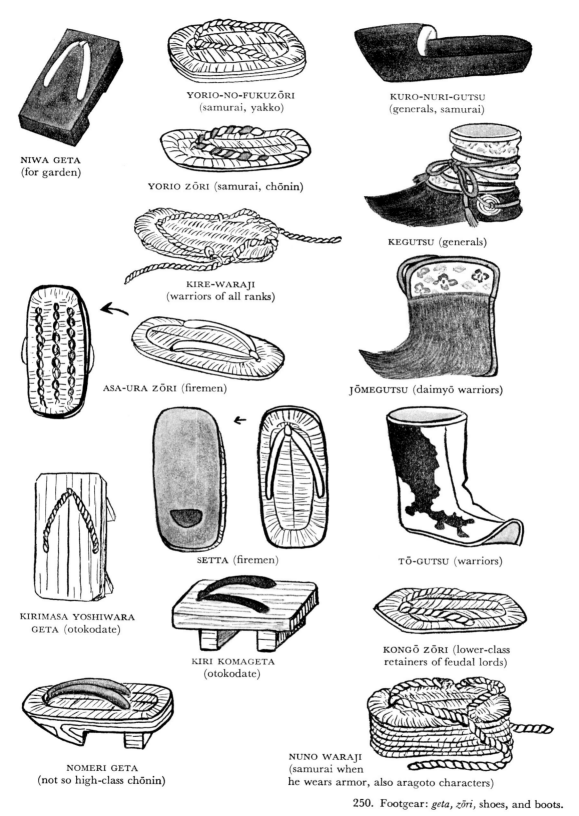

NIWA GETA
(for garden)

YORIO-NO-FUKUZŌRI
(samurai, yakko)

YORIO ZŌRI (samurai, chōnin)

KURO-NURI-GUTSU
(generals, samurai)

KEGUTSU (generals)

KIRE-WARAJI
(warriors of all ranks)

ASA-URA ZŌRI (firemen)

JŌMEGUTSU (daimyō warriors)

SETTA (firemen)

TŌ-GUTSU (warriors)

KIRIMASA YOSHIWARA
GETA (otokodate)

KIRI KOMAGETA
(otokodate)

KONGŌ ZŌRI (lower-class
retainers of feudal lords)

NOMERI GETA
(not so high-class chōnin)

NUNO WARAJI
(samurai when
he wears armor, also aragoto characters)

250. Footgear: *geta, zōri,* shoes, and boots.

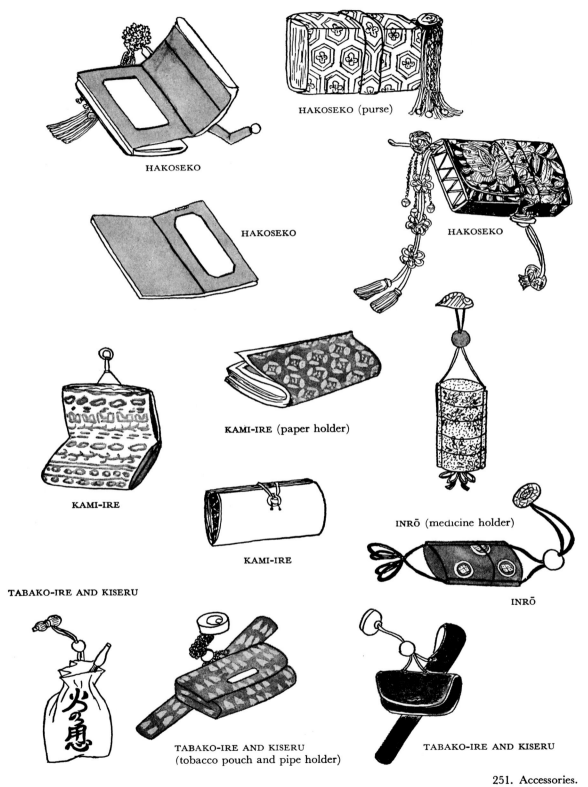

HAKOSEKO

HAKOSEKO (purse)

HAKOSEKO

HAKOSEKO

KAMI-IRE (paper holder)

KAMI-IRE

KAMI-IRE

INRŌ (medicine holder)

INRŌ

TABAKO-IRE AND KISERU

TABAKO-IRE AND KISERU
(tobacco pouch and pipe holder)

TABAKO-IRE AND KISERU

251. Accessories.

ISHŌ : COSTUMES  366

*tsukurimono-no-anesan-kaburi:* a *tenugui* which covers the head similarly to a *zukin*

*tamausagi-no-hachimaki:* a white headband worn by the rabbit in *Tama-usagi* and tied in front in deft imitation of a rabbit's ears

*eboshi:* all hats worn by men of all classes, other than *kammuri*

*kammuri:* all hats worn both indoors and outdoors by court nobles and civil and military officials

*kasa:* all reed hats used outdoors only, not including hats worn both indoors and out

*yoroi:* armor, including *kabuto* (helmet) and *kote-sune-ate* (arm and leg guards) and all other armor accessories

*hakimono:* all types of footgear

*ōgi* and *uchiwa:* folding fans and rigid fans

*katana:* swords of all types

The *ishō-ya* have a wealth of material at their command for making Kabuki costumes, and practically all are fabrics that were being loomed during Edo. The techniques of weaving *nishiki* (brocade) and *aya* (self-patterned silk with twill ground) had existed before the Heian period, but Kabuki costumes have never been made from such classic textiles as these. Probably the finest stuffs sewn into costumes have been patterned after those of Nō costumes of the Momoyama period.

The following are the principal Japanese textiles used for Kabuki costumes today. They are grouped into four divisions: silk and wool, hemp and ramie, cotton, and dyed stuffs. The parenthetical notation Nō means that the fabric is originally of Nō-drama use. The period of each fabric's first appearance in Japan is given parenthetically after the description: Nara (645–781), Heian (782–1185), Kamakura (1185–1392), Muromachi (1393–1573), Azuchi-Momoyama (1574–1602), and Edo (1603–1868).

SILK AND WOOL

*atsuita* (Nō): silk with lavish use of gold thread (Momoyama)

*birōdo:* velvet (early Edo)

*chirimen:* silk crepe (Momoyama)

*donsu:* silk damask with design in satin (late Momoyama)

*habutae:* plain silk (Nara)

*karaori* (Nō): brocade (Momoyama)

*kinran:* gold-brocaded cloth (Momoyama)

*omeshi:* flat silk crepe in striped or plaid design (late Edo, but not used in Kabuki until recently)

*rasha:* wool (Momoyama—imported)

*rinzu:* silk damask with geometrical background with small floral designs (early Edo)

*seigo* (Nō): silk of two kinds—one woven with thick weft (horizontal) threads, the other with degummed weft (Momoyama)

*sha:* silk gauze of soft-textured open weave (Nara)

252. *Kurombo*. The *kurombo* or *kuroko,* clothed entirely in black to suggest his invisibility to the audience, has the function of prompter and assistant stage manager, prompting the actors if they forget their lines, producing stools for them when they are required to sit, and handing them such accessories as fans and swords.

*shuchin:* brocaded satin (Momoyama)

*suzushi:* raw silk (Nara)

*tsumugi:* coarse pongee (Nara)

HEMP AND RAMIE

*katabira:* fine ramie cloth (Nara)

*nuno:* hemp cloth (Nara)

COTTON

*kasuri:* splash-designed cloth—also of hemp, cotton, or silk (Edo)

*kōshi:* checkered cloth (Nara or Heian, in silk only—popular in Momoyama and Edo in both silk and cotton)

*sarashi momen:* bleached cotton (Edo)

*shima:* striped cloth (Nara or Heian, in silk only—popular after Momoyama in both silk and cotton)

DYED STUFFS

*chūgata:* cloth with medium pattern dyed by stencil paste resist (Edo)

*kata-zome:* any cloth dyed by stencil paste resist (Momoyama)

*shibori:* tie-dyed cloth (Nara)

*yūzen* or *yūzen-zome:* cloth dyed by hand-drawn paste resist (Edo)

The glamorous costumes, with matching make-up and accessories, are the beautiful part of Kabuki that quickens the sensual pleasures and leaves strong, lasting impressions. It is to be hoped that Kabuki will never lose the visual and sensuous impact that it makes on an audience through color, costume, wigs, perfection in movement, and implication of detail.

Kabuki has always progressed through defiance of restrictions, and may it continue to do so without becoming so classic that it is static. The unique stage art of Kabuki, which "lies halfway between Chinese imaginative theater and Western photographic theater," as Sheldon Cheney in *The Theatre* expresses it, should continue as popular theater, not as museum theater, for its vitality as a dynamic theater art has much to offer not only to the Japanese public but also to the world at large.

# Glossary

*aburatsuki:* class of men's wigs in which back hair is pomaded, polished, and pressed close to head

*ai:* indigo, indigo blue

*ai-Benkei:* checkered textile pattern in blue and white, copied from *Benkei-gōshi*

*aibiki:* strings attached to wig for securing it in place

*aida-gire:* ornamental cloth wound around topknot in certain *onnagata* wigs; also called *tsurushi-gake*

*ai-mijin:* textile pattern of small blue and white checks

*aizome:* indigo dyeing

*aka:* red

*akahime:* (literally "red princess") role of princess, daughter of shōgun, or daughter of daimyō, for which costume is traditionally red

*akaito odoshi:* red-laced armor worn by youthful warriors; also called *hi-odoshi*

*akome ōgi:* many-staved folding fan with long streamers, carried as part of *jūni-hitoe* costume; also called *hi ōgi*

*akuba:* role of wicked or villainous woman

*aku-ōji:* role of wicked prince

*ame-ni-nure-tsubame:* textile pattern depicting rain and wet swallows

*ami-gasa:* large folding hat woven of rushes

*anesan kaburi:* young woman's style of wearing *tenugui* as headgear for travel or housework

*ao-iro:* yellowish-green "emperor's color"; also called *kikujin*

*aragoto:* grandiose, exaggerated, vigorously masculine style of acting

*araiso:* textile pattern depicting carp swimming in rolling waves

*arare:* textile pattern of hailstones, dots, or checks

*asa-gamishimo:* unlined *kamishimo* of ramie

*asagi:* light blue, flax blue

*asagi mompuku:* crested blue kimono

*asagi-no-kokumochi:* blue costume symbolizing the sea, worn by wives and daughters of fishermen

*asagi zukin:* blue *zukin* worn by characters of more gentle type

*asanoha:* hemp-leaf pattern in textiles

*asa-ura:* *zōri* with soles of braided hemp cords

*asobinin:* playboys, gamblers

*atama-awase:* fitting of *daigane* to actor's head

*atsuita:* stiff gold-brocaded silk; brocaded outer robe for men's roles in Nō plays

*atsuwata:* see *atsuwata-no-hirosode*

*atsuwata-no-hirosode:* thickly padded wide-sleeve garment worn over armor; also called *atsuwata*

*aya:* self-patterned silk with twill ground

*azuma-karage:* tucked-up style of wearing kimono, with hem pulled up by strings

*babā bōshi:* old woman's decorative headcloth

*beni:* red or deep red; red coloring used as rouge or lipstick in actor's make-up

*Benkei-gōshi:* textile pattern of oblong checks, usually black and white

*bin:* sidelocks; side pieces of wig base

*bingane:* metal piece inserted into sidelocks of wig to inflate them

*bingane-no-tsubo:* metal holder attached to wig base to secure *bingane*

*bin-no-mono daigane:* wig base with two side pieces and suspension bridge

*bin-sogi:* ceremony of cutting girl's hair to denote maturity

*birōdo:* velvet

*bō-chasen mage:* erect style of tea-whisk topknot in man's wig

*bō-jike:* pomade-hardened strands of hair at back of each ear

*bokashi:* gradation technique of applying *kumadori*

*bokutō:* wooden sword carried by samurai servants

*bōshi:* strip of cloth placed over forehead or crown of head as wig decoration

*bōzu:* Buddhist priest

*bōzu-bashori:* priest's style of tucking up back of kimono into obi

*bōzu-katsura:* see *maru-bōzu daigane*

*budōgoto:* forceful acting style in samurai revenge dramas

371

*buke-onna-no-mukō hachimaki:* samurai woman's style of wearing *hachimaki*

*bukkaeri:* version of quick change in which only top of a new costume is revealed

*bunkin-taka-shimada: onnagata* wig with tall topknot and back hair in mushroom shape

*bunko:* obi bow with loops curved slightly downward

*bunko-dome:* holes in base of *onnagata* wig for holding ornamental back hairpins

Bunraku: the puppet theater

*bushi:* early name for warrior, military man, samurai

*chasen mage:* tea-whisk style of topknot in man's wig

*chidori-gake:* stitches representing zigzag footprints of plover

*chikara-age:* shoulder pleat in kimono sleeve to give pushed-up effect

*chikara-gami:* paper wig decoration tied around topknot

*chikara-gane:* metal reinforcing strips at temples of wig base

*chirichiri:* tightly curled hair (actually fine wire) used in wigs for roles of masterful men

*chirimen:* silk crepe

*chōchō mage:* butterfly style of topknot for child's wig

*chōken:* semiformal dress of high-ranking samurai or generals (Kabuki term for *kariginu*); outer robe of silk gauze worn in both male and female dance roles in Nō

*chōnin:* merchants

*chōnin-no-mukō-hachimaki:* merchant-class style of wearing *tenugui* as headband

*chōnin tobi:* firemen maintained by merchant class

*chū-dachi:* flattened, somewhat loose style of sidelocks in wig

*chūgara:* see *chūgata*

*chūgata:* allover stenciled textile pattern of medium size; also called *chūgara*

*chūgen:* see *yakko*

*chūkei:* spread fan borrowed from Nō and used for *tachi-yaku* roles

*chūya:* see *kujira*

*daigane:* metal base of wig

*daimon:* shōgun or daimyō formal costume consisting of wide-sleeved top garment with large family crests and pair of *naga-bakama*

*daishō:* samurai's paired short and long swords, identical except in length

*daitō:* long sword; larger of samurai's paired swords

*dammari:* pantomimic scenes, usually occurring in darkness

*Danshichi-gōshi:* textile pattern of white and rust checks

*date:* dandy style, dandified

*date-basami:* gold-striped satin *tenugui* sometimes used as accessory to *yakko* costume; also called *hasami tenugui*

*date hachimaki: hachimaki* tied a little to left of center forehead, worn by *otokodate*, firemen, and palanquin bearers

*date-hyōgo:* courtesan wig featuring large globular topknot with wide division in center; also called *date-keisei*

*date-keisei:* see *date-hyōgo*

*deba-bōchō:* unsheathed kitchen knife carried by *sanjaku-mono*

*dō:* armor corselet

*dōchū-gasa:* samurai woman's *kasa* for traveling

*dōchū kaburi: tenugui* worn as headgear for traveling

*dōgane:* metal ornaments for scabbard

*dōgane-iri-saya:* scabbard decorated with *dōgane*

*dōgi:* sleeveless half-length undergarment

*dōji-gōshi:* textile pattern of alternating purple and white squares

*dō-juban:* sleeveless half-length *juban*

*dōmaru:* scale cuirass opening at the right side and tied at the waist (one of the three fundamental types of armor)

*donchō:* drop curtain

*donsu:* silk satin-damask

*dōnuki:* specially tailored courtesan kimono with upper and lower parts of different cloth

*eboshi:* nobleman's, samurai's, or court official's lacquered-paper hat

*eboshi-no-hachimaki:* headband attached to rim of *eboshi*

*Edo kanoko:* tie-dyed textile pattern in allover polka-dot style; also called *Kodayū kanoko*

*ende:* swallow-tail style of forelock in man's wig

*eri:* collar

*fuka-ami-gasa:* large, deep *kasa* completely covering head and face and having latticework "window" in front

*fukashi-bin:* inflated sidelocks of wig

*fuke-oyama:* role of elderly woman; also called *kashagata*

*fuki-nagashi kaburi: onnagata* headgear formed of *tenugui* draped loosely over head, with one edge held between the lips

*fukiwa mage:* topknot of *onnagata* wig looped over drum-shaped ornament

*fukurotsuki:* class of men's wigs with back hair in bag shape

*fukurotsuki-wakashu:* young man's wig resembling *shimada* but with topknot in masculine style

*fumi-hogo:* calligraphic design on *kamiko* worn for *nimaime* roles

*fundoshi:* see *shita-obi*

*fungomi:* woman's trousers—predecessor of *hakama*

*furisage musubi:* style of tying woman's obi in knot without loops but with long pendulous ends

*furisode:* young woman's kimono with long swinging sleeves

*furiwake-no-sumi-maegami:* center-parted forelock of man's wig, shaved at corners of forehead *fusa:* tassel

*futatsu-domoe:* crest design of two large comma shapes inverted to form slightly disjointed circle

*futatsu-ori ami-gasa:* folding *kasa* used for *wagoto* role

*futatsu-ori mage:* doubled or folded queue or topknot

*Genji-guruma:* crest or textile pattern basically representing two circles crossed by spokes radiating from center

*Genji-kō:* textile pattern composed of character for *hito* (man) repeated in groups of three; see also *Nakazō-jima*

*Genji-no-kammuri-shita:* style of man's tea-whisk topknot with end divided and curved to touch crown of head

*geta:* wooden clogs for outdoor wear

*gidayū-jōruri:* songlike narrative accompaniment in puppet-theater style

*gin hanagushi:* young woman's hair ornament with three to five rows of silvered metal flowers and butterflies

*gion-mamori:* crest or textile design of two-circle frame intersected by two horizontal lines, with inside circle crossed by two rolls of song scripts

*go-chūshin:* battle messenger

*gohon-bone:* five-ribbed fan used in "living-history" plays; also called *kawahori* or *musa ōgi*

*gojō kesa:* priest's surplice composed of five strips of cloth to form rectangular bag hung over left side by two shoulder straps

*gokenin:* lowest class of samurai

*goma:* gray hair; class of wigs with gray hair

*goma-no-marumage:* elderly woman's wig with mixture of black and white hair

*goma-shio:* mixed black and white hair in elderly character's wig

*Gonta hachimaki:* special *hachimaki* for role of Gonta in *Yoshitsune Sembon-Zakura;* white cotton *tenugui* dyed in navy-blue *mameshibori* and tied with ends upright in front

*Gorō kaburi:* type of *koshō kaburi* worn by young men in *jidai-mono*

*gosannen:* see *ori eboshi*

*goten jochū:* ranking lady-in-waiting at court of shōgun or daimyō

*gumpyō:* military troops

*guri-zaya:* red-lacquered (or occasionally black-lacquered) notched scabbard resembling shell of shrimp

*habutae:* plain silk; strip of silk on which hair is sewn to create wig hairline; class of wigs with this type of hairline; square of silk coated with pomade and oil and fitted tightly to actor's head as base for man's wig

*hachigane:* gold forehead decoration for battle *hachimaki*

*hachigane-tsuki hachimaki:* battle *hachimaki* with gold forehead decoration

*hachijō:* a soft plain-woven silk

*hachiken kusazuri:* eight-sectioned plaited skirt worn as armor

*hachiken ōgi:* a type of fan

*hachi-mai-bin:* sidelocks of wig made of four sheets of *mino-ge*

*hachimaki:* folded cloth worn as headband

*hada-juban:* woman's tight short-sleeved cotton undershirt; top underwear

*hadanugi:* version of *hikinuki* in which sleeve is slipped from right and then from left shoulder or from right only

*hakama:* pleated trousers, culottes

*hakeme:* brush-mark textile pattern

*hakimono:* footwear in general

*hako-bin:* box-shaped sidelocks in a wig

*hako musubi:* style of tying obi in square-shaped or boxlike bow; also called *karuta musubi*

*haku-sen:* ten-ribbed all-white folding fan used with *kamishimo* or *naga-gamishimo*

*hambakama:* see *han-bakama*

*hanagake:* scarf of *kanoko*-patterned cloth tied at root of topknot or queue in woman's wig

*hanagami:* paper handkerchiefs

*hanagushi:* woman's ornamental hairpin with three to five rows of silver flowers; see also *gin hanagushi*

*hanakazari-tsuki samurai eboshi: samurai eboshi* ornamented with red and white plum blossoms, worn in both male and female roles

*hana kōgai:* woman's bar-shaped hair ornament with flowers at each end

*hanamichi:* runway through audience from stage to rear of theater

*hanao:* thongs of *geta* or *zōri*

*hana yoten: yoten* costume with pattern of serpentine lines and conventionalized flower and leaf motifs on solid-colored ground

*han-bakama:* short *hakama* used mostly as part of *han-kamishimo*

*han-bōzu daigane:* priest's wig covering back half of head while waxed *habutae* covers front half

*hangire: hakama* with wide leg openings and stiffened back, made of single colored cloth patterned in gold

*han-juban:* woman's short undergarment

*han-kamishimo: kamishimo* with short *hakama*

*hannya-guma: kumadori* make-up for demon and ghost roles; also called *Heikurō-guma* and *kijo-guma*

*Hanshirō kanoko:* textile pattern of small-spot *shibori*

*hanten:* short outer coat worn by commoners, resembling *haori* but lacking ties

*haori:* short outer coat for men or women, fastened in front with ties

*happi:* short coat symbolizing armor in Nō plays; short topcoat

*happō-ware:* style of man's topknot divided in eight directions

*hara-awase:* see *kujira*

*haragake:* sleeveless, backless work shirt with crisscross back straps, worn by workmen or firemen

*haramaki:* scale cuirass opening at back and tied at

waist (one of the three fundamental types of armor)

*hari-bakama:* long red *hakama* worn by court ladies; also called *uchi-bakama*

*haritsuba mage:* topknot of man's wig with hair at end cut to resemble a rank of needles

*hasami musubi:* style of tying obi in plain overlooped bow with ends drawn through inside

*hasami tenugui:* see *date-basami*

*hashori:* raising or tucking up of kimono hem

*hatamoto:* direct feudatory of shōgun

*hattan:* a twilled silk

*hayagawari:* quick change of costume off stage

*Heikurō-guma:* see *hannya-guma*

*heyagi:* courtesan style of dress when entertaining guests; see also *dōnuki*

*hidari-zuma tori:* geisha style of holding up kimono hems tightly in left hand

*hikae yagura:* unlicensed theater management

*hikimaku:* Kabuki draw curtain

*hikinuki:* instantaneous on-stage change of costume

*hikitate eboshi:* tall pliable *eboshi* worn by *daimyō*, usually fastened with white ties

*Hikosaburō-gōshi:* textile pattern of diagonal stripes forming large diamonds which enclose interlocked *katakana* characters for *hi* and *ko*; also called *hikoza-gōshi*

*hikoza-gōshi:* see *Hikosaburō-gōshi*

*hime:* role of princess, daughter of shōgun, or daughter of daimyō; see also *akahime*

*hime hana-kanzashi:* ornamental hairpin with four rows of silver plum blossoms and butterflies, worn in *hime* roles

*himo:* strings or ties for various garments, hats, footwear, etc.; cloth band or belt worn over kimono before donning obi

*hi-no-hakama:* scarlet culottes worn as part of Heian noblewoman's attire; see *hari-bakama*

*hi-no-koromo:* high priest's scarlet coat with wide-open sleeves and knife-pleated flounce at bottom

*hi-odoshi:* see *akaito odoshi*

*hi ōgi:* see *akome ōgi*

*hirari bōshi:* folded *onnagata bōshi* pinned to wig above forehead; also called *Okumi bōshi*

*hirauchi:* woman's long flat ornamental hairpin

*hirosode:* "big-sleeve" apparel of the Nō

*hitatare:* samurai's large square-cut coat with cord-laced sleeve edges and short *hakama*; see also *yoroi-hitatare*

*hitoe:* any unlined kimono; unlined kimono worn under *uwagi* in *jūni-hitoe* costume

*hitoe-kariginu:* unlined *kariginu*

*hiyoku mon:* overlapping crests of *onnagata* and actor playing role of lover, used in *michiyuki* dual-style costumes

*hiza-yoroi:* belted two-piece armor resembling apron split in center, each flap extending from waist to knee

*hō:* outer robe of *sokutai*

*hōkamuri:* *tenugui* used as hood

*hommi katana:* stage sword with iron blade

*honke:* real hair used in a wig

*honke-no-mizuiri:* man's wig resembling long hanging wet hair

*hōsho:* Japanese paper used in wig decoration, as in *chikara-gami*

*hōshu:* textile pattern of fire-rimmed circle or "flaming gem"

*hotaru-uchi:* colored silk braid used to decorate topknot in men's wigs

*hyakunichi-no-tare:* man's wig with bushy hair covering top of head and long hanging hair tied at back

*hyōgo:* linked-chain type of decoration used on *tachi* scabbard; *tachi* with this type of scabbard; also called *hyōgo-gusari*

*hyōgo-gusari:* see *hyōgo*

*hyōgo mage:* large, globular, center-divided topknot of courtesan's wig

*hyōtan:* bottle-gourd for holding *sake* or water

*hyottoko kaburi:* *tenugui* headgear of clownish characters

*ichi:* part of topknot or queue nearest root; lower loop of topknot

*ichi-dome:* woman's hairpin

*ichimatsu:* see *Ichimatsu-zome*

*Ichimatsu-zome:* checkerboard textile pattern in various contrasting color combinations; also called *ichimatsu*

*ichime-gasa:* sedge *kasa* used in *shosagoto*

*ichimonji-gasa:* see *ichimonji suge-gasa*

*ichimonji kojiri:* straight-line chape for scabbard

*ichimonji suge-gasa:* sedge *kasa* worn by samurai

*ichō:* man's or woman's topknot in ginkgo-leaf shape

*ichō-gaeshi:* topknot in shape of pair of inverted ginkgo leaves

*igaguri maru-bōzu:* priest's wig imitating close-cropped head

*ikarizuna:* textile pattern of anchor ropes

*iki:* dandified appearance, spruceness, smartness in manner and costume

*ikinuki:* holes in base of *onnagata* wig for ventilation and for decreasing weight

*inaka musume:* role of country girl

*inaka nyōbō:* role of country wife

*inazuma:* "lightning" style of folding paper strips used as decorations for *onnagata* wigs

*inrō:* medicine box suspended by cord from obi

*ippon-tokko:* *chōnin's* obi pattern copying Buddhist ritual implements in claw-dumbbell shape

*ippon-guma:* single-line *kumadori* make-up

*iro-gamishimo:* young samurai's satin *kamishimo* in bright colors and large designs

*iro-nashi ōgi:* fan for madwoman roles in Nō

*iro-nonko:* another name for *iro-yakko*; general name for wigs worn by *iro-yakko*, featuring long topknot and highly polished back hair combed upward

*iro-yakko:* handsome or sensual *yakko*; also called *iro-nonko* or *shusu-yakko ishō:* costume, costumes

*ishō-kata:* man in charge of costume room

*ishō-no-tsukechō:* costumer's notebook listing actors, roles, and costumes for a production

*ishō-shirabe:* examination of costumes by actors prior to use

*ishō-tsuke:* dresser or costume specialist

*ishō-ya:* costumer

*issoku tabane:* style of man's topknot resembling bundle of straw

*ito-jike:* thickly twisted silk threads under sidelocks of *machi-musume* wig; looped strands of hair as in *kasshiki* wig

*ito-ori:* strong, durable silk woven from previously dyed yarn in pattern of medium-sized stripes

*itsutsu-ginu:* see *kasane uchiki*

*iyo-zome:* textile pattern suggesting sunlight shining through split-bamboo blinds

*jidai-mono:* plays loosely based on historical events

*jidai-sewa-mono:* historical-domestic plays representing commingling of samurai and plebeian families

*jimbaori:* sleeveless battle coat worn over armor

*jin-gasa:* battle *kasa*, usually worn by lower-ranking samurai

*jin-sen:* camp or battle fan

*ji-tabo:* class of *onnagata* wigs with natural-looking bag effect at back; natural-looking back hair without stretcher or padding

*jochū musume:* role of maidservant

*jōmegutsu:* step-in fur boots worn by daimyō in battle

*jōruri:* musical narrative in Kabuki and puppet plays

*jōshiki maku:* standard Kabuki curtain of black, reddish-brown, and moss-green stripes

*juban:* undergarment, underkimono

*jūni-hitoe:* Heian noblewoman's "layered" costume for formal occasions

*jūroku-musashi:* textile pattern of white zigzag lines intersected by white circles and an occasional black one—on a Kelly-green background

*jutte:* symbol of authority carried by *kuro yoten*

*juzu:* Buddhist rosary

*kabocha kaburi:* see *tōnasu kaburi*

*kabuki-mono:* outlaws or "free-life" people

*kaburi-mono:* headgear in general, except *tenugui* used as headband

*kabuto:* helmet

*kabuto-no-Hachiman-za:* top center of warrior's helmet, supposedly seat of war god Hachiman

*kachimushi:* dragonfly pattern

*kachishura:* type of Nō warrior fan

*kaemon:* actor's alternative crest for less formal wear

*kagoya:* urban palanquin bearers

*kagura:* ancient religious pantomimic dance form

*kaidan-mono:* ghost plays of grotesque theme

*kaidori:* see *uchikake*

*kaidori-karage:* woman's style of lifting both kimono and *kaidori* at hips and tying them with stitched belt or soft sash

*kaiken:* woman's dagger without guard

*kai-no-kuchi musubi:* style of tying obi in bow of shellmouth shape; also called *otoko musubi*

*kaki-iro zukin:* reddish-brown *zukin* worn by stronger characters

*kame-nozoki:* light blue

*kamiko:* calligraphic-patterned kimono for *nimaime* roles, originally of paper but now of satin or crepe; see also *fumi-hogo*

*kamishimo:* samurai costume consisting of ankle-length *hakama* and *kataginu* worn over *kitsuke*; see also *naga-gamishimo*

*kammuri:* hat worn by nobles and court officials in classical plays

*kamome-zuto:* seagull-tail shape of back hair in wig for temple page boys

*kamuro:* young girl attendant of ranking courtesan

*kangiku:* crest representing stylized chrysanthemum with stem split and brought up to blossom in circular shape

*kanoko:* fine-knotted *shibori* textile pattern resembling spots on fawn's hide

*kan tsunagi:* see *Shikan-jima*

*kanzashi:* woman's long ornamental hairpin

*kaomise:* "face showing," formal introduction of theatrical season

*Kaoyo Gozen* costume : standard costume for wives of feudal lords and court gentlemen, patterned after that of Lady Kaoyo in *Kanadehon Chūshingura*

*kappa:* raincoat

*karaginu:* loose short jacket with abbreviated sleeves, worn as outermost garment of *jūni-hitoe*

*karaori:* silk brocaded with colored floss or gilt-paper strips; brocaded outer robe of upper-class woman ; outer robe for women's roles in Nō

*kariginu:* outdoor dress of Heian nobleman

*karuta musubi:* see *hako musubi*

*kasa:* umbrella-shaped hat of sedge, rush, etc.

*kasane ōgi:* crest design of two overlapping fans

*kasane uchiki:* kimono with widely opened sleeve worn one on top of another in *jūni-hitoe* costume; also called *itsutsu-ginu*

*kasane waraji:* cotton-rope sandals with heel guards and laces for tying

*kasha-gata:* see *fuke-oyama*

*kasshiki:* wig with cloud-shaped hairline

*kasuri:* splash-designed fabric woven of pre-dyed silk or cotton threads

*kata:* stylized format of role, acting, costume, etc.

*kata-bashori:* see *shichisan-bashori*

*katabira:* fine ramie cloth; unlined summer kimono of ramie or hemp

*kata-eri:* padded collar or neckband

*kataginu:* man's jumper with broad winglike shoulders, worn with *hakama* or *naga-bakama* to form *kamishimo* or *naga-gamishimo*

*kataginu-hakama:* combination of *kataginu* with *hakama* of different pattern and cloth; also called *tsugi-gamishimo*

*katahazushi* costume: costume of upper-class samurai

wife or ranking lady-in-waiting at court of daimyō or shōgun—named for *katahazushi mage*

*katahazushi mage:* wig with asymmetrical topknot worn by upper-class samurai wife or ranking lady-in-waiting at court of daimyō or shōgun

*kata-ire:* kimono with shoulder inserts of different cloth to simulate patched garment

*katakawa:* see *kujira*

*kataki-yaku:* role of villain

*katana:* swords in general; sword with curved single-edge blade

*kata-wana musubi:* style of tying obi with one-looped bow

*kata-zome:* any cloth dyed by stencil resist

*kata-zuma tori:* woman's style of holding up left vertical hem of kimono in left hand or tucking it into obi

*katsuo-jima:* textile pattern suggesting bonito scales

*katsura:* wig

*katsura-no-tsukechō:* notebook listing wigs needed for a production

*katsura ōgi:* woman's fan used in Nō

*katsura-ya:* wigmaker

*katsureki-geki:* "living-history" play

*kawa-baori:* short leather coat worn by laborers' foremen

*kawahori:* see *gohon-bone*

*kazaori eboshi:* real-life daimyo's tall hat with crown flattened to one side—represented by Kabuki *hikitate eboshi*

*kazetōshi-no-ana:* ventilation holes in base of man's wig with *kōra*

*kegutsu:* low tie-on boots of bearskin, worn by generals in battle

*keisei:* courtesan

*keisei-kai:* dramas dealing with affairs of courtesans

*ken:* sword with straight double-edge blade; dagger

*kenjō-Hakata:* excellent-quality "dedication" silk from Hakata

*kenka kaburi:* *mameshibori tenugui* worn in fashion of a dandy

*kenuki-gata-no-tachi:* Heian-period *tachi* with hilt and blade of same metal and with hilt split through center

*kesa:* priest's robe or surplice

*keshin-mono:* animal costumes

*keshō:* make-up

*keshō-mino:* smoothly plaited hair used to finish wig hairline

*kichibishi:* crest in diamond shape representing stylized character for *kichi* (good luck)

*ki-hachijō:* yellow *hachijō* silk

*kijo-guma:* see *hannya-guma*

*kiku-byakunichi:* style of man's wig with lacquered layers of hair resembling chrysanthemum petals

*Kikugorō-gōshi:* crossbarred textile pattern with heavier lines forming main squares and lighter lines running through every other vertical and horizontal stripe and with characters *ki* and *ro* alternating in center of plain squares

*kikujin:* see *ao-iro*

*kindachi:* role of young nobles in Nō, or Nō warrior's fan used in Kabuki

*kin nawa:* gold rope for tying long loosely hanging hair in special men's wigs

*kinran:* gold-brocaded cloth

*kin sammi eboshi:* shōgun's gold hat

*kin tate eboshi:* gold *tate eboshi* worn by *onnagata* in dance plays

*kinu:* plain-woven silk

*kire-waraji:* cloth sandals dyed to simulate *waraji*; also called *nuno-waraji*

*kiriwara:* man's style of topknot resembling cut bundle of straw

*kitsuke:* top kimono under outer robe

*kizami-zaya:* notched scabbard resembling *guri-zaya*

*kizewa-mono:* domestic plays dealing with low life

*kobitai:* curved hairline at temples of wig

*kodachi:* woman's small sword

*Kodayū kanoko:* see *Edo kanoko*

*kodōgu:* hand properties; hand-properties department

*kōgai:* bar-shaped ornament for *onnagata* wigs

*kojiri:* chape of a scabbard

*kōken:* actor's assistant or property man

*kokumochi:* single-colored kimono with three to five appliquéd white circles imitating family crests

*ko-mage katsura:* wig with small topknot

*komageta musubi:* style of tying obi to resemble a pair of *geta*; also called *waribasami*

*komeya kaburi:* *tenugui* worn as headgear by rice dealers and for traveling

*kommurago odoshi:* laced armor pattern forming rectilinear design in blue and white

*komon:* small over-all dyed pattern in textiles

*komusubi:* six-tailed knot at back of *samurai eboshi*; also called *koyui*

*kon:* dark blue, navy blue

*kōra:* copper piece attached to wig base to represent crown of head

*kōraiya-gōshi:* textile pattern of white stripes forming squares on rust ground, with alternate stripes twice width of other stripes; also called *kōraiya-jima* or *okina-gōshi*

*kōraiya-jima:* see *kōraiya-gōshi*

*kōra-mono daigane:* wig base with metal plate representing crown of head

*Koroku-zome:* textile pattern of red and white oblique stripes; earlier known as *tazuna-zome*

*koroshiba:* murder scene

*korozen:* yellowish-brown "emperor's color"

*kōshi:* checkered textile patterns in general

*koshi-age hashori:* woman's style of raising kimono hems from lower hips, pulling them to right under obi, and tying them with stitched belt or soft sash

*koshi-gatana:* shorter of dissimilar pair of swords

*koshi-goromo:* priest's transparent black overskirt

*koshimaki:* (literally "waist wrapper") woman's loincloth or waistcloth *koshimoto:* daughter of samurai serving at court, lady-in-waiting, or wealthy merchant's daughter; costume for such a role

*koshō:* page boy

*koshō kaburi:* long *tenugui* tied under chin, worn by young men

*kosode:* small-sleeved kimono

*ko-suō:* *suō* with *han-bakama*

*kote:* arm guards worn with armor

*kouchigi:* aristocratic woman's coat used for both indoor and outdoor wear

*koyagake butai:* outdoor stage

*ko-yaku:* role of a child

*kozakura odoshi:* laced armor design with applied stencil pictures of cherry blossoms

*kozane:* small *sane* or armor platelets

*kozuka:* small dagger fitting into pocket in scabbard of *shōtō*

*kuge:* court nobles

*kuge-aku:* role of wicked nobleman

*kujira:* obi with each side of a different type of cloth; also called *chūya*, *hara-awase*, or *katakawa*

*kujō kesa:* priest's ceremonial surplice composed of nine strips of cloth

*kukuri-bakama:* hakama tied at the ankles

*kumadori:* nonrealistic stylized make-up for *aragoto* roles

*kumeza mage:* woman's divided or parted topknot in a wig

*kumo-ni-inazuma:* textile pattern of clouds interspersed with diagonal flashes of stylized lightning

*kumo-ni-ryū:* textile pattern depicting drifting clouds and dragons; also called *unryū*

*kumosuke:* highway porters

*kurai-boshi:* extra pair of dotted eyebrows above natural ones in woman's make-up

*kuri-gata:* hairline of a wig; cord knobs for attaching *obitori* to a *katana*

*kuri-ume:* purple with a tinge of yellow and red

*kuro:* black

*kuroko:* on-stage actor's assistant, prompter, and scenery changer; also called *kurombo*

*kuro-hachijō:* black *hachijō* silk

*kurohō:* black upper garment worn with *sokutai*

*kurohō-no-sokutai:* nobleman's formal court apparel with black upper garment

*kurombo:* see *kuroko*

*kuro-nuri-gutsu:* black-lacquered square-toed clogs

*kuro yoten:* *yoten* costume with all garments of black except for obi

*kuruma-bin:* stiffly lacquered sidelocks of man's wig combed into protruding flat strands resembling spokes of a wheel

*kushime:* style of wig with natural-looking back hair

*kusudama kanzashi:* young woman's hairpin decorated with long varicolored tassels

*kusun-gobu:* vagabond's or criminal's sheathed dagger

*kuwagata:* horn- or hoe-shaped crest on front of warrior's helmet

*kuwagata hachimaki:* *hachimaki* tied to resemble *kuwagata*

*kuwagata-tsuki hikitate eboshi:* daimyō's tall battle hat with attached headband and *kuwagata*

*kyahan:* leggings, gaiters

*kyōgen-kata:* production manager; stage director

*Kyōgen ōgi:* fans used in dance-dramas adapted from Kyōgen

*machi musume:* role of city girl

*machi nyōbō:* role of city wife

*machi yakko:* see *otokodate*

*mae-chasen:* tea-whisk topknot resting on crown of head in man's wig

*maedare:* maidservant's apron

*maegami:* forelock

*maekake:* apron worn by *inaka nyōbō*

*mae musubi:* style of tying obi in front

*mage:* queue, topknot

*mage-kakushi:* *eboshi* covering topknot only

*maiginu:* Nō robe of silk gauze for female roles in dance scenes

*mai ōgi:* dance fan used in *shosagoto;* also called *shiratake-no-ōgi*

*makeshura:* type of Nō warrior fan

*makie:* gold-sprinkled lacquer

*mameshibori:* tie-dyeing in small over-all pattern resembling beans, often used for *tenugui*

*manjū-gasa:* see *takenoko-gasa*

*maru-bōzu daigane:* priest's wig representing shaven head; also called *bōzu-katsura*

*maru-guke:* rope-style obi

*maru-juban:* full-length *juban*

*maru kojiri:* round chape for a scabbard

*marumage:* class of coiffure with rounded topknot worn by married women and sometimes maids or ladies-in-waiting

*maru-ni-chigai-takanoha:* crest depicting hawk feathers crossed in a circle

*maru-ni-fūjibumi:* crest representing tied letter paper in a circle, also used as textile pattern

*maru-ni-i:* crest composed of character for "well" in a circle

*maru-obi:* obi of one type of cloth only

*maru-shitagi:* full-length undergarment worn below *juban*

*maru-tabo:* class of *onnagata* wigs with back hair in rounded puff made with a stretcher

*matsubame-mono:* Kabuki plays of Nō origin

*matsuba-yamamichi:* textile pattern of pine needles on zigzag mountain path, often used for *tenugui*

*matsukawabishi-ni-tsuta:* crest design representing pine bark, ivy, and diamond shapes; also used as textile pattern

*matsuri ōgi:* a type of fan

*meisen:* type of medium-quality silk used by merchant class

*mekake:* role of concubine or mistress

*mete:* short sword with small guard worn at the right side

*michiyuki:* scene representing a journey, often of two lovers

*michiyuki kaburi:* headgear worn in *michiyuki* scenes

*midaidokoro:* role of wife of feudal lord or court gentleman

*midori:* very light green

*mie:* stylized cross-eyed pose

*mimasu mon:* Ichikawa actor's family crest representing three concentric squares

*mimasu tsunagi:* see *rokuyata-gōshi*

*mimikaki:* woman's long hairpin worn below topknot

*mimiwaki:* metal strip riveted to sides of wig base to secure connecting band at back

*mino-ge:* plaited hair attached to wig base to produce hairline in old-style wigs

*mino-no-yuiwata:* wig with topknot resembling tied silk wadding, worn by young *kokumochi*

*mino-shikoro-no-sagegami:* class of *onnagata* wigs with long hair hanging down in back

*mitsuba-no-kuro-nuri-geta:* high black-lacquered clogs worn by courtesan

*mitsu-dai-jima:* textile pattern using stylized character *dai* (large, great) in groups of three placed between rows of three closely spaced vertical stripes

*mitsu-ichō:* crest design of three ginkgo leaves, also used as textile pattern

*mizugoromo:* unlined topcoat worn by priests and sometimes by commoners in Nō

*mizu-iri:* man's wig simulating wet hair

*mo:* apron-train worn with *jūni-hitoe*

*moegi:* bright green

*moegi-no-kokumochi:* bright-green *kokumochi* costume for *inaka musume*

*momi eboshi:* "crushed" type of *eboshi* worn by commoners

*momohiki:* tight navy-blue cotton drawers

*mon:* family crest

*monsha:* woven silk gauze with pattern

*montsuki:* formal kimono with three or five family crests

*motoyui:* paper cord used for tying base of queue in a wig

*mukaibato:* crest representing two stylized pigeons facing each other

*mukō hachimaki:* *hachimaki* tied in flat bow at center of upper forehead

*munahimo:* breast tie of *daimon, hitatare,* and *suō*

*murasaki:* purple

*murasaki bōshi:* small flat purple *bōshi* usually placed on upper forehead and attached to wig

*musa ōgi:* see *gohon-bone*

*mushiri:* slight growth of hair on previously shaven part of man's head

*musume-gata:* role of young woman

*naga-bakama:* long trailing *hakama* used mostly as part of *naga-gamishimo*

*naga-gamishimo:* daimyō and samurai costume consisting of *kataginu* and long *hakama* worn over *kitsuke;* see also *kamishimo*

*naga-juban:* *onnagata's* long undergarment, similar to slip

*nagauta:* on-stage musical accompaniment by singers and orchestra

*naga-wakizashi:* *otokodate's* sword resembling samurai's *daitō;* medium-sized sword worn by commoners

*naginata:* halberd

*naimaze:* mixture of curly and straight hair used in certain wigs

*naka-no-tsuri:* lower of two suspension bridges at back of wig base; see also *tsuri*

*nakazashi:* woman's long bar-shaped hairpin thrust through base of topknot

*Nakazō-jima:* striped textile pattern employing *Genji-kō*

*namazu bōzu:* role of comic priest

*nanatsugane:* "seven-metals" type of *obitori* used for *tachi* scabbard

*narabi koshimoto:* a number of *koshimoto* moving and speaking as a group

*nari-tsuba katana:* sword with loosely made guard designed to produce ringing sound during swordplay

*ne:* base or root of queue in a wig

*nedori:* hair pieces of *mino-ge* attached to wig base to form complete coiffure

*nedori-no-ana:* holes in wig base for attaching topknot, etc.

*nedori-no-kane:* appendage at back of wig base for fashioning back hair in bag style

*nenneko:* full-backed garment designed to cover both mother and baby on her back

*nezumi-iro:* gray, mouse gray

*nihon-tokko:* samurai's obi pattern imitating two rows of Buddhist ritual implements in clawdumbbell shape

*niku-juban:* flesh-colored tights, sometimes with *kumadori* or tattooing

*nimaime:* actor portraying a young lover; see also *wagoto*

*ningyō-jōruri-shibai:* puppet theater

*nishiki:* silk woven or brocaded with colors and gilt or silver paper strips

*nishiki yoten:* *yoten* costume gold-brocaded in profuse designs

*nishoku-guma:* two-colored *kumadori*

*no-bakama:* *hakama* for outdoor wear

*Nō-chasen:* tea-whisk style of topknot in man's wig for roles derived from Kyōgen

*no-dachi:* paired short and long swords

*nōshi:* Nō costume representing court gentleman's long silk coat; court gentlemen's ordinary dress in Heian period

*noshime:* kimono with pattern across midriff

*nuihaku:* kimono decoration in imprinted gold or silver leaf and embroidery; woman's kimono so decorated *nuno:* cloth woven with vegetable fibers

*nuno-waraji:* see *kire-waraji*

*nureba:* erotic scenes

*nuri-gasa:* lacquered umbrella-shaped hat

*nurimi katana:* sword with black-lacquered wooden blade with red groove

*nusubito kaburi:* see *shinobi kaburi*

*nyōbō-gata:* leading female role

*obako mage:* divided, looped topknot in *onnagata* wig

*obi:* man's or woman's sash

*obi-age:* band for maintaining obi in place

*obijime:* narrow cord tied over obi to support it

*obitori:* loops through which *sageo* of sword passes

*ōchō-mono:* court dramas

*ōdōgu:* scenery

*odoshi:* laced or braided armor patterns

*ōgi:* folding fan

*ōguchi:* *hakama* of single-colored unpatterned cloth with large openings at ankles and extremely broad stiff back; also called *ōguchi-bakama*

*ōguchi-bakama:* see *ōguchi*

*ōhi:* priest's stole worn with *kesa*

*oie-mono:* dramas involving daimyō and other noblemen

*oiran:* courtesan of Edo period

*ō-jidai-mono:* historical dramas based on events of ancient times

*ō-jikken:* white or white-with-gold edges of *haku-sen* type used with *kamishimo*

*okagoshi:* samurai who carry shōgun's palanquin

*okifukusa bōshi:* purple *bōshi* worn exclusively by a feudal lord on pleasure excursions

*okina-gōshi:* see *kōraiya-gōshi*

*oki tenugui:* *tenugui* folded oblong and laid on top of head by indolent characters

*okoso zukin:* *onnagata zukin* covering entire head and forehead, with sides crossing under chin and ends draped over shoulders

*Okumi bōshi:* see *hirari bōshi*

*oku-seitai habutae:* *habutae* colored blue-black to represent shaven crown of middle-aged or old man's head

*okyōgen-shi:* women's Kabuki troupe

*omatsuri:* lacquered petal-like strands of hair above sidelocks in man's wig

*omeshi:* a flat silk crepe, usually with a woven pattern

*omigoromo:* leisure-style indoor attire of shōgun, daimyō, or general, consisting of large-sleeved floor-brushing brocaded coat with tuxedo collar, white kimono with large wadded obi, and white undergarments

*Omiwa hachimaki:* *hachimaki* formed of *tenugui* worn for role of Omiwa in *Imoseyama Onna Teikin*

*omodaka odoshi:* laced armor pattern stylizing arrowhead-shaped leaf of water plantain

*omote mon:* actor's main crest

*oni ōgi:* fan for demoness roles in Nō

*onnagata:* actor taking women's roles

*onna ōgi:* tasseled fan with one side gold and one silver, used for *hime* roles

*ori eboshi:* folded *eboshi* of lacquered paper; also called *gosannen*

*osae-mino:* small holes at hairline of wig base to which *mino-ge* is attached

*oshidori:* (literally "mandarin duck") topknot in *machi-musume* wig resembling mandarin duck in shape

*oshimodoshi:* *aragoto* role of hero who repulses a demon in concluding scene of a play

*ō-sode-mono:* "big-sleeve" apparel of the Nō

*otokodate:* chivalrous commoner of Edo period; also called *machi yakko*

*otokogata:* male roles in general; actors playing these roles

*otoko musubi:* see *kai-no-kuchi musubi*

*oyaji-yaku:* role of an old man

*ō-yoroi:* scale armor hanging from the shoulders and coming over the hips (one of the three fundamental types of armor)

*rasha:* felt-like material woven of wool

*rimbō:* textile pattern of circular frame with spokes extending beyond outer rim

*rinzu:* silk damask with fine pattern

*rōjo ōgi:* fan for roles of elderly women

*rokkotsu:* a type of fan

*rokubu-gasa:* deep *kasa* worn by Buddhist pilgrims

*rokuyata-gōshi:* textile pattern of linked *mimasu* (three concentric squares); also called *mimasu tsunagi*

*rōnin:* masterless samurai

*ryōbashori:* samurai style of tucking up kimono on both sides

*ryōmomodachi:* style of tucking up bottom of *hakama* into belt

*ryūjin-maki:* style of *suō*, usually for messengers, with stiff-standing right sleeve, worn over wadded brocade *uwagi*

*sabaki-yaku:* role of person influential in settling problems

*sagari:* decorative type of loincloth or apron worn by *yakko*

*sagegami:* woman's hair style with long hair hanging down in back to ankle length or longer

*sageo:* suspending cord for a sword, used chiefly as decoration

*saihai:* warrior's baton of command

*sakaiki-no-mono:* wig base with copper piece representing crown of head

*sakayaki:* shaven part of man's head in old-fashioned hair styles also called *sakaiki*

*sambasō:* New Year felicitation dance

*sambasō eboshi:* *eboshi* of gold paper worn in felicitous New Year pieces

*sammai-gasane zōri:* three-layer sandals with two-color thongs

*sammi eboshi:* lacquered black (sometimes gold) hat

worn *indoors or out* by samurai of highest class

*samurai eboshi:* black-lacquered *eboshi* turned down from crown into three-cornered shape

*samurai-no-mukō*; *mukō hachimaki* made of special cloth (cotton or silk) for the purpose

*sane:* platelets composing armor

*sanjaku-mono:* vagabonds or outlaws in *kizewa-mono*

*sanjaku* obi: "three-foot" obi worn by vagabonds and outlaws in *kizewa-mono*

*sankaku-ate:* white headband with triangular piece in front, worn on forehead by a corpse

*sanri-ate:* knee pads

*santome:* type of imported cotton cloth patterned with stripes; also called *santome-jima* or *tozan*

*sara-no-matsuri:* hanging short hair above sidelocks of warrior's wig

*sarashi:* bleached cotton or ramie cloth

*saru-guma:* monkey-type make-up

*sasa-rindō:* textile pattern consisting of symmetrical arrangement of bamboo-grass *(sasa)* leaves and gentian-like flowers *(rindō)*

*sashi-mono:* woman's ornamental hairpin

*sashinuki:* hakama gathered just above the ankles in Dutch pantaloon style

*saya:* scabbard, sheath

*seigo:* taffeta-like silk woven with thick weft threads

*seitai habutae:* habutae colored to represent shaven crown of young man's head

*setta:* zōri with rawhide soles, used for formal occasions

*sewa-mono:* realistic plays of the commoners

*sewa musubi:* style of tying obi in bulbous bow with ends protruding straight from sides

*sewa nyōbō:* role of samurai or *rōnin* wife

*sha:* soft-textured open-weave silk gauze

*shaguma mage:* globular *mage* of courtesan's wig

*shaku:* short stafflike implement carried by noblemen garbed in *sokutai*

*shibai:* (literally "play," "drama") familiar term for Kabuki

*shibori:* tie-dyeing; tie-dyed fabric

*shibu-sen:* a type of fan

*shichijō kesa:* priest's ceremonial surplice composed of seven strips of brocaded cloth

*shichisan-bashori:* asymmetrical style of tucking up kimono; also called *kata-bashori*

*shidagawa odoshi:* laced armor pattern employing leather printed with design of fern fronds

*shigoki:* soft obi

*shiitake mage:* topknot in mushroom shape

*shiitake-tabo:* class of *onnagata* wigs for feudal courtlady roles, with back hair in mushroom shape, highly pomaded and polished

*shikake-mono:* trick costumes for bit players

*Shikan-jima:* textile pattern with sets of four stripes, each separated by a row of linked drawer pulls; also called *kan tsunagi*

*shima:* striped cloth

*shimada:* woman's bouffant hair style

*shimada mage:* see *shimada*

*shimbō tachi-yaku:* role of man who suppresses emotions even when grossly provoked

*shinjū:* double love suicide

*shinobi kaburi:* tenugui worn as face-concealing headgear by thief or murderer; also called *nusubito kaburi*

*shioze:* thick silk resembling taffeta

*shirahone:* priest's folding fan with unpainted ribs

*shiratake mai ōgi:* a type of dance fan

*shiratake-no-ōgi:* see *mai ōgi*

*shiroito odoshi:* white plaited armor design

*shiro kosode:* small-sleeved white kimono worn under hitoe in *jūni-hitoe*

*shiromuku:* white silk kimono

*shiro-nuri:* all-white make-up

*shiro-ōguchi:* man's white *hakama* with wide pleats and stiffened back

*shiro yoten:* yoten costume with all garments white except for purple *shigoki*

*shitabaki:* type of loincloth worn by women

*shitagi:* undergarments in general

*shita-obi:* man's loincloth or breechcloth; also called *fundoshi*

*shita-uma:* unlined cotton undergarment resembling yukata, worn by common-class men

*shita-uma-tsuki:* combination of kimono and *shita-uma* worn as one garment

*shō-chiku-bai:* pine, bamboo, and plum combined to make an auspicious design

*shosagoto:* dance-drama

*shōtō:* short sword; smaller of samurai's paired swords

*shuchin:* brocaded satin

*shusu-yakko:* see *iro-yakko*

*shutara:* gold-braided cording worn with priest's ceremonial *kesa*

*Sōjūrō zukin:* special style of *zukin* used for *tachi-yaku* roles

*sokutai:* emperor's ceremonial costume; formal apparel of court nobles and special military officers

*sō-moyō:* kimono with allover pattern

*sora-iro:* sky blue

*soroban-dama-moyō:* obi pattern imitating beads or counters of Japanese abacus

*sōshō zukin:* zukin worn for roles of poetry and tea-ceremony masters

*suami:* net undershirt resembling chain mail

*suikan:* nobleman's court robe in ancient days

*suji-guma:* line make-up serving as foundation for *kumadori*

*Sukeroku hachimaki:* variant of *date hachimaki* in purple, used for role of Sukeroku in play of same name

*sumi:* black; black ink

*sumikirikaku-ni-hei-no-ji:* crest consisting of character hei (for Heiemon in *Chūshingura*) inside a square with corners cut off

*sumikirikaku-ni-hon-no-ji:* crest consisting of character hon (for Honzō in *Chūshingura*) inside a square with corners cut off *sumi-seitai habutae: habutae* colored blue mixed with black to represent growing hair on shaven crown of low-class man's head

*sune-ate:* leg protector, greave

*suō:* man's ceremonial costume with wide-sleeved top garment and *han-bakama* or *naga-bakama*

*suppori-no-mono:* man's wig completely covering crown of head

*surihagashi habutae: habutae* of same color as face make-up to represent bald head of elderly man

*surihaku:* gold- or silver-leaf imprint on silk; a kimono decorated in this fashion

*suso:* hem or bottom of garment

*suso-moyō:* kimono with plain upper part and patterned skirt

*suso-yoke:* woman's outer loincloth

*suttoko kaburi:* see *tōnasu kaburi*

*suzushi:* raw silk

*tabi:* bifurcated socks

*tabo:* back hair of a wig

*tabo-gane:* metal stretcher for back hair of wig; also called *tabo-kane*

*tabo-gane-dome:* holder for *tabo-gane* riveted on both sides of wig base at back

*tabo-kane:* see *tabo-gane*

*tabo-no-kane:* metal bridge at back of wig base for attaching back hair

*tachi:* long sword with two hangers on scabbard

*tachimawari:* fight scene; swordplay scene

*tachimochi:* sword-bearer

*tachine:* erect style of topknot in man's wig

*tachi-yaku:* actor of leading male roles; the roles themselves

*taikogawa:* "drum" type of *obitori* used for *tachi* sheath; *tachi* with such a sheath

*taisha:* brown or burnt sienna

*taishō mage:* style of wig worn by generals, daimyō, and court nobles

*taka-geta:* high-stilted wooden clogs

*taka-shimada:* see *bunkin-taka-shimada*

*takenaga:* starched paper strips worn as decoration for women's wigs

*takenoko-gasa:* bun-shaped *kasa* made of bamboo sheath; also called *manjū-gasa*

*tanzen:* bathhouse attire

*tanzen-roppō:* Kabuki plays of bawdy type

*tanzen-tate-gami:* man's hair style suggesting bathhouse dandy

*tare:* piece of crepe or foam rubber suspended at back of priest's wig to cover actor's own hair

*tasuki (-dasuki):* cloth band used to hold back kimono sleeves and free arms for action

*tate eboshi:* nobleman's, samurai's, or court official's tall lacquered-paper hat

*tatewaku:* textile pattern composed of two serpentine lines

*tate-ya-no-ji musubi:* style of tying obi in knot resembling *hiragana* symbol *ya* (や).

*tate-zashi:* woman's large upright hairpin

*tattsuke-bakama: hakama* with lower part in form of tight leggings

*tayū:* Edo-period courtesan of highest rank

*tazuna:* horse-bridle design of alternating bands of bright colors and gold; blade of *yakko* sword

*tazuna-zome:* see *Koroku-zome*

*tekka kaburi:* headgear consisting of *tenugui* tied under nose to conceal identity

*tekkō:* long cloth mittens covering lower arms and backs of hands

*tenchikin: haku-sen* type white fan with gold band along top and lower edges

*tengai:* deep tub-shaped hat with lattice "window," worn by mendicant monks

*tenugui:* hand towel, usually of cotton or ramie

*tōban tsunagi:* fireman's-staff textile pattern used for firemen's costumes

*tobi:* firemen; also called *hikeshi* or *tobi-no-mono*

*tobi-no-mono:* see *tobi*

*tobi-roppō:* leaping, arm-flinging exit of an actor over the *hanamichi*

*toko-yama:* wig dresser, coiffeur

*tombo-gashira:* part of froglike fastener that receives loop; see also *ukeo*

*tomesode:* short-sleeved kimono of married woman

*tomoe:* whirl pattern of circular shape formed of two or three comma-shaped figures

*tōnasu kaburi: tenugui* worn as headgear in pumpkin shape; also called *kabocha kaburi* or *suttoko kaburi*

*tonosama:* court lords

*toppei:* cone-shaped chape for a scabbard

*torioi-gasa:* grass or reed *kasa* worn by strolling female musicians

*tosaka:* cockscomb style of woman's coiffure with forelocks cut short, parted in middle, combed to side, and curved forward

*tō-santome:* see *santome*

*tō-sen:* a type of fan

*tōzan:* see *santome*

*tsuba:* sword guard

*tsubushi-shimada:* woman's low-puffed *shimada* coiffure

*tsugi-gamishimo:* see *kataginu-hakama*

*tsuka:* sword hilt

*tsukamitate:* pompon style of forelock in man's wig

*tsumadori odoshi:* laced armor pattern employing design of half pyramid in several colors against green background

*tsuma tori:* woman's style of holding up kimono hems loosely in one hand

*tsume-sode-mono:* "little-sleeve" garments

*tsumugi:* rough-textured pongee

*tsunokakushi:* cloth draped over headdress of a bride

*tsuri:* suspension bridge at back of wig base to support side pieces

*tsuru-no-maru:* crest representing impressionistic crane which forms a circular figure

*tsurushi-gake:* see *aida-gire*

*tsuyu-shiba-moyō:* textile design of dewdrops on a lawn

uchi-bakama: see hari-bakama

uchi-gatana: longer of dissimilar pair of swords

uchikake: woman's ceremonial outer robe; also called kaidori

uchiwa: rigid round fan used in sewa-mono and kizewa-mono

ue-no-hakama: outer hakama for formal dress of court nobles

ukeo: catching loop of froglike fastener; see also tombo-gashira

ukon: soft canary yellow

uma-no-shippo mage: woman's topknot resembling horse's tail tied up or folded over

ungetsu-sen: fan for priest roles in Nō

unohana odoshi: laced armor pattern in white and green depicting white deutzia flowers

unryū: see kumo-ni-ryū

ura-ume: crest design of plum blossoms viewed from back

uroko yoten: yoten costume of white silk with triangular pattern in silver leaf symbolizing scales of a snake

usagi hachimaki: hachimaki tied to resemble ears of a rabbit

ushiro hachimaki: common soldier's hachimaki tied at back

usuaka: pink or pale red

usugake: medium blue

usuzumi: gray

uwa-obi: band tied over obi

wagane: metal band connecting side pieces of wig base across back when wig is composed of two pieces

wagane-no-osae: holders near center edges for metal band connecting side pieces of wig base

wagoto: "soft" or gentle style of acting for role of a handsome young lover; see also nimaime

wakaimono: male servant attached to a brothel

waka-oyama: role of an unmarried girl

wakashu: role of a youth; also called wakashu-gata

wakashu-gata: see wakashu

wa kesa: priest's surplice for everyday wear

wakizashi: samurai's medium-length sword replacing smaller sword of daishō if mountings are not the same; also wealthy chōnin's sword

waraji: straw sandals

waribasami: see komageta musubi

wari-kōgai: woman's divided bar-shaped hair ornament

wata bōshi: onnagata bōshi of wata silk

watsunagi: textile design of overlapping circle outlines

yabo: naive, countrified character

yagasuri: arrow-patterned kimono worn by koshimoto

yagura: government-licensed theater of Edo period

yahazu: arrow-feather style of sidelocks in man's wig; crest design with two arrow feathers side by side in a circle

yakko: samurai's servant or footman; also called chūgen

yakko-no-nejikiri: man's style of tucking up entire hem of kimono

yakuza: gambler, idler, ne'er-do-well

yamabushi: mountain priest, itinerant priest

yamai hachimaki: hachimaki worn by ill or insane character, usually purple and always tied on left side of head

yamamichi: light-blue, white zigzag-patterned tenugui worn or carried by villainous characters

yanagi musubi: (literally "willow-tree knot") long-hanging style of tying woman's obi, now used only by geisha

ya-no-ji: see tate-ya-no-ji musubi

yare-gōri: textile pattern of cracked-ice tracery

yarō bōshi: man's bōshi of chirimen or plain-woven silk

yoki-koto-kiku: textile pattern of vertical stripes with hatchet (yoki), character for harp (koto), and stylized chrysanthemum (kiku) repeated in rows between plain stripes as play on words, with meaning of "good news"

yoroi: armor

yoroi-hitatare: warrior costume consisting of hitatare and short pleated hakama worn under armor

yoroi-shita: garment worn under armor in place of hitatare

Yoshiwara kaburi: tenugua worn as headgear on visit to the Yoshiwara

yoten: wide-sleeved garments with hems split at sides, worn by warriors, policemen, notorious thieves, sorcerers, etc.; wearers also called yoten

yotsu-hanabishi: crest or textile design of stylized four diamond shapes made up of four four-petaled flowers

yotsume-yui: crest design consisting of large square divided into four equal units with small square in center of each

yugake: leather gauntlets worn with armor

yuiwata: skein of silk, silk wadding tied in a bundle; woman's coiffure with topknot resembling wadded silk; crest design representing tied skein of silk inside a circle

yūjo: courtesan

yukata: unlined cotton or ramie kimono for summer and bath wear

yumoji: woman's loincloth; also called yumaki

yūzen: see yūzen-zome

yūzen-zome: fine-line resist dyeing with starch or rice paste

zangiri-mono: (literally "cropped-hair plays") realistic sewa-mono introduced during Meiji period

zōri: sandals with thongs

zukin: hood

# Bibliography

Abe Yutaka, ed.: *Butai no Omokage* (Memories of the Stage), Kōbunsha, Tokyo, 1919–22 (series)

Atsumi Seitarō: *Nihon Buyō Shi* (History of Japanese Dance), Yūzankaku, Tokyo, 1958

———: *Shibai Gojūnen* (Fifty Years of Drama), Jiji Tsūshinsha, Tokyo, 1956

Beck, L. Adams: "The Ghost Plays of Japan" (reprinted from *The Perfume of the Rainbow,* Dodd, Mead, New York, 1923), The Japan Society, New York, 1933

Benedict, Ruth: *The Chrysanthemum and the Sword,* Houghton Mifflin, Boston, 1946

Blakeney, Ben Bruce: "Rokudaime" (Onoe Kikugorō VI), *Contemporary Japan,* Tokyo, October–December 1949

Bowers, Faubion: *Japanese Theatre,* Hermitage House, New York, 1952

———: *Theatre in the East,* Thomas Nelson and Sons, New York, 1956

*Buyō Yosōi* (Dance Costumes), Buyō Yosōi Publishing Association, Tokyo, 1926

Cheney, Sheldon: *The Theatre,* Longmans, Green, New York, 1958

DeBecker, J. E.: *The Nightless City,* Probsthain, London, 1899

Dening, Walter: *The Life of Toyotomi Hideyoshi,* Hokuseidō, Tokyo, 1955

Dickins, Frederick V., tr.: *Chūshingura or The Loyal League,* Allen, London, 1879

Edwards, Osman: *Japanese Plays and Playfellows,* Heinemann, London, 1901

Ema Tsutomu: *A Historical Sketch of Japanese Customs and Costumes,* Kokusai Bunka Shinkō-kai, Tokyo, 1938

———: *Rekidai Fūzoku Shasei Shū* (Pictorial Collection of Historical Costumes), 16 vols., Geirindō, Kyoto, 1917–22

Ernst, Earle: *The Kabuki Theatre,* Oxford University Press, New York, 1956

———, ed.: *Three Japanese Plays from the Traditional Theatre,* Oxford University Press, London, 1959

Fenollosa, Ernest E.: *Epochs of Chinese and Japanese Art,* 2 vols., Stokes, New York, 1921

Ficke, Arthur Davidson: *Chats on Japanese Prints,* Tuttle, Tokyo and Rutland, Vermont, 1958

Fujii Otō: *Chikamatsu Monzaemon,* Kinkōdō, Tokyo, 1904

Fujinami Yohei: *Kodōgu: Fujinami Yohei* (Stage Hand Properties: Fujinami Yohei), Engeki Shuppansha, Tokyo, 1954

Gunsaulus, Helen C.: *Japanese Textiles,* The Japan Society, New York, 1941

Haar, Francis: *The Best of Old Japan,* Tuttle, Tokyo and Rutland, Vermont, 1954

———: *Japanese Theatre in Highlight,* Tuttle, Tokyo and Rutland, Vermont, 1952

Halford, Aubrey S. and Giovanna M.: *The Kabuki Handbook,* Tuttle, Tokyo and Rutland, Vermont, 1956

Hamamura Yonezō, Sugawara Takashi, Kinoshita Junji, and Minami Hiroshi: *Kabuki,* Kenkyūsha, Tokyo, 1956

Hasegawa Sadanobu: *Tadataka Kabuki Jūhachiban* (The Eighteen Best Kabuki Plays), Uchida Bijutsu Shoshi, Kyoto, 1941

Hironaga Shūzaburō: *Bunraku,* The Bunraku Theater, Osaka, 1959

———: *Bunraku: Japan's Unique Puppet Theatre,* Tokyo News Service, Tokyo, 1964

Honda Isao: *Monshō: Family Crests for Symbolic Design,* Japan Publications Trading Company, Tokyo, 1963

Iacovleff, A., and Elisséeff, S.: *Le Théâtre Japonais: Kabuki,* Meynial, Paris, 1933

Ihara Toshirō: *Kinsei Nihon Engeki Shi* (History of Modern Japanese Drama), Waseda University Press, Tokyo, 1927

———: *Meiji Engeki Shi* (History of Meiji-Era Drama), Waseda University Press, Tokyo, 1933

———: *Nihon Engeki Shi* (History of Japanese Drama), Waseda University Press, Tokyo, 1925

——— and Abe Yutaka, eds.: *Ichikawa Danjūrō*, Kōbunsha, Tokyo, 1933

Ise Teijō: *Kojitsu Sōsho Shōzoku Chakuyō Zu* (Ancient Practices Series: Costumes Actually Worn by Warriors and Women), Tokyo, 1779; reprinted, Tokyo, 1904

Iizuka Tomoichirō: *Kabuki Saiken* (Details of Kabuki), Dai-ichi Shobō, Tokyo, 1933

*Japanese Costume Through the Ages* (catalogue), Tokyo National Museum, Tokyo, 1962

*Japanese Noh Drama*, ten plays selected and translated from the Japanese by the Nippon Gakujitsu Shinkōkai, Tokyo, 1955

*Japanese Theatre Pictorial*, Tokyo Educational Institute, Tokyo, 1954

Joya, Mock: *Things Japanese*, Tokyo News Service, Tokyo, 1958

"Kabuki no Shin Kenkyū" (New Studies of Kabuki), *Journal of Theatre Art*, vol. III, no. 1, Chuōkōronsha, Tokyo, October 1952

*Kabuki Sōsho* (Kabuki Writings), Kinkōdō, Tokyo, 1910

Kagayama Naozō: *Kabuki no Kata* (Styles of Kabuki Acting), Sōgensha, Tokyo, 1957

Katayama Kuroemon, ed.: *Kwanze Ke Denrai Nō Men Shū* (A Collection of Nō Masks Treasured in the Kwanze Family), Hinoki Shoten, Tokyo, 1954

Kawakatsu Ken'ichi: *Kimono* (Tourist Library, vol. 3), Japan Travel Bureau, Tokyo, 1954

Kawatake Shigetoshi: *The Development of the Japanese Theatre Art*, Kokusai Bunka Shinkōkai, Tokyo, 1935

———: "Kabuki after the Opening of Japan," *Contemporary Japan*, vol. XXII, nos. 1–3, Tokyo, 1953

———: *Kabuki: Japanese Drama*, Foreign Affairs Association of Japan, Tokyo, 1958

———: *Kabuki Meisaku Shū* (Masterpieces of Kabuki), vol. I, Kōdansha, Tokyo, 1935

———: "Kabuki: Twelve Chapters on Japanese Drama," *Contemporary Japan*, vol. XXIII, nos. 7–12, and vol. XXIV, nos. 1–6, Tokyo, 1955–56

———: *Kawatake Mokuami* (Biography of Kawatake Mokuami), Toshihiko Wada, Tokyo, 1925

———, ed.: *Sandaime Nakamura Nakazō Temaemiso* (Biography of Nakamura Nakazō III), Hokko Shobō, Tokyo, 1944

———, ed.: *Geinō Jiten* (Dictionary of Theatrical Art), Tōkyōdō, Tokyo, 1954

Keene, Donald: *The Battles of Coxinga*, Taylor's Foreign Press, London, 1951

———: *Bunraku: The Art of the Japanese Puppet Theatre*, Kōdansha, Tokyo, 1965

———: *Living Japan*, Heinemann, London, 1959

———, tr.: *The Major Plays of Chikamatsu*, Columbia University Press, New York, 1961

———, ed.: *Anthology of Japanese Literature*, Grove Press, New York, 1955

Kikuchi Kan: *Tōjūrō's Love and Four Other Plays*, translated by Glenn W. Shaw, Hokuseidō, Tokyo, 1956

Kincaid, Zoë: *Kabuki: The Popular Stage of Japan*, Macmillan, London, 1925

*Kokon Yakusha Taizen* (All about Actors Old and New), Tokyo, 1750

*Kojitsu Sōsho Jokan Shōzoku Chakuyō Shidai* (Ancient Practices Series: Costumes Actually Worn by Court Ladies); late 18th century; reprinted, Tokyo, 1904

*Kojitsu Sōsho Reifuku Chakuyō Zu* (Ancient Practices Series: Ceremonial Costumes Actually Worn), late 18th century; reprinted (edited by Kosugi), Tokyo, 1904

Komiya Toyotaka, ed.: *Japanese Music and Drama in the Meiji Era*, translated and adapted by Donald Keene and Edward Seidensticker, Ōbunsha, Tokyo, 1956

Kotani Heishichi: *Monzukushi* (An Enumeration of Family Crests), 20th ed., Monzukushi Kankōkai, Kyoto, 1951

Kusano Eisaburō: *Stories Behind Noh and Kabuki Plays*, Tokyo News Service, Ltd., Tokyo, 1962

Lloyd, Arthur: "Notes on the Japanese Drama," *Transactions of the Asiatic Society of Japan*, Tokyo, May 1907

Lombard, Frank Alanson: *An Outline History of the Japanese Drama*, Allen and Unwin, London, 1928

Malm, William P.: *Japanese Music and Musical Instruments*, Tuttle, Tokyo and Rutland, Vermont, 1959

———: *Nagauta: The Heart of Kabuki Music*, Tuttle, Tokyo and Rutland, Vermont, 1963

Matsuda Seifū: *Kabuki no Katsura* (Kabuki

Wigs), Engeki Shuppansha, Tokyo, 1959

Matsuoka Tatsukata: *Kojitsu Sōsho Shōzoku Chakuyō Zu* (Ancient Practices Series: Costumes Actually Worn by Warriors), originally published *c.* 1779; reprinted, Kosugi, Tokyo, 1904

McClatchie, Thomas R. H.: *Japanese Plays,* W. H. Allen, London, 1890

Michener, James A.: *The Floating World,* Random House, New York, 1954

Minnich, Helen Benton: *Japanese Costume and the Makers of Its Elegant Tradition,* Tuttle, Tokyo and Rutland, Vermont, 1963

Mitford, A. B.: *Tales of Old Japan,* Macmillan, London, 1883

Miyake Shūtarō: *Kabuki Drama* (Tourist Library, vol. 7), Japan Travel Bureau, Tokyo, 1954

Miyamori Asatarō: *Masterpieces of Chikamatsu,* E. P. Dutton, New York, 1926

——: *Tales from Old Japanese Dramas,* G. P. Putnam's Sons, London, 1915

Miyao Shigeo: *Bunraku Ningyō Zue* (Pictures of Bunraku Puppets), Jidaisha, Tokyo, 1942

Murasaki Shikibu: *The Tale of Genji,* translated by Arthur Waley, Allen and Unwin, London, 1928

Nitobe Inazō: *Bushidō: The Soul of Japan,* Kenkyūsha, Tokyo, 1935

Nogami Toyoichirō: *Japanese Noh Plays* (Tourist Library, vol. 16), Japan Travel Bureau, Tokyo, 1954

——: *Japanese Noh Plays: How to See Them,* Nōgaku Shorin, Tokyo, 1954

——: *Seami and His Theories on Noh,* translated by Matsumoto Ryōzō, Hinoki Shoten, Tokyo, 1955

Noma Seiroku: *Masks* (Arts and Crafts of Japan, vol. 1), English adaptation by Meredith Weatherby, Tuttle, Tokyo and Rutland, Vermont, 1957

Nomura Shōjirō: *Ancient Chinese and Japanese Nishiki* (catalogue), The Copley Society, Boston, 1914

Odera Yūkichi: *Nihon Kinsei Buyō Shi* (History of Contemporary Japanese Dance), Yūzankaku, Tokyo, 1931

O'Neill, P. G.: *Early Nō Drama: Its Background, Character, and Development, 1300–1450,* Lund Humphries, London, 1958

Ōmori, Annie Shepley, and Doi Kōchi, trs.: *Diaries of Court Ladies of Old Japan,* Kenkyūsha, Tokyo, 1935

Onoe Baikō: *Ume no Shita Kaze* (Wind under the Plum Blossoms), edited by Inoguchi Masaharu, Noriki Shoten, Tokyo, 1930

Ortolani, Benito: *Das Kabuki Theater: Kulturgeschichte der Anfänge,* Monumenta Nipponica Monographs, no. 19, Sophia University Press, Tokyo, 1964

——: "Shingeki: The Maturing New Drama of Japan," in *Studies in Japanese Culture,* ed. Joseph Roggendorf, Sophia University Press, Tokyo, 1963

Ōta Gakō: *Kabuki Jūhachiban* (Eighteen Kabuki Plays: The Traditional Pieces of the Ichikawa Family), Gekiga Kankōkai, Tokyo, 1931

Ōtsuki Nyōden: *Bugaku Zusetsu* (Bugaku Picture Dictionary), Rokugōkan, Tokyo, 1927

Peri, Noël: *Le Nō,* Maison Franco-Japonaise, Tokyo, 1944

Priest, Alan: *Japanese Costume: An Exhibition of Nō Robes and Buddhist Vestments,* Metropolitan Museum of Art, New York, 1935

Robinson, B. W.: *The Arts of the Japanese Sword,* Tuttle, Tokyo and Rutland, Vermont, 1961

*Rokudaime Kikugorō* (Onoe Kikugorō VI), ed. Kikugorō Memorial Publishing Committee, Kaizōsha, Tokyo, 1950

Sadler, A. L.: *Japanese Plays: Nō, Kyōgen, Kabuki,* Angus and Robertson, Sydney, 1934

——: *The Maker of Modern Japan: The Life of Tokugawa Ieyasu,* Allen and Unwin, London, 1937

Sakanishi Shio: *The Ink-Smeared Lady and Other Kyōgen,* Tuttle, Tokyo and Rutland, Vermont, 1960

Salwey, Charlotte M.: *Fans of Japan,* Kegan Paul, Trench, Trübner, London, 1894

Sansom, G. B.: *Japan: A Short Cultural History* (rev. ed.), Appleton, New York, 1962

——: *The Western World and Japan,* Knopf, New York, 1950

Schiffman, Maurice K.: *Japan, the Land of Fans,* Foreign Affairs Association of Japan, Tokyo, 1954

Scott, A. C.: *The Classical Theatre of China,* Allen and Unwin, London, 1957

——: *Genyadana: A Japanese Kabuki Play,* Hokuseidō, Tokyo, 1953

——: *The Kabuki Theatre of Japan,* Allen and Unwin, London, 1955

——: *Kanjinchō: A Japanese Kabuki Play,* Hokuseidō, Tokyo, 1953

——: *The Puppet Theatre of Japan,* Tuttle, Tokyo and Rutland, Vermont, 1963

Sekine Mokuan: *Meiji Gekidan Gojūnen Shi* (Fifty Years' History of the Meiji Stage), Gembunsha, Tokyo, 1918

Shioya Sakae: *Chūshingura: An Exposition*, Hokuseidō, Tokyo, 1956

Shively, Donald H.: *The Love Suicide at Amijima*, Harvard University Press, Cambridge, Massachusetts, 1953

Siao, Eva; Alley, Rewi; and Liang Kuan: *Peking Opera*, New World Press, Peking, 1957

Sōma Akira: *Kabuki: Ishō to Funsō* (Kabuki: Costumes and Style of Dressing), Kōdansha, Tokyo, 1957

Statler, Oliver: *Japanese Inn*, Random House, New York, 1961

Sugi Gan'ami: *Butai Kansatsu Tebikigusa* (Handbook of Stage Observations), Engeki Shuppansha, Tokyo, 1957

Sugiyama Makoto and Fujima Kanjūrō: *An Outline History of the Japanese Dance*, Kokusai Bunka Shinkōkai, Tokyo, 1937

Sunaga Katsumi: *Japanese Music* (Tourist Library, vol. 15), Board of Tourist Industry, Japanese Government Railways, Tokyo, 1936

Suzuki Keizo: *Busō Zusetsu* (Armor and Armor Illustrations), Meiji Tosho Shuppansha, Tokyo, 1954

Takahashi Sei-ichirō: *The Japanese Woodblock Prints*, translated by Matsumoto Ryōzō, Yamagata Printing Company, Yokohama, 1955

Takano Tatsuyuki: *Jōruri Shi* (History of Jōruri), Shunyōdō, Tokyo, 1899

———: *Nihon Engeki no Kenkyū* (Study of Japanese Drama), 2 vols., Kaizōsha, Tokyo, 1926, 1928

———: *Nihon Kayō Shi* (History of Japanese Poetry), Shunjūsha, Tokyo, 1938

Takeda Izumo, Miyoshi Shōraku, and Namiki Senryū: *Chūshingura or The Treasury of Loyal Retainers*, translated by Inoue Jukichi, Nakanishiya, Tokyo, 1910

Tamura Nariyoshi, ed.: *Zokuzoku Kabuki Nendai Ki* (Third Kabuki Chronicles), Ichimuraza, Tokyo, 1922

Tanaka Ryō: *Kabuki Jōshiki Butai Zushū* (Kabuki Stage Designs), Kōdansha (for Dai Nippon Yūbenkai), Tokyo, 1958

Tobe Ginsaku: *Kabuki no Engi* (History of Kabuki), Engeki Shuppansha, Tokyo, 1956

Tosaka Kyōji, ed.: *Kabuki Techō* (Kabuki Notebook), Sōgensha, Tokyo, 1956

Toyo Kaishi: *Zoku Kabuki Nendai Ki* (Second Kabuki Chronicles), publisher and date unknown

Tsubouchi Shōyō and Yamamoto Jirō: *History and Characteristics of Kabuki*, edited and translated by Matsumoto Ryōzō, with an additional chapter, "Kabuki as Seen by Foreigners," by Ruth M. Shaver, Ediriweera R. Sarathchandra, and Faubion Bowers, Heiji Yamagata Printing Company, Yokohama, 1960

Tsubouchi Yūzō: *Geki to Bungaku* (Drama and Literature), Fuzambō, Tokyo, 1911

Ueda Makoto: "Chikamatsu and His Ideas on Drama," *U.S.A. Educational Theater Journal*, May 1960

Waley, Arthur: *The Nō Plays of Japan*, Allen and Unwin, London, 1954

Wells, Florence: "Hi-ogi: Japanese Cypress Fan," *Contemporary Japan*, vol. XXV, no. 4, Tokyo, 1959

———: "Uchiwa: The Round Fan," *Contemporary Japan*, vol. XVI, nos. 4–6, Tokyo, April–June, 1947

Yamamura Kōka and Machida Hiromi: *Shibai Nishikie Shūsei* (Collection of Theatrical Woodblock Prints), Seikasha, Tokyo, 1919

Yamanobe Tomoyuki: *Senshoku* (Dyeing and Weaving), Kōdansha, Tokyo, 1960

———: *Textiles* (Arts and Crafts of Japan, vol. 2), English adaptation by Lynn Katoh, Tuttle, Tokyo and Rutland, Vermont, 1957

Yoshikawa Keizō, ed.: *Tōken Zukō Buki Kōshō Dai-ichi* (Picture Dictionary of Swords), Meiji Tosho Shuppansha, Tokyo, 1952

Yumoto, John M.: *The Samurai Sword*, Tuttle, Tokyo and Rutland, Vermont, 1958

# Subject Index

*akahime:* costume for, 165–66, 280; roles, 165, 166
*akuba:* roles, 81, 84, 202; costume for, 202
*aku ōji,* 134
aprons, 138, 160, 195, 196, 209
*aragoto:* acting style of, 25, 48, 52, 60, 169, 341;
   costume for, 25, 49, 51–57, 59–60, 123, 230, 245,
   295, 296, 297, 343, 348, 355
armor: signified by *happi,* 28; garments with, 52, 98,
   101; arm guards with, 52, 89, 209, 212; leg guards
   with, 52, 89, 213; helmets used with, 97, 211;
   helmet horns with, 97, 211, 213; of paper, 171;
   battle costumes of, 203–13; corselets, 204, 209–10.
   212; *onnagata* use of, 204
*asobinin,* costume for, 266–67
*atsuita,* 28
*atsuwata-no-hirosode,* 52, 53

bared torso, 53
bare feet and legs, 52, 58, 69, 96, 136, 137. 157, 172,
   173, 176, 200
bathhouse dandy: costume for, 42–45; origin of role,
   42
batons, 136, 211, 213
beards, 96
bearers and porters: costume for, 242, 243, 261; roles
   243–44
*bōzu,* costume for, 139–42; *see also* priests, costume
   for
*budōgoto* scenes, 169
*bukkaeri,* 351–54
Bunraku, 48, 102; *see also* costume: relation to puppet
   theater and, *ningyō-jōruri-shibai*

carpenters, costume for, 242
*chōken,* 27, 143
*chōnin,* costume for, 167, 168, 241, 248, 271, 278, 293,
   298, 322; *see also* merchants, costume for
*chūgen;* see *yakko*
colors, indicative of: rank, 26, 63, 120, 204, 211,
   232; age, 28–29, 98, 114, 135, 138, 160, 162, 204,
   213, 232, 242, 296; personality, 53, 59, 60, 99–100,
   120–23, 133, 166, 172, 175, 242, 254–55, 279, 282,

296, 342–43; illness, 60, 242; emotion, 100, 342–
   43; nature, 232; sex, 255
commoners, costume for, 28, 82, 143, 254, 255
costume: realism of, 24, 25, 26, 28–30, 51, 53, 63, 69,
   81, 82, 89–91, 94, 95–98, 100–101, 105, 107–108,
   119, 120–23, 124, 133, 139, 143, 160, 163, 166, 167,
   172, 174, 193, 199, 203, 210, 212, 216, 232, 234,
   241, 247, 248, 254, 256, 262, 266, 270, 289–300,
   302, 337–43; innovations in, 24, 25, 53–60, 68–72,
   82–85, 89–91, 95–101, 103, 163, 166, 215, 216, 219,
   221, 224–25, 228, 229, 234–37, 239–40, 265, 295,
   338–43, 354, 358; relation to Nō, 25, 27–29, 59, 78,
   80, 83, 99, 120, 123, 124, 137, 140, 143, 157–58,
   161, 212, 278, 281–82, 302, 341, 342, 357–58, 367;
   relation to puppet theater, 25, 48–49, 67, 70–71,
   77, 123, 134, 167, 172, 219, 239–40, 279, 351, 354;
   legal restriction of, 25, 26, 27, 62–64, 71–72, 76–
   78, 80–81, 83, 88–91, 94, 120, 143, 203, 262; influence on popular attire, 26, 50, 69, 70, 84, 160,
   215, 221, 233, 254; illusory effects in, 27, 37, 59,
   77, 82, 99, 158, 160, 171, 209, 212, 240, 334, 335;
   seasonal variation of, 27, 29, 160; of Western dress,
   100, 103, 105; cost of, 63, 80–81, 357–58; ownership
   of, 64, 84–85, 90, 103, 266, 278, 289–90, 357; of
   legendary period, 108
courtesans: costume for, 27, 165, 193, 199–201, 272.
   280, 321; roles, 198
court gentlemen, costume for, 27, 134, 247, 262
court ladies, costume for, 161, 280, 306, 345, 350
crests, 26, 53, 57, 58, 80, 82, 120, 123, 138, 139, 142,
   162, 164, 174, 175, 198, 201, 229, 233–40, 253,
   266, 267, 273
cross-eyed pose, 60

*daimon,* 120–23, 124–33, 212, 240
*daimyō,* costume for, 77, 118, 120, 121–34, 211, 212–
   13, 248, 278, 295, 296, 298, 322
*dammari,* 96, 135, 222, 295
demons, costume for, 50, 101, 222, 282
designers: Kawachi Hanshichi, 49; Yoshioka Kembō, 69; Hasegawa Kambei I, 75; Sakai Hōitsu
   Inja, 81; Komura Settai, 216; Kubota Beisai, 216;

*shinjū,* 173

Shinko Engeki Jusshu collection, 101

shōgun, costume for, 120, 134

*shosagoto:* costume for, 70, 99, 113, 136, 244, 261, 265, 272, 282–84, 343, 357; focus on dancing, 70. 282–84

sleeves: outsized, 27, 29, 53, 134, 135, 143, 160, 212; tucked-up, 28, 135, 136, 137, 158, 212, 213; narrow-opened, 28, 29, 159; splinted, 53, 57, 123; ties & bands for, 57, 59, 82, 136, 137, 143, 213, 296; stiff-standing, 123; abbreviated, 160

*sokutai,* 96, 119, 157

straw-mat cape, 91

*suikan,* 37, 96, 143

*suō,* 53, 54, 123–24, 229, 253, 278

*surihaku,* 28

*suso-moyō,* 164, 165, 174, 198, 201

swords, 36, 45, 52, 53, 58, 59, 63, 69, 82, 124, 135, 136, 137, 143, 157, 164, 176, 210, 211, 213, 289–300

*tachimawari* scenes, 102, 134, 135–36, 137, 294

*tachi-yaku:* roles, 51, 84. 108; costume for, 84, 254, 278

*tanzen* costume; *see* bathhouse dandy: costume for

*tanzen-roppō* plays, 42–45

tattooing, 176, 267

*tenugui,* see hand towels

textiles and textile designs, 53–60, 62–63, 68–85 *passim,* 99, 114, 119–209 *passim,* 215–231, 234–72 *passim,* 279–82, 307–308, 354, 357–58, 367–69

tiger costume, 343

tights, 49, 124, 176

*tobi-roppō* scene, 135

*tomesode,* 196

*tsume-sode-mono,* 28

*uchikake,* 27, 80–81, 161, 162, 166, 199, 201, 350

umbrellas, 58, 230

undergarments, 57, 58, 59, 116, 118, 134, 137, 141, 160, 166, 168, 175, 194, 196–97, 201, 202, 209

*uwagi,* 53, 59, 123, 160, 229

villains, costume for, 50, 84, 102, 133, 134, 267, 297, 307, 322

*wagoto:* acting style, 48, 102, 169–71; costume for. 123, 171–73, 245, 256, 267, 298

*waka-oyama,* 50

*wakashu:* hair style, 36, 38; costume, 133. 174–75. 204, 296; roles, 51, 174

wigs: introduction of, 41, 81–82, 301; descriptions of, 52, 57, 77, 134, 135, 136, 138, 139, 160–61, 162, 163, 164, 165, 166, 169, 172, 175, 176, 194, 195, 196, 197, 198, 200, 201, 202, 211–12, 263, 304–36; men's, worn by *onnagata,* 263; making of, 302–21; dressing of, 321–24, ornamentation of, 324–34

*yagura,* 60–62, 107

*yakko,* costumes for, 84, 137–39, 255, 266, 294, 297. 298, 348

*yakuza:* costume for, 271, 346–47; roles, 271

*yamabushi,* costume for, 142

*yoten:* costume for, 25, 134–37, 222, 348; roles, 25. 134–35

*yukata,* 176, 201, 220, 224, 345

*zangiri-mono* plays, 100, 103, 107

# Index of Actors, Plays, and Roles